Aid Imperium

WEISER CENTER FOR EMERGING DEMOCRACIES

Series Editor
Dan Slater is Professor of Political Science,
Ronald and Eileen Weiser Professor of Emerging Democracies,
and Director of the Weiser Center for Emerging Democracies (WCED)
at the University of Michigan. dnsltr@umich.edu

―――――――――――

The series highlights the leading role of the University of Michigan Press, Weiser Center for Emerging Democracies, and International Institute as premier sites for the research and production of knowledge on the conditions that make democracies emerge and dictatorships endure.

―――――――――――

Ghosts in the Neighborhood: Why Japan Is Haunted by Its Past and Germany Is Not
Walter F. Hatch

*Struggles for Political Change in the Arab World: Regimes, Oppositions,
and External Actors after the Spring*
Edited by Lisa Blaydes, Amr Hamzawy, and Hesham Sallam

*The Dictator's Dilemma at the Ballot Box: Electoral Manipulation,
Economic Maneuvering, and Political Order in Autocracies*
Masaaki Higashijima

Opposing Power: Building Opposition Alliances in Electoral Autocracies
Elvin Ong

The Development of Political Institutions: Power, Legitimacy, Democracy
Federico Ferrara

*Aid Imperium: United States Foreign Policy and Human Rights in Post–Cold War
Southeast Asia*
Salvador Santino F. Regilme Jr.

Opposing Democracy in the Digital Age: The Yellow Shirts in Thailand
Aim Sinpeng

Normalizing Corruption: Failures of Accountability in Ukraine
Erik S. Herron

Economic Shocks and Authoritarian Stability: Duration, Financial Control, and Institutions
Victor C. Shih, Editor

Electoral Reform and the Fate of New Democracies: Lessons from the Indonesian Case
Sarah Shair-Rosenfield

AID IMPERIUM

*United States Foreign Policy and Human Rights
in Post–Cold War Southeast Asia*

Salvador Santino Fulo Regilme Jr.

University of Michigan Press
Ann Arbor

First paperback edition 2023
Copyright © 2021 by Salvador Santino Fulo Regilme Jr.
All rights reserved

For questions or permissions, please contact um.press.perms@umich.edu

Published in the United States of America by the
University of Michigan Press
Manufactured in the United States of America
Printed on acid-free paper
First published in paperback January 2023

A CIP catalog record for this book is available from the British Library.

Library of Congress Control Number: 2021947166
LC record available at https://lccn.loc.gov/2021947166

ISBN 978-0-472-13278-2 (hardcover : alk. paper)
ISBN 978-0-472-12950-8 (e-book)
ISBN 978-0-472-03927-2 (pbk.)

DOI: https://doi.org/10.3998/mpub.12036762

Cover illustration: Unsplash.com / USGS

Contents

Digital materials related to this title can be found on the Fulcrum platform via the following citable URL: https://doi.org/10.3998/mpub.12036762

Acknowledgments

This book had a long journey. My passion for human rights emerged from my undergraduate philosophy thesis about the universality of human rights vis-à-vis the East Asian values debate. My realizations about the practical significance of human rights inspired me to shift from philosophy to political science as I pursued graduate studies in Europe and the United States. In the mid-2000s, my brief stint as a civilian intelligence analyst for the Philippine government allowed me to see the contestations faced by political leaders as they deploy state violence toward their citizens. Those lived experiences, along with the realization that millions of people worldwide die annually from state violence, motivated me to write about physical integrity rights in the era of a transnational security crisis.

There is a long list of wonderful people to be thankful for, but unfortunately, far too many to acknowledge here. I could not have written this work without the support and advice of my mentor, Lora Anne Viola, an exemplar of intellectualism and generosity, and I thank her for her unwavering support, patience, and feedback. Susan Hyde provided valuable advice and warmly welcomed me during my time at Yale. Thomas Risse also supported my research in his capacity as my dissertation committee member. Moreover, I benefited from the advice and insights of many scholars, including Roland Czada, Ben Cashore, Julia Adams, Andreas Schedler, Ellen M. Immergut, Shannon Blanton, Margit Mayer, Emilie Hafner-Burton, Stathis Kalyvas, Claudia Derichs, Olivia Rutazibwa, Shirin Saeidi, Alejandro Portocarrero-Esguerra, Mark Thompson, Francisco Magno, Trinidad Osteria, Carolina Hernandez, Rainer Baumann, Katja

Freistein, Volker Heins, Lee Jones, Jeff Bridoux, Inderjeet Parmar, Nuno Monteiro, Alex Debs, Peter Barberis, Marian Döhler, Stephen Brown, Andreas Ufen, Frank Gadinger, Tobias Debiel, Ben Freeman, Jong Malabed, David Seaman, Ralf Kleinfeld, Christian Lammert, Boris Vormann, and Markus Kienscherf. Laura Sjoberg and Hitomi Koyama provided some very helpful publication advice, and I am grateful for their wisdom.

My research was made possible by the funding from the German Federal and State Governments' DFG Excellence Initiative Scholarship, the Fox International Fellowship at Yale University, the Center for Global Cooperation Research's Käte Hamburger Fellowship funded by the German Federal Ministry for Education and Research, and the Leiden Institute for History's sabbatical grant. I am also indebted to the staff and the administration of the Free University of Berlin's Graduate School of North American Studies (Gabi Bodmeier and David Bosold), the Macmillan Center for Area and International Studies at Yale (Julia Muravnik), and the De La Salle University's Robredo Institute for institutional support. This project benefited from the support staff and excellent resources of the Sterling Memorial Library, Center for Science and Social Science Information, and the Law School Library of Yale University. In Southeast Asia, I thank Jesus Macalinao and Henpritz Montalvo for their assistance in collecting hundreds of newspaper articles and primary documents. In Leiden, I thank Elif Polat for the excellent research assistance.

Several friends and colleagues provided moral support, advice, and feedback. I thank Curd Knüpfer, James Parisot, Philipp Reick, Evan Rodriguez, Wolfgang Gründinger, Winnie Chen, Lionel Beehner, Will Nomikos, Suparna Chaudhry, Marc Venhaus, Julian Gruin, Carina van de Wetering, Flavio Prol, Elise Roumeàs, Amrita Nandy, Stefan Thierse, Aaron Bartells-Swindells, Shawn Fraistat, Michael Weintraub, and Michael Blaakman. I also thank so many friends beyond academia for their moral support—including Stefan Evers, Johann-Sebastian Saile (formerly Diemann), Sebastian Bockrath, Sean Cornell, Chris King, Gregor Hintler, Rita Cucio, Peter Baum, Carmina Untalan, Seiko Mimaki, Haruko Satoh, Shaila Safaee Chalkasra, friends from the De La Salle Debate Society, my friends from my MA cohort at the University of Osnabrück, as well as my PhD cohort at the Free University of Berlin.

At the University of Michigan Press, I thank Elizabeth Demers and her team, including Haley Winkle, for their feedback, enthusiasm, and support for this project. The publication of this research would not be possible without the editorial guidance of Elizabeth Demers. I also thank Kevin Rennells and John Raymond for the excellent copyediting. I am grateful to the anonymous reviewers for the University of Michigan Press, Rutgers

University Press, and Manchester University Press for their constructive suggestions. Roger Haydon, Lisa Banning, and Peter Agree provided some helpful editorial advice during the preliminary stages of manuscript development, and I thank Rob Byron and Jon de Peyer for commissioning the reviews at Manchester.

I thank the organizers and participants of the following events and institutions for the opportunity to present my work and for the constructive suggestions: 2011 BISA US Foreign Policy Conference at the University of Oxford; MIT-Harvard-Yale Workshop on Political Violence; Manchester Metropolitan University's Politics Workshop; Heidelberg Spring Academy in American Studies; the Free University of Berlin's Kennedy Institute Politics Workshop; Humboldt Universität zu Berlin Comparative Politics Colloquium; De La Salle University; International Studies Association Conference in Providence (2013) and Toronto (2014); University of London's Institute for the Study of the Americas; Fox Fellowship Research Seminar; Yale International Relations' Student Workshop; Graduate School of North American Studies Graduate Conference 2013; Yale IPE Student Workshop; FoJuS Conference in Hannover; Whitney Center in Connecticut; and the International Institute of Social Studies in The Hague.

An earlier version of chapter 7 appeared as an open-access peer-reviewed article: S. S. F. Regilme, "Does US Foreign Aid Undermine Human Rights? The 'Thaksinification' of the War on Terror Discourses and the Human Rights Crisis in Thailand, 2001 to 2006," *Human Rights Review* 19 (1) (2018): 73–95. I thank Steven Roper, *Human Rights Review*'s editor, for permission to republish a revised version of that article. Chapter 2 was inspired by my earlier work on Colombia and US foreign aid: S. S. F. Regilme, "A Human Rights Tragedy: Strategic Localization of US Foreign Policy in Colombia," *International Relations* 32 (3) (2018): 343–65. I thank William Bain, coeditor of *International Relations*, for allowing me to reuse some of the passages in that article.

Words alone could not express my deepest gratitude to my father, Cesar, my mother, Annie, and my sister, Nica. I thank my dearest Anh Loan, my amazing wife, for her unwavering support and kindness that allowed me to remain optimistic amid life's cruelties. I dedicate this book to all human rights victims who suffered from all forms of state violence.

All errors in this work are my own.

Salvador Santino Fulo Regilme Jr.
Lansingerland, The Netherlands
January 30, 2021

Illustrations

Figures

Tables

Abbreviations

AFP	Armed Forces of the Philippines
AMLO	Anti-Money Laundering Office
APEC	Asia-Pacific Economic Cooperation
ASEAN	Association of Southeast Asian Nations
ASG	Abu Sayyaf Group
CHR	Commission of Human Rights of the Government of the Republic of the Philippines
CCHROT	Coordinating Committee of Human Rights Organizations in Thailand
COMELEC	Commission on Elections
CTIC	Counterterrorism Intelligence Center
DDS	Davao Death Squad
JUSMAG	Joint United States Military Assistance Group to the Republic of the Philippines
MCC	Millennium Challenge Corporation
MDT	Mutual Defense Treaty
MILF	Moro Islamic Liberation Front
MNLF	Moro National Liberation Front
NBI	National Bureau of Investigation (Philippines)
NHRC	National Human Rights Commission (Thailand)
NPA	New People's Army
PAF	Philippine Air Force
PNP	Philippine National Police
RAFI	Ramon Aboitiz Foundation Incorporated

SBPAC	Southern Border Province Administration Center (Thailand)
SONA	State of the Nation Address of the President of the Republic of the Philippines
TRT	Thai Rak Thai party
UN	United Nations
UNHCR	United Nations High Commissioner for Refugees
US	United States
USAID	United States Agency for International Development

ONE

Introduction

Human rights is the soul of our foreign policy, because human rights is the very soul of our sense of nationhood.
—US President Jimmy Carter during the 30th anniversary of the Universal Declaration of Human Rights, 1978[1]

The United States is by far the largest single foreign donor government, with nearly 200 recipient countries (McBride 2018). In recent years, the US has provided the largest amount of aid, greater than the next runners-up, Germany and France (Debusman 2011). In April 2017, just a few months after the inauguration of the Donald Trump presidency, the White House budget proposal revealed that the United States Agency for International Development (USAID), the quintessential government entity that is primarily responsible for official foreign assistance disbursements, would be absorbed by the US State Department—a bureaucratic restructuring that was expected to dramatically reduce US foreign aid by over one-third. The weak commitment to foreign aid coincided with the fairly consistent disregard for human rights principles in the foreign and domestic policy agendas of President Trump, who has undermined long-standing US bilateral relations with key partner countries, not to mention the future of US dominance amid the reemergence of non-Western powers, including China (Regilme 2019; Regilme and Parisot 2017). For advocates of the so-called American-led liberal order, the Trump presidency constituted a threat because "his happy-go-lucky disregard for basic norms . . . may do serious and lasting damage" (Jervis et al. 2018, xi).

Trump's disregard for upholding US foreign assistance and human rights diplomacy instigated a sense of precariousness in the future direction of American foreign policy (Chacko and Jayasuriya 2017; Karnitschnig 2017; Regilme 2019; Hamilton-Hart 2017). Foreign aid programs and human rights discourses constitute some of the prominent features of post–Second World War US foreign policy—starting from the Marshall Plan to war-torn Europe to the Millennium Challenge Corporation's development programs pioneered by the Bush administration (Walldorf 2008). Yet racist, authoritarian, and sexist discourses have recently gained traction in the transnational public sphere, while international human rights norms are being delegitimized if not instrumentally weaponized in ways that directly undermine human dignity (Regilme 2019). As the annual report of Human Rights Watch (2017, 3) warns, "truth is a frequent casualty . . . nativism, xenophobia, racism, and Islamophobia are on the rise," and this "dangerous trend threatens to reverse the accomplishments of the modern human rights movement." Unfortunately, anti-human-rights discourses have started shaping mainstream public debates, a trend that is reinforced by the international prominence of illiberal politicians such as Rodrigo Duterte of the Philippines, Recep Tayyip Erdogan of Turkey, Viktor Orban in Hungary, Vladimir Putin in Russia, and Donald Trump in the United States, among others.

This book addresses this core puzzle: Does foreign aid undermine human rights in recipient countries? If so, how and under what set of conditions does it impact human rights outcomes, particularly physical integrity rights? Although contemporary scholarship highlights the causes and consequences of human rights norms, ranging from civil rights to socioeconomic rights (Regilme 2014a, 2014b), I focus instead on physical integrity rights, or the freedom of the human person from extrajudicial killings, enforced disappearances, physical harassment, and torture (Risse and Sikkink 1999, 2–3). Indeed, human rights are widely entrenched in the international legal system. Following the 1948 Universal Declaration of Human Rights, the 1966 International Covenant on Civil and Political Rights, with more than 165 state parties and signatories, affirms that "every human being has the inherent right to life" and rejects "torture or cruel, inhuman or degrading treatment or punishment" (Articles 6 and 7). The European Union Charter of Fundamental Rights asserts that "everyone has the right to respect for his or her physical and mental integrity" (Article 3), and even in a region where full consolidation of liberal democracy has yet to emerge, the 2013 Association of Southeast Asian Nations (ASEAN) Human Rights Declaration maintains that "no person shall be subject to torture or to cruel, inhuman or degrading treatment or punishment." Bodily integrity, in this sense, needs protection not only from physical abuse but also from the more surreptitious and often more detrimental psychological or mental forms of harassment. Those international declarations unequivocally pledge the state's responsibility to protecting human dignity by condemning any form of mental or physical harassment.

Rather than using the term "foreign aid," I deploy the notion of *foreign strategic support*, which constitutes all forms of US foreign military and economic aid disbursements *and* the strategic political discourses and diplomacy that underpin them. Foreign aid only refers to the material resources given by a donor country, while foreign strategic support, as an aggregate term, includes material resources, political support, and other forms of a donor country's nonmaterial influence upon the partner government. Hence, foreign strategic support is a comprehensive approach to interstate diplomacy. Strategic support includes practices ranging from public diplomacy (*ideational-discursive*) to bilateral aid intended for military, economic, and political purposes (*material*). In material terms, strategic support includes financial aid, joint military and police training exercises, intelligence sharing, lending of military equipment, military advice, civil society support, and public infrastructure programs, among others.

Departing from the dominant social science literature that focuses on aid as a material resource (Morgenthau 1962; Riddell 2008; Ramalingam 2013), I underscore the role of political discourses and ideas in shaping and co-constituting the broader structural conditions that shape how and why a recipient government uses its own domestic resources and foreign assistance. The outcome of any material political resource also depends on the widely shared strategic intentions and ideas of the political actors that have the mandate to manage the use of *both* foreign aid and a recipient government's domestic resources. My theory[2] is integrative, rather than just a mere defense of *either* a material interest-centered explanation *or* an ideationally oriented causal framework. As such, Nicholas Wheeler (2000, 287) compellingly argues that "it is a categorical error to posit a separation between words and deeds when thinking about how the social world hangs together; the former constitute[s] the latter by establishing the boundaries of what is possible . . . words matter . . . the legitimating reasons employed by governments are crucial because they enable and constrain actions." The task of examining US foreign aid's impact requires a closer look into the donor and recipient governments' discourses. Those publicly articulated discourses, policy diagnoses, and beliefs illustrate relevant stakeholders' intentions in regard to the aims, justifications, and implementation goals of foreign aid programs. The term "foreign strategic support" offers a wider explanatory coverage than the term "foreign aid." Considering both the material and ideational aspects of US foreign policy,[3] I comprehensively map out the donor governments' concrete actions and publicly expressed intentions in ways that a mere focus on foreign aid amounts could not. Highlighting the discursive elements of foreign assistance, I show the scope of imagined political possibilities and structural constraints faced by donor and recipient governments. In her study of US foreign policy in India, Carina van de Wetering (2017, 475) argues that "underlying policy discourses create a dominant world view which restricts the foreign policy-makers' options," considering that "policy discourse constructs how security problems, objects, and subjects should be understood and how the security problems can be solved by articulating foreign policy options." When amounts of US foreign aid given to Thailand and the Philippines dramatically increased after 9/11, the overall discursive context focusing on the global war on terror facilitated the militaristic orientation of foreign aid and domestic resources in recipient countries. As Thomas Risse (2000, 5) rightly argues, "socially shared ideas—be it norms or social knowledge about cause-and-effect relationships—not only regulate behavior but also constitute the identity of actors." I contend that any kind of investigation about foreign aid's political consequences must go beyond the excessive analytic emphasis on quantitative aid data; instead, the shared discourses and publicly stated policy preferences of donor and recipient governments are reflective of how and in what ways foreign aid is most likely to be used. I find it analytically productive to study the impact of foreign aid in conjunction with the discourses, ideas, and publicly stated preferences, which reflect the underlying intentions, causal expectations, and priorities of leaders in both donor and recipient countries. Hence, foreign aid per se is neither good nor bad for human rights—relevant stakeholders' shared ideas and converging interests shape the material conditions and political opportunity structures that make foreign aid a potent tool for social transformation.

The Two Waves of Foreign Aid and Human Rights Research

The social science literature on human rights compliance is theoretically rich and empirically informative (Cardenas 2004; Hafner-Burton and Ron 2009; Landman 2005; Regilme 2014b, 2020a). Yet our knowledge about the causal relationship between foreign aid and human rights is still in its infancy, and this research field consists of two historical waves.

The first wave emerged in the 1980s, with the quantitative analysis of Lars Schoultz (1981a, 1981b), who postulated that US foreign aid tended to be allocated to South American governments that systematically repressed their members' physical integrity rights. Schoultz cautioned, however, that there could be a spurious correlation between aid and human rights, and it was not clear at that time which of the two was causing the other. In the 1980s, several quantitative studies focused on whether human rights practices in recipient countries influence foreign aid allocation decisions by donor countries, especially the United States (Schoultz 1981a, 1981b; Cingranelli and Pasquarello 1985; Stohl, Carleton, and Johnson 1984; Carleton and Stohl 1985, 1987; McCormick and Mitchell 1988; Poe 1990). Accordingly, US foreign aid allocation correlated with the human rights situation in recipient countries, and it was unknown whether aid programs improved human rights therein (Poe 1990).

The second wave of research, meanwhile, emerged after the end of the Cold War—an era when international policy debates focused on the role of US foreign policy on the human rights crisis in many recipient countries. Kathryn Sikkink's (2004) work on US policy in Latin America pioneered the second wave of research. While Sikkink's study is commendable for analyzing the evolution of US human rights promotion activities, it did not investigate the role of foreign aid and its domestic political outcomes in recipient countries. After Sikkink's work, various studies have deployed quantitative methods to tease out foreign aid's political consequences in recipient states, and those studies produced some interesting yet inconclusive findings. In recent years, several scholars explored how the human rights behavior of prospective recipient countries affects the foreign aid allocation decisions of donor governments (Lebovic and Voeten 2009; Dietrich and Murdie 2016). Several scholars maintain that the US government provides foreign aid based on the satisfactory human rights record of prospective recipients (Hafner-Burton 2014, 278–79; Demirel-Pegg and Moskowitz 2009). In contrast, some scholars suggest that the US government provides assistance to recipient states that implement high levels of domestic repression and human rights violations (Cingranelli and Pasquarello 1985; Petras 1997; Lai 2003; Robinson 1996; Wood 2003, 131–32), while Blanton (2000, 2005) shows that the human rights record of prospective recipient states is considered when assessing their eligibility for US arms transfers, particularly in the post–Cold War years. Another notable study investigates the impact of shaming a donor government's decision to support human rights-abusive states, and that outcome leads to the reallocation of funds to civil society actors in donor countries (Dietrich and Murdie 2016). Harrigan and Wang (2011) suggest that US strategic military interests impact the scope and conditions of foreign aid allocations.

Scholars from the second wave of human rights research investigate the political consequences of foreign aid in recipient countries. For example, the increased foreign aid commitment from the European Union (EU) might positively impact human rights compliance and democracy, as suggested by the evidence from EU donor countries and their former colonies (Carnegie and Marinov 2017). Barratt (2008) maintains that development assistance undermines economic development outcomes in recipient countries because of the donor's geostrategic interests. One study confirms that foreign aid increases paramilitary attacks and homicide in recipient countries (Dube and Naidu 2015), while another study suggests that it increases the legitimacy or "state reach" of recipient governments (Böhnke and Zürcher 2013). Other scholars posit that US foreign policy directly undermines human rights outcomes abroad (Callaway and Matthews 2008; Sandholtz 2016). Yet those studies are unable to provide a coherent story that specifies the causal mechanisms that link US aid with the domestic political factors in recipient countries.[4] Likewise, a recent quantitative study confirms that the four principal foreign policy instruments of the US government—military intervention, military aid, economic sanctions, and economic aid—are "either neutral in effect or linked to increases in the levels of state repression" (Choi and James 2017, 1). Unfortunately, Choi and James (2017) did not fully specify the general causal processes through which US aid interacts with other domestic conditions in ways that shape human rights outcomes. In recent years, quantitatively oriented political scientists have suggested the detrimental effects of US military aid in recipient countries. Specifically, Ahmed (2019) argues that US aid undermines political rights because the former reduces political accountability via the taxation route, while Jadoon (2017) maintains that both US development and military aid impact the likelihood of civilian killings in recipient countries. Both studies, however, neglected the role of donor and recipient governments' shared ideational beliefs and policy discourses and their impact on the patterns of domestic repression and respect for physical integrity rights.

Both waves of research impart useful insights regarding the relationship between aid and human rights. Yet the current state of knowledge on foreign aid and its plausible connection to human rights face some serious limitations, which my analysis seeks to redress. The majority of existing work on the causes of human rights violations in Global South countries focuses on two sources of explanatory factors: either *transnational* or *domes-*

tic factors. Yet many human rights outcomes in the Global South emerge out of the *dynamic* interactions of transnational *and* domestic factors. Just think about the protests of Palestinian activists against the role of US aid to the Israeli military, or the purported role of the Russian government's recent foreign assistance programs and foreign policy in the highly repressive government in Syria. Many states in the Global South depend on more powerful states for economic aid, political support, and even military assistance to varying degrees over time. This dependence usually has transformative consequences on the domestic social and political relations within small states, including their human rights situation. Those aforementioned studies, with the plausible exception of Robinson's (1996) work on Cold War era US foreign policy, have so far focused only on statistical correlations and broad global patterns and did not substantiate the causal mechanisms that link US foreign aid and human rights.

The important issue is whether foreign assistance shapes physical integrity outcomes in recipient countries. As Emilie Hafner-Burton (2014, 279) rightly contends, "the precise effects of foreign aid or its conditionality on human rights" are still unknown primarily because "most research has explored the effects of aid on development, or more broadly, good governance." The scholarly literature is unsettled regarding the purported direction of the causal relationship between foreign aid and human rights. This book offers the first comprehensive study that specifies the causal mechanisms and the ways in which foreign strategic assistance (aid and diplomacy) shape physical integrity rights in recipient states. I highlight the role of political discourses and ideas that shape how recipient governments use their own domestic resources and foreign strategic support. My contribution to this important debate on foreign aid is to provide an explanatory framework that illuminates how and under which conditions US aid facilitates domestic state repression and physical integrity rights abuses.

Preliminary Evidence: Linking Aid and Rights

Using a global dataset on US foreign assistance and physical integrity rights abuses in recipient states from 1976 until 2016,[5] the figure below shows the average total amount of US aid that matches with a particular severity of physical integrity rights abuses. Based on the Political Terror Scale (PTS), countries with a higher score (maximum of 5) experience the most severe and expansive state-initiated human rights abuses, while countries with a low score of 1 tend to experience very rare occurrences of political murders, torture, and political imprisonment within their borders. Figure 1.1 below demonstrates that countries with a score of 3 —or those that have rampant state-sanctioned extrajudicial killings and imprisonment of political dissidents—receive the highest amounts of US foreign assistance. Although extremely abusive states with a score of 4 or 5 in the PTS received low amounts of US aid, the US government, nonetheless, provided the largest amounts of money to countries with a problematic human rights record. While the US government's apparent intention was to use the aid to improve human rights in recipient states, it appears that the data inconclusively and indirectly suggest otherwise. Such results apparently support the conventional wisdom held by many practitioners and policy-makers, who uphold the idea that foreign aid has a negative impact on human rights in recipient countries (Petras and Veltmeyer 2002; Engel 2014). As figure 1.1 below shows, despite three decades of US aid, many countries in the Global South continue to face difficult obstacles in their democratization and human rights reform efforts. Of course, domestic state repression varies across historical time and political territories, and it is therefore erroneous to assume that all US aid programs need to be blamed for all cases of state repression in recipient countries. Notably, figure 1.2 below suggests that the top country recipients of US aid came from conflict-prone regions, where state violence against civilians is pervasive.

How did such global trends fare at the regional and national levels? Using Southeast Asia as the source of empirical analysis, I investigate the causal relationship between US strategic support and the physical integrity rights situation in Thailand and the Philippines over time. The Philippines and Thailand heavily depended on the United States in terms of political and economic support. Both countries are US mutual defence treaty allies, and their domestic policy elites generally maintain favorable perceptions of American power (Hagelin 1988; Hamilton-Hart 2012). Just to provide a quick preview, the total amounts of US aid over time, especially from 1990 until 2015, covary with the severity of human rights violations in Southeast Asia, particularly its core states, Thailand and the Philippines. Figure 1.3 shows the sudden increase of US military aid to the Philippines and Thailand in the 2000s after a decade-long slump in the 1990s, while figure 1.4 indicates that the number of state-initiated killings of civilians correlated quite well with the level of US military aid. In the early 1990s, both countries recorded high amounts of foreign aid and prevalent human rights abuses, yet the late 1990s recorded the decline of US aid together with a substantial improvement in human rights. In the early 2000s, the spike in

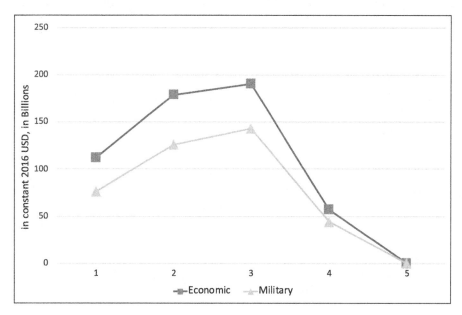

Fig. 1.1. US Foreign Assistance and Physical Integrity Rights, 1976–2016. The data used to create this figure is available on our Fulcrum platform at https://doi.org/10.3998/mpub.12036762.cmp.17

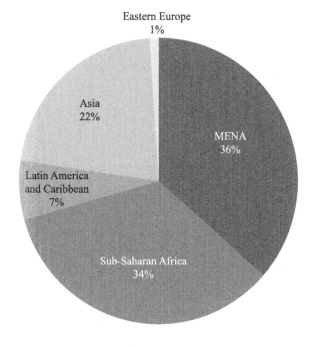

Fig. 1.2. US Total Amount of Economic and Military Aid Distributed per Region, 1976–2016

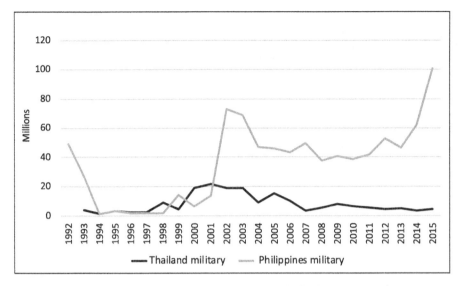

Fig. 1.3. US Military Assistance to the Philippines and Thailand, 1992–2015 (constant 2015 USD). The data used to create this figure is available on our Fulcrum platform at https://doi.org/10.3998/mpub.12036762.cmp.17

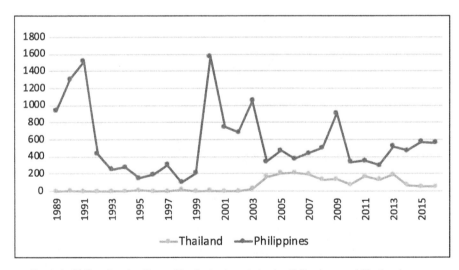

Fig. 1.4. Civilian Deaths Caused by State Agents in the Philippines and Thailand, 1989–2016. The data used to create this figure is available on our Fulcrum platform at https://doi.org/10.3998/mpub.12036762.cmp.17

US military aid coincided with the deterioration of physical integrity rights in recipient countries.

After the Bush administration designated Southeast Asia as the "second front" in the war on terror (Gershman 2002; Sidel 2007), the total amount of US foreign aid to the Philippines and Thailand remarkably increased, and the deterioration of human rights followed thereafter. After receiving post-9/11 US counterterror aid, the Philippines recorded an annual average of 23 cases of enforced disappearances and 132 instances of political killings per year from mid-2001 to 2009, compared to an annual average of only 5 disappearances and 33 political killings from 1992 to 1998.[6] Similarly, Thailand in the 1990s recorded very few state-sanctioned political killings. In contrast, the US-supported Thaksin Shinawatra administration implemented the highly repressive war against purported terrorists and narcotic drugs, which registered at least 2,500 killings of civilians in 2003 alone and hundreds more in the following years until the ouster of Thaksin in 2006.

One might argue that the post-9/11 human rights crisis might have caused the sudden increase and transformation in the focus of US aid. That counterargument, however, is ill-considered. As I show later, the core motivation for the dramatic increase of post-9/11 US military and economic aid to Southeast Asia pertains to the active role of the Philippines and Thailand in Washington's strategic interests. Both countries contributed to the American projection of global military power in the region and to the repression of armed Islamic extremist groups, which have made the southern Philippines (Mindanao) and Thailand (primarily in Pattani) their key hubs. The sudden increase of US aid after 2001 is remarkable, considering that the 1990s recorded a sudden slump in the amount of foreign assistance after decades of generous aid disbursements during the Cold War years.

The covariational relationship of US aid with human rights is not unique to the Philippines and Thailand. In recent years, the top recipients of US aid are widely known for their brutal and widespread human rights violations including Afghanistan, Israel, Iraq, Egypt, Kenya, and Colombia, among many others. For instance, Pakistan, which received US military aid amounting to 95.7 million USD in 2002 (from a meager amount of 1.2 million USD in 2000, or before the war on terror), has been experiencing a deteriorating human rights situation since the early 2000s, ranging from the killings of unarmed political dissidents to collateral civilian deaths due to US-supported counterterror operations. Amnesty International USA (2014) reported that "since 9-11, individuals suspected of having links with 'terrorist' organizations have been arbitrarily detained, denied access to lawyers, and turned over to U.S. custody or to the custody of their home country in violation of local and international law." Similarly, as the key US ally in the global war on terror on the African front, Kenya has been experiencing a deterioration of its human rights situation. For instance, Human Rights Watch noted that the "Kenyan police went on a 10-week rampage, torturing, raping, assaulting, extorting, and arbitrarily detaining at least 1,000 Somali and Ethiopian refugees and asylum seekers and Somali Kenyans," who were publicly branded as terrorists (Human Rights Watch 2013c). International NGOs confirmed that torture is widespread in contemporary Afghanistan, Uganda, Iraq, Jordan, and Pakistan — all of which were the world's top recipients of US aid in 2014 (Wickham 2014).

I chose Thailand and the Philippines as sources of case studies because they possess a lot of similarities to the extent that they can be meaningfully compared and analyzed with each other (Mahoney and Rueschemeyer 2003, 8; Diamond and Robinson 2011). As Jared Diamond and James Robinson (2011, 265) contend, "The natural experimenter should at least attempt to minimize the effects of individual variables other than those of interest, by choosing for comparison systems that are as similar as possible in other respects." Although Thailand was never formally colonized by a Western power, in contrast to the Philippines, both countries are signatories of a mutual defense treaty with the United States, thereby holding their relations with their most powerful donor country almost "constant." Both countries vigorously supported the US strategy of containing communism in the Asia Pacific region during the Cold War era and functioned as the core states in the US-led war on terror in the region (Gershman 2002; Sidel 2007). Classified as middle-income countries, Thailand and the Philippines belong to the same world region, and they therefore share a large set of fairly similar political, economic, and geostrategic challenges over time. The main point is about assessing the causal relationship (Tarrow 2010, 243–44). By beginning the comparison with "common foundations," my case selection strategy is "less likely to overlook unseen variables that might better explain the outcome under consideration" (Go 2011, 20). Both countries have similar political systems in many other respects, except for the key variables under considerations, specifically, the varying interest of donor and recipient governments as well as the magnitude of human rights abuses.

Methodologically, I employ theory-guided process tracing as a "strategy of causal assessment" (Mahoney and Rueschemeyer 2003, 363–65; Beach and Pedersen 2013, 33), which identifies the relevant causal mechanisms that link the explanatory variables with the outcome variable. I validate whether the empirical evidence in each case confirms or disconfirms the hypothesized sequences based on my interest convergence theory of aid and rights. Using the *within-country cases* comparative method, I examine the causes of the human rights situation in two cases pertaining to US-Thailand bilateral relations (before and after the 9/11 attacks) and three cases pertaining to the Philippines: pre-9/11 (1991–2001), the war on terror (2002–09), and post–war on terror (2010–15). In my case selection, I use a particular historical periodization that makes the war on terror (post-9/11) the focal reference point. The case studies on the Philippines allow me to control for other alternative variables not implicated in my theory, particularly because the country was able to maintain an electoral democratic system since the end of the Cold War until 2016. During the tenure of Philippine president Rodrigo Duterte (2016–21), the deterioration of the country's democratic institutions and the unexpected foreign policy shift toward China makes the most recent political period not comparable to previous cases—and therefore I excluded this period from the book. Moreover, the case on post-9/11 Thailand only refers to the time period from 2001 to 2006, because the country experienced a democratic reversal in 2006 followed by several intermittent military takeovers. I focus on the macro-political strategies of various important political leaders rather than the individual motives and impulses of specific human rights abusers committed by rank-and-file state agents (Kalyvas 1999, 246; Tilly 1975, 512). That is because the internal motivations of individual abusers "are usually hard to discern" (Tilly 1975, 512, cited in Kalyvas 1999, 246), while pieces of evidence that indicate the strategies of political leaders are much more accessible and reliable.

My personal interest in state repression and its detrimental consequences to human rights started in 2006. As a third-generation family member involved in the military, I worked as a civilian analyst for a top government intelligence agency in the Philippines, particularly at the time when the global war on terror was at its peak. That personal experience motivated me to deepen my understanding of America's war on terror, particularly by providing a theoretically informed account of its impacts in the Global South. I referred to at least 3,000 open-source documents that include both primary and secondary sources: news articles from leading international and domestic newspapers based in the United States and Southeast Asia; reports from reputable international organizations such as Human Rights Watch and Amnesty International and domestic human rights NGOs in Southeast Asia; open-access government documents; and policy briefs and academic analyses written by academics and area specialists. I present a causal story that best explains the variations in physical integrity rights outcomes during various time periods in Thailand and the

Philippines. Deploying data triangulation (Flick 2014, 184), I cross-verify empirical facts from documentary sources from a diverse range of actors or organizations with nominally different motivations (e.g., human rights NGOs, government commission reports, and media sources). I benefited from the abundant primary literature and secondary sources on Southeast Asia written by area specialists—a feature that facilitates good comparative analysis because theoretical arguments can be easily accounted for using a variety of empirical sources (Skocpol 1979, xiv–xv).

It is nearly impossible to trace how specific amounts of US aid could be linked to a particular incident of human rights abuse. Besides, there is a strong empirical and theoretical basis in previous studies supporting foreign aid as inherently fungible (Kono and Montinola 2009, 615; Feyzioglu, Swaroop, and Zhu 1998), which means that recipient states possess substantial leeway in redirecting aid from its original purpose to another aim unintended by its donor. Thus, I distinguish foreign military and economic aid programs *only* to show the broader motivations of the United States during a particular time period. In each chapter, I highlight the strategic purposes of foreign assistance through publicly invoked discourses and pronouncements of the donor and recipient government officials, allies, and other prominent political actors. Besides, donor governments "substitute" a particular foreign aid program for another, as was the case of the US government from 1990 to 2004, when it evaded foreign aid restrictions to human rights abusive-countries by giving the latter *food aid* instead, primarily because of Washington's strategic interests (Fariss 2010). Thus, the fungible nature of foreign aid makes the focus on the shared purposes of aid a more reliable strategy than blindly interpreting the registered amounts for each aid program.

The Puzzle and the Arguments

The principal questions that frame this study are does foreign aid, or what I call *foreign strategic support*, transform the physical integrity rights situation in recipient countries? If so, how and under what constellation of conditions does foreign strategic support impact human rights? I focus on the variation in human rights outcomes in Southeast Asia vis-à-vis the varying strategic purposes and amounts of US aid over time, particularly from the early 1990s to 2016. I systematically trace the relationship and patterns of influence between US strategic support and the physical integrity rights situation in Thailand and the Philippines in two ways: (1) during recent historical time periods *within* each of those countries, (2) and *between* the two countries.

In brief, I argue that the donor and recipient governments' converging interests, together with the domestic legitimacy of the recipient government, primarily shape the purposes of foreign aid programs and domestic policies. My core argument refutes the notion that recipient countries usually do not have the power to shape the strategic purposes and the implementation patterns of foreign aid programs. Although the economist Nancy Qian (2014, 1) maintains that "foreign aid is often determined by the objectives of donor countries rather than the needs of recipient countries," I demonstrate, in contrast, that aid recipient governments instrumentalize foreign aid in ways that bolster their domestic political legitimacy. The relationship between foreign aid and human rights outcomes is much more complex than a simple correlation. The following chapters demonstrate that, at least in the cases of post–Cold War US foreign strategic assistance to South East Asia, domestic politics in aid recipient countries shape the ways state actors use foreign assistance. Specifically, US foreign strategic assistance reinforces the dominant or emerging policy priorities of recipient governments and influential domestic political actors.

Foreign aid is usually characterized as either good or bad for Global South countries, particularly in terms of economic development, good governance, and even human rights. This book dispels the simplistic and blatantly ideological characterizations of foreign aid and its transformative consequences in aid recipient countries. Alternatively, I challenge the conventional wisdom, which often implies that material resources (e.g., foreign aid) have inherent properties, thereby making it either "good" or "bad" for recipient countries. As Wendt (1995, 75) rightfully argues, "social structures are real and objective, not 'just talk' . . . but this objectivity depends on shared knowledge." My theory underscores how donor and recipient governments' shared expectations and strategic purposes shape the patterns of use of foreign strategic support.

This book is part of the emerging research agenda in the social sciences that investigates the linkages between domestic and extranational factors in producing local political change, specifically in the Global South (Schmitz 2004; Krasner 2010; Regilme 2014a). Using analytic eclecticism (Sil and Katzenstein 2010; Regilme 2018a), I offer a novel theory of foreign aid and human rights by assessing the interaction between *ideational* factors and the *strategic-instrumental* motivations of both *extranational* and *domestic* actors. Whereas comparative politics and International Relations (IR) scholars often focus only on one spatial level of analysis (either domestic *or* transnational) in studying political violence and human rights, I offer a *multilevel* theory of how and under which conditions transnational factors can impact physical integrity rights outcomes in the Global South countries. At the macro-level, I show how critical junctures in the international system (e.g., the end of the Cold War or the global war on terror) enabled transformations in the ideational expectations and policies of the core state in the international system, particularly the United States. At the meso-level, I demonstrate how US foreign policy shapes and interacts with the domestic policy agendas and preferences of state leaders in partner states. At the micro-level, I illustrate various examples of how normative shifts and converging policy changes adopted by the United States and its partner governments affect the patterns of domestic state repression and an individual's physical integrity rights. Consequently, I establish how political transformations are generated by analyzing how ideas and policy actions are contested within and between states.[7]

Moreover, I emphasize the role of ideational factors in shaping the material consequences of foreign aid, considering that "the central factor overlooked in the literature on aid is ideational: ideas about goals and purposes of aid policy shape its formulation and implementation" (Van der Veen 2011, 2). That analytical focus on the relationship between political discourses and foreign aid is a missing yet important perspective in the mainstream literature on foreign assistance.[8] First, similar to Lene Hansen's (2006) groundbreaking discourse analysis of the Bosnian War, my analysis shows the integrative relationship of ideas and discourses vis-à-vis the material conditions, instead of demonstrating the significance of one over the other (Hansen 2006, 20). Second, I highlight the political agency of Global South actors as they negotiate and chart their political trajectories with powerful actors in the Global North. Whereas mainstream International Relations has historically discarded the role of peripheral actors, I deploy what Amitav Acharya (2014, 649) calls a "Global IR" approach, which "eschews exceptionalism" and "recognizes multiple forms of agency beyond material power, including resistance, normative action, and local constructions of global order." Third, I offer a causal story that maps out the mechanisms that link US strategic assistance and physical integrity rights outcomes in recipient countries, particularly in ways that previous quantitative studies on the topic have systematically ignored. Although such quantitative studies advance our understanding of the topic, many of those studies rely on what Mearsheimer and Walt (2013, 435–36) call "simplistic hypothesis testing" instead of offering "the big story" that meaningfully explains the relationship between foreign aid and human rights. In this book, I harness the explanatory strengths of both numerical and qualitative data analysis to understand the paths of influence through which US foreign policy shapes human rights outcomes. In teasing out the correlation between US aid and human rights, I refer to the quantitative data from the Uppsala Conflict Data Program, the Political Terror Scale, the USAID Greenbook, and local human rights data sources in the Philippines and Thailand. In understanding how those quantitative data relate to the politics on the ground, I implement comparative historical analysis of a wide range of qualitative data sources so as to provide a holistic, nuanced, and contextualized demonstration of the plausibility of my theory of foreign aid and rights. This balanced deployment of quantitative and qualitative data is necessary precisely because, as Sally Engle Merry (2016, 3) rightly argues, "despite the value of numbers for exposing problems . . . they provide knowledge that is decontextualized, homogenized, and remote from local systems of meaning." Fourth, this book differs from previous research on human rights in Southeast Asia, because so much of the International Relations and area studies literature on the region is mostly atheoretical[9] (Acharya and Stubbs 2006, 126). Indeed, the influential qualitative studies on human rights have focused on Latin America (Sikkink 1993; Lutz and Sikkink 2000, 2001; Gill 2004; Schmidli 2013).[10] Hence, I redress that gap by offering new theoretical insights developed primarily from the Southeast Asian region (Hafner-Burton and Ron 2007, 382).

Overview of the Book

This book is divided into three parts. The first part starts with this introductory chapter, which discusses the overarching puzzle about human rights and foreign aid and explains the overall scholarly and political significance of this study. Chapter 2 outlines the theoretical groundwork that guides my investigation of the relationship between US aid and human rights. Particularly, I demonstrate how and to what extent the donor and recipient governments' converging interests and policy preferences shape the scope and purposes of foreign aid programs, political discourses, and domestic state resources. Thus, the converging interests of donor and recipient countries, as an *ideational* component, affect how external assistance and domestic policies promote either intensified state violence or increased prioritization of nonmilitaristic priorities. Holding all other factors constant, aid recipient governments with weak domestic political legitimacy are more likely to instrumentalize foreign aid and their own

internal state resources to violently repress *both* unarmed and armed political dissidents. In contrast, recipient and donor states converging on a
wide range of policy preferences are more likely to use foreign strategic
assistance and domestic resources for nonmilitaristic aims. That scenario,
however, does not necessarily mean that all human rights abuses would
disappear; because of the long-standing institutional challenges within the
state apparatus, collateral abuses could still occur as state agents fail to
distinguish armed targets from ordinary civilians. I attribute those residual
abuses to the long-standing culture of impunity that is perpetrated by ineffective judicial institutions and the lack of professionalization in the coercive state agencies. In chapter 2, I elaborate those theoretical arguments,
which highlight the causal mechanisms that link foreign aid to domestic
political factors.

Subsequently, the second part is composed of five chapters. Each chapter therein zooms in on a specific case of human rights outcome, whereby
the relationship between US strategic support and the level of state repression in recipient countries is explored during a given time period. Chapters
3, 4, and 5 deal with three distinctive historical periods of human rights
outcomes in the Philippines. Chapter 3 presents evidence of how the converging interests of the administrations of US president Bill Clinton and
Philippine president Fidel V. Ramos on democracy promotion improved
the human rights situation in the Philippines. Chapter 4 confirms how
the administration of US president George W. Bush's "war on terror,"
as a response to the 9/11 attacks, enabled a dramatic increase in absolute
amounts of US aid to the Philippines. The terror-oriented US strategic
support and the domestic policy agenda of Philippine president Gloria
Arroyo focused on counterterrorism and national security. This convergence in counterterror agendas dramatically bolstered the capacities of the
Philippine security apparatus— particularly the police, military, and state
security agencies. That outcome led to a substantial increase in *systemic*
and *collateral* deaths of civilians due to deliberate state actions. In chapter
5, despite the departure of the Barack Obama and the Benigno Aquino
administrations from their predecessors' counterterror agenda, the impunity culture perpetrated by the military and judicial agencies facilitated the
emergence of *collateral* human rights abuses in the Philippines.

Chapter 6 explores how the improved human rights situation in Thailand resulted from the democratization reform efforts of the Clinton
administration and the emerging liberal democratic elites in Thailand.
Chapter 7 shows how the reforms in the 1990s were overturned when Thai
prime minister Thaksin Shinawatra took over the executive helm. Receiv-

ing increased US counterterror aid in the context of the global war on terror, the Thaksin administration—in its aim of consolidating its fledgling legitimacy amid domestic political opposition from Bangkok-based elites and the middle class—implemented pervasive systematic killings and the harassment of both unarmed and armed political dissidents. This unprecedented level of state repression under the Thaksin government was recorded as perhaps one of the most horrific periods in recent Thai political history. Several thousand people were killed in the 2003 war on drugs alone, when Thai government agents and state proxies extrajudicially killed alleged drug addicts, local political opposition members, and other civilians. Those victims perished as the result of Thaksin's mobilization of domestic state resources and US foreign strategic support toward counterterrorism.

Using the two-level game of diplomacy (Putnam 1988), I show how aid recipient governments strategically frame their discourses and interests in ways that adapt to the preferences of their own domestic public and the donor government. As shown in chapters 4 and 7, the emergence of Southeast Asian governments' terror-oriented focus was enabled by the strategic alignment of the policy preferences of the Bush administration, the Thai and Philippine governments, and the domestic public. At the international level, the Arroyo and Thaksin governments made the case that the terror threat to the United States was strongly linked to the armed Islamic insurgencies in southern Thailand and Mindanao in the Philippines, respectively (Banlaoi 2010; Sidel 2007; Singh 2007), which in turn motivated the Bush administration to provide counterterror assistance. At the domestic level, the overwhelming public insecurity due to the 9/11 terror attacks in the United States contributed to the perceived need for intensified state violence (Lopez and Crispin 2003).

In contrast, chapters 3, 5, and 6 show that the confluence of nonmilitaristic and pro-human-rights policy preferences of the United States and Southeast Asian governments in the 1990s generated an improvement in the human rights situation in Thailand and the Philippines. The pre-9/11 Thai and Philippine governments, which enjoyed strong domestic legitimacy, strategically localized discourses that sought (1) to respond to the emerging political demands of their domestic public and (2) to complement the US government's strategic purposes. Thus, in chapters 3, 5, and 6, I provide evidence that US strategic support complemented the Thai and Philippine government's domestic policies that sought to bolster economic development and human rights.

In the last part, the final chapter summarizes my key empirical findings on US foreign aid and human rights outcomes in Southeast Asia and their broader scholarly and practical implications. I reflect on how my theory of interest convergence can be used as a lens for understanding human rights crises elsewhere in the world, including Pakistan, Colombia, and Kenya. Moving forward in the next chapter, I present my theory of interest convergence, which serves as an explanatory framework for understanding how foreign strategic support shapes human rights outcomes in recipient countries.

TWO

United States Aid Imperium and Human Rights

On March 19, 2017, the *Los Angeles Times*[1] reported that President Donald Trump had proposed severe budget cuts to annual US contributions to the United Nations (UN). Trump's proposal generated serious concerns among members of the international aid community (Dixon 2017). The UN and its constituent agencies such as the World Food Program manage a wide variety of development projects in the Global South. These programs not only seek to foster long-term economic development but they also aim to alleviate the suffering of millions of people caught in humanitarian crises. Faced with the prospect of massive cuts in US aid, UN aid officials expected that more than 20 million people in Nigeria, Yemen, Somalia, and South Sudan would continue to suffer from starvation and hunger. That probable outcome was not only terrible because it endangered human lives, but, in the long-term, political instability could ensue without the much-needed US foreign assistance. Yet those who oppose foreign aid maintain that it does more harm than good in recipient countries (Moyo 2009), while others underscore how it improves the lives of those in the Global South (Wallis 2009). Both views, however, are not clear about the mechanisms linking foreign aid with several transformative outcomes in the Global South—ranging from improved public health, gender empowerment, good governance, and physical integrity rights, among many others. To redress that gap, I introduce an original theory that illuminates the relationship between foreign strategic assistance and the human rights situation in recipient states. My *theory of interest convergence* highlights the confluence of donor and recipient governments' shared interests and the recipient government's domestic legitimacy as the main independent variables.

The first part of this chapter discusses my theoretical framework and arguments, which will be applied in the case studies of post–Cold War US strategic assistance to Thailand and the Philippines. Next, I introduce the explanatory factors for human rights outcomes, particularly the convergence of the dominant policy preferences of donor and recipient governments, the nature of foreign strategic support, and the recipient government's domestic legitimacy. I explain how constant domestic conditions in recipient countries—a weak judiciary and a corrupt state security apparatus—generate human rights abuses even in the absence of the terror-oriented policy convergence of donor and recipient governments. The chapter elaborates the five key processes that link foreign aid policy convergence with the scope and extent of state-initiated human rights abuses: (1) strategic localization of discourses; (2) resource mobilization, which includes purpose-driven foreign aid and the internal resources of the recipient state; (3) selective political repression; (4) erroneous coercive practices; and (5) the culture of impunity.

Key Arguments: Foreign Aid Imperium and Human Rights

My main argument states that the convergence of the political interests and policy preferences of the donor and recipient countries' political elites—together with the recipient government's strength of domestic legitimacy—impact the magnitude of state repression, which in turn shapes physical integrity rights outcomes. When a recipient state with strong domestic legitimacy receives US strategic assistance, abuses tend to be less pervasive, particularly because domestic repression becomes unnecessary for regime consolidation. Yet, by fostering a culture of impunity, a corrupt coercive apparatus and a weak judicial system generate residual human rights violations even in the absence of a statewide policy of increased state repression. In contrast, shared interests in a militaristic agenda facilitate the escalation of state violence, which in turn engenders the proliferation of abuses. In this scenario, a recipient government is likely to use foreign aid and external political support in order to consolidate its power through the systematic domestic repression of all forms of political opposition. Regardless of the recipient government's domestic legitimacy, foreign aid amplifies the preexisting policy preferences of key political leaders in prospective recipient countries. As shown by panel data analysis covering 124 countries from 1960 to 2009, "aid makes already democratic countries more democratic and already dictatorial countries more dictatorial" (Dutta, Leeson, and Williamson 2013, 219). This amplification effect emerges as the outcome of aid giving, whereby "donors purchase policy support from recipients who use at least some of the assistance to ensure that they are securely ensconced in power" (Bueno de Mesquita and Smith 2007, 254). In the next chapters, I show how US foreign aid in the 1990s amplified the emerging demand in Southeast Asia for democratic governance and the constitutionalization of human rights protection. I demonstrate how US assistance bolstered the coercive capacities of the Thai and Philippine governments, which at that time faced considerable domestic challenges to their political legitimacy. In return, the Clinton administration in the 1990s expanded its access to Southeast Asian markets and promoted the legitimacy of democratic governance as the ideal system, while the Bush administration during the war on terror on the Southeast Asian front sought to quell armed Islamic rebel groups that were framed as linked to a global jihad against the United States.

Foreign aid operates within a world order that facilitates constitutive yet hierarchical relationships between a powerful donor state and a comparatively less powerful recipient country (including the political elites within and beyond those states). Although liberal internationalism, as the foundational ideology of the US-dominated postwar international system, considers foreign aid as constitutive of benevolent intervention, that order is underwritten by the logic of domination. The American foreign aid imperium legitimizes itself when US government officials emphasize foreign aid programs' purported benefits to a recipient government: either the framing is primarily for terror-oriented, militaristic goals or for a wide range of socioeconomic, nonmilitaristic purposes. Barnett (2011, 30) argues that the end of the Cold War until the present period constitutes the age of liberal humanitarianism, whereby liberal peace, economic globalization, and human rights are invoked to justify humanitarian practices. Yet, as Parmar (2016, 364) accurately notes, that "liberal internationalism silences about the order's underlying racial and imperial character, and the role of military violence in the periphery that proved fundamental to the order's construction and, via later wars, recalibration, obscure core features of the international system." Swedlund (2017) describes foreign aid politics as a "development dance," as it occurs through a back-and-forth process of negotiation, but that process is fundamentally asymmetrical. I show how the politics of aid giving emerges within the context of the American *aid impe-rium* and its core partner states in Southeast Asia. Similar to Peter Katzen-stein's conceptualization (2005, 208–48), imperium here refers to both the *territorial* (militaristic and geostrategic) and *nonterritorial* (informal forms of diplomacy and economic, cultural, and socioeconomic interventions) practices and expressions of American power, particularly in foreign poli-cies, aid programs, and public diplomacy. Similar to Julian Go's (2011, 7–9) notion of the American empire, I define imperium as the unequal power relations that constitute the processes through which a dominant politi-cal entity (such as the United States) shapes the sociopolitical formations, norms, and material distributive politics of subordinate states and societies. Constitutive of an asymmetrically dialogical relationship, the American imperium deploys foreign strategic assistance to promote its own interests and legitimizes that tool through the discourse of philanthropy and mutual benefit. In some ways, the imperium also demonstrates the reverse direc-tion of influence. Specifically, the US government responds to the politi-cal interests and policy preferences of subordinate partner governments; within its own territory, the United States adopts repressive tactics that were initially deployed in the peripheries of the imperium (McCoy 2009). Thus, I reject the analytic use of *empire*, which often implies a one-way form of control by the ruler and the absence of political agency on the part of the ruled subjects.

This aid imperium demonstrates the mutually reinforcing relationship between the powerful donor government and subordinate recipient gov-ernments. As the aid supplier, the United States provides foreign strategic support to reconfigure certain political, social, and economic facets of a recipient country, in ways that conform to the perceived strategic interests of the American imperium. Grewal (2017, 61) traces American humanitar-ianism's origins from "the project of Western humanitarianisms and their imperial histories," but with its own particularities: namely, "it builds upon common histories of 'charity,' missionary work, and the civilizing project enacted in the so-called developing world through war . . . and transnational NGOs." As shown in the succeeding chapters, this humanitarian imperium operated both during the noncrisis period in the 1990s (through various nonmilitaristic aid programs that promote trade, civil society activism, and other socioeconomic programs) and in the terror-oriented post-9/11 years (through counterterror and militaristic aid programs). In maintaining the imperium, the US government projects its strategic interests through a wide range of foreign strategic assistance programs ranging from disaster relief to foreign military financing. As Hattori (2001, 633) argues, foreign aid represents the "symbolic power politics between donor and recipient," and in many ways foreign aid "transform[s] material dominance and subordination into gestures of generosity and gratitude." That transformation of crude power assertion to a sense of generosity illustrates the American imperium's legitimization of unequal power relations between the giver and the receiver. Even neoclassical development economist William Easterly (2008, 2) admits that "foreign aid has been getting ever more imperial over the past quarter-century"—if only because in the last three decades or so, foreign military adventurism has been mixed with traditional civilian development aid work. Thus, foreign aid "is not a great act of generosity," for it can secure "things donors want—such as political support and economic advantage, whether directly for donor businesses or indirectly through policy change" (Glennie 2011, 5). Thus, donor and recipient states mutually co-constitute each other in the American aid imperium: through *inequality* in power and *differentiation* in terms of identity. These unequal and differentiated relationships in the international development sector reflect the fundamental logic of the international system—or, as Lora Viola (2013, 124) calls it, stratificatory differentiation as the constitutive principle of contemporary world politics.

On the demand side of foreign aid, recipient governments are not passive agents waiting to be controlled by the donor state. Rather, through the imperium's foreign strategic support, influential leaders and elites within the subordinate recipient countries assert their own interests and strengthen their legitimacy. As I discuss later, my theory zooms in on the recipient state's active role in the formation of its own domestic and foreign policies. Specifically, a recipient state deploys various legitimization strategies that justify the influx of foreign aid to an extent satisfactory to their own political survival and to the preferences of the domestic public and the donor government—in this case, the United States.

The Explanatory Power of Shared Interests in Foreign Aid

In linking foreign strategic assistance with human rights, I refer to three key explanatory variables: (1) the interest convergence of donor and recipient governments; (2) foreign strategic support; and (3) the domestic legitimacy of the recipient government. *Interest convergence* refers to the degree in which donor and recipient governments agree on the principal themes and substantive focus of their bilateral policy agenda. The substantive focus of this convergence shapes the overall trajectory of the recipient government's domestic policies and implementation patterns of foreign strategic assistance. I only refer to two essential and useful elements of the interest convergence concept: (1) "convergence of *policy goals*, a coming together of intent to deal with common policy problems," and (2) "*policy content*, defined as the more formal manifestations of government policy statutes, administrative rules . . . and so on" (Bennett 1991, 218; emphasis added). Hence, convergence consists of two distinct components: (1) foreign strategic support consisting of foreign aid as the material component and the donor government's strategic purpose as the ideational component; and (2) the recipient government's domestic motivations, which are primarily shaped by the strength of its domestic legitimacy.

The targets of state repression depend on the perceived *strength of the domestic political legitimacy* of the aid recipient government. My notion of legitimacy borrows the insights from Daniel Bodansky (1999, 601; see also 2008), who maintains that "authority has popular legitimacy if the subjects to whom it is addressed accept it as justified," and that "the more positive the public attitudes about an institution's right to govern, the greater its popular legitimacy." Thus, political legitimacy is not a question of "all or nothing but of more or less" (Bodansky 1999, 623). *Weak domestic legitimacy* increases the likelihood that the recipient government will resort to the systematic and violent repression *of all forms of political opposition*—a process that constitutes a broader strategy of regime consolidation. The aim is to strengthen domestic political support from various state agencies (especially from the military and the police) and to undermine political dissidence from the broader society. For a highly insecure chief government executive, the intensification of state violence becomes an appealing option especially in the context of a security crisis, considering that political survival is a key imperative for attaining other personal objectives (Bueno de Mesquita et al. 2005, 23). In contrast, if domestic legitimacy is considerably strong, then the central government is likely to limit state violence against armed political oppositionists.[2]

Domestic legitimacy has four observable attributes. The first aspect pertains to the public perceptions of the government's legitimacy. If most of the elites and civil society groups perceive that there are several equally (or almost equally) strong and viable contenders for political leadership that the incumbent faces, then the central government is considered weak. Second, the issue of timing of the leader's ascendancy to power vis-à-vis the sociopolitical context is also important. Leaders who are serving their term amid a sudden economic crisis or huge political scandals are more likely to be perceived as weak; such crises tend to be attributed to the leader's incompetence or administrative failures. Third, when dubious electoral procedures or extralegal methods (e.g., military coups) facilitated the appointment of the chief government executive, the strength of the central civilian government is highly likely to be fragile. Fourth, a weak civilian government is present when its elected top leader won only a small majority of the electorate. Various factors play a key role in ascertaining the strength of political legitimacy and survival of the regime. Those factors include political support from civil society actors, business elites, the broader domestic public, and key figures within the coercive apparatus including the police and military.

There are two primary ways through which a weak recipient government engages in the violent repression of *both* armed and unarmed political opposition. First, the elected incumbent gathers political support within the state's coercive apparatus, which in turn is tasked to deploy state violence against political dissidents (de Mesquita and Smith 2009; de Mesquita et al. 2005; Hafner-Burton, Hyde, and Jablonski 2014). This is common in many countries in the Global South facing an armed nonstate rebellion while receiving substantial foreign aid. Recipient states may still face threats from various warring elite groups, which sometimes resort to violence, despite these countries' formal transition to procedural democracy. Second, insecure recipient governments employ the state's coercive apparatus in violently repressing all forms of political opposition, including civilians. As my case studies demonstrate, a politically adventurous military institution is more likely to misuse foreign strategic support in ways that contravene human rights norms. In particular, the state's military and police agencies have been crucial in wielding "considerable political power" due to its "authoritarian past" (Croissant, Kuehn, and Lorenz 2012, viii). Several years after the democratic transition, the military and police agencies have yet to fully professionalize and to implement a rigorous system of accountability. For instance, even before the 2001 US-Pakistan agreement that facilitated the influx of more than 10 billion USD worth of covert and 12 billion USD worth of overt terror-oriented US military and economic aid from 2001 to 2009, "money from such unsupervised budgets had enabled the [Pakistani] Army to become one of the richest and largest industrial, banking, and landowning bodies in Pakistan" (Ibrahim 2009, 4). This preexisting condition also constituted the military's vast webs of political clientelism, considering that terror-oriented foreign aid is usually tagged as confidential in the state's coffers. Although foreign aid could deliver welfare-maximizing effects in recipient countries, terror-oriented aid often eludes the various systems of checks and balances and public transparency (Easterly 2008, 13–14). More often than not, recipient governments invoke national security to justify why the use of some of their domestic resources and foreign aid should be hidden from public scrutiny.

Severity of Physical Integrity Rights Abuses

I classify state-initiated human rights violations into two types, which are primarily based on the recipient government's motivations in implementing domestic political repression. First, collateral violations emerge as outcomes of *erroneous coercive state practices*, which pertain to the state agents' actions resulting from regular counterterror, policing, and military operations. Such abuses become more widespread especially in societies with a highly entrenched culture of impunity. Many abusive state agents go unpunished as the leadership of the military and police shield their own comrades from legal prosecution. Second, state-initiated human rights abuses emerge as outcomes of *selective political repression*, whereby state violence is systematically employed to repress many forms of political resistance, including civilian activists.

Impunity Culture as the Enduring Domestic Condition

Particular enduring domestic conditions—a weak judiciary and a corrupt coercive apparatus—generate state-initiated *collateral* human rights abuses, *regardless* of the substantive content and magnitude of a foreign strategic support. The bureaucratic defects in the judiciary and the coercive state agencies are difficult to change, especially in a short period of time. Those defects produce *collateral* human rights abuses *irrespective* of the recipient government's degree of legitimacy—and even in the absence of militaristic or nonmilitaristic foreign aid. The two key factors that are likely to reinforce the magnitude of collateral abuse include (1) the role of the military in democratic civilian politics and (2) the effectiveness of the judicial system. The next two subsections discuss how these enduring domestic political conditions shape human rights outcomes, regardless of the scope and purpose of foreign aid. Such long-standing factors are important because, as Paul Pierson (2004, 10) argues, "the institutional 'rules of the game,' and even citizens' basic ways of thinking about the political world will often generate self-reinforcing dynamics."

Notwithstanding bilateral convergence on a nonmilitaristic policy agenda and the recipient government's strong domestic legitimacy, residual human rights abuses still persist. Those violations emerge because of the enduring *culture of impunity* generated by a corrupt judiciary and coercive state agencies. Legal scholar Diane Orentlicher (2005, 6) defines impunity as "the impossibility, *de jure* or *de facto*, of bringing the perpetrators of violations to account—whether in criminal, civil, administrative or disciplinary proceedings—since they are not subject to any inquiry that might lead to their being accused, arrested, tried and, if found guilty, sentenced to appropriate penalties, and to making reparations to their victims." Impunity refers to the systemic dispensation from "accountability, penalty, punishment, or legal sanction for perpetrators of illegal acts" (Opotow 2001, 149). An impunity culture generates human rights violations, particularly when commanding military and police officers fail to investigate, prosecute, and punish suspected state agents for abusive use of power (Bienert 2018, 78). That failure "sends a message to subordinates that their superiors at least do not care about unlawful conduct or—even worse—tacitly endorse or even expect such behaviour" (Bienert 2018, 78). A rigorous system of oversight and accountability mechanisms is likely to prevent such abuses, which in turn could undermine an impunity culture. The Human Rights Committee of the United Nations (2004, 118) considers the failure to investigate and to prosecute suspected abusers as constitutive of a human rights violation on its own. As the anti-impunity norm remains the core element for the prevention of human rights abuses (Sikkink 2011; Engle 2016, 15; Jorgensen 2009), judicial institutions as well as the police and military leadership play a key role in ensuring fair trials, speedy prosecutions, and just punishment of abusive state agents. While elected governments come and go over time, the long-term reformation of the criminal justice system is likely to prevent state actors from committing human rights abuses. Notably, "prosecutions are considered to be an unalloyed good: they deter future abuses, promote the rule of law, restore the confidence of citizens in government, guarantee respect for human rights, and ensure justice for victims of atrocious crimes" (Engle, Miller, and Davis 2016, 1). After all, the threat that convicted human rights abusers are very likely to face incarceration and other criminal justice punitive measures tends to deter prospective abusers (Hafner-Burton 2013, 38–39).

Even with a shared pro-human-rights agenda of donor and recipient governments, state agents still harass activists and civilians for several reasons. First, seeking to undermine civilians who obstruct their commercial interests, business actors contract state agents in exchange for financial rewards. Those collateral abuses emerge in societies that do not have professionalized coercive agencies and an impartial judiciary, which jointly function as credible signals of deterrence to potential state abusers. The culture of impunity remains pervasive in the Global South, including Thailand and the Philippines (Haberkorn 2018; Franco and Abinales 2007). In the context of Colombia's US-funded war on drugs, the absence of democratic oversight of the armed forces that enjoyed high levels of US security assistance facilitated the strong sense of impunity enjoyed by the Colombian armed forces (Fajardo-Heyward 2015, 18; Regilme 2018b). I show why collateral abuses emerged despite a pro-human-rights agenda of the United States and recipient governments in three case study chapters: (1) the Philippines in the post–Cold War 1990s, (2) Thailand in the post–Cold War 1990s, and (3) the Philippines in the post–war on terror period, 2010–16.

Indeed, terror-oriented US foreign strategic support intended for consolidated liberal democratic states (e.g., Japan, Australia, New Zealand, Canada) is more likely to be used solely for the purpose of targeting armed rebel groups, rather than in the systematic repression of unarmed political dissent. That is likely the case because of favorable conditions, such as the government's strong domestic legitimacy, professionalized coercive agencies, and effective judicial systems. Human rights abuses, however, can still emerge as outcomes of erroneous policing practices rather than the systematic targeting of peaceful political dissent. Thus, state-initiated abuses in the Global North, which were once confronted with the post-9/11 terror threat, were less prevalent than in the Global South.

State Security Agencies' Intervention in Civilian Politics

Ideally, the military and police forces should be subservient to the leadership of a democratically elected civilian government. Yet that is far from the case, especially in many electoral democratic countries in the Global South, where the likelihood of a potential military coup is quite high compared to the relatively more professionalized military bureaucracies elsewhere (Maniruzzaman 1992). In contrast to a highly interventionist armed forces, the officers and agents of a politically disengaged and highly professionalized security apparatus consistently display expertise, responsibility, and corporateness (Huntington 1957).

The patterns of state violence can be viewed either in terms of aspirational neutrality *or* political partisanship—a binary opposition that must be viewed as a matter of degree. In a politically partisan form of state violence, the civilian government and armed state agents "transform into criminal enemies those who publicly criticize the state," or those more commonly known as "dissenters" who "believe they can lawfully advocate radical change through the spoken word and achieve it through public persuasion" (Brodeur 1983, 512; see also Brodeur 2007, 28).

A highly interventionist state security apparatus displays several features. First, state security officials are directly involved in politics either as full-time politicians or political appointees in top civil service positions. Second, the armed forces' recent historical record of coups and insurrections also suggests strong interventionist tendencies. Both of these qualities demonstrate the enduring political interventionism of state security agencies, which in turn makes them vulnerable to the whimsical ambitions of civilian politicians. As chapters 3 through 7 show, contemporary Thailand and the Philippines demonstrate such persistent forms of political adventurism in ways that generate abuses even in the absence of a statewide policy of increased repression.

The sudden influx of foreign strategic support, especially the highly fungible counterterror aid, is likely to trigger rent-seeking activities among state security officers (Djankov, Montalvo, and Reynal-Querol 2008; Maren 1997; Remmer 2004). Motivated by long-standing institutional corruption and unattractive compensation packages, state security agents kill civilians in return for financial gain or other forms of personal enrichment. The quality of recipient countries' state institutions "mediates the impact of unearned foreign income on government survival," particularly through government patronage in more authoritarian or newly democratized societies (Ahmed 2012, 48). In countries with a weak central government, state security agents are likely to convert public resources into private gains, which contribute to state-initiated human rights abuses (Gupta, de Mello, and Sharan 2001, 752–53). As shown in the next chapters, the sudden influx of foreign strategic assistance to recipient governments with weak domestic legitimacy fueled the incentives of military and police agencies to target civilians—a phenomenon that is widely confirmed in the theoretical literature (Barratt 2004; Bräutigam and Knack 2004; Jablonski 2014; Kono and Montinola 2009; Nielsen et al. 2011; Poe 1990; Savun and Tirone 2011). Co-opting a civilian government with weak domestic legitimacy, state security agencies seek to kill armed nonstate rebels and to eliminate political opposition. Because of their low compensation and the pervasive culture of corruption, state agents easily acquiesce to the political ambitions of the incumbent civilian leader and his or her allies. Determined to strengthen its rule, the incumbent government diverts foreign aid to coercive state agencies, which are then tasked with repressing political dissidents. That tendency is amplified when a donor government pushes for a militaristic agenda in its bilateral relations, as was the case in US foreign relations during the Cold War or the post-9/11 periods.

Ineffective Judiciary

How does an ineffective judicial system facilitate human rights abuses, especially collateral abuses, and regardless of the presence of foreign strategic support? There are three notable qualities of an ineffective judicial system: (1) the propensity of courts and state prosecutorial services to be easily subjected to external pressures (*lack of judicial independence*); (2) institutional inefficiencies in the bureaucratic management of case investigation, prosecution, and adjudication (*judicial inefficiencies*); and (3) the lack of adequate and timely laws on human rights protection (*legal vacuum*). Judicial independence promotes a "constitutional culture, which teaches state actors that the legal bounds of the system cannot be transgressed for the achievement of partisan political gains" (Larkins 1996, 607). Courts must be committed to "the principled enactment of justice" as well as ensuring that its "judges should not be used as tools to further political aims nor punished for preventing their realization" (Larkins 1996, 608–9). By ensuring that courts are "politically insular" (Fiss 1993), suspected violators would be deterred from bribing courts in order to get favorable legal decisions. Also, the following institutional qualities demonstrate judicial independence: (1) guaranteed terms of office; (2) finality of decisions; (3) exclusive authority on decisions based on competence; (4) bans against exceptional or military courts; (5) fiscal autonomy; (6) separation of powers; and, (7) merit-based selection of judges (Keith 2002, 196–97).

In contrast, a highly partisan judicial system tolerates military and police agents coercing political dissidents without fear of immediate legal reprisal. That is particularly the case when human rights victims find legal remedies costly and when relevant laws that promote successful prosecution of abusive state agents remain absent. A highly partisan judiciary is likely to accede to the demands of the central executive government, particularly to the latter's efforts to derail, if not totally hinder, the prosecution of abusive state actors. For example, the case of the Guantanamo military commissions, which were created by the US Military Commissions Act of 2006, shows that the lack of judicial independence undermines the timely delivery of justice.

Institutionalizing an effective judicial system is all the more necessary in so-called transitional societies. UN Human Rights Special Rapporteur

Philip Alston (2010) highlighted the importance of an effective justice system in transitional societies that just went through a human rights crisis. Informed by his official investigations in Nigeria, Kenya, and Guatemala, Alston (2010, 363) keenly observes that "prosecution services are generally understaffed and under-resourced, and they too are often available to the highest bidder . . . corrupt judges can let people off, or find them guilty of much lesser offences, or simply delay trials for long enough that the case lapses, either in law or in practice." Thus, judicial institutions play an important role in promoting human rights (Sikkink 2011). As shown in chapter 5, when newly democratized states fail to implement meaningful judicial reforms (Olsen, Payne, and Reiter 2010), residual human rights violations persist regardless of the converging interests of donor and recipient governments. The efficient and fair human rights prosecutions of high-ranking officials deter prospective human rights violators (Orentlicher 1991) precisely because they "demonstrate the willingness, capacity, and effectiveness of courts in challenging impunity" (Olsen, Payne, and Reiter 2010, 997). Effective judicial prosecution functions as the "most effective insurance against future repression" because it "inoculates the public against future temptation to be complicit in state-sponsored violence" (Orentlicher 1991, 2543).

Causal Mechanisms and Social Processes

This section discusses the five transformative social processes through which foreign strategic support shapes human rights in recipient countries. As they "should be conceptualized as insufficient but necessary parts of an overall mechanism" (Beach and Pedersen 2013, 30), these social processes include (1) strategic localization; (2) resource mobilization; (3) selective political repression; (4) erroneous coercive state practices; and (5) a culture of impunity. In figure 2.1, I visualize how the convergence of policy preferences influences human rights outcomes in recipient countries.

Strategic Localization of Political Discourses

Strategic localization refers to the recipient government's discursive articulations of political agendas, which aim to win the support of two important stakeholders: (1) its own domestic public (2) and the donor country. Discourses can either be primarily militaristic (post-9/11 period) *or* pro–human rights along with a wide range of nonmilitaristic objectives

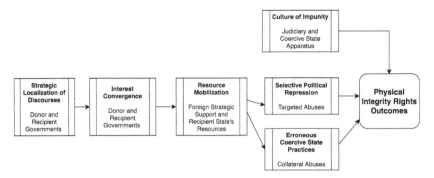

Fig. 2.1. Explanatory Model: Interest Convergence and Physical Integrity Rights

(pre-9/11 period). Strategic localization has two basic attributes. First, a coalition of state actors (elected civilian officials, military, police, local politicians) redefines a specific transnational security discourse or norm (e.g., human rights) "to further their own particularistic interests in domestic policy debates" (Acharya 2009, 16). With the support of a "winning policy coalition" (Risse 1995, 25), the aid recipient government expects that customizing a transnational security discourse will strengthen its political legitimacy within and beyond the state apparatus, considering that the state leaders' primary goal is political survival (de Mesquita et al. 2005). Strategic localization could be a more effective way of persuasion compared to the simplistic importation of transnational norms and ideas into the domestic context. Second, recipient governments are "norm-takers" because they seek to resolve the "contestation between emerging norms [international] and existing local beliefs and practices" (Acharya 2009, 4). By localizing those transnational discourses, recipient governments seek the domestic public's acceptance of the core purposes of foreign strategic support. In contrast to foreign aid scholars who assume that donors primarily set the agenda for recipient states (Lancaster 2007), I maintain that aid programs emerge from the political contestations between donor and recipient governments embedded in a broader society. Based on her study of foreign aid to pharmaceutical industrialization in East Africa, Nitsan Chorev (2020, 11) argues that "parties [donor and recipients] are hardly equal—bargaining occurs in the shadow of power." Consequently, less powerful states "can gain concessions by constructing priorities and choosing battles based on the opportunity structures in place . . . even when countries with minimal bargaining leverage are not necessarily passive recipients of gifts bestowed on them . . . they are active manipulators of opportunities when these exist" (Chorev 2020, 8).

In general, prospective recipient governments strategically adapt to the preferences of two important stakeholders: (1) the recipient country's domestic public and (2) the donor government. Recipient states strategically reframe and reinterpret transnational and domestic discourses in ways that garner support from the donor government and the recipient country's domestic public—an ideational process that I call *strategic localization*. My concept of strategic localization borrows insights from Robert Putnam's two-level game theory, which posits that an "executive negotiating a deal with foreign country is playing two interacting games that have to be balanced: a domestic game to secure ratification of a final deal, and an international game to secure the best possible deal" (Beach 2012, 239; Putnam 1988). Putnam's two-level game in diplomacy suggests that bilateral negotiations succeed when they are "recognized as legitimate in both international and national political processes" (Winn 2009, 188). In his study of US foreign policies on genocidal events abroad, Mayroz (2020, 124) shows that "discourse does matter . . . many other elements of foreign policy, domestic and international legitimacy [are] sought, gained, or lost through discourse." As such, potential aid recipient governments engage in this delicate politics of balancing interests because foreign aid is one of those "international benefits" that "are frequently targeted toward states possessing valued characteristics" (Hyde 2011, 9). Donor countries respond to a prospective recipient government's strategic localization through foreign aid provision. Through strategic localization, a recipient government makes the case that its policy preferences appear to match those of the prospective donor country, and, in doing so, foreign could be provided. Thus, the "meaning and effects" of "material power and interests" ultimately "depend[s] on the social structure of the system," or, more precisely, on the shared expectations and ideas of relevant stakeholders in any given policy issue (Wendt 1999, 20).

Yet strategic localization differs from Amitav Acharya's notion of constitutive localization, which is a "process that enables norm-takers to build congruence between the local and external norms" (Acharya 2009, 4). While we both agree that "norm diffusion strategies that accommodate local sensitivities and contexts are more likely to succeed than those seeking to dismiss or supplant the latter" (Acharya 2009, 15), I differ to the extent that the recipient government redefines external norms as a deliberate *political strategy*, whereby the foremost goal is to enhance political legitimacy and regime survival. Finnemore and Sikkink (1998, 913) rightly contend that "frequently heard arguments about whether behavior is norm-based or interest-based miss the point that norm conformance can often be self-interested, depending on how one specifies interests and the nature of the norm." Whereas Acharya's discussion appears to be silent on the importance of material interests, strategic localization recognizes how local actors redefine external norms because of an underlying instrumentalist perspective (Hyde 2011). As a social process, strategic localization demonstrates how the logics of appropriateness and consequences form one causal process (Goldmann 2005; March and Olsen 2006). Thus, I fully recognize the underlying instrumentalist perspective that political actors initially consider on why and how they should alter or embrace international norms. If "human rights today are legitimated by their origins in transnational consensus-building processes and packaged by translators into local cultural terms" (Merry 2006, 180), then it is also possible that local actors reinterpret international security threats and militaristic policy preferences in light of the domestic context.

Strategic localization is a more nuanced form of securitization. In the International Relations literature, securitization occurs when a given issue attains the status of security (Jetschke 2010, 47; see also Hayes 2012, 6) and consists of three important steps: (1) the designation of an existential threat by an actor, (2) the actor's assertion that such a threat requires "emergency action or special measures," and (3) the acceptance of such designation by a critical mass of the relevant public (Buzan, Waever, and de Wilde 1998; Jetschke 2010). The success of localization depends on whether the broader public accepts such a framing. Indeed, strategic localization is "a process rather than a singular event" (Hayes 2012, 67; see also Stritzel 2012). Discourses function as action-oriented sets of directions that political actors can act upon (Goldstein and Keohane 1993). Elites and key stakeholders use their material resources and social capital in order "to create, challenge, change or amend existing meaning structures, potentially establishing new discursive hegemonies in history" (Stritzel 2012, 551). They create and reinforce new public discourses in order to justify their chosen political actions and to promote new policies and ideas. State actors and elites use various discursive tools to interpret specific events as "key moments of change" (e.g., 9/11 attacks), thereby requiring significant policy and institutional changes, and using the available "political opportunity structures" to strategically pursue their aims (Hay 2006, 58–59). In this way, state actors interpret particular critical junctures such as the 9/11 attacks through political discourses, which are articulated and negotiated in the public sphere.

Notably, the recent scholarship on foreign aid employs the notion of securitization to understand the effects of foreign aid framed in "security terms," primarily from the donor government's perspective (Brown and Grävingholt 2016, 3). Alternatively, my concept of localization emphasizes the crucial role played by recipient governments in shaping foreign strategic support's impact in recipient countries. Demonstrating the role of the recipient state is essential because the broader public discourses in the Global North often portray political actors in the Global South as passive agents subjected to the whims and caprices of powerful patron governments.

Following Schmidt (2008), I conceptualize that the discursive policy shift from human rights protection to a counterterror emphasis (and vice-versa) happens in two crucial spheres: "coordinative discourse" involves government policy elites in the United States and the policy circles of its partner Southeast Asian countries, and "communicative discourse" pertains to how policy actors communicate with the general public. As shown in chapters 4 and 6, the evidence from post-9/11 Southeast Asia demonstrates the shift in the policy emphasis from human rights and democracy to a militaristic version of national security. American and Southeast Asian policy elites interpreted the 9/11 attacks as representative of an unprecedented threat to liberal democracy, and consequently, they advocated for a militaristic approach. This shift in coordinative discourse happened during the post-9/11 period, considering that the domestic public's fear of terror attacks facilitated the relative success of a policy focus on counterterrorism.

There are two primary ways in which transnational events generate new policy paradigms. First, large-scale events, such as the 9/11 terror attacks, motivate politicians and elites to identify new causal ideas in order to justify policy changes as a way of adapting to a crisis. In foreign policy, causal ideas "respond directly to uncertainty by reducing it," while principled ideas "enable people to behave decisively despite causal uncertainty" (Goldstein and Keohane 1993, 16). Policy elites anticipate the far-reaching consequences that could emerge due to the perceived changes in the transnational order. Such changes facilitate a sense of political uncertainty, which in turn often calls for a fundamental shift in policy priorities. First, elites undertaking strategic localization blame old policy paradigms as responsible for the crisis and therefore consider them untenable. Second, faced by a crisis, political actors rethink some of their fundamental values (e.g., human rights, democracy, military security) that shape foreign aid programs and domestic policies—a process that could lead to a change in "principled ideas." International Relations scholars call this transformative phase "ideational collapse" (Legro 2005), "circumstances of reflection" (Philpott 2001), and "ideological crisis" (Owen 2010).

Political elites legitimize policy shifts, including the core purposes of foreign strategic support, through several discursive tactics. Notwithstanding social resistance, "discourse may intersperse technical and scientific arguments with more generally accessible narratives that fit together the specialists' arguments with accounts of events, emblematic cases, and even doomsday scenarios to generate compelling stories about the causes of current problems, what needs to be done to remedy them, and how they fit with the underlying values of the society" (Schmidt 2008, 309). Various political actors offer new *diagnostic justifications*, which refer to the descriptive and normative statements by politicians and policy-makers about their own understandings of the nature of the political problem (*diagnosis*) and the policy goals and actions needed to address the relevant problem (*justification*). Political actors engage in coalition building, which involves the formation of transnational and domestic alliances among state and nonstate actors, who will then promote the new narratives and discourses that emphasize either military security or a more diverse range of interests. This process generates strategic partnerships among key stakeholders, who form "winning policy coalitions" (Risse 1995, 25) that publicly support newly created norms in a more coordinated way. Such coalitions advance new norms and practices because they have a perceived benefit in doing so. Considering post-9/11 Southeast Asia, I refer to the perceived threat of nonstate terrorism, which generated the policy shift toward military security. In the next chapters, I demonstrate that the shift to military security was highly contentious, especially in some factions of the domestic civil society network in Thailand and the Philippines.

Resource Mobilization: The Impact of Purpose-Driven Foreign Assistance

When there is bilateral convergence on militarism, how does a recipient government mobilize its own domestic resources and foreign strategic support? In that scenario, the enormous amounts of foreign aid are then channeled into the recipient state's coercive apparatus, particularly the military and police agencies. Material support includes joint military training exercises, military advisors, military equipment, intelligence sharing, joint military strategy planning, counterterror training, and surveillance technologies, among others. The military and police agencies use such resources and newly learned counterterror techniques in state violence against the broader population. That is the case especially in countries with state security agencies that are highly dependent upon a powerful patron country, as demonstrated by US support to the Philippines and Thailand, whereby the absence of external support is likely to constrain severely the magnitude of state repression.[3] In those cases, police and military operations require tremendous amounts of resources that include manpower, intelligence funds, and political support that are usually not existent if not for the support of a more powerful donor country. Thus, I show in my post-9/11 Southeast Asian case studies that their governments required substantial resources in order to bolster their repressive capacities, and the only way to do so was to seek US strategic support. Remarkably, countries with small elite constellations and very scarce governmental resources are more likely to receive US strategic support (de Mesquita and Smith 2007, 279). As Boutton (2019) rightly argues, although the US government "prefers a reliable government with apolitical, inclusive security forces capable of ensuring stability, the priority of a vulnerable leader [in a recipient country] is to consolidate power and coup-proof his regime." When it is given to a leader with weak domestic legitimacy, terror-oriented foreign aid generates a political opportunity structure whereby "a weak leader feels emboldened to consolidate more aggressively" (Boutton 2019, 2). Deploying state violence, a recipient government redirects all foreign strategic support and its own domestic resources to bolstering the capacities of its military and police agencies. Faced with a security crisis, a recipient government enjoys wide administrative discretion in defining the targets of state repression. A powerful donor country usually gives to recipient governments considerable discretion in spending aid because of the high political uncertainty emerging from a crisis, thereby "calling into question the 'existing rules of the game'" (Acharya 2009, 16; see also Ikenberry, Lake, and Mastanduno 1988, 234).

Recipient governments use foreign strategic assistance in ways that are perceived to deliver mutually beneficial outcomes to the donor and recipient states. In many cases, recipient governments may deviate from the intended outcomes of aid while concurrently deceiving the donor government, thereby making cooperation possible amid deception. While misperceptions and false beliefs are often associated with conflict, "cooperation is enhanced when actors believe that intersubjectivity— common knowledge, common norms, or common identities—exists even when they are wrong" (Grynaviski 2014, 5). The role of misperceptions in aid provision—and the ensuing leeway that the recipient government enjoys—should not be understated. For example, the Bush administration, in its global war on terror, aided Southeast Asian governments based on the false belief that local armed Islamic insurgencies therein were directly connected to the Al-Qaeda network. The connection between the terror networks in the Middle East and Southeast Asian terror groups was not conclusively proven (Sidel 2007). Yet the US government vigorously branded Southeast Asia as the "second front" in the war on terror based on questionable evidentiary standards.

Donor and recipient governments justify intensified state repression and expansion of counterterror operations based on a perceived climate of "clear and present danger" (Zenko and Cohen 2012). Various economic-development-oriented projects such as public infrastructure and other social welfare initiatives are subsumed under the central goal of quelling perceived domestic threats. In the case of Western donor governments, "aid for development has been regarded as a means of dampening the social discontent that can strengthen the temptations of communism or feed terrorist impulses" (Lancaster 2007, 14), which became more prevalent during the Cold War and post-9/11 era. For example, foreign economic aid intended for infrastructure projects is redirected to regions where military operations require them, thereby making economic aid a hostage of counterterror policy priorities. In case of convergence on a wide range of policy preferences, the recipient government mandates that the state security establishment cooperate with civilian state agencies in undertaking non-militaristic tasks. When the recipient government enjoys strong political legitimacy, domestic state repression is likely to focus only on armed political dissidents.

Selective Political Repression and Intended Human Rights Violations

Selective political repression involves the systematic identification, harassment, and killing of political opposition, *including* peaceful political dissidents, that are deemed threats to governmental authority. By targeting all forms of political opposition, the government can selectively repress whoever it wants. It emerges when the aid recipient government promotes strategically localized discourses that brand both violent *and* peaceful political opposition as security threats. This tendency to repress political opposition is quite consistent with the basic assumption in governance: "rulers by definition possess the apparatus of the state and all being equal we would expect them to use it to consolidate their power over time by reducing domestic ideological opposition" (Owen 2010, 48). Given a converging interest in a militaristic policy agenda, state agents marshal foreign aid and domestic resources to violently repress both *armed and unarmed* dissidents.

State agents identify, harass, and kill nonviolent and innocent civilians[4] whose political advocacies and actions are perceived to be against the interests of the central executive government, the security apparatus of the state, and their nonstate allies (e.g., provincial elites and private business actors). With the support of the state security establishment and the ruling civilian government, rank-and-file state agents target civilian oppositionists and subject them to brutal techniques of physical and psychological harassment, and at times deliberately kill them. Selective political repression includes the following: extrajudicial killings; enforced disappearances; torture; rape; illegal arrests; destruction and divestment of private property; forceful restriction and violent dispersal of mass gatherings; imprisonment; forceful use of civilians in police/military operations as guides; violation of domicile; and forced eviction and demolition of residence, among others.

Limiting state repression *only* to *armed* political dissidents is likely to emerge when the recipient government enjoys strong domestic legitimacy within and beyond the formal state apparatus. In this scenario, a regime's toleration of peaceful opposition is consistent with a domestic public's demand for open political competition, which in turn bolsters the legitimacy of the ruling regime. Selective political repression does not necessarily mean, however, that human rights norms do not exist. As Kratochwil and Ruggie (1986, 768) rightly argue, "neither the violation of norms, nor, in special circumstances, even their 'nonexistence,' necessarily refutes their validity." As the next chapters show, human rights norms, which gained traction in the early post–Cold War years, did not necessarily cease to exist during the post-9/11 war on terror period. Moreover, counterterror laws weaponize the legal system to justify selective political repression. They provide state leaders broad leeway in formulating the criteria for what constitutes a security threat, thereby enabling the state to identify peaceful yet openly critical civil society actors as potential targets. Such laws allow the comprehensive expansion and restructuring of the national security apparatus in order to effectively implement the first two functions.

Erroneous Coercive State Practices and Collateral Abuses

Erroneous coercive state practices generate collateral human rights abuses that emerge from intensified state violence targeting violent, nonstate, armed actors. When state security agencies do not have reliable accountability mechanisms from civilian state leadership and civil society, military and police officers are likely to subject civilians to various forms of abuse. Unattractive compensation packages make police and military agents more vulnerable to nonstate actors, who privately contract state agents for their own personal agendas. For instance, powerful mining corporations hire military and police officers to harass and, in some cases, to kill unarmed political dissidents who oppose large-scale mining projects—an outcome that could cause collateral abuses. They are collateral human rights abuses to the extent that a statewide policy of full repression of all forms of dissidence is absent.

Because the implementation of state violence is not a perfect science, the reliance on false intelligence inadvertently leads to the physical harassment and killings of innocent individuals wrongfully accused of being armed dissidents. Hannah Arendt (1970, 4) astutely identified this sense of randomness during conflicts: "While the results of men's actions are beyond the actors' control, violence harbors within itself an additional element of arbitrariness; nowhere does Fortuna, good or ill luck, play a more fateful role in human affairs than on the battlefield." Robert Jervis (2010, 2) defines an intelligence failure as "a mismatch between the estimates and what later information reveals." Errors in carrying out state violence, many of which result from intelligence failures, usually occur in the following situations: operations in conflict-prone areas; military-induced displacements; destruction of private property; use of public places (e.g., schools and churches) for military purposes; and errors in distinguishing combatants from civilians, among many others. Even in Global North democracies, individual state agents commit human rights abuses even when constitutional guarantees and state institutions publicly condemn such violations, while other countries generally condone such abuses in a climate of judicial impunity (Ignatieff 2004, 18–19). A clear example of this is the case of Rizwaan Sabir, a graduate student at the University of Nottingham in England, who was held under secret police custody for nearly a week and was even subjected to "psychological torture" (Curtis and Hodgson 2008). Under the legal provisions of the UK's Terrorism Act, Sabir was charged with illegally downloading a "copy of the al-Qaida training manual from a US government website for his research into terrorist tactics" (Curtis and Hodgson 2008).

There are several reasons why failures in policing, military, and counterterror operations emerge, especially at the level of intelligence gathering (Jervis 2010, 2–3). First, state actors fail to articulate "testable hypotheses" about a particular security problem, and their actions and strategies rely on preexisting beliefs and biases that cannot be disproved by evidence. Second, state actors fail when they are unable to closely examine the underlying assumptions about their security strategies. Third, state actors commit failures when existing empirical evidence does not support the causal assumptions of their security strategies. Even some well-intentioned state actors end up accidentally killing unarmed individuals, even if their original aim was to target only the armed ones. As Stathis Kalyvas (2006, 180–192) maintains, "It is fair to surmise that political actors frequently fail to discriminate between the guilty and the innocent." For instance, in 2003, the Colombian military arrested and detained hundreds of individuals in various provinces based on very few denunciations, while "seventy-four people were arrested in the small town of Cartagena del Chaira on the strength of a single denunciation by a man who many locals accused of malice" (Semana 2003, cited in Kalyvas 2006, 188).

When given to other liberal democracies in the Global North, terror-oriented US strategic support is most likely to be used solely for the purpose of targeting domestic armed rebel groups, rather than using it for state violence against peaceful political dissent. That is likely the case because of their governments' strong domestic legitimacy, professionalized coercive agencies, and effective judicial systems. Violations, however, can still emerge as outcomes of erroneous policing practices rather than a state's systematic repression of unarmed political dissent. Thus, state-initiated human rights abuses in consolidated democracies, which were once confronted with the post-9/11 terror threat, are less pervasive than those in Global South societies.

Despite interest convergence on a nonmilitaristic agenda, collateral violations still emerge as residual effects of corrupt state security agencies and an ineffective judicial system. As I show in my comparative case studies of pre-9/11 Thailand and the Philippines, some collateral abuses emerged when individual police officers and military agents were co-opted by private businessmen and local politicians to harass peaceful activists (e.g., environmental activists against massive commercial projects). Those violations confirm the detrimental consequences of merging economic development imperatives within a broader human security framework (Duffield 2007). Residual human rights abuses emerged in the 1990s precisely because of the enduring defective qualities of the coercive and judicial agencies of the Thai and Philippine states. Table 2.1 below schematizes my case studies and how the human rights outcomes therein are generated by domestic conditions and foreign strategic assistance.

Using the term "collateral abuse" does not mean that I condone state repression. All forms of state abuses are morally despicable, especially

TABLE 2.1. Typology of Cases: Interest Convergence and Physical Integrity Rights

Interest Convergence vis-à-vis Human Rights Outcomes in Recipient Countries					
Independent Variables				*Outcome Variable*	
Foreign Strategic Support		**Domestic Variables and Enduring Conditions**		Type and Magnitude of Human Rights Violations	*Empirical Cases*
Foreign Resource Allocations (Material)	Powerful Donor Government's Strategic Purpose (Ideational)	Domestic Legitimacy of the Recipient Government			
More foreign aid	Comprehensive range of security interests	Strong Legitimacy	Culture of Impunity	**Fewer Human Rights Abuses**	Post–War on Terror Philippines (2010–16)
	Counterterrorism/ militaristic	Weak Legitimacy		**Pervasive Human Rights Violations**	Post-9/11 Philippines (2001–2009) and Thailand (2001–6)
Less foreign aid	Comprehensive range of security interests	Strong Legitimacy		**Fewer Human Rights Abuses**	Pre-9/11 Philippines (1992–2000) and Thailand (1992–2000)

because they undermine the dignity of the human person. When branding an abuse as a likely instance of collateral damage, I only suggest that it likely emerged in the absence of a statewide policy of condoning violence against civilians. When human rights abuses were fewer, particularly in the 1990s, many state institutions still held some discriminatory biases against minoritized groups. Such abuses persisted because of the enduring culture of impunity where many abusive state agents remain unpunished—an outcome facilitated by the institutional deficiencies in the judicial system and the state security establishment. Even in the case of conflict with nonstate armed rebel groups, states have a moral responsibility to use all the available nonviolent means to address the structural causes of armed rebellion rather than resorting to a full-blown militaristic approach.

This chapter discussed my core arguments pertaining to the conditions under which foreign strategic assistance shapes the human rights situation in selected cases in Southeast Asia. I contend that the shared interests of donor and recipient governments, combined with the level of domestic legitimacy held by the recipient government, transform the human rights situation in recipient countries over time. The empirical part of this study begins with chapter 3, which probes the plausibility of my theory using the evidence from US-Philippine bilateral relations vis-à-vis the human rights situation in the 1990s.

THREE

Human Rights Renaissance in the Philippines, 1990s

For the first time, more people live under democracy than dictator-ship. . . . Every dollar we devote to preventing conflicts, to pro-moting democracy, to stopping the spread of disease and starvation brings a sure return in security and savings.

—US President Bill Clinton, State of the Union Address, February 4, 1997

The scope of human rights has expanded to include not only the right to life and liberty but also special concerns such as alterna-tive cultures, minorities, indigenous people, women, children and other disadvantaged sectors, and lately the right to a healthy envi-ronment. . . . we Filipinos [have] provided a new standard for human rights for the twenty-first century.

—Philippine President Fidel V. Ramos, speech on Human Rights Day, December 10, 1993[1]

This chapter examines how and under which transnational and domestic conditions strong human rights protections emerged in the Philippines in the 1990s. I argue that the comprehensive and nonmilitaristic development agenda of US foreign strategic support, together with the strong domestic legitimacy of the Ramos administration, reinforced the emerging domestic public's demand for constitutionally guaranteed human rights protection. American and Filipino government officials and elites vigorously supported democratization and economic development, which resulted in two key domestic outcomes: (1) a low priority status for domestic armed counterin-surgency, thereby resulting in fewer collateral human rights violations; and (2) the state's high tolerance for unarmed political opposition, which elimi-nated the need for a statewide policy of selective political repression. Such domestic policies, which were bolstered by pro-human-rights US strategic support, generated fewer state-initiated human rights abuses.

To demonstrate those findings, I first analytically describe the human rights situation vis-à-vis America's foreign policy goals and bilateral aid to the Philippines. Second, I compare the emerging post–Cold War expec-tations of American and Filipino political elites and the broader domes-tic public that generally favored stronger human rights protection. This section traces the process through which the post–Cold War Philippine government strategically localized US foreign policy discourses on human rights, democracy, and economic development in ways that suited the domestic political context. Third, I demonstrate that this shared agenda of the United States and the Philippine governments expanded the public sphere for political contestation, facilitated pro-human-rights constitu-tional reforms, and widely tolerated unarmed political opposition. Finally, I provide some illustrative evidence that represents some of the key pat-terns of human rights violations that emerged during this period. In the 1990s, human rights violations resulting from selective political repression were nearly absent, while collateral abuses persisted in the late 1990s, when the Joseph Estrada administration declared an "all-out-war" against armed Islamic rebels in Mindanao. The next section presents a general compara-tive overview of the human rights situation in the Philippines in the 1990s and the scope of US strategic support resulting therefrom.

Overview of the Human Rights Situation in the Philippines and US Foreign Policy

The large amounts of Cold War-era US military aid coincided with the proliferation of human rights abuses committed by Philippine president Ferdinand Marcos's authoritarian regime. After the fall of the Marcos dic-tatorship and the end of the Cold War, the US government dramatically reduced its foreign aid to the Philippines, which also experienced remark-able human rights improvement. Whereas the US government provided aid that amounted to 1 billion USD from 1993 to 2001, the Philippine gov-ernment received generous financial aid from the United States amount-ing to almost 5 billion USD in the preceding period (1984–92). In the

1990s, the number of human rights violations in the Philippines decreased. Figures 3.1 and 3.2 show the fluctuations in the magnitude of physical integrity rights violations in recent historical periods in the Philippines. Specifically, the human rights situation in the Philippines during the war on terror period (2002–10) worsened compared to the preceding decade (post–Cold War period, 1992–2001).

As shown above, the human rights situation consistently improved from the late 1980s up to the late 1990s when compared to the Martial Law period (1972–86). Did the US government's foreign policy change in response to the domestic Philippine public demands for democracy and stronger human rights protection? In the early 1990s, various liberal democratic Filipino politicians emerged in mainstream politics and vigorously opposed the return of authoritarian practices that were pervasive during the Martial Law period. After the peaceful demonstrations that toppled the US government-supported leadership of Ferdinand Marcos (1972–86), constitutional democracy was restored in 1986 (Robinson 1996; Villegas 1987), when the overwhelming majority of Filipinos elected President Corazon Aquino (1986–92). The 1987 Constitution guaranteed fundamental human rights to Filipino citizens, including the toleration of peaceful political opposition. The Ramos administration released hundreds of political prisoners who were detained during the Marcos dictatorship. Warrantless arrests and extrajudicial killings became less pervasive. All of these significant developments were sustained during the tenure of Presidents Fidel Ramos (1992–98) and Joseph Estrada (1998–2001). Whereas approximately 7,500 victims died because of state-initiated enforced disappearances and extrajudicial killings in any given year during the Marcos era (1965 to 1986), the number of killings dramatically decreased to less than 300 in the 1990s. Consequently, the Philippine state's commitment to the protection of the physical integrity rights of its citizens dramatically improved in the post–Cold War period (Weismann 1994, 252).

Remarkably, state abuses during the term of President Arroyo (2001–10) were more widespread than during the pre-9/11 period (1992–early 2001). Fewer than 300 extrajudicial killings and enforced disappearances were reported during the presidential terms of Ramos (1992–98) and Joseph Estrada (1998–2001), compared to a conservative estimate of 1,500 cases during the Arroyo regime. The Task Force Detainees of the Philippines (TFDP 1998) reports that the average number of cases of politically motivated imprisonment was reduced from 20,523 in 1986 to only 2,459 in 1991, and the numbers consistently decreased since then until 2001. Thus, in the words of Blas Ople (1994, 33), a highly influential statesperson in

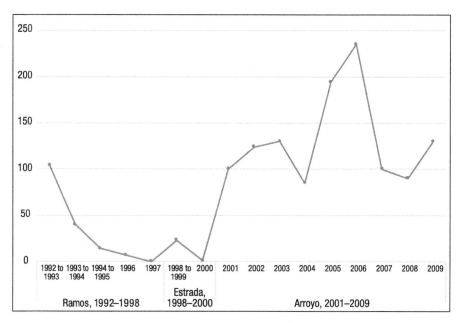

Fig. 3.1. Annual Number of Political Killings per Year in the Philippines (approximate), per Presidential Administration. The data used to create this figure is available on our Fulcrum platform at https://doi.org/10.3998/mpub.12036762.cmp.17

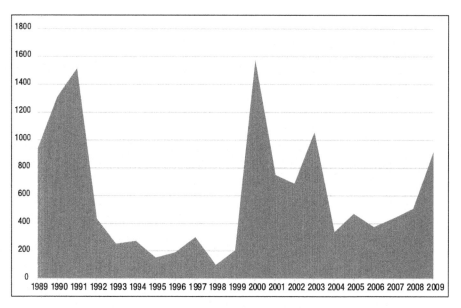

Fig. 3.2. Annual Data on State-Based Violence (Recorded Deaths) in the Philippines, 1989–2009. The data used to create this figure is available on our Fulcrum platform at https://doi.org/10.3998/mpub.12036762.cmp.17

the country, "the Philippines, like other states in its Asia-Pacific neighborhood, welcomes the stability brought about by the end of the Cold War." That political stability emerged after the human rights reforms were introduced under the Ramos administration.

The substantial reduction in the number of abuses coincided with the dramatic decrease of US military and economic aid to the Philippines. Whereas US military aid reached as high as 300 million USD in 1991, the amount plummeted to a meager 50 million USD in 1992, and US bilateral economic and military aid continued to be at relatively low levels until 2001. Moreover, US economic assistance, which was valued as high as 636 million USD in 1989, eventually dropped to as low as 55 million USD in 1994. These reductions in US aid suggest that "with the end of the Cold War, Washington's strategic interest in the Philippines has sharply diminished" (New York Times 1992a, 16)—with strategic interest referring to a militaristic US foreign policy. Responding to demands from civil society groups, the Philippine Congress in 1992 voted to remove all US forces and military bases in the archipelago, including Clark Air Base and the Subic Naval Base (Cooley 2008, 80–82). The expulsion of all permanent US military forces and facilities in the country indicates the dramatic shift of Manila's priorities in its bilateral relations with Washington, DC, whereby the necessity of military security greatly diminished.

After the Cold War, the United States emerged as the most powerful country in the world, marking a position of "unprecedented preponderance" (Waltz 2000). In the Asia-Pacific, the perceived absence of a communist threat and a serious challenger to the United States explains why military assistance needed to be reduced to a minimum. Consequently, the American public's relative lack of interest in foreign policy issues at that time was consistent with the Clinton administration's focus on domestic issues, except for a foreign policy agenda that advocated for human rights, democracy promotion, and global trade (Brinkley 1997).

The human-rights-oriented policy convergence can be seen in several instances. During the first visit of Philippine president Fidel Ramos to the White House, President Bill Clinton heralded "a new partnership" that moved away "from the once-dominant issues of aid and military security" (Briscoe 1993b). Specifically, the Ramos administration promoted the idea that the Philippines is uniquely positioned in the region for foreign investments because of its democratization and trade liberalization reforms. Ramos argued that regional security should not depend on a militaristic agenda but on socioeconomic development and contended that the presence of US military bases in the country should be abandoned because

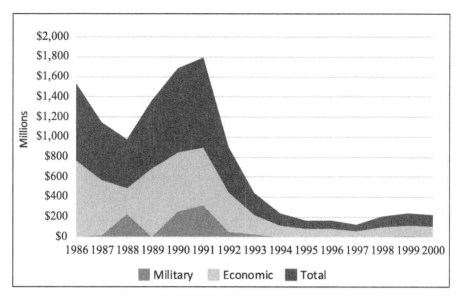

Fig. 3.3. US Foreign Aid to the Philippines, 1986–2000 (constant 2016 USD).
The data used to create this figure is available on our Fulcrum platform at
https://doi.org/10.3998/mpub.12036762.cmp.17

the Cold War had formally ended (Briscoe 1993a). Clinton (1993, 8) said post–Cold War US foreign policy in the Philippines should be founded on "a renewed partnership, based on long historical association, our shared values, our expanding trade and our investment links, our bilateral security cooperation and our common dedication to democracy and human rights." Such statements demonstrate the shift from the militaristic security alliance during the Cold War to more comprehensive bilateral relations focusing on democratization.

Yet that shift in US foreign policy was not unique to the Philippines. The retrenchment of US military forces worldwide, including from the Philippines, temporarily facilitated a sense of uncertainty concerning US security guarantees (Yeo 2011, 154; Cibulka 199, 115). In one of his speeches during his 1994 Asian tour on free trade, President Clinton contended that, in many federal-level policies, bipartisan support "was used to apply to national security defined in military terms [during the Cold War]; today [post–Cold War/1990s], it applies to national security defined in economic terms" (Clinton 1994, 2405). While the US commitment to military security and political stability remained, Clinton maintained that the "balance of our (American) relationship with Asia has tilted more and more to trade." Hence, the emergence of this economic-centered foreign policy did not require huge military aid to Asian countries in the 1990s. Clinton's public diplomacy approach to the Philippines and Asia fostered multilateral trade forums such as the Asia Pacific Economic Cooperation summits and the numerous US-funded programs on civil society development and human rights promotion in the Philippines. Consequently, the US government dramatically reduced monetary assistance to the Philippine armed forces and police agencies in the 1990, which in turn decreased the incentives to bolster domestic state repression. During the 1990s, such reductions in US military aid undermined the previous pervasiveness of human rights abuses.

Philippine Government's Strategic Localization of Pro-Human-Rights Discourses and Resource Mobilization

The Philippine government's strategy aimed at winning the support of two important constituencies. First, the majority of Filipinos demanded deep-seated democratic reforms as the fitting response to the abuses during the two-decade Martial Law period (1972–86). Many elected national governments and local politicians committed to strong human rights protection in order to boost their legitimacy. Second, the US government in the 1990s shifted its foreign policy priorities toward nonmilitaristic priorities, specifically for programs that sought to expand civil society activities and to promote human rights in the Philippines. The bilateral relations focused on a comprehensive development agenda that undermined the role of the Philippine military and police agencies, which are historically known as perpetrators of human rights abuses during the Cold War.

The Philippine government maintained that sustainable economic growth must be fostered through stronger human rights protection. Hijacking the hype on democratization, Presidents Ramos and Estrada deployed political discourses that were less militaristic than the previous decade. During Ramos's tenure, the dominant policy discourses were couched under the rubric of "Philippines 2000"—an ambitious socioeconomic strategy that aimed to position the country as a newly industrialized economic powerhouse (Briscoe 1993a, 2004; Schirmer 1997). That strategy advocated for the privatization of the transportation systems, communications industry, and other utility services. Ramos maintained that long-term economic development could flourish only when democratic openness and stronger human rights protection are in place. In response to the policy recommendations of the World Bank, the International Monetary Fund, and the US government, the Ramos administration implemented progressive taxation in order to boost state capacity for social services and infrastructure building programs (Bello et al. 2004).

Believing that sustained economic growth requires democratization, the Ramos administration promoted the country as one of the most vibrant economic and tourist destinations in Asia. Ramos boasted the government's democratic and human rights reforms in order to attract investments from the United States and the Global North. During the official visit of President Ramos to the United States in 1993, various international and local media accounts reported that the Filipino president had won the admiration of many economic and political elites in Washington, DC and beyond (Crisostomo 1997, xiv). That visit to the United States started the trend in the 1990s when high-ranking Filipino government officials actively welcomed American investors to the country, which indicated the focus on economic development-oriented diplomacy. The overwhelming support of the US foreign policy establishment for the Ramos administration's democratization and liberalization reforms emerged, quite surprisingly, even after the Philippine Senate voted in 1992 to kick out US bases in the Philippines (Kirk 2005).

President Ramos unveiled his grand strategy as "development diplomacy" (Pattugalan 1999; Tible-Caoyonan 1994), which resulted in a dramatic increase in exports of Philippine products to the United States and elsewhere. Remarkably, Ramos holds the record for the largest number of official trips abroad while in office in comparison to his predecessors from the 1930s until 2013. He prioritized not only economic issues in his meetings with government officials, but his administration organized high-level meetings with CEOs and members of various chambers of commerce in key parts of the United States. The numerous trips of Ramos to the United States facilitated the influx of new investments to the Philippines (Crisostomo 1997, xiii). Consequently, the Philippine government received around 2.5 billion USD worth of new American investments, "mostly in power generation, in response to a new political stability and economic reforms for which Ramos can honestly take credit" (Crisostomo 1997, xiv). Instead of employing the military-affairs-focused diplomacy that defined US-Philippine relations during the Cold War, the Philippine government in the 1990s actively welcomed American investments rather than military aid and counterterror assistance.

The Philippine government's nonmilitaristic policy strategy reflected the overall Filipino public's sentiment at that time, when 85 percent of the

respondents in a 1993 survey believed that the government must prioritize job security, economic growth, and democratic openness (Sandoval,
Mangahas, and Guerrero 1998). New policy paradigms such as the Ramos
administration's long-term economic development vision called "Philippines 2000" and the "development diplomacy" strategy represented the
state establishment's support for the growing public demand for nonmilitaristic policy priorities (Acop 2006; Lobo 1999; Ramos 1995, 2010).

The strong appeal of democratization and the post–Cold War human
rights agenda inspired Filipinos to discard military security as the principal
policy goal. In his widely televised speech to the Philippine Congress in
1995, President Ramos argued that the path to development should prioritize democracy and human rights and not authoritarianism (Ramos 1995,
3): "the Filipino can succeed in the struggle for development, carry ambitious programs to their conclusion, and succeed, not by taking the authoritarian road but by democratic consensus and collective effort." Moreover,
President Ramos made the "economy his chief priority" (Reid 1992). In
response to the widespread human rights abuses during the Martial Law
period, the Philippine government in the 1990s established and empowered the Commission on Human Rights (CHR), which is the independent
government agency created by the 1987 Freedom Constitution. With the
focus on civil and political rights, the CHR's central role is to execute independent investigations of all reported violations committed by state actors.
The establishment of the CHR is remarkable because "at the start of the
post-Cold War period, only the Philippines had a national human rights
commission" in the Asia-Pacific region (Ciorciari 2012, 705).

The Ramos administration strategically framed international human
rights norms as the key prerequisite for long-term local economic
development—the political justification that facilitated the influx of nonmilitaristic American aid. Starting in 1994, Clinton's foreign aid package
to the Philippines almost eliminated military aid, and US policy explicitly
classified all forms of US aid as "sustainable development" funding, which
focused on the development of renewable sources of energy and socioeconomic development programs that also facilitated the proliferation of various progressive civil society groups (Tira-Andrei 1994). In 1994, the total
amount of combined US military and economic aid to the Philippines was
valued at 72.6 million USD. Reflecting the priority given to sustainable
development and democratization, American funding was largely made up
of the following programs: "$15,504,000 to support broad-based economic
growth; $7,334,000 to build democracy; 26,131,000 to stabilize popula-
tion growth; $12,683,000 to protect the environment; $1 million to con-

tinue the international military education and training (IMET) program, an amount that is allocated for the use of non-governmental organizations operating in the Philippines" (Tira-Andrei 1994, 11). Such nonmilitaristic programs reinforced the converging human rights agenda of the American and Philippine governments (Inter-Press Service 1992; Morea 2008).

The Philippine armed forces and local police agencies also fulfilled various nonmilitaristic tasks in support of democratization reforms and sustainable development. Thus, the post–Cold War era "saw the effective reassertion of civilian elected officials' authority over the military," with the reassignment of the Philippine military to marginal violent clashes against communist and Islamic armed insurgencies in remote areas of the archipelago as well as guarding the Philippine-claimed areas in the disputed South China Sea region (Hedman and Sidel 2000, 57–58). This shift made the police and military agents less engaged on the battlefield, resulting instead in intensive involvement in socioeconomic development programs initiated by elected civilian government officials. President Ramos promoted the view that civilians play a crucial role in promoting political stability in their communities, and that the military and police must actively support socioeconomic development projects such as public infrastructure development, sports programs, and even public health missions. In his 1997 State of the Nation Address, Ramos introduced the new work approach, which the Armed Forces of the Philippines and the Philippine National Police adopted in the 1990s (Armed Forces of the Philippines 1997, Letter of Instructions 14/97, 15):

> Developmental activities encompass non-traditional activities conducted by the AFP [Armed Forces of the Philippines] independently or in coordination with other government agencies and units, nongovernment organizations (NGOs), and people's organizations (POs) within its capabilities intended to promote the general welfare and well-being of the members of the military organization and their dependents, reservists and retirees, and the community; and to contribute to nation building and national growth. These activities consist of socio-economic upliftment; search and rescue, relief, and rehabilitation; enhancement, protection, preservation and conservation of natural resources and environment, and civil works.

Ramos promoted the notion of an "integrated approach" as the new organizational paradigm of the police and military agencies. That approach stood in contrast to the Cold War period's dominant paradigm that under-

scores state terror against all forms of political dissidence. The so-called
integrated approach contended that sustainable economic development
could be achieved through an active partnership between the state and the
civil society, while ensuring that the armed forces remain under democratic
civilian control. Thus, President Ramos explained his new policy paradigm
(Radyo ng Bayan Quezon City 1992, 62) by arguing that poverty is the
root cause of armed rebellion:

> I will intensify this integrated approach because the problems that
> gave rise to insurgency, cessation [secession] and military rebellion,
> did not come out of military conditions. And so, if we can alleviate
> poverty, which is one of the major causes of insurgency or rebel-
> lion, if we can distribute, through devolution, decentralization and
> democratization, the goodies in this country for a greater propor-
> tion of our people, then that will be part of the approach. If we
> can also improve education, information, thereby eliminating igno-
> rance, which is also a major cause of insurgency, secession and rebel-
> lion. The military will be there only in support.

Ramos committed to a full transition to a vibrant democracy through
the active inclusion of left, right, and centrist parties into mainstream electoral politics. This unprecedented initiative successfully integrated former
armed communist rebels into peaceful mainstream politics. With the backing from the Philippine Congress, the Ramos administration successfully
repealed the law that banned communists and left-wing groups from form-
ing political parties that were eligible for electoral party competition. This
policy motivated left-wing political leaders to seek elected government
positions rather than seeking political change through armed struggle
(Toronto Star 1992). Presidents Ramos and Estrada extended the post-
1986 Aquino-era political amnesty to former armed rebels of the communist New People's Army and even broadened the scope of eligibility
to other armed rebel groups. In his first month in office, Ramos repealed
Republic Act 1700 or the Anti-Subversion Act, which formed the legal
basis for the violent repression of unarmed communist party members and
sympathizers. In an unprecedented move, the Philippine government also
established a National Unification Commission that was responsible for
"open peace talks with the rebels" and pushed for the extensive "review
of all cases of suspected rebels" (Human Rights Watch 1993b). Because
of the right-wing coup attempts, around 20,523 political prisoners were
detained (but many eventually freed) during the six-year term of President

Corazon Aquino (1986–92). Under the Ramos administration, the country witnessed the "diminishing number of political prisoners," considering that there were only around 2,549 political prisoners during his term—a significant 87 percent decrease compared to the previous period (Task Force Detainees of the Philippines 1998). Echoing Clinton's emphasis on democracy promotion, President Ramos explained his main policy agenda, which encouraged armed rebels to embrace peaceful democratic politics (Ramos 1998, xi):

> My first concern, on assuming the Presidency in June 1992 had been to deal with endemic instability by *bringing the three-armed dissident groups back into the political mainstream.* I offered an honorable truce to the mutinous young officers who had mounted seven coup attempts against my predecessor, former President Corazon C. Aquino; initiated peace negotiations with Muslim separatists in the southern island of Mindanao; proclaimed a general amnesty for the Communist guerrillas of the "New People's Army"; and legalized the Communist Party, which had been banned for almost 50 years.

The ratification of the Party List System Act (Philippine Republic Act No. 7941) in March 1995 expanded the range of social movements and marginalized groups that can formally participate in mainstream national politics. This law mandates the proportional representation of marginalized groups (peasants, labor unions, the urban poor, women's rights movements, ethnic communities) in the election of members from a certain percentage of the total number of seats in the House of Representatives. That innovation in the national electoral system facilitated the effective integration of social democrats and former armed rebels into mainstream national politics, thereby reducing the manpower and domestic public support for armed rebellion against the Philippine state. During the 1990s, the government exhibited its full commitment in empowering leftist parties and marginalized interest groups, many of which became eventual targets of extrajudicial killings in the post-9/11 presidency of Arroyo. Such developments "brought about a formal restoration of political rights and a widening of the democratic space" (Holden 2009, 381).

US military aid to the Philippines was allocated to human rights awareness programs for the Philippine military and police agents. For example, the pre-9/11 governments of Aquino, Ramos, and Estrada implemented the Unlad-Bayan (Develop the Nation) programs within the military and police institutions. Those programs involved three types of projects. The first type referred to confidence-building strategies that initiated regular dialogues between the armed state agencies and civil society groups about human rights. The second type pertained to community service programs that "focused on providing direct services to communities . . . that were once strongholds of communist insurgents" (Hernandez and Ubarra 1999, 47). It included health care and medical mission programs as well as public infrastructure investments that involved the assistance of the Philippine military. Third, it also introduced interagency cooperation, whereby the military and police took up other civilian policy tasks under the leadership of civilian cabinet departments. The new civilian tasks of police and military agencies can be grouped into several new themes: "(1) infrastructure development, (2) human resource development, (3) crisis management, (4) reserve force utilization, (5) humanitarian and social services, (6) environmental activities, and (7) livelihood opportunities and income generating projects" (Hernandez and Ubarra 1999, 47).

The Ramos administration, which received substantial USAID assistance for local civil society groups, strongly encouraged the establishment of human rights and other civic organizations. In 1993, the US Congress allocated 40 percent of its total aid to the Philippines for purely democracy promotion-oriented projects through the Multilateral Assistance Initiative (Human Rights Watch 1993b). Many of these important programs lasted until the late 1990s. With the financial support from the USAID democracy promotion projects, "the Aquino and Ramos administrations provided limited-period amnesty and financial assistance to former communist rebels" (Hall 2006, 4). Through the "rebel-returnee" programs, the Clinton administration, in partnership with the Philippine government, "funded livelihood projects for cooperatives" operated by ex-rebels. One of these programs include the Balik-Baril (Return Your Firearms) project, "which encouraged rebels to surrender their firearms in exchange for seed money to start a livelihood program" (Hernandez 2006, 5). In 1994, various social programs benefited "an estimated 39,000 ex-rebels," who "have received 12,500 pesos for starting a small business, one-time emergency assistance of 4,500 pesos and national health insurance coverage" (Hall 2006, 5). According to the study of the Development Academy of the Philippines, an independent Manila-based policy think tank, and the CHR, various US-supported programs promoted human rights within the police and military. The report underscored the effectiveness of these programs by substantially increasing the awareness of human rights principles among military officers and soldiers (Hernandez and Ubarra 1999, 42–43).

The Philippine government cooperated with the USAID on the

Growth with Equity (GEM) Program in conflict-ridden Mindanao, which provided almost 441 million USD from 1995 to 2000. According to a US State Department report, the GEM Program (1995–2000) helped more than "56,000 farmers double their incomes by producing higher value crops, adopting improved technologies, and selling crops to new and more profitable markets." Producing almost 77,000 new jobs in Mindanao, GEM assisted 13,000 former armed rebels and their families to start "commercial-level production of hybrid corn, rice and seaweed" (GEM Program Office, Philippines USAID 2002). Around 151 public infrastructure projects were built during this time in Mindanao, while the regional government units in Mindanao dramatically increased its infrastructure budget from 11 percent in the 1980s to around 27 percent at the start of the new millennium (GEM Program Office, Philippines USAID 2002). The infrastructure projects included the construction of the airport in General Santos City worth 48.6 USD million, the 15 million USD expansion of the Makar port, and the 63.3 USD million cost of building the extensive road network linking 10 towns to General Santos City (Bureau of Economic and Business Affairs 2000). The US ambassador to the Philippines, Thomas Hubbard, explained that "the purpose was to try to build an infrastructure that would draw in the private sector . . . that would draw in the fisheries industry . . . that would lead to economic development in this region" (Filipino Express 1997, 5). The GEM project provided technical and financial support to families and businesses located in conflict-ridden regions in order to boost economic development. The GEM Project was just one of the many US-supported projects that demonstrated the "holistic and developmental nature" of the Ramos administration's programs focusing on "social reform agenda"—a marked contrast to the militarism that was prevalent during the Cold War and the war on terror periods (Hernandez 2006, 5).

USAID and other private US-based organizations, including the Ford Foundation and the Asia Foundation, substantially aided the proliferation of vigilant civil society organizations, especially those that advanced the interests and rights of marginalized groups (Andrei 1999; Briscoe 1993a; Cruz 1993; Fisher 1999; New York Times 1992a). Between the early and mid-1990s, "the number of registered NGOs in the Philippines grew by 160 percent" (Clarke 1998, xxvi), and a large number of civil society groups expanded their activities because of the seed funding provided by USAID and US government funds channeled through other American NGOs (e.g., Asia Foundation) operating in the country. USAID in the Philippines differentiated the work of NGOs engaged in "democracy-through-governance" and others that are preoccupied with "democracy-through-development" (Racelis 2000, 172–73). While the former refers to aid primarily aimed at governments as target recipients (such as the Philippines' Commission on Human Rights), the latter is designed to support projects that bolster civil society through community organization and other socioeconomic development programs. USAID promoted the expansion of civil society spaces by providing substantial amounts of financial support to "coalition-building programs among basic-sector groups like fisher folk, the urban poor, indigenous people, women and children working in the informal sector, coconut farmers, and microfinance groups" (Racelis 2000, 173). In Cebu, the second largest city in the archipelago, the Ramon Aboitiz Foundation Incorporated (RAFI) emerged as the key player in the local civil society sector within the region. The influence of the Ramon Aboitiz Foundation increased when it received substantial USAID funding that facilitated the construction of a "purpose-built six-story building to house other NGOs and to host NGO conferences and training seminars" and numerous capacity-building workshops for other smaller NGOs that promoted human rights and private economic entrepreneurship (Clarke 1998, 137).

The desire for democracy and human rights emerged out of the demands from American and Filipino elites and the broader Filipino public. At the transnational level, the end of the Cold War provided an impetus for the Clinton administration to focus on promoting democracy and American economic interests abroad (Brinkley 1997). The US government no longer had to rely on militarism in order to combat the "domino effect" of the spread of communism—a threat that was widely perceived as irrelevant in the 1990s. At the domestic level, the strong domestic disdain against human rights violators emerged in response to the widespread abuses committed by the US-supported regime of Ferdinand Marcos, who only agreed to step down from the presidency after "the US government made it clear that it would no longer provide the massive amounts of military and economic aid that kept his regime in power" (Chenoweth and Stephan 2011, 168). In fact, nearly 90 percent of the budget of the Philippine military during the Marcos regime came from the United States through loans and grants (De Castro 1999, 122).

The images of the eventual collapse of the Marcos regime in 1986 and the end of the Cold War bolstered the significance of human rights and democratic procedures in national governance (Montiel 2006, 173). The policy agendas of Filipino reformist politicians gained more traction especially with the end of the Cold War. Anti-Marcos politicians, progressive civil society leaders, and Liberal Party leaders strategically interpreted the end of the Cold War as the fundamental failure of autocratic political systems, thereby making the case for open societies that prioritize human rights as the most appealing alternative. Thus, they discredited the moral standing of Marcos cronies as they laid the constitutional foundations for democratic governance (Thompson 1996).

How did policies emerging from the convergence of US and Philippine governments' shared expectations bolster human rights? The human rights situation in the Philippines during the pre-9/11 period shows how domestic politics and US foreign policy reinforced each other in ways that contributed to human rights improvement. At the domestic level, the late 1980s and the early 1990s witnessed an expanding civil society movement (Villegas 1987, 203). During this period, a new cadre of younger and pro-liberal-democratic politicians became more prominent and influential in mainstream national and local politics, while the human rights agenda was first explicitly introduced in the 1987 Freedom Constitution (Thompson 1996, 197). Following the fall of the two-decade-old dictatorship of Ferdinand Marcos in 1986, several important political developments effectively addressed the emerging domestic political demand for a stronger commitment to human rights. The growing influence of civil society movements in the early 1990s kept the elected governments of Corazon Aquino, Fidel Ramos, and Joseph Estrada committed to human rights. At the international level, democracy and human rights promotion gained traction as constitutive elements of US foreign policy and global governance agendas (Russett 1993).

Human rights protection emerged not only as mere policy rhetoric. The Armed Forces of the Philippines, the Philippine National Police, and other state security units—all of which were widely implicated in the human rights crisis during the Martial Law and post-9/11 eras—made human rights one of the core elements of their institutional strategic plans. That transformation was shown in a comparative case study by Rosalie Arcala Hall (2006), who examined civil-military relations in 20 "military frontline" villages in Panay Island in central Philippines. During the Cold War, Philippine military units focused on conducting "more offensive operations" by terrorizing the community (Hamilton-Hart 2010, 121; McCoy 2006, 75–78). The US involvement in domestic state repression in the Philippines during the Cold War is well documented. As Hamilton-Hart (2010, 121) explains, the "CIA maintained close ties with Philippine military, police and intelligence personnel, at a period when the use of torture and extrajudicial killing by these agencies was particularly high, even by the standards of authoritarian regimes." In contrast, during the 1990s, soldiers and local residents, particularly those in conflict-prone areas, received intensive human rights training and awareness programs conducted by the Commission of Human Rights and USAID-funded civil society groups.

The aforementioned domestic and transnational developments reflected the two-level logic of shared expectations among US officials and political actors and the domestic public in the Philippines. The human rights reforms emerged from the confluence of interests of key domestic political constituencies in the Philippines and the United States.

Why and how did the Philippine government, especially the Ramos administration, decide to widely tolerate peaceful political opposition— the policy stance that was absent during the Cold War and post-9/11 periods? The elected central civilian government's strong domestic legitimacy, which was derived from its commitment to democratic openness and human rights, played a key role here. In the 1990s, the Ramos and the Estrada administrations consistently enjoyed high public satisfaction ratings, ranging from +65 percent to +10 percent, compared to their successor post-9/11 administration of Gloria Arroyo with a consistently negative rating of as low as –50 percent. Public satisfaction can be a good indicator for politicians to gauge public perceptions of their leaders' domestic legitimacy (Social Weather 2014, as cited in Sabillo 2014). Subsequently, the Ramos and Estrada administrations had a weak incentive to repress the legal political opposition in order to gain legitimacy. Remarkably, President Ramos argued that the "tension between the government and human rights NGOs is a necessary element in democracy" (Clarke 1998, 179).

Had this human-rights-oriented strategic support from the United States and the emerging norm for greater human rights protection been absent, we could expect that the scope and extent of violations would have been much higher. In effect, these important post–Cold War legal and political developments guaranteed the protection of marginalized people's interests and provided a congenial space for open political opposition. With financial and political support from the US government, domestic policies by the government in Manila substantially deterred potential abuses by making it more difficult to extensively implement the systematic repression of peaceful political opposition.

The post–Cold War policy aims of the US and Philippine governments converged with the Filipino public's preferences for stronger human rights protection. That preference for a wide variety of development goals constrained the expansion of state repression in conflict-ridden regions of the archipelago, which in turn improved the physical integrity rights situation in the Philippines. The Philippine government deliberately promoted the idea that human rights protection is crucial to long-term national economic development. Such strategic reinterpretation won the support of the majority of the Filipinos, who suffered from the abuses of the Martial Law period. The discursive commitments of the Ramos administration to democratization and human rights encouraged the US government to provide political support and material resources that were intended for that purpose. Taken together, these developments generated the improved human rights situation during the 1990s.

Two Types of Human Rights Abuses in the 1990s

In the 1990s, many instances of human rights violations emerged as *collateral consequences* of the government's armed operations against communist and Islamic rebels, who refused to join the emerging peace talks in the early to mid-1990s. Except during the short-lived presidency of Estrada (1998–2000), the Philippine government did not launch a large-scale national counterinsurgency campaign against armed rebel groups to an extent comparable to the scale of post-9/11 operations or the Cold War period. That policy agenda consequently restricted the scope of violent operations of the Philippine military and police agencies. The reduction in the scope of state security agencies' operations dramatically reduced the number of extrajudicial killings, torture, and enforced disappearances. Yet two types of collateral human rights abuses emerged: (1) as indirect consequences of regular operations by the military and the police agencies and as (2) indirect consequences of the socioeconomic modernization programs initiated by the Ramos administration.

Despite the democratic reforms in the 1990s, why did some residual human rights abuses emerge? The body of evidence from this period suggests two important patterns of state behavior that ultimately led to human rights violations. First, some erring police officers and military agents committed abuses precisely because of the individual financial motivations (e.g., bribery by private firms) and other financial reasons brought by the rapid economic growth of the 1990s. That was especially the case considering the substantial growth rates recorded during the period, from 1.3 percent annual GDP growth rate in 1991 to 3.7 percent in 1997 (World Bank 2017), a record that was stimulated by the economic neoliberalization programs of the Ramos administration. That program, however, led to a different type of human rights abuses, but not necessarily state-led and as heinous as it was during the Marcos years: "massive dislocation of the peasantry, including the national minorities; labour contractualization and the suppression of wages; rising abuses on Filipino OCWs [overseas contract workers]; commercialization of education; the commodification and white slavery of women; and increasing abuses on children" (Karapatan 1997, 3). Second, many human rights abuses, which were committed during the 1990s and the decades before that, have yet to be effectively addressed in the country's judicial system. For example, the inability of the Philippine state to provide monetary compensation to the estimated 7,000 human rights victims of the Marcos regime represented the enduring institutional problems within the judicial system. Instead of the Philippine Supreme Court taking responsibility, human rights claimants had to resort to the courts of the state of Hawaii (where the Marcos family fled to in 1986) in order to receive compensation. As Jerry Orcullo, one of the leaders of an NGO representing political detainees (Selda), argues: "*Mas maayo pa ang hustisya sa Hawaii kay sa ato dinhi sa Pilipinas*" ("The justice in Hawaii is better than ours here in the Philippines") (Managbanag 2014, 15). The aforementioned problems represent the persistently corrupt culture in the justice system and state security establishment (Agabin 2012). Based on the World Bank survey conducted in 2000, 72 percent of the Filipino respondents "called the amount of corruption in the government to be very large or somewhat large," with the judiciary and police/military agencies appearing on top of the list (World Bank 2001, i–ii). That same survey revealed that around 50 percent of the total number of respondents expressed distrust of the Supreme Court, 47 percent for the local judges, and 55 percent for the police institutions. Accordingly, "the proportion of Filipinos who believe that most or many judges can be bribed remained unchanged at 57 percent from April 1997 to December 1999, the corresponding percentage for lawyers increased from 60 percent to 65 percent during the same period" (World Bank 2001, ii). This culture of corruption in the judiciary undermined the effectiveness of the human rights reforms in the 1990s, thereby facilitating the persistence of an impunity culture.

Despite the Ramos and Estrada administrations' strong public legitimacy, human rights abuses persisted because of some erring police officers and soldiers. This reflected the institutional inertia of some pockets of the state security apparatus from fully committing to human rights. As the renowned Filipino economist Bernardo Villegas opined: "We thought our institutions were so strong that it no longer really mattered who was president. . . . now we realize there's a limit to that" (Frank 2000, 8). Those limitations pertain to institutional deficiencies within the Philippine military and the Philippine National Police, in which some of their individual officers and rank-and-file agents succumbed to corrupt practices (Hernandez 1995, 2006; Hernandez and Ubarra 1999; McCoy 1999). For example, some police officers and soldiers stationed in rural provinces connived with private investors to provide security to local business interests, many of which were heavily resisted by local residents. Facing peaceful resistance from local residents, state agents responded with violence, largely because of the financial incentives offered by wealthy private investors.

Collateral Abuses of Regular Police and Military Operations

Many human rights violations emerged because of the individual mistakes of agents of the Philippine military and police agencies rather than as outcomes of a nationwide policy of domestic repression. For example, the range of violations included the false identification of ordinary civilians as armed rebels; the inability of the government to efficiently process the legal claims of political prisoners held captive during the Cold War years; claims of torture committed by individual police officers or soldiers; and personally motivated physical abuses committed by the state-sponsored Civilian Armed Forces Geographical Units (CAFGUs). Since the establishment of the CAFGU in the late 1980s, around 800 legal cases of human rights violations were filed against its 1,001 members as of the year 2000 (Philippine Commission on Human Rights 2000).

In the late 1990s, the Philippines witnessed an upsurge of kidnapping of wealthy individuals. According to the Philippine National Police, the number of kidnapping cases nationwide increased from 25 in 1991 to a peak of 179 in 1996 (McCoy 2009, 454). In 1999, the Commission on Human Rights disclosed that Philippine National Police officers "were responsible for almost 22 percent of the human rights violations involving deaths," while other instances were attributed to the Armed Forces of the Philippines and the CAFGU (US Department of State 2000, 9). The crime problem in the late 1990s, particularly during the term of President Joseph Estrada, was so severe that daily TV news shows regularly reported the kidnapping incidents of wealthy Filipinos.

One of the widely known cases of human rights violations emerging from regular criminal policing operations is the Kuratong Baleleng incident (US Department of State 1998). The Kuratong Baleleng was an organized crime group involved in several illegal activities, including drug trafficking. It was widely believed that the group was established by the Armed

Forces of the Philippines in Mindanao in the mid-1980s in order to fight communism in the region. The incident occurred in 1995 when Philippine National Police general Panfilo Lacson apparently commissioned the brutal killings of 11 men suspected of robbery. It took almost four years before Lacson faced a court trial, whereby he and his colleagues were eventually acquitted. The acquittal of Lacson, who started his term as an elected senator in 2001, was largely seen by the Filipino public as the failure of the judicial system to subject some of the most powerful state officials to the rule of law. The Kuratong Baleleng incident demonstrated that the shared expectations of elected Filipino officials and the US government about human rights protection were not enough to obliterate all state-initiated human rights abuses, despite the absence of a deliberate national policy of killing civilian dissidents. This incident indicated that regular police operations were inevitably vulnerable to the inadvertent killings of civilians, thereby contributing to residual human rights violations that emerged despite the democratization reforms. Notwithstanding the various US-sponsored programs on judicial reforms (Blair and Hansen 1994; Messick 1999) and the Philippine government's democratization efforts, domestic legal justice remained largely inaccessible to many human rights victims (US Department of State 2000). That institutional frailty enabled some erring military agents and police officers to continue with their abusive actions regardless of the shifts in the strategic policy goals of the central civilian government.

As the Philippine economy boomed in the 1990s, domestic tourism gained traction and local economies in peripheral provinces expanded, while the increasing urbanization in big cities generated new governance challenges, particularly in maintaining public security. Consequently, the scale of state repression increased in the southern Philippines, with its newly expanded economy in the 1990s. While there was no national government program that promoted the violent repression of civilians, the Estrada administration tasked the military and provincial police units to intensify their offensive operations against kidnap-for-ransom groups, which proliferated during the economic boom. Estrada's decision to carry an all-out war against armed civilians was not limited to ordinary criminal syndicates in Metro Manila but extended to other armed groups in the provinces including those in the conflict-ridden Mindanao Island in the southern region. The US Special Forces assisted in the operations in Mindanao during this time (Kirk 2005; McCoy 2009). Reacting to this surge of kidnapping incidents that even escalated to a diplomatic crisis, Estrada vowed to "crush the kidnappers and reduce them to ash" (Spillius 2000, 6). In fact, the Abu Sayyaf Group took several Europeans and Americans as hostages for ransom, while the most prominent kidnapping case, which occurred in May 2000, even involved high-level diplomatic talks between the Philippine government and the respective national governments of the victims. The hostages were taken from a Malaysian island resort to the Sulu Islands in the southern Philippines, which are known for general lawlessness, piracy, and smuggling (McCarthy 2000, 8). In April 2000 the Abu Sayyaf Group captured 50 individuals on Basilan island and demanded that the Philippine government ask President Clinton "to release Yousef, the World Trade Center bomber currently serving a 240-year sentence in the U.S."—a request that Philippine President Estrada easily dismissed (McCarthy 2000, 8).

Violations as Consequences of Socioeconomic Programs

Some human rights abuses emerged as collateral consequences of the ambitious socioeconomic modernization programs of the Ramos administration (Bello et al. 2004). To a large extent, the US government promoted neoliberal economic development programs (Andrei 1999; Bello et al. 2004; D. Briscoe 1993a; Tira-Andrei 1994; Weissman 1994) in many Global South countries including the Philippines. Yet their collateral costs included the forced displacement of thousands of citizens from their original settlement with the aim of converting their residential lands into highly profitable commercial spaces. The provincial governments deployed local police and military units when communities resisted these projects. The commercial projects were discursively sold to the public either as economic development initiatives that emerged from domestic public-private partnerships or as strategic economic ventures between the Philippine government and the private sector, including American companies (Bello et al. 2004; Kelly 1997; Shatkin 2000). Various companies and firms surreptitiously contracted some groups of the military and police units in forcibly displacing local inhabitants, which sometimes led to violent encounters between civilians and armed state agents. Those incidents suggest that apparently well-intentioned socioeconomic development programs could inadvertently lead to human rights violations. The corrupt tendencies within the military and police units to connive with private interests even thrived during a period when shared expectations on human rights vis-à-vis economic development dominated. Many victims, who often came from a financially poor background, were unable to file a case in domestic courts primarily because of the exorbitant costs of legal services.

The collateral abuses emerging from the implementation of socioeconomic programs persisted both in the rural areas and in Metro Manila. Thus, a good example, which illustrates the violent implementation of socioeconomic programs, pertains to the Public Estate Authority–Amari Development Corporation deal in the mid-1990s. The project included the government's sale of reclaimed lands in Manila Bay to the Amari Corporation, with the aim of establishing luxury real estate development projects. Private security men and government police forces violently relocated thousands of poor families from Manila Bay's fishing communities. A large sector of the Filipino public saw the project as an "immoral, illegal, and grossly unconstitutional state venture" (Corpuz 2003, 6). In 1998, the Ecumenical Commission for Displaced Families, a local NGO, documented seven cases of forced displacements in Metro Manila because of the government's demolition of houses in Manila Bay. Those demolitions harmed the lives of around 15,876 individuals in 2,646 families, as government agents physically harassed many of those civilian residents during the relocation process (Corpuz 2003). There is no evidence, however, of a national government–sanctioned policy that explicitly and directly allowed violent demolitions by local police units.

Despite national economic growth, indigenous communities suffered immensely due to the deterioration of their traditional ways of livelihood, land dispossession, and sometimes the militarization of their homeland. In the rural areas, private companies contracted some members of the local military and police units in order to provide security to powerful business actors while commercial construction projects were being undertaken. Some Filipino police officers and soldiers stationed in rural areas harassed unarmed local residents who were against massive commercial projects. In the process, state agents have undermined indigenous peoples' rights. Although the landmark Indigenous Peoples' Rights Act was enacted in the mid-1990s, the physical harassment and killings of people from indigenous communities persisted—an outcome that likely resulted from the dramatic proliferation of economic development projects. Calling the various government programs forms of "development aggression," the indigenous communities lost their ancestral lands to an unprecedented magnitude in favor of large-scale economic development projects that were first seen in the 1990s (Bauzon 1999, 263). Those economic projects included the building of hydroelectric dams, mining operations, and private real estate projects brought by increased foreign direct investment from the United States. For example, in April 1993, the Bugkalot Tribe in the northern Philippines opposed the construction of a 300-megawatt dam near their communities because the project was expected to "submerge 3,600 hectares of their land and displace 18,000" members of their tribe (US Department of State 1994b, 52). In Bukidnon Province in the southern Philippines, several local police units killed two members of the Higaonon indigenous tribe as well as a local civilian and injured three others including an eight-year-old girl. The incident occurred on July 20, 1997, when local security forces cooperated with provincial police units "in the course of forcibly removing" the Higaonon tribe "from lands that they claimed as ancestral domain but to which a powerful local family also laid claim" (US Department of State 1998, 9). The initial aim was to remove more than 600 members of the tribe from these contested lands. Police officers claimed that it was an accident and insisted that some members of the tribe were also armed during the demolition incident.

The aforementioned abuses suggest that the human rights violations occurred without a deliberate command from the central government in Manila, or from the US government. Because many of the collateral abuses occurred in rural areas, indigenous peoples became top targets of state repression. These incidents of repression occurred despite the landmark political reforms that sought to improve the plight of indigenous communities. With the political support of the US government, in 1997 the Philippine government ratified the Indigenous Peoples' Rights Act, which legally recognized the ancestral claims of these tribes to their lands and created the National Commission on Indigenous Peoples, an autonomous government agency responsible for promoting the welfare of such marginalized groups. After the establishment of the National Commission on Indigenous Peoples, the US government funded many local NGOs that promoted the welfare of indigenous communities and provided financial support for grassroots organizations that advocated for stronger protection of indigenous communities. The growth in the 1990s of such NGOs, functioning as effective deterrence against state abuses, was unprecedented. In the words of USAID mission director Patricia K. Buckles in October 1999 during an annual conference for funding partners, the Philippines is an "NGO superpower" because "the amazingly rich and diverse experience of civil society organization in the Philippines now benefits not only Filipinos, but also people beyond the country's boundaries" (Racelis 2000, 162). Toward the end of the 1990s, various NGOs, many of which were funded by USAID, substantially contributed to "redefining the content of politics" because "topics that would once have been deemed inappropriate for legislation—rape, other violence against women, the rights of indigenous people—have now become subjects of debate and successful parliamentary legislation" (Racelis 2000, 171). That being so, the shared goals among US and Philippine officials for stronger human rights protection were realized when local human rights NGOs—many of which received USAID grants—contributed to a "large, highly organized, and politically prominent civil society" (Silliman and Garner 1998, 13). In effect, these organizations consistently pressured police and military agents to tolerate peaceful political opposition.

Conclusion: Stronger Human Rights Protection in the 1990s

In closing, this chapter presented illustrative evidence from the pre-9/11 Philippine human rights situation vis-à-vis nonmilitaristic US foreign strategic assistance. The evidence confirmed the central tenet of my theory of interest convergence: the conjunction of the donor and recipient governments' interests fundamentally shapes the ways in which domestic policies and foreign strategic support can affect human rights. That conjunction of interests optimized US strategic support and local political reforms in ways that widely tolerated peaceful political opposition and promoted other nonmilitaristic policy goals. I established that the Philippine government's strategic reinterpretation of human rights as crucial to long-term economic development legitimized the influx of pro-human-rights strategic assistance from the US government and the domestic policy prioritization of socioeconomic development. The Clinton administration's democracy promotion initiatives inspired the Philippine government's policy on the integration of former armed communist rebels back into mainstream peaceful electoral politics. Those converging nonmilitaristic interests and policy strategies contributed to the absence of state repression against peaceful dissidence.

Yet several collateral abuses still emerged because some private companies contracted lowly paid military and police agents to provide security amid the booming private sector economic activities in the 1990s and the enduring culture of impunity in the military. The actions of these contracted state agents contributed to the harassment and killings of some civilians in areas affected by expanding economic activities. The inability of the courts to effectively provide justice to human rights victims did not send a credible signal of deterrence to potential abusers within the policy and military agencies. Moving forward, the next chapter examines how and why the Philippines' human rights situation deteriorated during the war on terror period, from 2001 to 2009.

FOUR

From the War on Terror to the Crisis in Arroyo's Strong Republic

I felt that when we formed the global coalition against terrorism, then we were no longer alone. I welcome the support of the world, and I welcome the support of the U.S. in our war against terrorism.

—Philippine President Gloria Macapagal-Arroyo

I remember right after September the 11th, President Arroyo called me, and there was no doubt in my mind where she stood. It was more than the condolence call. It was a let's-get-after-them call. And I knew that we had—I had a strong ally and friend when it came to chasing these people down, which is precisely what we have to do. And she knows that, and that's the strategy she's employed.

—United States President George W. Bush, news conference with President Arroyo, White House, May 19, 2003

The US-led global war on terror constituted the intensified militaristic cooperation of key allies worldwide. As the epigraphs above suggest, Philippine president Gloria Arroyo and US president George W. Bush facilitated the sudden and transformative turn of US-Philippine bilateral relations from the comprehensive socioeconomic agenda in the 1990s to the counterterror policy focus in the 2000s. Why did the Arroyo and Bush administrations suddenly adopt counterterrorism as the priority despite the democratization and economic development reforms of the previous decade? How did such a transformative policy shift impact the level of state repression and physical integrity rights situation in the Philippines after 2001?

This chapter examines how and under which conditions the severe human rights crisis emerged in post-9/11 Philippines from 2001 to 2009. Using my interest convergence theory of aid and human rights, I demonstrate that the terror-oriented strategic support from the US government bolstered President Gloria Macapagal-Arroyo's violent repression of political dissidents. The Arroyo administration's weak political legitimacy and the terror-oriented policy discourses of American and Filipino officials resulted in two transformative policy patterns. The first pattern refers to the Arroyo administration's intensified domestic counterinsurgency program against armed Islamic, secessionist, and even communist rebels—an outcome that led to the massive mobilization of US aid and domestic state resources to the military and police agencies. The second pattern pertains to the highly selective employment of state repression against civilians deemed as "state enemies," particularly through the widespread killings of legal political opposition members, critical media personnel, and unarmed student activists.

This chapter consists of five parts. First, I provide a general characterization of the human rights situation vis-à-vis US strategic support to the Philippines from 2001 to 2009. Second, I examine the shared policy expectations of American and Filipino political elites as well as the broader Filipino public in light of the post-9/11 security context. Third, I show that the terror-oriented agenda was realized in the domestic policies strategically crafted by the Philippine government led by President Gloria Macapagal-Arroyo. Fourth, this chapter provides an analytical survey of the forms of human rights violations that emerged during this historical period. Finally, I explain the implications of the evidence from the post-9/11 US-Philippine counterterror cooperation.

Post-9/11 Human Rights Situation in the Philippines

In contrast to the human rights improvements in the 1990s, the situation in the Philippines deteriorated from 2001 to 2009. In the 2000s, domestic human rights groups recorded 700 summary executions or extrajudicial killings of civilians by state agents under the Arroyo administration (Karapatan 2009). Based on other sources, around 300 cases of "enforced" or "involuntary" disappearances were reported from 2001 to 2010 (Asian Federation Against Involuntary Disappearances 2010). The number of extrajudicial killings under the Arroyo regime is substantially higher compared to the previous decade. Despite the conflicting reports of various organizations concerning the exact number of state-sanctioned abuses, local and transnational human rights groups and scholars alike agree that the Arroyo presidency was the worst in terms of human rights protection since the end of the Cold War in the Philippines (Katigbak and Pareño 2002; Conde 2005; Curato and Arugay 2010; Wilson 2010). At least that is the case when one analytically discards the rampant abuses committed by the administration of President Rodrigo Duterte (2016–), who, during his tenure as Davao City mayor, was a loyal provincial ally of Arroyo (Simangan 2018; Regilme 2020b). In the 2007 official report to the UN Human Rights Council (Francia 2007, 16; Alston 2007, 16), UN representative Philip Alston reported that, from 1986 to 2002, the number of journalists "killed averaged between 2 and 3 per year" in contrast to the years from 2003 to 2006 when "the number killed averaged between 7 and 10" (Alston 2007, 15). The UN reported that "some killings had been perpetrated to prevent journalists from exposing information related to the crimes and corruption of powerful individuals" (Alston 2007, 16), most especially local and national politicians supportive of Arroyo.

The graph below demonstrates the fluctuations in the amount of US bilateral aid to the Philippines from 2001 to 2009. Figure 4.1 shows the sudden drop in military aid following the end of the Cold War, and US foreign aid was maintained at a minimal level until 2000. After the 9/11 attacks, US military aid skyrocketed from less than 10 million USD in 2001 to almost 74 million USD in 2002. The Philippine government received high amounts of US aid from 2002 until the end of that decade, which greatly exceeded the minimal average amounts of aid recorded in the 1990s. Figure 4.1 shows that the combined amounts of US economic and military aid dramatically decreased in the 1990s compared to the levels recorded during the Cold War period, but it increased substantially after 2001. US foreign aid to the Philippines after 2001 reflected a militaristic and terror-oriented emphasis, considering that the amount of military aid was much greater than economic aid.

This chapter illustrates that the Philippine government under President Arroyo reinterpreted terror-oriented discourses in ways that linked the internal security situation in the Philippines to the perceived threat of global armed Islamic fundamentalism. This strategy bolstered the political appeal of the US-led counterterror policy agenda in the eyes of the Filipino public. Yet the Arroyo administration's strategic localization of US terror-oriented discourses provided the Philippine government some normative justifications for the violent repression of unarmed political opposition and peaceful political critics. Such a localization of international terror-

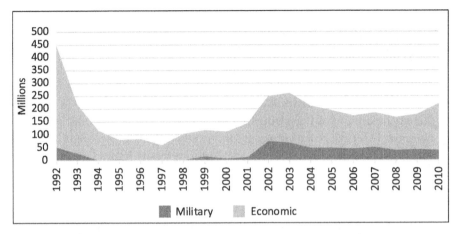

Fig. 4.1. US Military and Economic Aid to the Philippines, 1992–2010 (constant 2016 USD). The data used to create this figure is available on our Fulcrum platform at https://doi.org/10.3998/mpub.12036762.cmp.17

oriented discourses facilitated the influx of counterterror assistance from the United States, which legitimized the increased magnitude of domestic state repression and human rights abuses in the Philippines. I show that the Philippine government's sudden shift to counterterrorism, as an overarching policy emphasis, was politically possible because of the two-level public support from the American government (transnational) and Filipino public (domestic).

Strategic Localization of Security Discourses: Legal Political Opposition as Targets of State Violence

After the 9/11 attacks, the Philippine government actively localized international counterterror discourses, mostly emanating from the US government, in order to advance two main goals. The first aim was to secure the US government's support so that domestic armed rebel groups in the Philippines could be eliminated, and the second objective was to secure the support of the Filipino public for increased state repression (Sidel 2007; Soliven 2003; Holden 2009). For the US government, assisting Southeast Asian allies, especially the Philippines, was a crucial component of the global war on terror because homegrown terrorist groups especially in the Mindanao region were purportedly linked with the Al-Qaeda network (Sidel 2007; Simon 2002). The Philippine government actively lobbied in

Washington, DC to convince the US government that terrorism in Southeast Asia is operationally linked to the Al-Qaeda terror network (Guevarra 2007). The minority view, however, suggests that the link between Al-Qaeda and regional terror groups was fabricated (Sidel 2007). The Philippine government considered the influx of US counterterror assistance as one of the most effective ways to curb armed rebel groups in the country (e.g., communists and Islamic secessionist groups) and to implement violent repression against peaceful political opposition.

Despite the state's constitutional mandate to *only* target armed rebels, the Arroyo administration later arbitrarily redefined the targets of the state repression strategy (Quimpo 2007; Franco and Abinales 2007; Rodriguez and Balce 2004). Whereas both the US and Philippine governments publicly agreed that armed nonstate rebels were the primary targets of counterterror operations, the Arroyo administration added that left-wing political opposition members and vocal critics of the state must be violently repressed. This strategy was reflected in the Arroyo administration's frequent public justifications that the left-wing political opposition constituted a grave threat to state security. Yet the Bush administration and its officials did not publicly tolerate the Philippine government's repression of unarmed political dissidents. While post-9/11 US aid reached more than 100 million USD per year after 2001, with the bulk of that amount allocated to foreign military financing, the Bush administration only withheld 2 million USD of military aid in 2008 in response to domestic and international pressures not to support the Philippine military suspected of human rights abuses (Pangilinan 2012; Karapatan 2009; Olea 2009; Philippine Star 2007).

The Philippine government deployed several justifications for the increased domestic repression against many forms of armed and unarmed political dissidence. As early as 2002, the Arroyo government hinted that the US-led war on terror against armed Islamic rebels ought to be implemented through the inclusion of unarmed leftist political opposition parties as targets of state coercion (Capulong 2002; Sy and Villa 2004; Amnesty International 2006b; Sales 2009). That strategy conflated terrorists with peaceful activist groups that were critical of government policies. In the absence of credible and publicly available evidence, the Philippine military designated key members and sympathizers of leftist political parties as fundamental security threats, while the Arroyo administration widely tolerated the Philippine military's vigorous public harassment of peaceful political dissidence (Amnesty International 2006b; Davao Today 2007; Romero 2007). That process occurred despite the fact that Philippine law recognizes unarmed leftist political parties as legitimate political organizations. Many of the biggest left-leaning parties have consistently fielded candidates for "party-list positions" in the House of Representatives since 2001. Civil society organizations that are now major political parties include Bagong Alyansang Makabayan (New Patriotic Alliance); Nation First; Kabataan (Youth) Party list; Gabriela Women's Party; Anakpawis (Toiling Masses, the electoral wing of the radical labor union movement); and Kilusang Mayo Uno (May 1 Movement, a less radical labor union movement). These parties had enjoyed significant political support from the Filipino public as indicated by their consistent electoral success since the first party-list elections to the Philippine Congress. Whereas the ambitious program of granting political amnesty for communist rebels and the reactivation of competitive electoral processes emerged in the 1990s, post-9/11 domestic politics overturned those democratic and human rights reforms by violently undermining the progressive political opposition.

Responding to social democratic politicians, who disclosed that a US army soldier killed a local and unarmed tribesman in the midst of counter-terror operations, President Arroyo discredited such elected progressive politicians by branding them as human rights violators themselves (Calica and Villanueva 2002): "We shall not relent in the fight against terrorists and criminals hiding behind the veil of human rights advocacies or other seemingly, deceptively legitimate political advocacies." Many Philippine government officials believed that the elected officials of left-leaning political parties had been transferring their "pork barrel funds" (discretionary budget as a member of Congress) to the rural-based communist armed insurgent groups—particularly, as alleged financiers of the Communist Party of the Philippines and the New People's Army. Each Filipino senator receives 200 million pesos (3.8 million USD) annually, while a member of the House of Representatives gets 70 million pesos (1.3 million USD) (Merueñas 2011). Yet there is no credible evidence of leftist politicians' financial support to the armed communist rebellion, considering that the Arroyo administration made that allegation against those politicians in order to deflect criticisms against her own government's abuses (Alston 2008). In fact, President Arroyo even asserted how state repression would be used to curb all forms of political opposition:

> The war on terrorism does not distinguish between ordinary terrorists and those espousing a political ideology. . . . We will wage war against criminals, terrorists, drug addicts, kidnappers, smugglers, and those who terrorize factories that provide jobs. (Capulong 2002)

The Philippine government vigorously deployed political discourses that framed the country as the indispensable partner in the US-led war on terror strategy in the Asia-Pacific region. Arroyo contended that US counterterror assistance and intensified domestic repression against all forms of political dissidence were crucial to the elimination of security threats (Bhattacharji 2009; Guevarra 2007). Arroyo was the first Asia-Pacific leader to express support to prospective US military-oriented responses to terrorism, particularly referring to the probability of using facilities in the Philippines for the US military. During the 50th anniversary of the Mutual Defense Treaty between the United States and the Philippines, Arroyo visited the White House in November 2001 and reframed the Mutual Defense Treaty as the core foundation of the renewed counterterror agenda at that time (Bush and Arroyo 2001a, 2001b; Gunness and Arroyo 2001; Lehrer and Arroyo 2001; Locsin 2001; Agence France-Presse 2003). To further enjoy the monetary benefits of counterterror cooperation, Philippine national security adviser Norberto Gonzales in 2005 signed a contract with the Washington, DC-based law and lobbying firm Venable LLP, which was hired to pressure the White House to provide additional military aid to the Arroyo government, including the massive counterterror training of the Philippine National Police and Armed Forces of the Philippines (AFP) officers (Guevarra 2007). According to US Justice Department records, the Arroyo administration sought to secure 800 million USD worth of military equipment. The contract signing in 2005 coincided with Arroyo's confession on national TV that she had cheated during the 2004 elections. This was a crucial time when the perceived strength of Arroyo's leadership was at an all-time low.

During the first few years of the US-Philippine counterterror cooperation, Arroyo enjoyed wide administrative discretion from the Bush administration, particularly in using US strategic support for domestic counterterrorism. Indeed, the Bush administration granted the Arroyo-led government considerable discretion in determining who and what constituted a "security threat" (Sy and Villa 2004). Due to Arroyo's public endorsement of the US counterterror policies, the Philippine government enjoyed some form of policy autonomy in determining the domestic security threats that needed to be eliminated using US aid (Bush and Arroyo 2001a, 2001b; Laude 2002; Romualdez 2003; Soliven 2003). President Arroyo offered the US government the use of military bases and hosted US military advisors to assist the Philippine military in domestic counterterror operations (Simon 2002). On October 2, 2001, barely a month after the 9/11 attacks, President Arroyo announced to the international media that her government was fully committed with the United States in the war on terror. During the first few hours after the 9/11 attacks, Arroyo telephoned Bush and promised him that the Philippine government would "help in whatever way we [Philippine government] can to strengthen the global effort to crush those responsible for this barbaric act" (Bhattacharji 2009, 11). Remarkably, President Arroyo offered crucial military resources to the US government: "intelligence, logistical help, and the use of Philippine air space" (Landler 2001, A5).

In response to Arroyo's "unequivocal" support for the "war on terror" (Gonzalez 2001b, 1), the US government, on September 29, 2001, asked the Philippine Department of Foreign Affairs for the use of local airspace "whenever it needs" during this "war." The Arroyo administration offered "blanket legitimacy" for all American military vessels, aircraft, and transport facilities to use Philippine territories for "refueling and other purposes" except for building a long-term military base (Gonzalez 2001b; Talosig 2001a, 2001b, 2001c; Clapano 2003). Bush sternly responded that Arroyo enjoys full US support "in any way she suggests in getting rid of the ASG [Abu Sayyaf Gang]" (Today 2001, 4). Because of Arroyo's extensive personal ties with the US foreign policy establishment, the Philippine government enjoyed considerable latitude in its war against unarmed political opposition and government critics.

Despite resistance by local civil society groups against renewed US intervention in Philippine politics, the Arroyo administration attempted to justify its terror-oriented US-Philippine bilateral cooperation by leveraging various narratives that seemed sensible and appealing to the broader Filipino and American public spheres. President Arroyo and the state establishment promoted the idea that the sudden influx of US aid after 9/11 could be the most effective panacea for the centuries-old armed conflict between the Muslim minority in the southern Philippines and central authorities in Manila. The Philippine government heightened the security threat in the country by consistently referring to the Islamic rebel group Abu Sayyaf Gang's abduction in May 2001 until early 2002 of Martin and Gracia Burnham—an American couple who spent some time in Mindanao as Protestant missionaries. In doing so, the Arroyo administration successfully linked internal security threats to the broader international terror problem. That discursive strategy solidified the purported importance of the country in the global war on terror.

Similarly, the Arroyo administration juxtaposed counterterrorism with its antipoverty policy agenda, which clearly resonated with many Filipinos. To commemorate the 50th year of the Philippines-US Mutual Defense

Treaty, President Arroyo visited the White House in November 2001 in order to increase counterterror assistance to Manila. During that meeting, Arroyo emphasized that the war on terror supports the war on poverty, thereby suggesting that counterterrorism is good for poverty reduction and economic growth (Capulong 2002; Philippine Star 2006; Arroyo 2002; Agence France-Presse 2003; Sy and Villa 2004). This discursive linkage of poverty to terrorism demonstrates the Arroyo administration's strategic localization of the US government's "winning hearts and minds" strategy, particularly by seeking to legitimize increased state violence so as to repress political dissidence against her regime. In 2002, amid vociferous outcry from the unarmed political left, which opposed the growing presence of US forces, the Social Weather Station (SWS) survey revealed that 81 percent of the total respondents believed that US military forces were indispensable in the Philippine government's fight against domestic terrorism (Social Weather Station 2001; Lagniton 2002).

The implementation of intensified counterterror and military operations in the Philippines occurred amid the overwhelming domestic public anxiety over terror threats. Based on the November 2001 national survey (Social Weather Station 2001), nearly 70 percent of the Filipino respondents responded that they were "very worried" about the "possibility of a major terrorist attack," compared to the nearly 40 percent of US respondents, based on a *Washington Post* survey conducted October 9, 2001. Meanwhile, around 70 percent of Filipino respondents confirmed that they "strongly approve[d]" the militaristic US-led war on terror (November 3–21, 2001), compared to around 40 percent support in the Gallup poll survey conducted in the United States (November 2 to 4, 2001) (Social Weather Station 2001). In the same SWS survey, close to 65 percent of respondents maintained that US forces should be "allowed to pass through Philippine territory" in the context of the war on terror (Social Weather Station 2001), while the net trust of the United States in the Philippine public consistently remained at no less than 40 percent during the years 2001 to 2009, a remarkably favorable rating that was much higher than trust in any other major external power, such as Japan, Australia, and China (Social Weather Station 2001).

Due to the domestic public anxiety over the perceived terror threat, the Arroyo administration easily framed the potential US-Philippines counterterror cooperation as a compelling proposition, particularly by linking domestic security threats to international terror networks. In effect, the Filipino public seriously considered US-Philippine counterterror cooperation as indispensable and timely in quelling local armed Islamic rebels. US

President Bush contended during the 2001 visit of Arroyo to the White House:

> I'm willing to listen to President Arroyo; I'm willing to work with her in any way that she wants to. We've had a discussion about Abu Sayyaf. *She's got a clear vision about how to fight Abu Sayyaf, and I'll let her speak for herself.* But the Philippines are a great ally. They're close friends, and *we will cooperate in any way she suggests* in getting rid of Abu Sayyaf and other threats. (emphasis mine; Bush and Arroyo 2001a, 2001b; Locsin 2001)

Bush's statement reflected Washington's unwavering belief in Arroyo's abilities in addressing the domestic security threat. The statements of Bush and Arroyo attested to two important transformations in the belief systems of security policy-makers in both Washington and Manila at that time. The first point refers to the *causal* idea that the human rights–oriented policy paradigm after the Cold War had to adapt to the unprecedented security challenges of the post-9/11 security context. Thus, President Bush underscored the necessity of emphasizing public security as the appropriate response to a state of emergency (Jervis 2005, 49): "The United States is under attack . . . and at war, the President needs to have the capacity to protect the national security interests and the safety of the American people." The second shift occurred in the content of *principled* ideas that justified the new counterterror partnership between the United States and the Philippines. Many policy-makers in Manila and Washington believed that human rights and the liberal democratic system can only thrive if national security is guaranteed through extensive state repression and counterterrorism (Acop 2006; Egco 2001; Montemayor 2001). From the perspective of the Arroyo administration, making other civilian development goals subservient to the overarching counterterror strategy was the only way to secure the long-term survival of the Philippine state. In a BBC World Service opinion poll, 63 percent of the respondents who were asked after Bush's reelection in 2004, confirmed that the United States under the Bush administration would be a big boost for international peace— thereby making the Philippines the most pro-US country in a sample of 18 nations (Yujuico 2011, 62). That being so, the dominant communicative discourse, or the interactive dialogue between the Filipino and American policy-makers and the public, advanced the idea that human rights values were somehow subservient to state security (San Juan 2007, 164). Such a belief meant that "the security of the state and quite frequently of the political regime itself are privileged over that of the individual"—a belief that gained traction in post-9/11 Asia because of the "presence of many intrastate conflicts in Asia, which reflect the disjuncture between territorial and ethnic boundaries" (Foot 2005, 418).

To sell her counterterror agenda, the Arroyo administration introduced the notion of a "Strong Republic" or Matatag na Republika (Corpuz 2002; Dimond 2006), which refers to the policy strategy that underscores the critical role of a robust national security apparatus, with a focus on domestic counterterrorism. Arroyo's notion of a strong republic evokes the former Filipino dictator Ferdinand Marcos's long-term developmental strategy called Bagong Lipunan (New Society). Both regimes enjoyed huge amounts of financial aid and political support from Washington. In that regard, Arroyo's Strong Republic marks "three significant thrusts of the regime: 1) the grand comeback of U.S. Special Forces through *Balikatan* (joint exercises with Filipino soldiers) and the Mutual Logistics and Support Agreement (MLSA); 2) the open use of repressive measures against critics and perceived foes; 3) and the all-out implementation of neo-liberal policies at the expense of domestic industries" (Corpuz 2002, 3). This discursive framing of Strong Republic was persistently used as a political justification for harassing and killing nonviolent political dissidents and civilians amid the post-9/11 US-Philippine counterterror cooperation. For that reason, Fernando Hicap, who was the chair of the country's largest progressive alliance of fisherfolk organization, contended that Arroyo was "reversing history's verdict on Marcos . . . by reviving the brutal regime of Marcos . . . [through the] Strong Republic" (Albert-Corpuz 2002, 4).

The Arroyo-led government argued that human rights must be subservient to public security, if only temporarily. President Arroyo (2002, 87) hinted that human rights must be treated as deferential to public security: "at stake in this war is the very life of society, the very possibility of basic rights and liberties, which have been under attack for too long." That sentiment was evident in her 2002 State of the Nation Address, which was delivered before the joint session of the Philippine Congress. Arroyo (2002, 49) highlighted the symbolic and material gains of her country's participation in the global war on terror

> As a result of our decisive action after September 11, the Philippines is now a recognized player in world affairs. The President of the Philippines was the first head of government to emphasize the interconnection between the war against terrorism and the war against poverty. . . . We have gained powerful allies in our domestic

war against terrorism. I am certain that our increased international visibility will continue generating capital inflows for the Philippines.

Filipino and American security officials invoked the necessity of militaristic "emergency actions" or "special measures" as the most effective response to the terror attacks. Yet, such militarism has to be justified through the legal system. Inspired by the USA PATRIOT Act and strongly encouraged by the Bush administration, the Philippine government enacted in 2007 its own version of a counterterrorism law called the Human Security Act (HSA) (see also Jha 2007; Romero 2007; Rauhala 2010; Eadie 2011). The HSA considers acts of terrorism as one of the most severe legal violations that an individual can commit within the Philippines' territorial boundaries. The new law permits preventive detention and arrests of suspects without a writ of habeas corpus. Strangely enough, the HSA identifies 12 acts of violent yet "ordinary" crimes against individuals such as piracy, murder, arson, kidnapping, and rebellion as "acts of terrorism." Consequently, military and police agencies found it convenient to invoke the HSA in order to harass unarmed political opposition members. The HSA lowers the standard of evidentiary requirements for ordinary crimes, which consequently made it easier for the police and the military to frame political dissidents as "terrorists" (Jha 2007; Abaya 2007). The Supreme Court, led by a key Arroyo ally, Chief Justice Renato Corona, upheld the constitutionality of the HSA in 2010, almost a year after the presidency of Arroyo. The US Embassy in Manila publicly supported the ratification of the HSA in 2007 under the impression that it would give more leeway for US and Filipino security forces to conduct effective anti-terror operations (Laude 2004; Jha 2007). Civil society groups viewed the new counterterror laws as detrimental to human rights because they "stifle legitimate public dissent, suppress progressive militant groups and political parties, and prepare the way for an all-out authoritarian rule conceivably worse than the criminal Marcos dictatorship that People Power overthrew in 1986" (San Juan 2007, 164). On February 24, 2006, Arroyo placed the entire country under a "state of emergency" through Presidential Proclamation (PP) 1017, ironically on the same day that the entire nation was commemorating the 20th anniversary of EDSA revolution that toppled the authoritarian regime of Ferdinand Marcos (Arroyo 2006; Pangalangan 2011). PP 1017 was the first formal government document since the end of Martial Law in the late 1980s that castigated the nonviolent political left as cooperating with armed insurgent groups. Arroyo's PP 1017 echoes the sinister state terror embedded in Proclamation 1081, which was the official government policy in the 1970s that officially established Martial Law rule under President Ferdinand Marcos. To rebut criticisms of the PP 1017, Arroyo (2006, 8) alleged that peaceful political opposition members were directly engaged with armed terror groups and that they "constitute a clear and present danger to the safety and the integrity of the Philippine State and the Filipino people."

Resource Mobilization: The Influx of US Counterterror Aid

When I first became President in 2001, I inherited a commitment of military assistance from the U.S. of $1.9 million only. . . . Today, that American assistance to our military support is now $400 million and still counting. In other words, from 1.8 million dollars, as I entered the presidency, our security relationship with the United States today is worth about 400 million dollars and still counting. Still counting because we are now a major non-NATO ally of the U.S. and other assistance and priorities go with that.

—President Gloria Macapagal-Arroyo, March 2004 (Official Gazette of the Philippine Republic 2004, 5–6)

The impact of US aid to the Philippine state's coercive apparatus is substantial, particularly because of its severe budgetary constraints. The largest chunk of the Philippine military's budget is usually spent on personnel salaries and regular operational expenses, rather than defense capability programs and massive counterterror operations (Jacobson 2013). That is why, if not for US aid, the extent and scope of counterterror operations could have been much more limited, thereby decreasing the probability of human rights abuses. The post-9/11 influx of US foreign aid bolstered the counterterror capacities of the Philippine military and police agencies, ranging from regular and upgraded training exercises, joint combat operations, and additional military equipment. In 2002, US military forces trained around 5,000 Filipino soldiers, mostly in Basilan Island in the southern Philippines (Amnesty International 2002, 7; Francia 2007). Aimed at counterterrorism, US training assistance to the rank-and-file soldiers of the Philippine armed forces in 2002 was worth 22.4 million USD. In the same year, the US government spent around 1.3 million USD for sending Filipino military and police officers to several US military schools for specialized training in psychological operations in counterterrorism. The Arroyo administration reported that the US-funded military modernization program included the Squad Automatic Weapons Acquisition

Project, worth around 2.8 million USD (Philippine Presidential Management Staff 2003). The project enhanced the Philippine military's combat capacities and increased the number of troop deployments in the southern provinces (Mindanao) and other communist rebel-inhabited regions in northern Luzon (Philippine Presidential Management Staff 2003). The Arroyo administration reclassified some US military assistance and regular Philippine government funds as "intelligence funds" in order to evade a stringent public audit (Olea 2004). Because of the influx of post-9/11 US aid, the national security agencies' operating budget dramatically increased, as shown by the notable 35 percent increase of 2 billion PhP (45.7 billion USD) in 2003 to 2.7 billion PhP (62.7 billion USD) in 2004. The top three biggest recipients of US aid were all agencies of the Philippine state security apparatus—all of which were implicated in human rights abuses (Olea 2004): the central intelligence services of both the military (6 million USD) and the police (8 million USD) as well as the National Intelligence Coordinating Agency (5.9 million USD). The strategic use of these external resources included two important aspects: (1) the adoption of a "total-offensive approach" (Caballero-Anthony 2003; Holden 2009; Sidel 2007; Soliven 2003) among all the units of the police and the military, and (2) the reorientation and subordination of traditional nonmilitary projects (e.g., socioeconomic development initiatives) under counterterrorism as the overarching policy goal.

Consequently, American and Filipino state officials embraced a full-blown militaristic conception of state security. The Arroyo administration promoted a "high-policing" orientation in both the coercive and civilian agencies of the state, particularly by synchronizing and optimizing its resources in curbing, repressing, or eliminating perceived internal security threats. The Arroyo administration, with the financial and political support of the Joint United States Military Assistance Group to the Republic of the Philippines (JUSMAG), created the multiagency counterterrorism task force that was composed of US military officials and 34 Philippine government agencies responsible for security, socioeconomic, and political work portfolios (US State Department—Office of the Coordinator for Counterterrorism 2005). The goal of JUSMAG was to harmonize state policies, US counterterror assistance, and cabinet departmental portfolios all under the office of President Arroyo. The JUSMAG spearheaded the implementation of various humanitarian activities and socioeconomic development projects such as the building of roads, bridges, and other forms of public infrastructure in conflict-ridden areas such as Basilan, Palawan, Zamboanga, and Batanes (Briscoe 2004; International Coordinating Secretariat in Utrecht and IBON Foundation 2007; Sidel 2007; Simon 2002; Walley 2004). Even these civilian policy portfolios of the state were then redefined as subservient to post-9/11 counterterror aims, particularly by ensuring that these civilian projects went to conflict-prone areas such as Mindanao, rather than the more geographically widespread allocation in the 1990s.

Thousands of Filipino military and civilian security officials participated in US-funded joint military exercises, war games, counterterror seminars, and military professional education exchanges to the United States within the framework of the International Military Education and Training Program (Mogato 2002; Balana 2009). As early as July 2002, American and Filipino military officials, who convened the US-Philippines Mutual Defense Board, conceived the "Five-Year Work Plan" that guaranteed "increased and sustained counter-terror cooperation" (De Castro 2004, 202). Many incidents of repression occurred in conflict-prone areas, especially in Mindanao and in communist-controlled regions in the northern Philippines, where most, if not all, of US counterterror assistance was allocated (Docena 2007a, 2007b).

Philippine national defense secretary Eduardo Ermita contended that the unprecedented amount of post-9/11 US military aid was a "testament to the Philippines' leading role in the Southeast Asian war on terrorism," and that "all these gains are seen in the context of stronger Philippines-US relations . . . because of a common threat which is terrorism" (Philippine Star 2003b, 12). Referring to US-Philippine security relations from 2001 to 2004, Ermita enumerated the significant components of US aid, including the designation of the Philippines as a major non-NATO ally and an unprecedently long list of military equipment and vessels that were geared for counterterrorism (Ermita 2004, 200). The Bush administration's designation of the Philippines as a "major non-NATO ally" legitimized Arroyo's counterterror policies, which were already beginning to create collateral damage to human rights as early as 2002 (Pamintuan 2003; IBON Foundation 2005).

Various US agencies directly contributed to the planning and implementation of counterterror operations in the Philippine archipelago. The US Pacific Command (PACOM), which is the unified combatant command under the US armed forces and the Defense Department responsible for the Pacific areas, provided "extensive and tactical command advantage over the Armed Forces of the Philippines (AFP)" (International Coordinating Secretariat in Utrecht and IBON Foundation 2007, 74). After 2001, America's more intensively engaged strategic leadership over the Philippine military emerged through various organizational instruments jointly headed by Filipino and American security officials. Specifically, the post-9/11 joint leadership bodies of US and Filipino officials included JUSMAG, the Defense Policy Board, the Security Engagement Board, and the Joint Defense Assessment. In effect, these joint leadership initiatives "strengthened the US hand over the AFP, the police and paramilitary forces to make them more compliant with America's military objectives in the Philippines and in the region as a whole" (International Coordinating Secretariat in Utrecht and IBON Foundation 2007, 74).

Evocative of the Bush administration's Operation Enduring Freedom and substantially financed by US bilateral aid, Oplan Bantay Laya (Operation Security and Freedom) was the official name of the Philippine government's internal security campaign against violent and nonviolent political opposition (Del Rosario-Malonzo 2010; Lucas and Shahshahani 2014). It was part of the US-led global war on terror, which was carried out in various conflict-prone territories especially in Iraq, Afghanistan, the Horn of Africa, and Central America. The Philippine military and police vigorously fought in all conflict-prone areas of the Philippine archipelago, while the Arroyo administration publicly justified intensified state violence as part of the "neutralization campaign" against communism and other armed Islamic terrorists. The Arroyo administration branded progressive and nonviolent organizations, which were critical of specific government policies, as terrorists (Corpus 2010; Government of the Philippine Republic 2012). In the 2008 official report to the UN, Special Rapporteur for Human Rights Philip Alston (2008, 9–10; Human Rights Watch 2012a) explained that delegitimizing unarmed political opposition also involves domestic state violence:

> The public vilification of "enemies" is accompanied by operational measures. The most dramatic illustration is the "order of battle" approach adopted systematically by the AFP and, in practice, often by the PNP. In military terms an order of battle is an organizational tool used by military intelligence to list and analyze enemy military units. The AFP adopts an order of battle in relation to the various regions and sub-regions in which it operates. A copy of a leaked document of this type, from 2006, was provided to me, and I am aware of no reason to doubt its authenticity. The document, co-signed by senior military and police officials, calls upon "all members of the intelligence community in the [relevant] region . . . to adopt and be guided by this update to enhance a more comprehensive and concerted effort against the CPP/NPA/NDF." Some

110 pages in length, the document lists hundreds of prominent civil society groups and individuals who have been classified, on the basis of intelligence, as members of organizations which the military deems "illegitimate." While some officials formalistically deny that being on the order of battle constitutes being classified as an enemy of the state, the widespread understanding even among the political elite is that it constitutes precisely that.

Another official Philippine military document classified mere participation in lectures and symposia deemed to be critical of the government as sufficient condition for inclusion on the target list of the military (IBON Foundation 2006). Critics from civil society contended that the military's criteria for inclusion were formulated to specifically target peaceful political dissent (Corpus 2010, 13).

The second aspect of policy transformation pertains to the reclassification of traditionally nonmilitaristic projects as subservient to counterterrorism (Banlaoi 2010, 80–81). The majority of USAID humanitarian and civilian projects were allocated in Mindanao, where armed Islamic rebels have been waging a rebellion against the Philippine state for several decades (Philippine Star 2003b; Natsios 2006). That shift was shown by the sudden allocation of at least 60 to 70 percent of post-9/11 US economic and military development aid to the less populated but conflict-prone Mindanao, whereas before 2001 it was only 30–40 percent (Today 2001; Casino 2007). In exchange for Arroyo's support, the US government bolstered the coercive capacities of the Philippine military and police agencies (International Coordinating Secretariat in Utrecht and IBON Foundation, 74–75; emphasis added): "The US has increased military aid to the Philippines by 1,111 percent. The *military aid in the form of grants and loans has been used by the Arroyo government for its counterinsurgency program leading to the escalation of human rights violations and crimes against humanity.*" The large chunk of post-9/11 US aid was largely reconfigured to the various counterterror programs of the US and Philippine governments. The US and Philippine government officials spent funds tagged as "development aid" for counterterror purposes and not for economic development (Docena 2008, 1):

In General Santos City, the US constructed a deep-water port and a modern civilian airport and built one of the country's best roads to connect them. At Fort Magsaysay, where US troops routinely deploy for training, the local airport was renovated and its runway strengthened to handle the weight of C-130 planes. In Basilan and

Sulu, also US training venues, the US Agency for International Development has built roads and ports that allow huge ships to make berth.

Even the US-based think tank Center for Strategic and International Studies characterizes "the civil engineering and humanitarian projects of US troops in the country as linked to the counterterrorism mission" (Del Rosario-Malonzo 2010, 54). Similarly, the Manila-based IBON Foundation observes that "it is thus unsurprising that engineering projects such as roads, airfields, and wharfs are structurally designed to accommodate large vessels and aircrafts used for US combat operations here and abroad" (Del Rosario-Malonzo 2010, 54) instead of serving the local community's daily needs. This reorientation of development aid stood in contrast to the situation in the 1990s, when aid was evenly distributed to various regions in the Philippine archipelago, devoid of an overarching military security objective.

In sum, the human rights crisis under the Arroyo regime can be attributed to two transformative policy patterns. *First*, the Philippine government included left-wing political opposition, critical journalists, government critics, and local political opposition as targets of state violence. Because of her perceived weak leadership, President Arroyo used US foreign strategic assistance to gain the political support of her military and police officers, most especially the Armed Forces of the Philippines. Consequently, the military and police agencies obtained more discretionary intelligence funds, modern equipment, and counterterror training sponsored by the US government. *Second*, backed by US strategic assistance, the Philippine government expanded the scale of counterterror operations against armed Islamic and communist rebels, which consequently generated the build-up in the number of collateral deaths and injuries of civilians in conflict-ridden areas. Thus, Manila's support for Washington's war on terror "essentially opened channels for increased US military assistance" that empowered the military and the police "to gain the upper hand in its fight against local Islamist terrorist and secessionist groups" (Morada 2003, 228; Arroyo 2002; Capulong 2002; Philippine Star 2006). The longstanding armed domestic insurgency problem was no longer an exclusive concern for the Philippine government; instead, it was incorporated into the global US-led war on terror. In effect, extensive counterterror operations in the post-9/11 Philippines generated an increase in collateral human rights violations.

The deterioration of the human rights situation in post-9/11 Philippines emerged from the close entanglements between US foreign policy and Philippine domestic politics. At the transnational level, the American public widely supported the Bush administration's war on terror and the various forms of intensified US military engagements with other allies (Gershkoff and Kushner 2005; Landau 2004). This domestic public support enabled the Bush administration to provide enormous amounts of terror-oriented material support to allied countries. At the domestic level, the Arroyo administration launched its increased armed operations against armed rebels in the southern regions based on exaggerated characterizations of the domestic terror threat and its links to international terrorism. The Filipino public widely supported US assistance to the Philippine government's counterterror agenda. The terror-oriented US-Philippines bilateral agenda emerged precisely because of the convergence of American and Filipino public support for such a policy focus.

Had the US government not provided terror-oriented aid to the Arroyo administration, would the Philippine government have targeted both armed and unarmed civilian targets? The emerging consensus among several scholars suggested that the post-9/11 counterterror campaign against peaceful and armed political opposition was largely the outcome of domestic politics (Rivera 2005; Chambers 2012; Franco and Abinales 2007). Absent the terror-oriented US foreign strategic support, the Arroyo administration might have resorted to targeting both armed and unarmed opposition in order to strengthen her political rule. That diagnosis, however, is misguided. First, widespread counterterror operations in the Philippines require willing and well-funded military and police agents. In conducting their counterinsurgency campaigns or even in undermining political opposition, the Philippine armed forces and the police would require at least the latent political support of the United States. Without US support for Arroyo's leadership, neither an expansive counterinsurgency campaign nor extrajudicial killings of civilians would be possible. This is precisely because the regular government budget allocated for state security is usually diverted to the salaries of the military and police personnel. Any form of large-scale counterinsurgency efforts would normally require enormous funding that the Philippine state normally does not have. Second, the perception of an emerging public insecurity after 9/11 was widely shared by the US and the Philippine political elites as well as the domestic public. This made it easier for President Arroyo to sensationalize the threat of both armed and unarmed political dissidence and consequently justify well-funded counterterror operations, which were discursively sold to the public by highlighting the overriding importance of public security over human rights. Historically, foreign assistance has been indispensable to the Philippine military considering that the US government substantially funded almost all of the post–World War II counterinsurgency campaigns against communist, Islamic, and other secessionist armed rebel groups (Blum 2004, 38–43).

Intervening Factors: The US-Led War on Terror and Domestic Politics in the Philippines

President Arroyo's problems in securing legitimacy motivated her to pursue two important goals during her tenure: (1) winning the support of the military and other state security agencies in order to prevent potential coups, and (2) weakening all forms of political opposition that could undermine her legitimacy (Bernas 2007). As such, the Arroyo administration rewarded influential factions within the state security establishment in order to subvert the possibility of a military takeover or a political defection (Gloria, Rufo, and Bagayaua-Mendoza 2011; Gloria 2013; Curato and Arugay 2010; Corvera 2003a). Arroyo appointed 12 generals to the position of chief-of-staff of the AFP during her 10-year term, "subsequently shifting them into civilian posts after retirement," thereby indicating the "increase in military influence on political institutions since 2001" (Mietzner 2011, 5–6; Arugay 2011). Before Duterte, Arroyo holds the record of having the largest number of cabinet officials and high-level diplomatic posts assigned to retired military and police officers[1] (Adriano 2008). In return, President Arroyo contracted state security agencies to kill and harass the legal political opposition. Because of their strong support base for left-wing politics especially outside of Manila, the social democratic-oriented and communist organizations became the immediate targets of state violence. To a lesser extent, incumbent local leaders, who were formally allied to President Arroyo, targeted their own respective political opposition challengers. Media critics, student activists, and sympathizers of left-wing politics became clear targets of violent state repression.

The post-9/11 US foreign strategic assistance to the AFP and the Philippine National Police provided various rent-seeking opportunities for the state security agencies (Bhattacharji 2009; Gloria, Rufo, and Bagayaua-Mendoza 2011). The suicide of Angelo Reyes, Arroyo's defense minister and former AFP chief-of-staff, shows the extent of corruption resulting from the post-9/11 aid shock. Reyes, a Harvard-educated military official, committed suicide allegedly because of the corruption charges against him and the fledgling political legitimacy problems of the Arroyo government. In the words of the Filipino political scientist Nathan Quimpo: "Corruption in the Philippine armed forces and police has plagued the fight against terrorism. . . . At the height of the Abu Sayyaf kidnappings, the Philippine media frequently reported the collusion of soldiers with terrorists, selling them guns and ammunition and getting cuts from ransom payments" (Quimpo 2007, 8; Gonzalez 2001b, 1). By providing enormous funds to the Philippine military, Arroyo temporarily secured the political support of the state's coercive agencies in expanding the scale of state repression against all forms of political opposition. Amid the expansion of counterterror operations, "Arroyo became less inclined to challenge military prerogatives in internal security, and as such, gained the support of many soldiers" (Chambers 2012, 129). Thus, "Arroyo's embrace of the United States and the acquisition of US aid increased her standing vis-à-vis the armed forces" (Chambers 2012, 154; see also Clapano 2003; M. Gonzalez 2001a; Talosig 2001a, 2001b, 2001c). Worst of all, the ineffective judiciary and the enormous financial and nonmonetary costs involved in the prosecution of suspected military and police violators provided the military and police officers a sense of immunity from any form of legal punishment.

The Arroyo presidency registered consistently low levels of public support since the return of electoral democracy in 1986 (Social Weather Station 2010). Arroyo's highest public satisfaction rating was recorded in 2001(at a mere 25%), yet the rating at that time was comparably very low relative to her predecessors' record. In 2004, Arroyo was elected by approximately 1 million votes ahead of her challenger—the only year in which President Arroyo enjoyed a very high rating compared to all the years of her presidency. Nevertheless, that positive approval rating eventually dipped in June 2005 when the "Hello Garci!" scandal broke out. The scandal began when an audio recording of a phone conversation between Arroyo and a Commission on Elections commissioner, Virgilio Garcillano ("Garci"), was released to the public and the media. The conversation between Arroyo and Garci occurred several months before the 2004 presidential elections. Incumbent President Arroyo asked Garci to manipulate the national election results for the presidency, particularly by ensuring that she should have at least one million more votes than her nearest rival. Eventually, the official results in the 2004 elections indicated a one million lead against Fernando Poe Jr., a very popular movie star. On June 27, 2004, a teary-eyed Arroyo appeared on national television and acknowledged that it was indeed her voice on the audio recording but denied that the 2004 elections were rigged. Ironically, she apologized and was known, since then, by her famous line: "I am sorry." Arroyo, surprisingly, conceded her wrongdoing, yet managed to remain in power. Thus, Arroyo's claim to legitimacy was fragile, thereby making state repression against dissidence a more viable option.

Another enabling domestic political condition concerns the lack of restraint on the military against engaging in civilian politics. In the case of the Philippine state, two enduring institutional qualities remain obvious: (1) the consistent meddling of the military and police actors in national and local politics; and (2) the severe infighting and persistence of conflicting factions within the Philippine military, thereby demonstrating the lack of coherent institutional leadership and professionalism (McCoy 1999; Arugay 2011; Abinales 2005). Considering the highly politicized nature of the military, the Arroyo administration rendered political favors to the most important actors within the military leadership. Her administration used large amounts of intelligence funds (largely from US aid), wide administrative discretion in implementing wide-scale counterterror operations, and high-profile cabinet positions within the civilian government to lure influential military and police commanders into leading the government's repressive practices against armed and unarmed opposition (Corvera 2003a, 2003b).

The Philippines lacks a highly effective judicial system. First, this practically means that external political pressures easily influence the judicial system. The 2012 report by the Heritage Foundation's Index of Economic Freedom Report lists some of the enduring problems in the Philippine judicial system: "the legal framework is deficient in independence and efficiency . . . cumbersome court system and loose regard for contracts continue to be causes for concern" as well as the susceptibility of the courts to overt political interference (Miller, Holmes, and Feulner 2012, 340). Second, the judiciary has been facing the problem of case congestion. The Philippines' National Statistical Coordination Board reported that the "judiciary faces serious difficulties in addressing case backlogs, and that additional investments will be required to improve the adjudication process" (Bacani 2013, 1). Accordingly, lower courts had a very high vacancy rate in the number of judges at 24.3 percent from 2006 to 2009, and that "over a million cases swamped in the lower courts a year also mean that each judge need[s] to handle an annual caseload of 644 cases or about three cases to be resolved each working day" (Bacani 2013, 6). Because of that backlog, many human rights victims were unable to make a successful legal case in these courts, while abusive police and military agents enjoyed impunity.

Selective Political Repression against "Enemies of the State"

This section presents several observations from 2001 through 2009 that depict the scope and type of human rights abuses at the micro-level. The narratives of severe physical harassment and extrajudicial killings of unarmed and legal political opposition members, civil society activists, and journalists illustrate the brutality and pervasiveness of violent harassment employed by the military and the police. These abuses emerged as outcomes of selective political repression, because they occurred as part of the nationwide policy of the Philippine government, which deliberately targeted legal political opposition members and other civilian activists.

The Maguindanao massacre is an infamous example of state violence during this period (Perez and Dimacali 2009; Rauhala 2010; Beehner 2010). *Time Magazine* named the Maguindanao Massacre the world's "single worst attack on journalists ever recorded" (Rauhala 2010, 3). On November 23, 2009, a convoy of journalists, lawyers, and relatives of Vice-Mayor Esmael Mangundadatu ("Toto") were on their way to support and to cover the filing of Toto's certificate of candidacy for provincial governor in a local Commission on Elections office in Maguindanao Province. Since 2001, when President Arroyo named Andal Ampatuan Sr. as her most loyal political ally in the region, Maguindanao Province had remained under the political control of the Ampatuan political clan. Since then, a member of the Ampatuan family had occupied almost all key elected positions in the province. According to witnesses and official accounts by various government agencies, Toto's group was at a police checkpoint when a group of nearly 100 armed individuals suddenly intervened and took over the lead of the convoy. The Ampatuan clan employed these armed men as paid employees of the provincial government. Women were raped and sexually mutilated before being killed. In the final tally, 57 unarmed men and women were found dead, 30 of them journalists who wanted to cover the filing of the candidacy of the electoral challengers of the Ampatuan clan.

A few days after the incident, the independent national government investigation launched an inspection of the Ampatuan clan's mansion and discovered "a big weapons cache consisting of light artillery and heavy infantry weapons (including commando weapons, explosives, and ammunition) as well as military uniforms" (Perez and Dimacali 2009, 29). Accordingly, the investigators "uncovered a hidden armory behind a concrete wall, with ammo cases for M-16, M-14, and possibly M-203 rifles also bearing the mark of the United States Department of Defense Arsenal"

(Perez and Dimacali 2009, 30). It is likely that the new military ammunition from the United States came into the hands of the Ampatuan family
because of their close links with the Arroyo administration and the Philippine military. That belief is not surprising considering that "most US military assistance goes to military equipment and US military training of local
troops," compared to the stark emphasis on nonmilitary concerns prior to
9/11 (Hall 2010, 33).

The 2009 Maguindanao massacre illustrates how the Arroyo regime
used US strategic assistance to buy the political loyalty of local politicians
as well as the loyalty of provincial police and armed forces units. The dis-
covery of US military resources in Ampatuan's private residence points to
that conclusion. Local politicians, in turn, marshaled military resources
and regional units of the military and police to physically harass and to kill
political opponents in the rural provinces. The local media reported that
the Ampatuan clan's unprecedented access to various instruments of political violence was a result of the Arroyo administration's naming of Mindanao as a priority area for post-9/11 counterterror operations. That designation as a conflict hotspot facilitated the influx of US aid to the region
through the Arroyo-led government based in Manila.

The strategic alliance between the Ampatuans and the national executive government galvanized the political legitimacy of Arroyo in the
southern Philippines. After the Maguindanao massacre, local media outlets reported that the Ampatuan political clan was crucial in delivering the
landslide victory for Arroyo during the 2004 presidential elections and
the senatorial candidates of Arroyo's political party. Arroyo withstood the
numerous scandals that plagued her presidency because of the local coalitions that she forged, while "her closest ally in Central Mindanao was the
Ampatuan family whose brutal grip over the region ensured the president
the one million votes she needed to win the 2004 elections" (Abinales and
Amoroso 2017, 302–3). In 2005, most of these votes from the southern
Philippines were disclosed as fraudulent, which led to the eventual public
apology of President Arroyo in prime-time national television for committing electoral fraud.

Local media reports in Mindanao suggested that the Ampatuans, prior
to the massacre, implemented a massive political propaganda campaign
that discursively branded the emerging opposition politicians as detrimental to local security. That incident demonstrates the strategic localization of
post-9/11 security discourses, whereby pro-Arroyo politicians used counterterror justifications to undermine the credibility of local politicians.
Moreover, the local media discourses in the Ampatuans' locality contrib-

uted a sense of legitimacy to the killings of the local opposition (Human Rights Watch 2010b; Rauhala 2010). The Ampatuan family framed their political challengers as "local terrorists" who purportedly threatened the political stability in the province that had been controlled for such a long time by pro-Arroyo politicians. A Mindanao-based human rights activist interviewed by Human Rights Watch claimed that "the Ampatuans used the AFP to run after their political enemies," while another peace worker confided about the Philippine military officers' admission of their involvement with the Ampatuans (Human Rights Watch 2010b, 60).

Another example of an attempt at regime consolidation at the local level was the politics of post-9/11 violence in Davao City, where its mayor, Rodrigo Duterte, sanctioned many of the abuses in that city. Known as one of the staunchest allies of Arroyo, Duterte served as the presidential adviser on peace and order and security issues concurrently while serving as the elected mayor of Davao City. Before assuming the presidency in 2016, Duterte was widely known for being in full command of the extrajudicial killings in the city. For that reason, *Time Magazine* named him "The Punisher," while the local media branded him the "Dirty Harry of the Philippines" (Zabriskie 2002; Breuil and Rozema 2009; Human Rights Watch 2009). Similarly, Human Rights Watch, Amnesty International, UN Special Rapporteur for Human Rights Philip Alston, and domestic civil society groups blamed Duterte for his blatant political and material support for killing suspected criminals, street children, and drug addicts, among many others. Although the state-sanctioned death squads in Davao City started as early as the mid-1990s, local and international NGOS reported a dramatic increase of killings starting in 2001 (Breuil and Rozema 2009). The brutality and pervasiveness of Duterte's human rights violations increased after the Philippines joined the US-led war on terror. In the first phase of the Philippines' US-supported war on terror, Duterte "would announce the names of 'criminals' on local television and radio—and some of those he named would later become death squad victims" (Conde 2014, 3). The victims' surviving family members did not launch a legal case against suspected government agents due to the fear of retribution. Human rights violations under Duterte's command emerged because the local government effectively hijacked the sensationalized political discourse on public security amid the "war on terror." The pervasiveness of the killings soared after 2001 to the point that "if you want to kill anybody in the Philippines, now [post-9/11 period] is the best time" (Conde 2005).

Arroyo's political support for Duterte was indeed remarkable. In January 2004, despite the Davao Death Squad's reported killings of 34 civilians, the Arroyo administration awarded the Davao City police force as the country's best for 2004 (Conde 2005). Arroyo openly and consistently endorsed Duterte's political leadership and praised his performance in Davao City for strengthening public security amid a region beset with nonstate terrorism. Many elected local officials openly endorsed the killings in their city, thereby reinforcing the role of the local government in the formation of the death squads (Conde 2005). At least 16 percent of the victims in 2001 and 2002 were minors, and in 2005 at least 30 percent of the killings targeted children (Breuil and Rozema 2009, 417). The Philippine Commission on Human Rights concluded that there was "a pattern of selective and systematic extrajudicial killings of 206 individuals accused or suspected of committing various offenses by a vigilante group in Davao City from 2005 to 2009" (Regalado 2012, 1). Apparently, the local government contracted retired soldiers, who led groups of active local military and policy units that were responsible for the assassinations. At the height of the international uproar against the human rights violations committed in Davao City, Mayor Duterte in 2009 unashamedly contended that all suspected criminals deserved to be killed (Philippine Daily Inquirer 2012, 4):

> If you are doing an illegal activity in my city, if you are a criminal or part of a syndicate that preys on the innocent people of the city, for as long as I am the mayor, you are a legitimate target of assassination.

The modus operandi of the Davao Death Squad had been replicated in other parts of the country, primarily through the initiatives of local government leaders with strong political alliances with President Arroyo. For example, the mayor of Cebu City, the second largest city in the country, located in the Visayas region, also supported the idea of local government-sponsored "death squads" under the rubric of counterterrorism. President Arroyo's State of the Nation Address at the start of her term in 2001 also branded ordinary criminals and drug addicts as "internal security threats" that must be considered as legitimate targets of counterterrorism. In 2004, Cebu City's mayor, Tomas Osmeña, openly encouraged local police "to be more aggressive" against criminal suspects, while coincidentally "death squad" operations similar to Davao emerged in Cebu. Osmeña proudly confessed that he told police officers that "if you encounter a crime in progress, don't be shy. Pull the trigger and I'll give you a bonus" (Conde 2005, 24).

To boost her legitimacy, President Arroyo—in cooperation with provincial politicians—contracted with local police and military to kill unarmed political dissidents. That deal between the central government in Manila and the local provincial authorities became effective using two political mechanisms. First, Mayor Duterte capitalized on Arroyo's Strong Republic paradigm, which contended that violent state repression of all forms of political dissidence is needed to maintain security and democracy. Located in Mindanao in southern Philippines, Davao City and its surrounding regions became the focal point of counterterror operations. The strategic importance of Davao and Duterte's support for Arroyo's political survival led one analyst to assert that "a presidential aspirant would need his [Duterte's] endorsement" (Gonzalez 2005, 5). Second, the widespread activities of the "death squads" required tremendous amounts of material resources, and the influx of US counterterror aid fueled the state's machinery of domestic violence, which proliferated after 2001. In return for support from the Arroyo government, Duterte facilitated the extensive intelligence gathering and violent operations of US Special Forces in Mindanao as well as consolidating local political support for President Arroyo (Regalado 2007).

There were two key observable patterns of state repression during this period: (1) state killings were implemented to eliminate all forms of political opposition to the Arroyo administration, and (2) state violence occurred in more prevalent ways where there were military detachments (Asian Human Rights Commission 2006). These patterns show that the state's increased use of political violence is a double-edged sword: whereas counterterrorism was explicitly aimed at combatting armed rebellion, it was also used to undermine peaceful political dissent.

The Tokyo-based NGO Human Rights Now (Amnesty International 2006a; Davao Today 2007; Human Rights Now 2008; Romero 2007) reported that "the majority of targets are people who are lawfully criticizing governmental policies by means of peaceful measures such as speeches, writing, and mobilizing people." In an interview with a high-ranking civil society activist in northern Philippines, William Holden (Holden 2009, 382; see also Calica and Villanueva 2002) noted that "the more vocal people are, the more vulnerable they become." Many victims of extrajudicial killings were directly involved in various activities that "go against the interests of the Arroyo regime," including human rights defenders, union leaders, student activists, and religious leaders, among others (Human Rights Now 2008, 17). Some victims were ordinary bystanders who were later on incorrectly tagged by government agents as terrorists.

The 2006 abduction of Karen Empeño and Sherlyn Cadapan, who were prominent student activists from the University of the Philippines, represents the Philippine government's selective political repression of left-wing activism. The incident illustrates the direct involvement of the Philippine military in the violent repression of organized political dissent and criticism (Philippine Daily Inquirer 2011; US Department of State 2008). Considering that Empeño and Cadapan were active in grassroots politics and numerous student protests against the US-Philippines counterterror partnership, government agents kidnapped Empeño and Cadapan, who were conducting interviews with peasant farmers in northern Philippines for their academic research. Most likely because of their left-wing political beliefs and involvement in progressive student organizations, the military considered the students as enemies of the state and subjected them to violent harassment. The Empeño and Cadapan case confirms how the Arroyo administration implemented the systematic repression of nonviolent left-wing politics, particularly those of a social-democratic or Marxist persuasion. Similarly, in 2003, the Philippine National Police arrested Ninez Cacho Olivarez, who was the publisher and editor of the *Daily Tribune*, which published a series of articles that implicated Arroyo's closest associates in the corruption scandal pertaining to the construction of terminal 3 of Manila's international airport (Sison and Felipe 2003).[2] The national media framed this incident as the "first arrest of an editor since 1986," when the two-decade authoritarian leadership of Marcos ended (US Department of State 2004a, 98). Thus, even ordinary activists and journalists fell victim to selective political repression.

Those aforementioned incidents of state repression occurred and persisted through two primary strategies. First, the Arroyo administration and the Philippine military publicly justified the massive purges of peaceful political dissidents as "legitimate" by offering a counternarrative that the targets were surreptitiously aiding armed rebellion in the rural areas. Second, the Filipino police and military used US military resources and advanced post-9/11 counterterror techniques in order to effectively implement widespread political repression (Laude 2002; Villanueva and Brago 2003).

Collateral Consequences of US-Philippines Counterterrorism

Many state agents killed civilians under the unfounded suspicion that the latter were members of the armed communist movement. These collateral violations emerged amid counterinsurgency operations and military deployments in conflict-prone rural areas in "Southern Tagalog, Bicol and Central Luzon; Samar, Leyte and Negros in the Visayas; and North Eastern (Caraga), Southern (Compostela Valley) and North Central Mindanao" (Karapatan 2009, 40). The widespread counterterror operations caused the displacement of communities, the destruction of private property, and the detrimental psychological effects of military operations to civilian residents living in conflict-prone areas (Foot 2005). The map of the Philippines below shows the number of civilian deaths due to state-based violence during the period from 2001 to 2010. Of the 5,543 cases, the large majority of those incidents were concentrated in the southern islands of Mindanao, where the Philippine government implemented counterterror military operations against armed Islamic rebels. The other cases of civilian deaths, meanwhile, were scattered in the various northern and middle parts of the archipelago, where armed communist insurgents (the New People's Army) mainly operate.

State agents erroneously identified civilians as terror suspects, thereby contributing to the increase in the number of erroneous detentions during this period. Many civilian residents in Mindanao, central Luzon, and other conflict-prone rural areas of the archipelago were killed, injured, and psychologically harassed. These abuses occurred while Filipino soldiers and agents of US Special Forces were stationed in their victims' communities as part of the widespread counterterror operations against armed Islamic or communist rebel forces. In other instances, many schools, homes, and private properties of ordinary residents were destroyed, while government forces engaged in combat operations against armed Islamic rebels in Mindanao or communist rebels in rural areas in Luzon and the Visayas Islands. Such incidents are outcomes of processes that I collectively call erroneous intelligence and policing practices.

The 2009 detention of Muhamadiya Hamja is a telling example of the collateral abuse emerging from the government's false identification of a suspected rebel (Philippine Commission on Human Rights 2009; Penney 2011). Hamja, who lives in the Muslim-dominated Quiapo neighborhood of Manila, was erroneously accused by police of being a member of the Abu Sayyaf Gang, the notorious kidnap-for-ransom Islamic rebel group. The suspicion was based on a report from a neighbor who expected "to win more than $1000 from the American-funded 'Rewards for Justice' programme, which gives cash prizes to citizens who identify terrorists" (Penney 2011, 15). In the official Philippine Commission on Human Rights report (2009), the police conceded that the arrest of Hamja was a big mistake. The CHR cited the reasons of Hamja's defense attorney, who asserted that the arrest warrant was intended to capture "Madja Hamja,"

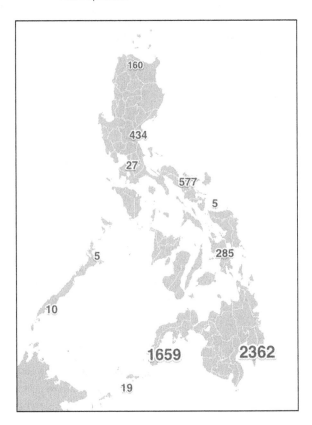

Fig. 4.2. Geographic Location of Civilian Deaths due to State-Based Violence in the Philippines, 2001–2010. (Data from Uppsala Conflict Database. Map of the Philippines by Michael Gonzalez, via https://commons. wikimedia.org/ wiki/File:BlankMap-Philippines.png)

whereas her client's name is "Muhamadiya Hamja." The same CHR report lamented the fact that Hamja "had also been arrested sometime in 2001 for fifty-two cases of kidnapping and illegal detention but was never identified after the presentation of more than sixty witnesses, leading to the dismissal of the cases against him" (Philippine Commission on Human Rights 2009). In 2009, the police secretly detained Hamja, but he was later released after the police confessed that Hamja's detention was a case of mistaken identity.

The destruction of private property and the torture of erroneously identified suspects in several conflict-prone areas proliferated during this period. The massive counterterror and surveillance operations in the southern Philippines led to forced displacement, violation of privacy rights, and destruction of private property (Docena 2007a). Many civilian children were not spared from the far-reaching effects of US-Philippine counterterror cooperation. The Arroyo administration's counterinsurgency program in the southern Philippines killed 423 children during the government soldiers' encounter with armed rebels in January to March 2008 (Children's Rehabilitation Center 2008). In early 2008, the human rights organizations Children's Rehabilitation Center and Karapatan reported that 126,850 children were detrimentally affected by the US-supported Philippine military operations in Mindanao from 2001 to 2005 (Children's Rehabilitation Center 2008), including "580 direct victims, 138 indirect victims, 17 children political detainees, and 126,115 children displaced due to indiscriminate firing, strafing, bombing, destruction and divestment of properties" (Children's Rehabilitation Center 2008, 5). From 2001 to 2005, Mindanao had the largest number of underaged victims of human rights violations. The instances of violations primarily resulted from the numerous military operations that affected the psychological well-being of the children residing in conflict-prone areas. Many of these reported violations occurred in Mindanao, where US Special Forces operated in joint missions with the Philippine military on several occasions from 2002 to 2008.

Indigenous people also suffered from the far-reaching detrimental consequences of counterterror operations. Based on the official 2008 report of indigenous peoples' rights networks to the UN High Commissioner for Human Rights, indigenous communities in the country "are estimated to be around 12 to 15 million, or 15 per cent of the total population" and "they occupy more than 10 million hectares of the total landmass of 30 million hectares" (Indigenous Peoples' Rights-Monitor Philippines et al. 2008, 4). Based in isolated conflict-prone areas, indigenous groups face the risk of death or physical harm by the state's security forces during armed encounters between the military and armed rebels. Such abuses can be classified into two types: (1) indigenous leaders mistaken for being direct supporters of armed nonstate rebel groups, and (2) forced displacement from their ancestral lands due to regular counterterror operations. Various domestic and transnational human rights networks reported that 120 indigenous civilians were killed from 2001 to 2007 (Indigenous Peoples' Rights-Monitor Philippines et al. 2008, 4). The Lumads of Mindanao and the Igorots of the Cordillera in the southern and northern parts of the country, respectively, suffered the most due to the increased militarization of their areas. From 2003 to 2006, state agents killed, in separate incidents, four indigenous persons in the Cordillera region in the northern Philippines after the victims were mistaken for being communist rebels. Yet the victims were using firearms solely for food gathering as they conducted their indigenous hunting practices (Indigenous Peoples' Rights-Monitor Philippines et al. 2008). The displacement and deaths of indigenous residents illustrate the collateral consequences of intensified counterterror operations in many of the rural regions where they live (Alston 2008; Miller 2008). In late 2007, the Philippine army launched violent operations against communist rebels in Surigao del Sur, the northeastern province of Mindanao. That operation resulted in the forced displacement of around 1,500 Manobo indigenous residents, while a cholera epidemic worsened the situation in the evacuation centers. The problem was so severe that the Philippine Senate called it a humanitarian disaster (Senate of the Philippines 2007). While the displacement lasted for almost two months, the Manobos, who eventually returned to their lands after the military clashes, witnessed their homes completely destroyed, including their animal farms.

In many rural areas, some factions of the Philippine military recruited indigenous people as part of the Philippine government's paramilitary units.[3] As recipients of post-9/11 US aid, the Philippine military had the wherewithal to expand its violent operations in many places where armed rebel groups persisted. Considering the rugged terrain in many of these conflict-prone areas, the Philippine armed forces had to rely on local residents for reliable domestic intelligence and additional logistical support. Because of the financially impoverished situation in these militarized areas, indigenous communities were forced to join the government's paramilitary units in exchange for money. Indigenous people were underpaid in their collaboration as paramilitary support forces of the Philippine military, and many of them were coerced to join government forces out of sheer financial motivations or incomplete understanding of the situation. In August 2009, Lumad indigenous communities in northeastern Mindanao failed in their plea to the Armed Forces of the Philippines' 401st Infantry Battalion for government forces to leave their ancestral lands. The militaristic operations in their ancestral land, home to around 1,700 indigenous residents, caused a food blockade in the area as well as the extremely coercive conscription of some Lumad male members to be part of the government's paramilitary organization (Bulatlat 2009).

Notably, American forces worked closely with Filipino troops in conflict-embattled zones. In November 2002, the Philippine military staged armed combat operations against purported members of the Abu Sayyaf Gang. They targeted the Moro National Liberation Front, "a group whose peace agreement with the government has frayed but which is not tagged a 'terrorist group' by either Manila or Washington," at least until November 2002 (Docena 2007b, 14). Yet the AFP launched various military operations with assistance from the US Special Forces covertly stationed in Mindanao. According to testimonies from residents in the Sulu Islands in the southern Philippines, US Special Forces troops were leading combat operations together with the Philippine military officers. That incident demonstrated that the US military forces based in the Philippines had a more direct role with the commission of collateral violations in a few instances such as when

> they [Americans] were seen aboard military trucks with their Filipino counterparts and in rubber boats, mounting heavy artillery, operating military equipment, removing landmines, or evacuating casualties. Throughout the clashes, a spy plane—which locals claim had been flying over the skies for months—was seen hovering above the area where fighting was ongoing. (Docena 2007a, 14)

The Moro National Liberation Front, which was established in the 1960s, advocates for the establishment of a "Bangsamoro" land in the southern Philippines, or a desired autonomous state that is governed by Islamic law. Before 9/11, the Philippine and US governments as well as UN Security Council reports had never classified the Moro National Liberation Front as a "terrorist group." This is because of the group's commitment to ongoing peace negotiations with Manila about the terms of political autonomy of Mindanao.

The joint operations of US and Filipino military agents led to the destruction of private properties, physical injuries, and civilian deaths. For example, from January to August 2002, joint American-Filipino military operations against the Islamic terror group Abu Sayyaf Gang resulted in the displacement of around 90,000 rural residents in the southwestern Philippines and destruction of private properties and residential buildings (Norwegian Refugee Council 2002; Simon 2002). Similarly, from January until September 2005, US-guided Philippine military operations against the Abu Sayyaf Gang and other Islamic rebel groups in the southwestern Philippines led to the inevitable displacement of residents, among many other collateral damages (International Coordinating Secretariat in Utrecht and IBON Foundation 2007).

Reinforced by the pro-government bias of the mainstream news media, the Arroyo administration was largely successful in deterring news coverage of the collateral damages of the US-led operations in Mindanao. For example, in 2003, 60 percent of the news articles of the five Philippine newspapers with the broadest circulation primarily used official government sources (Cole 2006, 62). Whereas national media agencies persistently emphasized the gains of counterterrorism, reports concerning the horrific plight of thousands of victims from the countryside were rare.

Media agencies focused on the brutality of the targets of state violence, which practically meant that "most media practitioners used the 'terrorist' label to encompass the actions of guerrilla fighters, bandits, kidnappers, arsonists, murderers and terrorists" (Cole 2006, 63).

Conclusion: Philippine Human Rights Crisis after 9/11

This chapter confirmed my theoretical expectations, as set out in chapter 2. Specifically, increased foreign strategic support will lead to human rights deterioration if both the donor and recipient governments' interests converge on a counterterror agenda and the recipient government has a weak domestic legitimacy. The aid recipient government's decision to include the unarmed political opposition as targets of violence depended on the perceived need of the central civilian government to assert its political legitimacy amid serious legitimacy problems. I demonstrated that the post-9/11 Philippine government used terror-oriented US foreign strategic assistance to harass peaceful opposition and to increase the scale of domestic counterterror operations, both of which resulted in a spike of collateral and intended human rights abuses. Long-standing institutional defects within the state security apparatus and the Philippine judiciary facilitated the further deterioration of the human rights situation during this period.

Did the human rights situation in the Philippines improve after the US-led war on terror and its localized policies in Southeast Asia somehow formally ended? The next chapter shows that US strategic support facilitated positive outcomes in human rights protection in the Philippines in the years from 2010 until 2016.

FIVE

Overcoming the Human Rights Crisis

Reforms under Obama and Aquino

As for our common defense, we reject as false the choice between
our safety and our ideals. Our founding fathers, faced with perils
that we can scarcely imagine, drafted a charter to assure the rule of
law and the rights of man, a charter expanded by the blood of generations. Those ideals still light the world, and we will not give them
up for expedience's sake.

> —United States President Barack Obama, Inaugural Address,
> January 20, 2009

Today marks the end of a regime indifferent to the appeals of the
people. . . . I will dedicate my life to making our democracy reach
its fullest potential: that of ensuring equality for all. My parents
sought nothing less and died for nothing less than democracy, peace
and prosperity. I am blessed by this legacy. I shall carry the torch
forward.

> —Philippine President Benigno Aquino, Inaugural Address,
> June 30, 2010

During his 2008 presidential campaign, Barack Obama rejected the subser-
vience of human rights principles under the veneer of public safety and state
security. Deploring the abuses of the Arroyo administration, Philippine
president Benigno Aquino III committed his administration to democracy,
peace, and economic development, as he discarded counterterrorism and
state security as overarching policy priorities. How and to what extent did
these preliminary political commitments lead to transformative outcomes

in the Philippines? My objective in this chapter is to examine how and under what set of transnational and domestic conditions the strong human rights protection reemerged in the Philippines during the post–war on terror period (mid-2010 to 2016). Using my theory of interest convergence, I explain why the minimal number of residual human rights violations still transpired during this period, despite the emerging pro-human-rights agenda and the strong domestic legitimacy of Philippine president Aquino. This case study of the Aquino administration's human rights record shows an intriguing observation: the increase in US bilateral aid coincided with the substantial decrease in the number of human rights violations.

I argue that the pro-human-rights approach of the Obama administration reinforced the emerging domestic political climate in the Philippines, whereby the newly elected government and the domestic public demanded stronger human rights protection and democratic deepening. The convergence of the pro-human-rights expectations of American and Filipino political elites, together with the strong legitimacy of the elected government in the Philippines, resulted in two key domestic policy patterns: (1) a low priority status for domestic counterinsurgency vis-à-vis the minimal collateral abuses, and (2) a domestic policy that widely tolerated peaceful political opposition. Notwithstanding, residual state-initiated abuses persisted because of the ineffective judicial system and the corrupt practices of some agents in the Philippine state security establishment.

The Philippine government's human rights agenda in the late 2000s coincided with the Obama administration's departure from his predecessor's counterterror agenda—at least in the case of US foreign policy in the Asia-Pacific. Philippine president Benigno Aquino III, whose electoral success was largely based on a campaign agenda of good governance and human rights, justified the shift to human rights protection in two important ways. First, the Aquino administration actively sought human-rights-oriented and nonmilitaristic bilateral aid from the White House based on the diagnostic justification that pinpointed government corruption as the root of poverty, economic underdevelopment, and human rights deterioration. That strategy stood in contrast to the more militaristic notion of Matatag na Republika (Strong Republic) by Aquino's predecessor, President Arroyo. Second, the Aquino administration justified that US strategic support must be primarily reoriented toward nonmilitaristic aid, most especially by lobbying for a 500-million USD Millennium Challenge Grant from the US government. In that way, the US government acceded to such a demand because of the Obama and Aquino administrations' shared interests in strong human rights protection in the Philippines. Similarly, the

Filipino public supported that policy shift in reaction to the human rights crisis that emerged in the previous period. As I show later, the success of the Aquino administration's human rights agenda relied on the strategic localization of reemerging global demands to redress the abuses of the US-led war on terror through a stronger commitment to human rights.

In this chapter, I first provide a general assessment of the human rights situation vis-à-vis America's foreign policy goals and bilateral aid to the Philippines from 2010 to 2016. Second, I analyze the emerging expectations of American and Filipino political elites and the broader domestic public, who generally favored stronger human rights protection. Third, I demonstrate that the domestic policies of the central government in Manila as well as the aid programs of the US government reflected a strong human rights and nonmilitaristic policy orientation. The chapter concludes by presenting the theoretical implications of the evidence from the Philippines during the post–war on terror period.

Human Rights Situation and US Strategic Support

The human rights situation during the tenure of President Benigno Aquino III dramatically improved compared to the conditions during the tenure of President Gloria Macapagal-Arroyo (2001–10). Yet domestic human rights groups recognized the limits of Aquino's success, and the human rights situation was in no way comparably better than in the 1990s. The annual rate of 56 extrajudicial killings for the period from July 2010 to August 2013 was substantially lower than the annual rate of 124 incidents recorded during the term of President Arroyo (2001–early 2010) (Karapatan 2009, 49; Karapatan 2013, 3) . Yet both rates recorded after 2001 were still dramatically higher than the rate during the pre-9/11 period (1992–95), which was pegged at approximately 30 killings per year (Clarke 1998, 190). The post–war on terror period (2010–13) registered a striking decline in the annual rate of enforced disappearances, with a low average of 4 incidents per year, or a total of only 19 incidents for three years (Karapatan 2009, 6). Even so, the post–war on terror period's annual rate of enforced disappearances was still comparatively higher than the annual rate of 4.6 from 1992 to 1998, or a total of 21 reported incidents (Clarke 1998, 190). The Aquino administration, nonetheless, received reports of abuses committed by some police officers and military soldiers, who were involved in "80 cases of torture, 608 cases of illegal arrest, and more than 30,000 forced evacuations" (Oreta, Salvador, and Tolosa 2012, 10).

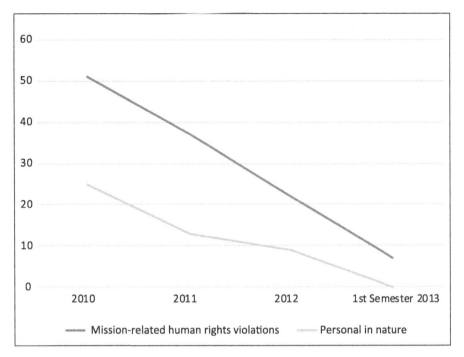

Fig. 5.1. Human Rights Violations Incurred and Reported by the Philippine Military, 2010–2013. The data used to create this figure is available on our Fulcrum platform at https://doi.org/10.3998/mpub.12036762.cmp.17

Domestic civil society groups actively demanded legal justice for human rights victims and a more effective judicial prosecution of abusive state agents. In his 2013 public letter addressed to President Aquino, Human Rights Watch Asia director Brad Adams underscored that "the number of serious human rights violations by the military has significantly declined" and the "public rhetoric on human rights by senior military officers has improved" (Human Rights Watch 2013b, 7). Adams, however, demanded that the abusive military and state security officials during the Arroyo regime should be prosecuted.

Similarly, the Philippine military reported a decline in the number of human rights violations committed by its officers. The bar chart shown above illustrates the remarkable decrease in the recorded number of military abuses. The magnitude of collateral damage from military operations is illustrated by the bar graph's dark-colored line (fig. 5.1), while abuses committed by military agents for personal reasons are captured by the

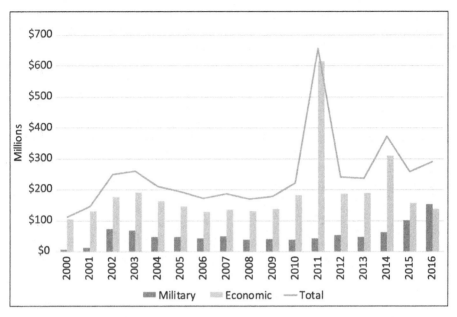

Fig. 5.2. US Foreign Aid to the Philippines, 2000–2016 (in constant 2016 USD). The data used to create this figure is available on our Fulcrum platform at https://doi.org/10.3998/mpub.12036762.cmp.17

light-colored line. I consider these two categories of violations classified by the Philippine military as subtypes of *collateral human rights abuses* resulting from *erroneous policing and intelligence practices*—a subject that I discuss later in the chapter. The Philippine military noted the absence of human rights abuses resulting from selective political repression, primarily because neither the Aquino administration nor the AFP's leadership had an official policy of killing unarmed activists.

The graph in fig. 5.2 illustrates the substantial increase in the average annual amount of US aid to the Philippines, from 151 million USD per year (2001 to 2009) to 396 million USD (2010 to 2011). The increase in total US aid emerged from changes in US economic assistance (fig. 5.2), which rose from 244 million USD in 2010 to 611 million USD in 2011. Much of the aid for this period came from the "compact aid grant" of the US government-funded Millennium Challenge Corporation (MCC).

Although the Arroyo administration lobbied for US counterterror aid right after the 9/11 attacks, Aquino focused instead on economic diplomacy, particularly by welcoming US initiatives on economic development and human-rights-oriented programs. In 2010 the Aquino administration hired the influential Washington, DC law firm Covington and Burling "to help win a reported $439 million Compact with the Millennium Challenge Corporation" (Jaleco 2010, 1). Unlike other forms of US assistance, MCC funding is normally given to specific countries based on a given set of indicators that seek to measure recipient countries' performance in economic and democratic governance. The provision of the MCC grant demanded that US-Philippine bilateral relations should work toward equitable economic growth and strong democratic governance during the post–war on terror period. The MCC grant was an outcome of the Aquino administration's strategy of adapting to the interests of the Obama administration. Whereas the previous period recorded a boom in US military aid to the Philippines due to Arroyo's counterterror agenda, the Obama administration promoted good governance and human rights, especially by making them key prerequisites for the continuous receipt of the MCC grants. Bolstered by Aquino's reformist policy agenda, the Philippines qualified for the MCC aid that aimed to promote economic growth and anticorruption as poverty-reduction measures (Millennium Challenge Corporation 2010). MCC's chief executive officer, Daniel Yohannes, explained that "the Filipinos have articulated a clear vision to improve the quality of their lives through a technically, environmentally and socially sound plan" (Jaleco 2010, 13). The Philippine government used that aid in three key projects that were implemented from 2010 through 2014, with around 434 million USD in total value: (1) 54 million USD for more efficient tax collection activities; (2) 120 million USD for rural development projects; and (3) 214 million USD for infrastructure development.

The Philippine government received a dramatically lower amount of US military aid, with a 50 percent decline from 2009 until 2012, compared to the early years of the US-led war on terror. Yet US military aid to the Philippines increased from 12 million USD in 2011 to 30 million USD in 2012, while the Philippine Department of Foreign Affairs confirmed that the US government increased its military aid for the rest of the term of the Obama administration. From late 2010 to 2016, the US government allocated its increased military assistance to the Philippines primarily for the modernization of the Philippine navy and other units of the armed forces (Lucas and Shahshahani 2014). Responding to Beijing's intensified military assertiveness in the disputed South China Sea maritime area, the increased US military aid to the Philippines aimed to counter the growing Chinese military presence in the highly disputed Spratly Islands and nearby maritime regions (Regilme 2018a; Mogato

2015; Regilme and Parisot 2020, 189). The US government increased the frequency and number of ship visits and joint military training (especially with the navy) as a form of political showmanship in the Pacific region. That development was seen as a response to increased Chinese naval activities in the South China Sea (Clinton 2011). Taken together, those policies emphasize the external-security-oriented focus of the Philippine military, which abandoned the domestic counterinsurgency agenda during the war on terror period. The Philippine military's change in strategic focus generated a reduced number of combat operations conducted against domestic security threats, thereby contributing to fewer collateral and systemic human rights violations. That development coincided with the very limited amount of US military aid aimed to support some domestic counterinsurgency operations against armed communist and Islamic rebels (De Jesus 2014).

Why did the human rights situation improve despite the increase in US foreign economic assistance during the post–war on terror period? My analysis of the post–war on terror period proceeds in four parts. First, I present evidence of how American and Filipino political elites have intentionally shifted their policy priorities from internal security to external security— that is, from domestic counterterrorism to a more comprehensive range of priorities with a focus on the rise of China as a perceived security threat. This transformation in policy priorities redirected the Philippine government's efforts and resources away from counterterror operations against domestic armed rebels, which resulted in a general decline in the number of collateral human rights violations. The second part explains that strong human rights protections emerged partly because of the Aquino administration's reformist agenda, which widely tolerated peaceful political dissidence, especially from the members of the leftist political opposition. That reform was the key factor for the *absence* of selective political repression, or a statewide policy that condemns peaceful political opposition. Focusing on the long-standing corrupt tendencies within the state security establishment and the inefficiencies within the judicial system, I demonstrate why some violations persisted despite the bilateral policy approach that focused on human rights protection. Next, I present some illustrative examples that characterize the patterns of repression and human rights violations and differentiate their main characteristics from those incurred during the War on Terror period. The final part of the chapter summarizes the main findings from the case of the Philippines during the post–war on terror period, and I analyze how the evidence fares in comparison to the expectations of my interest convergence theory.

Strategic Localization of Human Rights Norms: From Counterterrorism to Stronger Human Rights Protection

How did the Philippine government persuade the US government and the Filipino public of the urgency of strong human rights protection? I argue that the Aquino administration strategically localized international human rights norms vis-à-vis the domestic political context in order to accomplish two key goals. The first aim refers to the need to attract substantial amounts of US bilateral aid and to secure political support from the Obama administration. The second goal pertains to linking Obama's policy agenda of rectifying the policy failures of the war on terror to the Filipino public's demand for strong human rights protection, thereby abandoning Arroyo's counterterror agenda. The Aquino-led government reframed the country's security imperatives by emphasizing the "rise of China"—or the perceived geostrategic and military threat posed by China as a reemerging global power. The perception of China as an emerging security threat forced the Philippine military to focus on external security rather than internal security concerns, thereby sidelining domestic counterterrorism against political opposition members and armed rebels. By discursively linking government corruption with material poverty and human rights violations, the Aquino administration successfully persuaded the US government to optimize its foreign aid programs for external military security, economic development, and human rights. Discourses that pinpointed corruption as the main factor for the human rights crisis in the previous regime resonated with the domestic Filipino public, while the Aquino administration reallocated domestic state resources for civilian development objectives and external security objectives concerning the territorial disputes in the South China Sea.

The ascendancy to power of President Barack Obama in 2009 and President Benigno Aquino III in 2010 marked the transformation in the substantive focus of US-Philippines bilateral relations (Regilme and Untalan 2016, 151–55). The post–war on terror period shows that the Philippine government shifted its policy agenda away from internal counterterror strategies in response to intense public criticism of the Arroyo administration's human rights practices (Mertus 2008). Whereas the Bush administration stringently focused on counterterrorism, the Obama administration reoriented US foreign policy to Asia toward the "rise of China" problem and the promotion of human rights in the Philippines (Landler 2012; Obama 2013; Sutter 2009). Consequently, the range of America's security interests in the Asia-Pacific expanded to various policy priorities ranging from maritime security, territorial disputes (e.g., the South China Sea dispute), nuclear proliferation on the Korean Peninsula, the rise of China as an economic power, counterterrorism, democratic governance, and the protection of human rights.

Whereas the Arroyo administration focused on intensified counterterrorism, nonmilitaristic political threats such as widespread government corruption became prominent in the shared agenda of the Obama and Aquino administrations. As a former torture victim during the authoritarian period in the 1980s, Human Rights Commissioner Loretta Rosales noted that the Aquino administration promoted "a paradigm shift from a militarist/hawkish approach to internal peace and security to one that is 90% political and only 10% military-oriented" (Maaten and Sanchez 2011, 15). In contrast to the Arroyo administration, which promoted the idea of a "Strong Republic" that linked economic security with effective counterterrorism, the Aquino administration actively framed poverty and government corruption as compelling and urgent security threats. Thus, President Aquino consistently leveraged a strong pro-human-rights rhetoric: "cases of extrajudicial killings need to be solved, not just [to] identify the perpetrators but have them captured and sent to jail" (Karapatan 2010, 2).

The US government deployed policy discourses that explicitly undermined the importance of counterterrorism in its relations with the Asia-Pacific region, especially with the Philippine government. While the Bush administration focused too much on the Middle East and Southeast Asia as the primary fronts of the US-led war on terror (Singh 2007), the Obama administration focused on a wide range of security concerns in the Asia-Pacific region. For example, US Secretary of State Hillary Clinton (2011, 1) contended that "the future of politics will be decided in Asia, not Afghanistan or Iraq, and the United States will be right at the center of the action." Yet that statement does not suggest an exclusively military-oriented engagement of the US government toward Asia. Secretary Clinton (2011, 6) clarified that post–war on terror US foreign policy constituted a diverse range of policy priorities ranging from the promotion of "freedom of navigation in the South China Sea . . . to ensuring transparency in the military activities" of America's allies. Even Tom Donilon (2011, 6), President Obama's national security advisor, conveyed that "security in the region requires that international law and norms be respected, that commerce and freedom of navigation are not impeded, that emerging powers build trust with their neighbors, and that disagreements are resolved peacefully without threats or coercion"—the pledge that effectively discards state terror as a primary instrument for development. At a time when China overtook Japan in 2011 as the second world's largest economy after the United States, President Obama launched a series of high-profile visits in the Asia-Pacific region (Barboza 2010; Morrison 2013, 1). President Obama (2011, 11) maintained that the war on terror was over, at least on the Southeast Asian front, and committed to expanding the scope of policy priorities beyond terrorism: "the larger purpose of my visit to this region—our efforts to advance security, prosperity and human dignity across the Asia Pacific," which included the creation of economic opportunities in the United States and Asia.

The US and Philippine governments upheld the rise of China as the quintessential regional security concern, focusing especially on the South China Sea dispute. Because of the widespread perception that China was becoming more aggressive in asserting its claims over the disputed islands in the northwestern Philippines, the Obama and Aquino administrations mutually agreed in August 2011 "to focus their efforts on the development of a framework for increased bilateral and multilateral security and maritime domain awareness" (De Castro 2012, 2). Those joint efforts included a "US rotational presence in the Philippines to assist the AFP in developing its own capability for territorial defense; bilateral maritime security activities; development of joint-use maritime security support facilities; improved bilateral information sharing; and, coordinated and integrated maritime security initiatives between US Pacific Command and the AFP" (De Castro 2012, 2). Secretary of State Hillary Clinton, during her 2011 official visit in Manila, explained that bilateral cooperation had shifted from domestic counterterrorism to the maritime security challenges brought by the rise of China: "Our long mutual defense treaty and alliance relationship with the Philippines has to be updated . . . and that will require working with the Philippines to provide greater support for external defense particularly maritime domain awareness, defensive ones, and maritime boundaries" (Cheng 2011, 13). Moreover, the Obama and Aquino administrations' perception of military security focused on "interoperability in humanitarian assistance, as well as in the areas of disaster relief, maritime security, and maritime domain awareness" (Filipino Reporter 2012, 9).

Similarly, US foreign policy discourses that focused on socioeconomic issues other than counterterrorism were matched by similar public pronouncements by President Aquino, who promoted three significant policy themes and goals from 2010 until 2014: (1) the prospect of a final peace agreement with Islamic rebel groups and the end of the armed conflict in Muslim Mindanao; (2) a strong and unconditional pledge for human rights; and (3) the importance of other socioeconomic priorities such as good governance and equitable economic development.

First, the sustained commitment of the Aquino administration in forging a peace agreement with the Moro Islamic Rebel Front (MILF) reduced the frequency of armed encounters between the military and the rebels. In 2010, the Aquino government initiated a peace agreement with the MILF. In early 2014, the MILF agreed to full disarmament of all its members (around 12,000) and to prepare them for integrating into civilian life. In return, the Aquino government pledged to provide autonomy to a new administrative region to be called Bangsamoro in Mindanao and the southern islands, where the majority of the Filipino Muslim population live. The peace agreement emerged primarily because of Aquino's pledge of more equitable economic development in the region. Aquino explained that the agreement "means that hands that once held rifles will be put to use tilling land, selling produce, manning work stations and opening doorways of opportunity for other citizens" (Whaley 2012, 12). Support for the peace agreement increased because of the promise of sustained financial assistance from the US government. In cooperation with the local government and civil society groups, USAID implemented socioeconomic development projects in the southern Philippines. US Secretary of State John Kerry commended the Philippine government for "concluding negotiations toward an historic, comprehensive agreement" as "both sides are moving closer to the vision of a just and peaceful solution as outlined in the October 2012 Framework Agreement on *Bangsamoro*" (Kerry 2014, 1–3).

The eventual dissolution of paramilitary forces, often contracted by the Philippine armed forces for domestic counterterror surveillance, had always been a key goal of elected governments since the return of electoral democracy in 1986 (Sidel 1999; van der Kroef 1986). The Philippine Interior and Local Government Department reported that the Aquino government "has dismantled almost half of the private armies in the southern island of Mindanao" (Human Rights Watch 2012b). On January 25, 2014, the Philippine government and the MILF, one of the key rebel groups that were subjected to US-Filipino counterterror operations shortly after 9/11, signed a peace agreement that "lays out the process of decommissioning the MILF's armed forces" and "delineates a maritime territory for the future autonomous entity" (Alipala and Rosauro 2014, 2). Consequently, "Muslim rebels agreed to disband guerrilla forces, surrender weapons, and rebuild their communities while the government gives them self-rule with wider powers to control their economy and culture" (Reuters 2014, 2). President Aquino welcomed the peace agreement and exhorted: "Let us exchange our bullets for ripening fruit, our cynicism for hope, our histories of sorrow for a future of harmony, peace, and prosperity" (Reuters

2014, 5). Committing to substantial USAID funding and political support
for the eventual establishment of the autonomous Muslim region, Secretary of State Kerry congratulated the Philippine government for brokering
a "historic, comprehensive peace agreement" that "offers the promise of
peace, security, and economic prosperity now and for future generations in
Mindanao" (Santos 2014, 4).

The prospects for sustained financial assistance and political support
from the US government lent credibility to Manila's offer for peace to
armed rebels in Mindanao. Without the promise of sustained USAID
funding in Mindanao's development and the commitment of the Aquino
government, it would have been difficult for the MILF and its other allied
rebel groups to surrender their arms for the sake of a peace agreement.
First, the US government's guarantee of long-term financial assistance
provided political credibility to the Aquino administration's vision of peace
in Mindanao. The Muslim population in the southern Philippines has been
historically skeptical of the central government's willingness to invest in
sustained funding for long-term development plans. Second, the Aquino
administration's unconditional pledge for stronger human rights protection
signaled a serious commitment to shift from a militaristic, violent approach
toward a more conciliatory and economic-oriented emphasis when dealing
with the politics in Mindanao. As a son of the leading political opposition
figure during the authoritarian period under Marcos, Benigno Aquino III
launched his electoral campaign in 2009 and early 2010 based on a policy
platform that highlighted strong human rights protection and good governance. Similar to Obama, who capitalized on the shortcomings of his
predecessor in terms of human rights, President Aquino (2010, 4) used his
personal background to boost his credibility as a human rights advocate:

> I grew up in an era where human rights were often violated. My
> father, together with many others, was a victim. Our family and
> their families were victims too. . . . We know more than anyone that
> the blatant disregard of liberties will only bring us further into the
> dark.

During Aquino's tenure, many high-ranking US and Filipino government officials rarely focused on themes such as terrorism, national security,
and military security. In contrast to his predecessor, who was often silent
about the human rights abuses during the war on terror period, the US
ambassador to the Philippines, Harry Thomas, consistently and vigorously
expressed the US government's support for the human rights initiatives of

the Aquino administration. During the 63rd anniversary of the Universal Declaration of Human Rights celebrations, Thomas noted that "the Aquino family has long championed human rights . . . and has proven to be a staunch ally in efforts to promote human rights" (Santos 2011, 2).

The Aquino government focused on "issues such as weak governance and poverty . . . as structural deficits that can be overcome through the collaboration of state and non-state actors" (Curato 2013, 8). Aquino maintained that government corruption is the root cause of poverty, human rights violations, and other social ills. Aquino's appealing election campaign slogan reflected that message: "*Kung walang kurap, walang mahirap*" (If there is no corruption, then there is no poverty). That paradigm, which discursively linked human rights abuses with government corruption and economic stagnation, is now widely known in the national media as *Aquinomics*, "which equates good governance with good economics" (Curato 2013, 8). During Aquino's tenure, all government agencies were required to publicly reveal their operational budgets, financial statements, procurement strategies, and bids for outsourced projects, most especially some of the biggest expenses in the Philippine military and police agencies (Official Gazette of the Government of the Republic of the Philippines 2012a). The US-supported programs of the Aquino administration on the "fight against corruption, good governance, and poverty alleviation" facilitated the impressive economic growth recorded for the country since the 2007/2008 financial crisis (Bower 2012, 3). Aquino promoted what he and his allies called *tuwid na daan*, a very insightful and catchy phrase in the local vernacular that means "straight path," which called for all government officials and employees to act according to the public interest rather than for private gain. In policy terms, that included a substantial increase in the salaries of all government employees, including rank-and-file soldiers and police officers, which in turn undermined the likelihood that politicians and wealthy businessmen would contract state agents for private gain.

President Aquino won the admiration of American political and economic elites, which resulted in the influx of enormous amounts of US foreign economic aid solely intended for good governance reforms. As early as the first year of Aquino's term, Ambassador Thomas advised the Philippine government that "there is a serious interest on the part of investors who want to know what's in store for them if they invest in the Philippines" (BBC 2010, 2). In 2010, for instance, Aquino's short visit to the United States "generated $2.4 billion in new investments for the Philippines" and the "commitment of at least 43,650 new jobs in the next three years, including some 4,500 in construction-related jobs and because of the multiplier effect we estimate 200,000 more jobs to benefit our country" (Filipino Reporter 2010, 1). This economic success was complemented by the Obama administration's almost half-billion dollar MCC compact grant, which funded USAID projects on good governance, private entrepreneurship, and bureaucratic reforms. The US economic assistance strategy primarily focused on economic livelihood projects, increased civil society activities, and other nonmilitary initiatives in conflict-prone regions such as Mindanao. That strategy constituted the bilateral "Partnership for Growth" program, which was known for "catalyzing [a] joint effort to promote anti-corruption and rule of law, improved fiscal performance and regulatory quality and inclusive fiscal growth" (White House 2012, 6). Reminiscent of the close bilateral trade relations in the 1990s, the Obama administration intensified economic relations through the Bilateral Trade and Investment Framework Agreement together with President Aquino (Filipino Reporter 2012). American and Filipino government officials invested on large-scale economic and good governance programs in Mindanao and elsewhere in the country.

Judicial reparations for human rights victims also emerged as a key priority of US-Philippine bilateral relations in the post–war on terror period. The US government aided the Philippine Commission on Human Rights, particularly in building the professional competencies of its investigators and prosecutors and in financially supporting domestic judicial reforms (Human Rights Watch 2013b). The US government supported the enactment of a law that mandated compensation of all human rights victims using 11 billion Philippine pesos (245 million USD) worth of recovered ill-gotten wealth from the Marcos family. On December 2012, Aquino signed the Anti-Enforced Disappearance Act, or the Desaparecidos Law, which imposes a maximum term of life imprisonment and the denial of any prospective presidential amnesty for any state actor who is convicted of committing enforced disappearances. One of the most important provisions of this law was the prohibition of the military and police agencies' drafting of an "order of battle," which refers to a Philippine military's list of people targeted for surveillance, harassment, and assassination. The military arbitrarily drafted the list without any direct command from civilian agencies. Historically, the order of battle was frequently used during the Cold War years when President Marcos led a two-decade authoritarian rule and during the post-9/11 period during the tenure of President Arroyo. In both periods, the AFP received substantial funding from the US government and targeted anybody who was openly criticizing government policies. The law prohibits succeeding governments from nullifying the law even in cases of war or security crises. The Desaparecidos Law is the first legal instrument introduced in the Asia-Pacific region that imposes severe penalties for state-initiated enforced disappearances (Casauay 2012; Human Rights Watch 2012a; Government of the Philippine Republic 2012). That law mandates that convicted high-ranking officers and rank-and-file agents should receive the same penalties whenever it is relevant. All new high-ranking appointments in the military and police have to be vetted based on their previous human rights records.

In 2010, President Aquino established the Human Rights Office within the Philippine Armed Forces, headed by a senior rank general who leads independent investigations of all internal human rights complaints forwarded by newly installed human rights officers of each regional military command (Official Gazette of the Republic of the Philippines 2012b). Similarly, the police leadership assigned an independent human rights desk officer to each of its units nationwide, widely distributed human rights handbooks to its various regional commands, and regularly conducted refresher courses on the human rights obligations of the police.

The Philippine government enacted some unprecedented measures that aimed to promote judicial remedies for human rights victims. The Aquino administration allocated substantial government resources to prosecuting the suspects in the 2009 Maguindanao massacre and initiated an investigation into former Supreme Court chief justice Renato Corona's financial record, which led to his eventual impeachment over corruption charges. This was an important political move because Corona, a former chief-of-staff to President Arroyo, was widely perceived as complicit in the human rights violations of the Arroyo administration. Amid the corruption scandal of Corona in 2010, US ambassador Thomas publicly demonstrated his "conspicuous display of support for Aquino" during Corona's impeachment trial (Santolan 2012, 16). That support demonstrated the significant shift from the post-9/11 US government's public diplomacy: particularly, from being complicit with military and police abuses during the war on terror period to being unequivocally supportive of the anticorruption and pro-human-rights agenda of the Aquino government.

Reminiscent of the 1990s, the Philippine military's comprehensive role in peace and development was reinstated. The military was once again mandated to be equally responsible for assisting in the civilian government agencies' projects as well as leading regular military operations. The country's highest ranking military general, Emmanuel Bautista, argued that "the Armed Forces of the Philippines (AFP) does not only protect human rights, we also work to uplift human lives" (Romero 2013, 13).

For example, the AFP actively deployed their soldiers in engineering and infrastructure projects that totaled several billions of pesos (Acop 2012).

Various branches of the Aquino government optimized the processes related to the investigation and prosecution of suspected human rights violators. The creation of a high-profile interagency committee, which oversees the coordination of various civilian and military agencies within the government, facilitated the efficient and sustained investigation of extrajudicial killings. The enforced disappearance of peasant activist Jonas Burgos was one of those cases subjected to the fast-tracked investigation and legal prosecution program supported by the Aquino administration. In early 2013 the Supreme Court directed the military leadership to present documents, albeit confidentially, confirming the whereabouts of military officers involved in the abduction of Burgos. In response, the military cooperated with the court, while the Department of Defense promised that the military leadership "adheres to the Rule of Law in all its undertakings . . . it is one with the Filipino people in search for truth and justice" (Carcamo and Diola 2013, 20). Determined in leading the investigations of reported cases of disappearances and torture, Philippine Defense Department Secretary Voltaire Gazmin emphasized that his agency "will cooperate and make sure that the people or the personnel needed in the investigation will come out . . . will cooperate with the legal system" (Carcamo and Diola 2013, 16).

Why did the Philippine government suddenly abandon counterterror discourse? The US and Philippine governments shifted from a terror-oriented perspective to a more diverse set of security problems through three important strategies. First, American and Filipino elites did not perceive peaceful political opposition as security threats. As such, President Obama and President Aquino diversified the range of security issues that defined their bilateral relations since 2010. Many of these issues were predominantly political (good governance, anticorruption, and human rights protection) and economic (increased bilateral trade, welfare subsidies, and regional economic growth) in nature. Consequently, military-oriented problems that focused solely on domestic insurgency had a low priority. The modest scale of US military assistance primarily focused on maritime security, particularly because of increasing Chinese military assertiveness in the South China Sea. The Obama administration's policy was to provide an "enlarged rotation presence" of American forces in the Philippine archipelago, especially in the highly disputed territories in the South China Sea (Calonzo 2014, 17). This policy stance resulted in the signing in April 2014 of the Enhanced Defense Cooperation Act, which aims to contain Chinese naval incursions and not necessarily to engage in combat operations against internal security threats.

The second step in the shift from counterterrorism to human rights refers to domestic policies that supported the shared agenda of the US and Philippine governments. For instance, the high-profile anticorruption measures, including the eventual detention and prosecution of President Arroyo and the impeachment of Supreme Court Chief Justice Corona over corruption and plunder charges, constituted key priorities of the Aquino administration (Baviera 2012; Ronas 2013). Even US Ambassador Thomas publicly lauded those accomplishments, a political gesture that was significantly different from the public diplomacy approaches employed by his American predecessor. This change in the attitude of American diplomats in Manila was significant because, during the War on Terror period, US Ambassador Kristie Kenney remained a good friend and supporter of Arroyo amid the human rights crisis and the 2004 electoral manipulation scandal.

President Aquino's nonmilitaristic policy agenda received substantial amounts of financial support through the MCC from 2012 to 2016. Reminiscent of the 1990s, the Philippine military played a modest role in terms of its involvement in combat operations during the post–war on terror period. Subsequently, the Philippine military's resources and strategic planning were divided between the limited counterterror operations and the numerous civilian development projects in Mindanao and post-disaster humanitarian assistance elsewhere in the country. During this time, the military redirected its substantial manpower and engineering technologies "amounting to not only millions but also billions of pesos in infrastructure projects throughout the country" (Acop 2012, 105). The military played a crucial role in leading the disaster relief operations in the Visayas region affected by Typhoon Haiyan (or Yolanda), which was one of the deadliest tropical cyclones ever recorded in the country. The Philippine military's support for the Aquino administration was reflected in the policy strategy called Operation Plan Bayanihan (Helping Out), which aimed to "improve the Philippines' Global Peace Index rating between January 1, 2011, until the end of President Aquino's term in 2016 and to comply with the human rights requirements of international humanitarian law through effective community development programs" (Acop 2012, 105).

The final step that facilitated the successful policy shift from counterterrorism to human rights was the consolidation of the Filipino public's political support for stronger human rights protection. This was evident in a Social Weather Station's national survey (Social Weather Station 2012), which tracked responses from 2010 to 2012 and found that the top three "most important problems in the country" were the economy with 44 percent, social services with 13 percent, and infrastructure with 12 percent support. It is interesting to note that "crime" and "security" (military), as policy issues, were rated of very low importance, at 5 percent and 2 percent support, respectively. Those findings stood in marked contrast with the survey results from the war on terror period when "criminality and terrorism consistently ranked in the top five urgent national concerns in nationwide surveys" (Office of the Presidential Adviser on the Peace Process 2013, 1).

I consider two forms of post–war on terror discourses through which shared expectations for human rights protection became dominant: (1) coordinative discourses and (2) communicative discourses. First, the coordinative discourses refer to the interactions based on official policy statements and public pronouncements of the officials of both the Obama administration and the Aquino administration. As I show in this section, the discourses of Filipino and American officials indicated that their governments abandoned a terror-oriented policy paradigm and instead shifted the focus to a more comprehensive range of development priorities. There was a clear conjunction of political interests in undermining the overarching importance of counterterrorism as the focal point of US-Philippine bilateral relations. Second, the communicative discourses pertained to the Philippine and US governments' articulation of their policy aims to the Filipino public. The Filipino public substantially changed their policy preferences from 2010 to 2013, particularly by considering economic development and good governance as far more important than domestic counterterrorism.

Domestic Politics and the Aquino
Administration's Policy Priorities

Although the violent repression of unarmed political opposition became the official policy during the war on terror period, the Aquino government tolerated left-wing political activism and open public criticism by the media and other civil society activists. Why did the Aquino government tolerate unarmed political opposition, whereas the predecessor government did not? The strong domestic legitimacy of President Aquino made it unnecessary to repress unarmed political opposition. Aquino's electoral success can be partially attributed to the support of left-wing political parties after some of its members were subjected to physical harassment and torture by the Arroyo administration. Aquino won the 2010 presidential elections under the "rainbow coalition" party network that was composed of all opposition parties including left-wing and social democratic parties. Loretta Rosales, the human rights commissioner under the Aquino administration, was a former Congress member during Arroyo's presidency. Rosales was often subjected to death threats and harassment because of her leadership role in the Akbayan Party, or what former chief-of-staff of the Arroyo administration, Rigoberto Tiglao (2012, 8), called "a small association of mostly armchair revolutionaries who had been living off from donations of leftist European NGOs."

Compared to his recent predecessors, President Aquino enjoyed strong political legitimacy. He won the presidential elections in 2010 based on a substantial electoral mandate, with 40 percent of the total votes, or five million votes more than the next candidate (Aquino and Bradley 2010). The record of voter support is unprecedented in the country's recent political history, with one of the highest voter turnout rates since 1986. Roughly throughout his term as president, from 2010 until 2016, Aquino consistently enjoyed high public satisfaction ratings. The Social Weather Station survey reported in the fourth quarter of 2010 that "73% of adults [were] satisfied and 9% dissatisfied with the general performance of the National Administration" (Social Weather Station 2010). From 2010 until 2014, the Aquino administration recorded consistently high public satisfaction ratings ranging from 50 percent to 75 percent at any given quarter during those years. The record stood in stark contrast with Arroyo's performance from 2001 to 2009, when she received negative quarterly ratings, from a high of only 20 percent in 2001 and a low of a net negative rating of 58 percent in 2008. The high satisfactory ratings of Aquino reflected the public's favorable "perceptions of his strong political will in going after his predecessor Arroyo, who stands accused of many wrongdoings committed during her incumbency" (Baviera 2012, 242). Thus, Aquino's high public satisfaction ratings demonstrated his consistently strong political legitimacy, with exceptionally good ratings in the policy areas of human rights promotion, counterterrorism, and reconciliation with Muslim rebels (Social Weather Station 2010). President Aquino realized the importance of the domestic public's political support for his reform agenda. Pertaining to corruption and human rights abuses, Aquino vowed in 2010 that "as president, we [I] will be in a position to effect the necessary changes," and that "with the backing of the people, I don't think anything is impossible" (Teves 2010, 2). Because of Aquino's strong electoral mandate, the option of resorting to state repression became politically unnecessary.

Many human rights activists and the families of victims during the war on terror period demanded the arrest of high-ranking military officials who had commanded the killing spree at the height of counterinsurgency in the Philippines in the 2000s. An open letter to President Aquino from Edita Burgos—mother of Jonas Burgos, who was abducted by military agents in 2007—expresses dissatisfaction with the judicial system (Inquirer News 2014, 3):

> Our hope was anchored on your promise to do what you could "on the basis of evidence" when I, accompanied by my son, personally pleaded for your help. This was almost four years ago, May 2010. . . . In spite of the unfulfilled Supreme Court order to produce Jonas, no one has been penalized or found accountable.

Notwithstanding the Human Rights Commission's report that explicitly named AFP major Harry Baliaga Jr. as the principal suspect, the military did not surrender their own officer as mandated by the Supreme Court. Direct pressures from President Aquino did not suffice in compelling the military to surrender all of the officers implicated in the various human rights violations. Aquino issued several directives to the Department of Justice and the National Bureau of Investigation to invest resources in a "focused, dedicated and exhaustive investigation on the Jonas Burgos case . . . to ferret out the truth" (Inquirer 2014, 8). This lack of cooperation from some factions within the military defied the pro-human-rights political pressures emanating from the Aquino administration, transnational-domestic civil society networks, and the US diplomats in Manila. Some factions within the military leadership refused to surrender their own abusive officers to the judicial process. Specifically, AFP general Jovito Palparan, known as Arroyo's executioner or the *berdugo*, went into hiding after a provincial court issued an arrest warrant in 2011 for the 2006 killings of two University of the Philippines student activists. President Arroyo promoted Palparan to the rank of major general even at the height of the extrajudicial killings in 2006 to 2007. He was the commanding officer of several regions in the archipelago where state-initiated killings were rampant (Lucas and Shahashahani 2014). In August 2014, Palparan was captured after a three-year manhunt and eventually underwent judicial prosecution. Described as one of the most significant achievements of the Aquino administration, the arrest of Palparan led one prominent news editor to express his optimism that "he [Palparan] will have his day in court. He will be given fair trial and due process, human rights which he never gave to his tortured victims whose cries of pain and suffering will forever haunt him to the end of his days" (Barcenas 2014, 18). On September 2018, a local court convicted Palparan for the extrajudicial killings and sentenced him to life imprisonment.

Despite the direct policy command from the Aquino administration and the top military leadership for them to surrender, many high-ranking military officers, who were allies of Arroyo, went into hiding (Melo 2007). The inability to capture erring state agents was largely seen by the public as a major drawback in Aquino's human rights reform agenda. Yet the successful prosecution and indictment of state violators is not only a matter of temporal shifts of shared expectations among civilian political elites. Instead, the problem in capturing the suspected violators demonstrates the enduring institutional defects in the Philippine national security apparatus. Within the Philippine military, a culture of protecting their own peers, despite continuous deviations from civilian law, persisted even when human rights norms were gaining traction. These strong bonds among military officers are akin to being "closer than brothers"—a relationship that breeds corruption later on in professional life (McCoy 1999).

Many legal cases of human rights violations that occurred during the war on terror period remain unresolved. From the perspective of human rights victims' families based in rural areas, the costs of hiring a lawyer, the prospects of retaliatory actions from the local police and military, and the expectation that courts can be bought by bribes constitute significant hindrances to obtaining justice. During this period, one of the most serious problems faced by the judges serving in provincial courts was the prospect of being physically harassed or killed by police officers who had been contracted by local politicians. On February 28, 2014, Reynerio Estacio, a regional trial court judge in the southernmost province of Zamboanga, and his wife were killed by several gunshots by local police officers (Cupin and Falcatan 2014; de Quiros 2014). Provincial media reports suggested that Estacio's judicial rulings did not usually favor local politicians and even castigated the local police for abuses. In response, Supreme Court chief justice Maria Lourdes Sereno was quick to condemn the killings (Cupin and Falcatan 2014, 11): "When lawless violence claims one of our own, it wounds us more grievously not only because we would be one good man less but also because the rule of law is diminished by the sheer force of arms." Sereno further admitted that the "judiciary does not have the resources to combat violence against its members but can only rely on the police to protect them" (Cupin and

Falcatan 2014, 12). In this context, Secretary of State Kerry reminded Philippine government officials of the importance of prosecuting the previous
regime's violators: "Defending human rights is not some high-minded exercise, it is about accountability, it is about ending impunity" (De Quiros 2014,
10). Even with the pressure from the US government, which represented
the most influential external donor government of the Philippine military,
the Aquino administration sometimes failed to stop abusive military agents.

Patterns of Human Rights Violations

Although the Aquino administration introduced human rights reforms,
which enjoyed US strategic support, those policies were not enough to
fully eliminate human rights abuses. While the human rights situation
improved during the time of Aquino, residual abuses persisted because of
the long-standing structural defects of the Philippine state security agencies as well as the judicial system. The endemic culture of corruption in the
military and police agencies influenced some of its members to contract
with private firms and local politicians. The goal was to kill or to harass
peaceful political dissenters who opposed some of the commercialization
projects planned by private, nonstate firms. Of course, the conspiratorial
activities of the individual soldiers and police officers occurred in defiance
of the preferences of the Aquino administration and the domestic public.
Some state agents during the post–war on terror period committed abuses
because of the assumed low possibility that they would face a successful
legal prosecution. Although there were pending investigations on many
suspected abusive state agents, only high-ranking politicians and officials
such as former president Arroyo, Supreme Court chief justice Corona, and
other prominent executive officials were formally prosecuted (Ronas 2013).

How do we make sense of such residual human rights violations? Many
of these state-initiated abuses can be meaningfully classified (1) as intended
outcomes of individual motivations of actors within the military or the
police, and (2) as collateral violations emerging from the ongoing counterterror operations in conflict-prone area in Mindanao and the communist
rebel-controlled regions in Luzon.

Premeditated Abuses

The first type of abuses refers to premeditated violations resulting from
a very limited form of selective political repression in which state agents

deliberately targeted civilians based mostly on personal-related reasons rather than a broader political goal of systematically undermining legal political opposition. Those "premeditated violations" during the post–war on terror period have several features. First, the state agent had a prior intention to harass and kill civilians. Second, the collective leadership of either the military or the Aquino administration did not directly and explicitly command military and police officers to kill or to harass the unarmed targets. Rather, the motivation for the killing was based on the state agent's expectation of an individual reward (financial or career-oriented) and other personal reasons. Third, violations had a blatant political dimension only to the extent that military and police officers abuse their individual powers in their capacity as state agents, while such agents and conniving nonstate actors (e.g., mining companies) benefited. In some cases, local politicians in the provinces tasked their respective police and military units to kill opposition members and critical journalists.

Various premeditated abuses involved the cooperation of state security agents with mining companies to quell the peaceful resistance of local communities. Because President Aquino openly welcomed foreign investments as part of his economic-development-centered agenda, American and other foreign mining companies actively conducted their mining operations in the country, most especially in Mindanao (Holden and Jacobson 2013). Many of these mining sites were located in conflict-prone regions, where either communist or Islamic armed rebel groups have sometimes destroyed government facilities and private infrastructure. In response, the Philippine military formed state-sponsored paramilitary groups in those regions "such as the Special Civilian Armed Auxiliary (SCAA) as force multiplier to secure mining corporations and other similar economic development-oriented projects" (Karapatan 2011, 3). Mining initiatives constituted the economic development strategy jointly funded and implemented by public and private agencies. For instance, on April 12, 2011, several suspected military agents in Pantukan, Compostela Valley in the southern Philippines shot 49-year-old Santos Manrique dead in front of his family. Manrique was a prominent community organizer of a group of small-scale miners who peacefully lobbied against the new operations of the Philippine company Napnapan Mineral Resources and its US partner, Russell Mining and Minerals. It is widely believed that those foreign companies paid some form of financial compensation to soldiers, police officers, and state-organized paramilitary forces assigned to its operation sites. Before and after the death of Manrique, local NGOs "documented several cases of human rights violations such as forcible evacuation, threats, harassment and intimidation, violation of domicile and use of civilians as guide in military operations in the sitios of Anibugan, Ibwan, Oraya, Ayan and Kamarin, all in Napnapan, Pantukan, Compostela Valley" (Karapatan 2011, 3).

Another instance of premeditated violation was the killing of Juvy Capion and her two sons, Jan, 8, and Jordan, 13, in their own residence in Kiblawan, Davao del Sur Province in the southwestern part of the country. The case is widely known in the country as the "Tampakan Massacre," named after the Tampakan mining site. The husband of Juvy Capion was a prominent environmentalist and antimining leader, who peacefully advocated for responsible mining in Davao del Sur's Tampakan gold and copper extraction project, which covered around 23,571 hectares of land and was managed by the global mining giant Sagittarius Mines Inc.—Xstrata. The mining project was valued at around 5.2 billion USD (Davao Today 2013). Testimonies from the community indicated that several soldiers from the Philippine Army's 27th Infantry Battalion raided the farm and residence of the Capion family. When some relatives pleaded with the military not to kill the children while the raids were ongoing, one of the soldiers sternly responded: "*Mas maayo nga tiwason ang mga bata para wala'y witness*" (Better to finish off the children so that there will be no witnesses) (InterAksyon 2012, 14). Several days after the incident, the mayor of Kiblawan Province, Marivic Diamante, confessed that the mining company provided a monthly allowance of around 7,500 Philippine pesos (168 USD) to individual members of state-sponsored Citizens Armed Force Geographical Unit and the Philippine Army assigned to the mining sites (Karapatan 2013, 15). While massacres of antimining activists were more prevalent and widely tolerated during the time of President Arroyo, the number of incidents during the post–war on terror period was much lower. The Aquino administration spent its political capital and resources in investigations of the killings, while its public rhetoric condemned the erring actions of military and paramilitary agents who surreptitiously connived with the mining companies (Maaten and Sanchez 2011).

Several local civil society groups accused some units of the Philippine Army of using the "peace and development" agenda of Aquino as a cover-up for intelligence gathering that sometimes led to the physical harassment and intimidation of civilians. For example, several Philippine Army soldiers presented themselves sometime in 2011 to their assigned communities in Guinobatan, Albay Province, in southwestern Luzon Island, as members of the "peace and development teams" that were assigned to conduct preliminary interviews, focused group discussions, and a census for the planning of community development projects. These tasks reflected President Aquino's new policy strategy, whereby military and police operations were integrated with the overall economic development strategy in conflict-prone regions. Yet some military units apparently failed to understand the merits and intended goals of President Aquino's new paradigm in counterinsurgency. In Albay Province, for instance, the Alpha Company of the 2nd Infantry Battalion of the Philippine Army headed by Lt. Basibas had concurrent deployments in 11 communities. From July to August 2011, these soldiers introduced themselves as conducting a census for the Department of Agriculture in order to determine the area's most impoverished families, who can qualify for relief packages. Nonetheless, local reports documented that (Karapatan 2011, 1)

> the soldiers summoned for tactical interrogation residents they suspected of being supporters of the *pasmado*, a derogatory military term for the New People's Army (NPA). The residents were "interviewed" one by one inside the detachment and their photograph taken holding a tag with his/her name plus an alias provided by the soldiers. They were made to sign a blank document, which supposedly proved that they were cleared of suspicions of being NPA supporters. Those who refused to have their picture taken were required to report to the camp three times a day. Some victims were coerced into reporting every day for two weeks without any cause.

Several American and Filipino soldiers purportedly committed premeditated abuses because of personal reasons. For instance, the mysterious death of Gregan Cardeño in February 2010 illustrated how individual motivations of erring state agents, rather than a direct command from the central government in Manila, could explain the emergence of collateral human rights abuses. Gregan was a 33-year-old interpreter hired by US troops (Joint Special Operations Task Forces) based in the military barracks of the 103rd Brigade of the Philippine Army in Marawi City in Mindanao. On February 1, during his first day of work, Gregan was immediately assigned to an American barracks within a Philippine Army camp in Marawi City. Three days after reporting for work, unidentified US soldiers brought the dead body of Gregan from Marawi City to Zamboanga City and reported to the Philippine police that the interpreter committed suicide by hanging himself in one of the rooms of the American barracks located within a Philippine military camp in Marawi City. Yet Gregan's family did not believe the US soldiers' report. This was because the US and Philippine Army refused to conduct any autopsy, and the testimonies of Filipino soldiers and police did not corroborate the story presented by the American soldiers. The story of suicide did not sit well with the fact that Gregan's cadaver shows an "enlarged scrotum, the enlarged opening of his anus, a deep wound on the upper right part of his neck, and three injuries on his head" (Abella 2010, 2; Bulatlat 2010). During the second day of his work, Gregan called his wife over the phone and said: "What they are asking me to do is very difficult. . . . If I do not get out of here, this could be the cause of my death. . . . If I ever go home, would you still accept me?" (Abella 2010, 2). Before ending the short phone conversation, Gregan told his wife that he was not doing any kind of language translation work and that "those with me are all Americans." Known as a local Christian pastor in his town, Gregan's personal background did not show any hint of a strong motive for suicide. Because of the physical injuries of Cardeño's dead body, his wife hinted, "they [US soldiers] made him a pet . . . they probably played with him" and that it was plausible that her husband was "sexually abused and tortured" (Abella 2010, 2).

In response, the Aquino administration's civilian cabinet agencies quickly commissioned independent investigations of the incident. The Human Rights Commission immediately cooperated with the National Bureau of Investigation in conducting a thorough investigation. Yet the military and the police obstructed the investigation, as they refused the CHR and National Bureau of Investigation officials access to the joint military barracks of American and Filipino soldiers in Marawi City. Hence, the CHR presented "inconclusive" findings about Cardeño's death. The unique legal and social status of US soldiers operating in Philippine territory ultimately hindered independent Philippine government institutions from conducting a thorough investigation of the case.

Collateral Violations

The violent skirmishes between the military and the armed rebels led to the physical harassment, mental abuse, and deaths of civilians residing in conflict-prone areas, especially in the northern and southern Philippines. Although the number of reported collateral violations substantially declined during this period, the US State Department (2013, 73) noted that "clashes between the AFP (Armed Forces of the Philippines) and separatist forces as well as incidents of inter-clan vendetta leading to violence continued in central Mindanao resulted in civilian deaths and the displacement of thousands of individuals." Many abuses emerged as the collateral effects of regular military operations.

One of the most prominent instances of collateral killings committed by the military was the death of the nationally renowned University of the Philippines biology professor Leonard Co and two of his security officers. They were killed while collecting some seed samples in the forest of Leyte Island in central Philippines as part of their scientific research (Ong and Ingle 2011). Co and his associates were conducting some botanical work as consultants for a private energy firm. Yet they were "reportedly caught in the crossfire between the troops of the Army's 19th IB and communist rebels in Upper Mahiao, Barangay [village] Lim-ao" in the central Philippines (Philippine Daily Inquirer 2012, 1). The Justice Department and the National Bureau of Investigation conducted a joint investigation of the incident for two months and found that the military should not be liable for the deaths of these civilians. The CHR conducted its own investigation and hinted that there was no cross fire between the military and the communist rebels. Local residents suggested that Co and his companions were falsely identified as armed rebels and that government soldiers immediately killed them. Consequently, Justice Secretary Leila de Lima formed a panel of state prosecutors who conducted a preliminary investigation for the legal case filed against Army 1st Lt. Ronald Odchimar and 37 other soldiers who were suspects in the killing of Leonard Co and two other individuals. This incident showed serious errors on the part of a handful of soldiers stationed in the area where Co and two others were conducting their botanical research.

Because many indigenous communities live in regions often populated by armed rebel groups, the Philippine military sometimes erroneously identified unarmed indigenous peoples as members of armed rebel groups. In the post–war on terror period, some of these civilian residents were inadvertently killed while the military was conducting bombing operations. Some indigenous communities were forced to evacuate their ancestral lands, and in cases of their peaceful resistance, the military violently harassed them. In 2010 to early 2014, the Kalipunan ng mga Katutubong Mamayan ng Pilipinas (KAMP, or the Coalition of Indigenous Peoples of the Philippines) "recorded 16 incidents of forced evacuations of indigenous peoples involving approximately 9,754 individuals, including peasant settlers" and the evacuations occurred in several indigenous communities in five major provinces in the southern Philippines (Karapatan 2014, 71). For example, on August 30, 2013, the Kakanaey people in Sagada town, Mountain Province in the northern Philippines, experienced severe physical injuries during a bombing raid conducted by the Philippine Air Force's 1st Division's Strike Wing that had pursued a group of suspected communist guerrilla forces. The military forces bombed the farms and water facilities of the indigenous tribes, an incident that left severe psychological trauma among many children.

In Agusan del Norte and Surigao del Norte Provinces in northeastern Mindanao, the Philippine Air Force launched sustained and weekly air and ground-based artillery bombardment operations from February to August 2012. Philippine Air Force agents believed that most of the targets were suspected Islamic armed rebels based in remote mountainous areas. Hundreds of members of the Lumad indigenous community, however, were also living in most of the areas considered to be military targets. The operations not only stopped the livelihood of the Lumad people, but caused the massive evacuation of 500 indigenous civilians to a small basketball court in Butuan city, 50 kilometers away from the indigenous communities' ancestral domains. While some Lumad adults complained of some physical injuries, many children experienced psychological trauma caused by the sustained bombing operations. Faced with the grievances of the Lumad communities, the Philippine military expressed its sympathy to civilian residents but justified the necessity of the military operations by underscoring the security of the community (Mascarinas 2012).

Even as President Aquino prioritized economic development, some economic development projects generated collateral human rights abuses. The Aquino administration actively implemented the National Land Reclamation Project in various areas, with the projected target area of 38,272 hectares of coastline for land reclamation in the areas of Manila Bay, Cebu, Davao, and other parts of Visayas and southern Mindanao (Karapatan 2014). The land reclamation projects led to violent evacuations of families living in the affected areas. In some cases, the police forces resorted to demolishing violently the properties of residents as well as physically harassing the residents. Similar to cases in the 1990s, some police officers received bribes from private firms that were involved in large-scale real-estate projects in exchange for the speedy relocation of local residents to be facilitated by state security forces.

Conclusion: Human Rights after the War on Terror

The decrease in the scale and frequency of counterterror operations against armed Islamic and communist rebel groups contributed to the comparatively fewer collateral deaths of civilians based in conflict-prone regions. Some police and military officers nevertheless cooperated with private firms and even local politicians in return for some illegal rent. This led to the escalation of state violence against indigenous communities and peaceful dissenters. The cases of land reclamation and rapid real estate development projects and their detrimental effect on civilian resident communities, especially on indigenous tribes, demonstrated the typical instances of state abuses motivated by the rent-seeking motives of some military and police agents.

The Aquino administration widely tolerated peaceful political opposition and integrated peaceful left-wing political opposition into mainstream politics, whereas both strategies were absent in the previous administration's policy agenda. The absence of a central government policy that violently quelled peaceful political opposition substantially deterred state security agents from committing human rights abuses. In effect, the police and military agencies carried out abuses that were mostly motivated by distinctive individual reasons. Various human rights abuses including the death of Gregan Cardeño, the Tampakan Massacre, and the deaths of anti-mining protesters suggest that a well-intentioned presidential administration does not automatically fully prevent the entire state security establishment from violating their human rights commitments.

There were two key factors in US-Philippine bilateral relations that facilitated the improvement in the human rights situation during this period. First, the convergence of shared interests and intended policy outcomes of the Obama and Aquino administrations shifted resources away from counterterrorism toward a more comprehensive range of nonmilitaristic policy interests. This development prevented the proliferation of collateral abuses precisely because it forced the Philippine state security agencies to shift their resources and attention away from domestic counterinsurgency. Second, the Aquino administration's strong legitimacy made violent state repression of unarmed political dissidence completely unnecessary. The Aquino administration implemented two important policy strategies that led to an eventual decline in the number of human rights abuses: (1) allocate US strategic support and more domestic state resources away from counterterrorism toward the implementation of pro-human-rights policies, and (2) influence the attitudes and cognitive predispositions of the state security agencies that peaceful political opposition should be widely tolerated. Taken together, those two elements contributed to the decline in human rights abuses.

To what extent did political discourses shape the policy priorities of the donor and recipient governments? In what ways did the American and Philippine governments' political discourses contribute to stronger human rights protection? The Aquino administration's success in advancing a human rights reform agenda depended on the strategic localization of discourses. First, Aquino's policy platform discursively framed government corruption as the root problem of many social ills and economic decay in the country, including human rights violations. Second, a domestic pro-human-rights constituency, which enjoyed political support from the US diplomatic mission headed by Ambassador Thomas, leveraged various prescriptive policy discourses that sought to combat government corruption.

Those aforementioned domestic and transnational developments reflected the two-level logic of shared expectations among US officials and Filipino political actors. Particularly, the first level of negotiation that produced such shared human-rights-oriented policy expectations pertained to the bilateral relations between the US and the Philippine governments. Their bilateral relationship emphasized that the perceived diminished threat posed by international terrorism required the prioritization of strong human rights protection, democratic reforms, and economic development in the Philippines. On the US side, the election of Barack Obama as president and the growing domestic and international uproar against the human rights toll of the US-led war on terror galvanized public and elite support for a US human rights-oriented foreign policy agenda. The second level, meanwhile, referred to the negotiations and interactions among the officials of the Obama and Aquino governments. Aquino and his Liberal Party's reformist agenda coincided with President Obama's vigorous support for human rights. Because of that interest convergence, the Aquino administration enabled various domestic policies and permitted US-funded programs that complied with the Philippine state's constitutional guarantees for physical integrity rights.

This chapter illustrated how US strategic support contributed to the improvement of the human rights situation in the Philippines under the leadership of President Aquino. In my interest convergence theory, I hypothesized that the convergence of donor and recipient government's interests on a wide range of policy goals together with the strong domestic legitimacy of the recipient government are more likely to generate stronger human rights protection. In this scenario, several residual violations would persist because of the intractable and long-term defects in the military and police agencies as well as the judiciary. That expectation can be seen in the case of the Philippines from 2010 to 2016, when the Obama and Aquino administrations mutually shared a more diverse range of strategic interests other than domestic counterterrorism. This chapter concludes the analysis of the human rights situation vis-à-vis US-Philippine bilateral relations from the 1990s until 2016. The forthcoming chapter examines how US strategic support for Thailand in the 1990s led to improved human rights outcomes.

SIX

Human Rights Renaissance in Thailand, 1990s

I am very delighted to be back in the United States. . . . Ours is a friendship which goes back 165 years. . . . it is a friendship which is now based upon a growing convergence of values, especially those related to democracy, freedom, social justice, and the rule of law.

> —Thailand's Prime Minister Chuan Leekpai, speech at the
> Council on Foreign Relations and the Asia Society,
> New York, March 11, 1998

A rising tide of freedom has lifted the lives of millions around the world. . . . And from the Philippines to . . . Thailand, freedom has reached Asia's shores, powering a surge of growth and productivity.

> —President William "Bill" Clinton, June 29, 1998

Similar to the political trajectory of Philippine politics in the 1990s, Thailand successfully transitioned to a constitutional liberal democracy, reintroduced national elections, and recorded stronger human rights protection when compared to the Cold War and the post-9/11 eras.[1] What explains Thailand's improved human rights record in the 1990s? In this chapter, I examine why and under which conditions strong human rights protections emerged in the 1990s in Thailand. I argue that the pro-human-rights and less-militaristic approach of US strategic support reinforced the emerging domestic political norms in Thailand that called for stronger human rights protection and democratization. The convergence of American and Thai

136

government elites' interests resulted in two key policy patterns that generated improved physical integrity rights protection: (1) the low priority for domestic counterinsurgency, which generated a decrease in collateral abuses; and (2) the tolerant policy toward unarmed political opposition, which obliterated the need for selective political repression of activists, journalists, and other nonviolent dissenters.

This chapter unfolds in five parts. First, I provide a general assessment of the human rights situation vis-à-vis America's foreign policy and bilateral aid programs in Thailand. Next, I examine the emerging post–Cold War expectations of American and Thai political elites and the broader domestic public that generally favored stronger human rights protection. Third, I demonstrate that the convergence of Thai and American policymakers toward a pro-human-rights agenda resulted in transformative domestic policies and US aid programs that promoted democratic openness and improved physical integrity rights outcomes in Thailand. Consequently, I characterize the scope and magnitude of state-initiated human rights abuses that emerged during this period. The chapter concludes by explaining the theoretical implications of the evidence from Thailand during the pre–war on terror period.

Overview: Human Rights Situation and US Foreign Policy in Post–Cold War Thailand (1992 to Early 2001)

During the Cold War and the post-9/11 periods, the Thai state emerged as one of the largest recipients of US military aid in order to reinforce the shared geostrategic interests of the US and Thai governments in the region (Bamrungsuk 1988; Chambers 2004; Linantud 2008; McCoy, Read, and Adams 1972; Busbarat 2017). During the Cold War, Thai political leaders cultivated a "special relationship" with the US government; specifically, Bangkok provided political support and use of its territory for the US military's anticommunist war efforts in the region, while Washington bolstered the Thai military amid the looming threat of Vietnamese forces' invasion of Cambodia (Busbarat 2017, 256; Fineman 1997). During the Cold War, the American government's support to the Thai armed forces' weapons program and other military modernization projects was indeed unmatched by other third-party countries (Wattanayagorn 1998, 232). As the key sponsor of Thailand's coercive state machinery, the US government fueled the violent repression of armed communists and bolstered the Thai armed forces' claim that they are the "guardian of the nation," particularly by repressing "domestic enemies, claiming to protect the state and, at the same time, cementing its power network in politics" (Chachavalpongpun 2011a, 47). As early as 1953, the US National Security Council considered Thailand as the "anti-communist bastion in order to extend US influence—and local acceptance—throughout the whole of Southeast Asia" (Tyner 2007, 190; see also Wah 2000). In fighting communism, the Thai military implemented widespread extrajudicial killings, torture, and enforced disappearances—targeting especially those who were suspected as armed communist rebels.[2] As the Cold War historian Arne Kislenko (2004, 1) notes, "For the US, Thailand represented a bastion of anti-communism in a region full of political uncertainty . . . represented a valuable Asian ally in the Cold War, a model of economic development . . . and a strategic base from which to prosecute both overt and clandestine operations in Indochina."

That enduring militaristic bilateral policy agenda gained traction once again in the post-9/11 years, particularly through joint counterterror efforts against domestic and regional security threats posed by armed Islamic insurgents (Busbarat 2017). That counterterror agenda meant that "for the United States, the Bush administration was able to count on Thailand's wide-ranging cooperation in counterterrorism, including a greater compilation and sharing of intelligence and toughened law enforcement" (Pongsudhirak 2016, 69). Bangkok consistently enjoyed a good relationship with Washington "because it was viewed as a front-line state in the war against communism, and, as such, was privy to substantial U.S. military and development assistance" (Asia Foundation 2002, 1). The Thai military received enormous amounts of financial aid from the US government, which in turn expanded the scope of military and counterterror operations in Thailand. To the extent that it prioritized geostrategic security in the region over human rights protection, the Thai government actively supported the genocidal policies of Cambodia's Khmer Rouge, which directed and implemented the mass killings of around two million Cambodians (Haberkorn 2013).

Thailand in the 1990s experienced a dramatic improvement in its human rights record, as Amnesty International underscored that "Thailand has made progress in safeguarding human rights since mass prodemocracy street protests in 1992" (Associated Press 1999, 1). During this period, state-initiated extrajudicial killings and disappearances were very rare (see fig. 6.1[3]). Most of the abuses likely emerged as outcomes of the individual motivations of state agents, devoid of any public support from

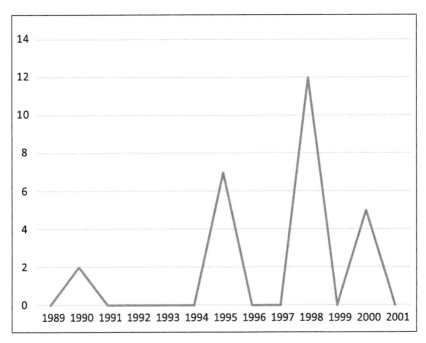

Fig. 6.1. Civilian Deaths Caused by the Thai Government, 1989–2001. The data used to create this figure is available on our Fulcrum platform at https://doi.org/10.3998/mpub.12036762.cmp.17

the central civilian government or the central military command. The improvement in human rights outcomes in the 1990s can be attributed to Thailand's democratization reforms after the infamous Black May incident on May 17–20, 1992, when the Thai police killed at least 52 civilians and injured hundreds of people during a protest in Bangkok. The protesters peacefully opposed the appointment of General Suchinda Kraprayoon as prime minister (Uniyal 2000, 13). Around 200,000 people peacefully protested against the authoritarian rule of General Suchinda Kraprayoon.

Viewed as one of the most violent cases of police abuse in post–World War II Thailand, the Black May incident signaled a new dawn in Thai politics because it forced General Suchinda Kraprayoon to resign from his seat as prime minister. The resignation marked the end of almost three decades of military rule. Consequently, in September of that year, Thai voters elected the Democratic Party's Chuan Leekpai as the new prime minister. The standoff between the military and the protesters ended when the Thai royal family mediated between those two groups. The royal intervention produced a compromise in which the prime minister needs to be elected by a popular majority vote. The Black May event facilitated the emergence of national consciousness that underscores the need for democratic civilian rule over the state's coercive apparatus, considering that "the 1992 uprising made many educated Thais realize that economic growth without political liberalization can dangerously destabilize the country" (Eng 1997, 172; Charles 1996). After the Black May incident, "an unprecedented period" emerged in which "the military, shamed and chagrined, withdrew from political life, while the progressive spirit inspiring the democracy movement had freer rein than, perhaps, ever in Thailand's history, and further, it gained an institutional presence, unseen previously" (Selby 2018, 1). Consequently, human rights and democratization reforms gained traction through institutional reforms within the state, strengthened civil society activism, and prevented the military from intervening in civilian politics—all of which contributed to the decline in state-initiated physical integrity rights abuses of Thai citizens.

Spearheading the shift of US foreign policy toward strong human rights protection, US president George H. W. Bush responded to the Black May 1992 incident by publicly criticizing the military-led Thai government and urged Thai officials to resolve the crisis peacefully. The White House also ordered a brief interruption of joint US-Thai military exercises, but resumed those trainings after Thailand conducted the national election in September 1992. A Pentagon spokesperson explained: "We think it makes common sense in a time of problems in Bangkok not to have [a] picture of U.S. forces storming the beaches in Thailand" (Human Rights Watch 1993a, 19).

In the 1980s, US military and economic aid to Thailand was valued between 150 to 350 million USD annually, whereas in the 1990s the average amount plummeted to less than 50 million USD per year. In the 1990s, the US government expanded its trade portfolio, which included nonmilitaristic policy priorities such as trade, economic development, democratization, and human rights protection. The substantial reduction in human rights violations in the 1990s correlated with the dramatic decrease of US bilateral aid to Thailand. What explains this correlation of three notable outcomes in the 1990s—fewer human rights abuses, less militaristic US aid, and the ascendancy of liberal Thai political elites to power? The next section discusses how and why US and Thai government officials, politicians, and civil society actors converged toward a reformist human rights and democratization agenda.

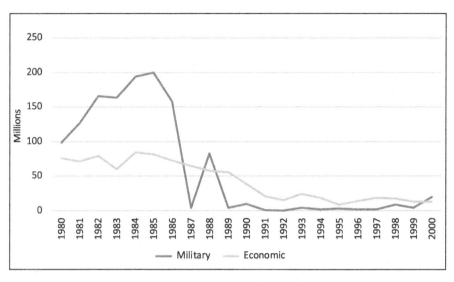

Fig. 6.2. US Military and Economic Aid to Thailand, 1980–2000 (constant USD). The data used to create this figure is available on our Fulcrum platform at https://doi.org/10.3998/mpub.12036762.cmp.17

US and Thai Governments' Shared Expectations for Stronger Human Rights Protection in Thailand

During the Cold War, the Thai state aimed for the consolidation of all anticommunist forces as the core objective of domestic repression, whereby state agents were tasked "to tarnish virtually all opponents, including those who called for a constitution and parliamentary forms" (Hewison 1997, 13). In contrast, the post–Cold War period witnessed a remarkable shift in policy priorities toward human rights, democratization, and economic development. Specifically, the absence of a perceived security threat from the communist rebels required the abandonment of a militaristic approach to US-Thailand bilateral cooperation. Kusuma Snitwongse (2001, 205), a prominent Thai public intellectual, observed that "the Thai-U.S. relationship has, however, since the Cold War years, changed from one of patron-client to one of equal partnership," and that "the end of the Cold War resulted in a difference in geopolitical outlook between the United States' global strategic outlook and that of Thailand's regional power balancing outlook and its perception of local threats." In addition, the US government relegated Thailand to a "lesser level of importance," particularly in terms of geostrategic military significance (Chambers 2004, 460). Departing from their predecessors' militaristic agenda, post–Cold War Thai prime ministers Chuan Leekpai (1992–95, 1997–2001) and Banharn Silpa-Archa (1995–96) strongly committed to political openness, human rights protection, and equitable socioeconomic development. Sharing the emerging prodemocratic stance of other Asian leaders, including the Thai delegation, US assistant secretary of state for East Asian and Pacific Affairs Winston Lord in May 1993 during the ASEAN Summit in Brunei contended that "democracy and human rights are components of a broader definition of security" (Tat 1993, 7–8). That statement suggests that military cooperation was never abandoned, considering that the Thai military greatly benefited from US strategic culture (Wah 2000, 13). Yet Bangkok and Washington in the 1990s widely expanded their scope of cooperation in ways that the overarching framework constituted a commitment to human rights and democracy, which were systematically undermined during the Cold War (Phongpaichit and Baker 1995, 125–29; King and LoGerfo 1996; Pathmanand 2001).

Many liberal democratic-oriented political parties based in Bangkok emerged as key figures in this reform movement. The most notable stakeholder among these movements is the Democrat Party, which eventually ruled Thailand in the 1990s. The Thai Democrat Party is known for its liberal democratic and promarket leanings. It became the dominant force in Thai politics especially in the aftermath of the 1992 Black May incident. This was because the Democrat Party spearheaded the protests against the military junta, and thereafter it became known for its vigorous opposition against all forms of military intervention in Thai politics (Bunbongkarn 1993; Phongpaichit 2004; Ufen 2008, 338). Thai political elites reframed and strategically localized the importance of human rights norms by causally linking them to sustainable economic growth. In the 1990s, Chuan's government and his highly influential Democrat Party envisioned a Thai state that was effective in protecting its citizens from human rights abuses—a commitment that could make Thailand a model for its peers in the region. That ambition was reflected by the Chuan administration's commitment to the "transformation of the Indochinese battlefields to marketplaces" (Acharya 2003, 382), which suggests the departure of the Thai state from its hawkish domestic and foreign policies during the Cold War to a more diverse set of policy aims in the 1990s. Thus, in the 1990s Thailand witnessed the "emergence of a liberalizing middle-class population actively seeking democratic transformation" (Acharya 1999, 420). Governing the most rapidly growing economy in the region at that time, the Thai state focused on human rights and socioeconomic development because of the appeal of "economic expediency, or the actual lure of Indochinese resources and markets" and "sheer geopolitical ambition, or to develop a Thai-dominated Southeast Asian heartland as implicit under the government's revival of the traditional Thai Golden Peninsula concept" (Acharya 2003, 382). Promoting the causal belief that a militaristic and authoritarian policy agenda undermines the economy, the Thai government prioritized nonmilitaristic concerns, especially in promoting equitable economic development and political openness.

The Clinton administration strongly supported the human rights and democratization reforms advocated by Thai political elites and civil society. It spearheaded a "more comprehensive approach to East Asia as it meant of American interests beyond the Cold War policy of containment," particularly when "economic cooperation and the promotion of human rights, reflected the United States' new agenda for the post-Cold War era and mirrored the Wilsonian cum liberal tradition of an earlier stage" (De Castro 2000, 65). In his landmark speech in 1996 at Chulalongkorn University, President Clinton asserted that, despite the differences between the United States and Thailand, both countries "share a common vision— the dream of an Asia-Pacific region where economic growth and democratic ideals are advancing steadily and reinforcing one another" (Agence France-Presse 1999; Purdum 1996, A11). That causal idea, which associated sustainable economic development with human rights protection, gained traction among Bangkok's most influential political elites, especially the new cadre of young politicians from Prime Minister Chuan's Democrat Party, the Thai monarchy, and the military leadership. Many Thai elites considered the disappearance of the armed communist threat and the eventual disintegration of the Thai Communist Party in the 1990s as failures of an authoritarian political culture in sustaining economic development. At the transnational level, increasing economic globalization effectively pushed the Thai military to implement transformative reforms on human rights, anticorruption, and free trade (Samudavanija 1997, 51). Thai politicians and the Clinton administration promoted the causal idea that adopting a democracy-oriented agenda is necessary to sustain economic growth. Liberal Thai politicians justified democratization by arguing that economic growth depends on the "relaxation of state power and the degree of liberalization in matters such as deregulation, privatization, and the internationalization of capital"—a political choice that ultimately demanded the breakdown of the authoritarian regime (Samudavanija 1997, 43). Consequently, Prime Minister Chuan aimed to make Thailand "the center of gravity for economic activities in the region" and vowed to continue the democratic reforms of his predecessor, particularly by strengthening representative institutions (Lehner and Owens 1992, 15).

Thai civil society groups highlighted the horrific abuses of the Thai military during the Cold War and advocated for constitutional guarantees for human rights protection and democratization. Thailand's leading human rights activist and former political prisoner Somchai Homlaor observed that the post–Cold War era brought tremendous improvements in human rights: "We may not be among the top 10 (nations) in human rights, but compared to other countries in the region, we are much better . . . more attention will be paid to these as civil society gets stronger" (Uniyal 2000, 4). Seeking to undermine the overwhelming power of state security agencies by pointing out their historical record of abuses, liberal Thai politicians blamed state security agencies for their support of the Khmer Rouge's genocidal policies in Cambodia during the Cold War. Hence, political power shifted from the military and monarchy to "being contested by a variety of sociopolitical forces, both old and new" (Phongpaichit and Baker 1997, 21). This contestation demonstrates the expansion of the public sphere and the diffusion of power within Thai society.

The Thai government's policy discourses and initiatives demonstrated the importance of human rights. In response to a 1999 Amnesty International report, which claimed that Thailand was making significant progress in meeting international standards for human rights protection, Prime Minister Chuan's spokesperson argued that "as far as Thailand is concerned, we have been trying very hard. . . . If you look at the new constitution and the various organic laws, I would say we are giving a lot more emphasis to human rights than in the past" (Associated Press 1999, 6; Cook 2007). Also responding to the report, the deputy director-general of the Ministry of Foreign Affairs, Jullapong Nonsrichai, emphasized his government's commitment to human rights and admitted that some abuses had emerged from time to time without the authorization of the central government (Agence France-Presse 1997). Those pronouncements from high-ranking Thai officials signified the state's full commitment to international human rights norms. As such, Thailand "took major steps, however, toward instituting a more accountable and transparent political system and became the first country in Southeast Asia to sign the Rome treaty establishing the International Criminal Court" (Human Rights Watch 2001, 1; Christensen and Siamwalla 1993). In October 1996, Thailand signed the International Covenant for Civil and Political Rights, thereby signaling its commitment to international human rights norms. In 1994, Prime Minister Chuan Leekpai's government permitted a group of Nobel Peace Prize laureates to visit Bangkok and campaign for the release of the Burmese leader Aung San Suu Kyi (Human Rights Watch 1994), consequently signaling the government's desire to assert Thailand's crucial role in regional human rights diplomacy.

Meanwhile, the Clinton administration strongly advocated for a pro-human-rights agenda that converged with the policy priorities of the newly installed electoral democratic regime in Bangkok. Several official interactions between Prime Minister Chuan and President Clinton and their respective high-ranking cabinet members demonstrated that commitment. For example, the official pronouncements of high-ranking Thai and US officials at the ASEAN and the APEC (Asia-Pacific Economic Cooperation) summits consistently placed human rights and economic development at the core of US-Thailand bilateral cooperation (Bangkok Post 1996; Chachavalpongpun 2005; Kendall 1994). In 1995, Jeffrey Garten, the US undersecretary of commerce for international trade, affirmed that the United States was unprecedentedly determined to focus on trade and investment in Southeast Asia, particularly in Thailand. The post–Cold War period witnessed the US government's newly found economic interest in Thailand, which was then considered as "one of the 10 'big emerging markets' identified by Washington in a new drive to boost US exports and investments" (Agence France-Presse 1995, 3).

The US government in the 1990s began referring to the human rights practices of the Thai government in deciding the scope of their bilateral trade relations. This foreign aid conditionality emerged when the Clinton administration identified Thailand right after the Black May incident as the "priority foreign country for special scrutiny by the US Government under Section 301 of the 1988 US Trade Act," which in turn made foreign aid conditional upon strong human rights protection (Bangkok Post 1993, 4; Economist 2008). Responding to the US government's pressure to expand the space for civil society, Thailand's interior minister, Sanan Kachornprasart, declared in February 1999 that the government was nullifying the law passed in 1952 that sought to ban all communist-related activities (Cooper 1997; Human Rights Watch 1999). The abolition of this law undermined "security officials' wide powers of arrest, search, and detention" (Human Rights Watch 1999, 7), which they previously held during the Cold War. Those changes in the constitutionalized powers of the military resulted from "US foreign and trade policy and its support of human rights and democracy" and the "rapidly declining significance of security concerns" based on the perceptions of the Thai elites and the general public alike (Samudavanija 1997, 53).

Several events of mass social mobilization against state abuses served as a wake-up call for institutionalizing human rights protection in Thailand. Such incidents of violent crackdown of street protests occurred in the early 1990s, culminating in the Black May incident in 1992, when 52 protesters were killed and around 3,500 to 4,000 activists were imprisoned by the military. The horrifying abuses during the 1992 Black May incident galvanized politicians and proreform movements to undermine the legitimacy of military rule, which increased the political viability of human rights reforms and bolstered the argument for greater democratic civilian rule over the Thai armed forces. Considering the dominant belief that the end of the Cold War meant the end of military rule, Pavin Chachavalpongpun (2011a, 49) alluded to the effect of images, perceptions, and impressions brought about by the Black May incident: "With the massacre of protesters disgracing the military in the eyes of Thai society, the military was subsequently forced to go into 'hibernation' throughout the 1990s."

Various Thai political elites reframed the incident as the pivotal point when the military could be dethroned from power. The White House pressured the Royal Thai Armed Forces to stop its violent crackdown on peaceful protests, especially in the critical years of 1991 to early 1992. During his testimony at the House of Representatives East Asian and Pacific affairs subcommittee hearing, Assistant Secretary of State Richard Solomon pressured the Thai military junta (National Peacekeeping Council) to cede its power to a civilian government to be elected by the Thai people (Reuters 1991, 2–3). Likewise, the US Department of Defense in 1991 and 1992 postponed all joint military exercises with the Thai military and fervently warned the military-led government to stop any of its plans to violently quell peaceful prodemocracy protesters (Agence France-Presse 1992). A series of violent military crackdowns of mass protests in Bangkok in the early 1990s, which eventually resulted to the Black May incident in 1992, provided the impetus for the postponement of joint US-Thai military exercises. That concrete policy action from the US government was complemented by tougher American aid sanctions on Thailand, as explained by State Department spokesperson Margaret Tutwiler: "In view of the continuing violence in Bangkok, we have put resumption of economic and military assistance on hold and suspended all combat elements of the (joint) military exercises," while pressuring the Thai armed forces to "refrain from the use of deadly force as a means of resolving the issues that divide the opposition and the government" (Agence France-Presse 1992,

2). Those political pressures demonstrated the US government's judicious use of its long-standing influence and ties to the Thai military in order to generate reforms in Thailand. Together with the pressures from the Thai public and the emerging cadre of liberal democratic elites from Bangkok, US public diplomacy and its aid sanctions eventually undermined the power of the Thai military and state security agencies. This outcome eventually led to the downfall of the military regime and the emergence of Thai liberal democratic politics.

In the 1990s, the US government started to maximize the use of aid, economic trade, and military assistance as "levers to promote political pluralism and individual liberties in countries that put greater emphasis on stability and social control" (Richardson 1993, 4). In 1993, just a year after the Black May incident, US Secretary of State Warren M. Christopher proudly asserted that stronger human rights protection is "a cornerstone of US foreign policy" (Richardson 1993, 8). The reason for the shift, according to the US government, was because of the declining social legitimacy of autocratic rule and the increasing public demand for political openness and human rights guarantees. That being so, Winston Lord, the US assistant secretary of state for East Asian and Pacific Affairs, highlighted the benefits of democratization in Thailand (Richardson 1993, 8–10):

> Open societies do not attack one another. . . . They make better trading partners. They press for environmental reform. They do not practice terrorism. They do not produce refugees . . . (there had been) encouraging strides toward more democratic and humane societies in Thailand.

After the Black May incident and the return of competitive elections, Thailand's domestic civil society flourished and consistently became more vigilant against state-initiated human rights abuses. Moreover, Thailand became a regional hub with the largest number of important regional human rights networks in Southeast Asia, even surpassing the Philippines, which had a much longer exposure to electoral democracy and political openness (Acharya 2003, 385). The emergence of Thailand as the regional hub for human rights had two important consequences. First, these organizations deployed strong political pressures on the central government in Bangkok to comply with its human rights commitments. This was a crucial development because Thai bureaucrats, the monarchy, and the military dominated pre-1990s Thai politics, with a highly repressive state apparatus and a limited space for political opposition (Acharya 2009; Ferrara 2010).

In contrast, the increase in the number of civil society groups in the 1990s made political discourse and contestation more pluralistic and highly competitive. Second, the proliferation of domestic and transnational human rights organizations signified the determination of Chuan's administration to advance norms of political openness and active civil society engagement. As early as 1992, Prime Minister Anand Panyarachun had forecast the indispensable role of human rights organizations and other democratic reforms, which the military institution had to pay attention to: "They cannot go against the trend of public opinion. They cannot go against the global trend which moves towards a market economy and more democratic society" (Girling 1996, 86).

The Thai government, especially during the tenure of Prime Minister Chuan, adopted a more interventionist stance on human rights issues in other Southeast Asian countries. On November 20, 1997, Prime Minister Chuan gave a speech to the parliament and reaffirmed a human rights-oriented Thai foreign policy and the country's firm commitment to domestic human rights promotion. Chuan reaffirmed that one of the key goals of the state is "the participation by Thailand on the international stage in the protection and promotion of democratic values and human rights" (Snitwongse 2001, 192). Defying the norm of "nonintervention" in the affairs of other member countries of the Association of Southeast Asian Nations (Acharya and Tan 2006; Kohn 1997), the Thai government aspired to be a human rights leader in the region. That political tactic became effective in 1993, when the Thai and US governments jointly promoted human rights norms in Burma. For instance, General Charan Kunlawanit of Thailand's National Security Council noted that the Thai prime minister and Foreign Ministry officials actively cooperated with the US State Department, especially Deputy Secretary Clifton Wharton, in brokering a series of peace dialogues with the Burmese government and Burmese minority groups. Remarkably, General Charan proudly acknowledged that it was Thailand's role to broker peace dialogues and argued that "once peace materializes, democracy will follow" (BBC 1993, 10)—a stance that represented a clear departure from the authoritarian impulses of the Thai military before the 1990s.

The US government capitalized on the importance of its enduring economic relations with Thailand, particularly by linking sustainable economic growth to stronger human rights protection (Bennet 1998; Manihandu and Sawatsawang 1996; South China Morning Post 1998). In its diplomatic relations with other Southeast Asian countries, the US State Department and Bangkok officials persistently alluded to Thailand as an exemplary model that showed how strong human rights protections facilitate sustainable economic development. That kind of rhetoric proved to be persuasive especially at the height of the East Asian values debate on human rights, primarily spearheaded by Singapore's prime minister, Lee Kuan Yew, and Malaysia's prime minister, Mahathir Mohammad, both of whom had cast serious doubts on the universality of human rights (Barr 2007; Emmerson 1995; Thompson 2001).

Even in times of economic crises, the Clinton administration provided financial assistance to the Thai government and deployed political discourses that highlighted democratic openness and transparency as crucial to good economic governance. The political appeal of such a link between economics and democratic politics gained traction after the 1997 Asian financial crisis, when Thai and American politicians attributed the crisis to the insufficiency of democratic reforms and political openness carried out in the early 1990s (Bridges 1999; Rodrik 1999). Considering that the United States was Thailand's second largest trading partner after Japan, the Clinton administration ensured Thailand's economic survival in the thick of the 1997 Asian financial crisis when it "assembled a package of aid worth about 1.7 billion USD for Thailand, including trade assistance and investment in power projects" (Bennet 1998, A5). Bangkok's response to US strategic assistance was predominantly positive, to the extent that Prime Minister Chuan acknowledged that his country was "undergoing a period of financial and economic crisis" and that his government appreciated "the help and support of friends," especially from the United States (Bennet 1998, A5). The US assistance to Thailand during the 1997 Asian financial crisis had some important ramifications in fully realizing the shared bilateral agenda on human rights and good economic governance. As Larry Diamond and Juan Linz argued, "economic crisis represents one of the most common threats to democratic stability" (Przeworski et al. 1996, 2). Had the Clinton administration not chosen to assist the Thai government, the credibility of the US-supported human rights agenda could have been derailed. Had Thailand not survived the economic crisis, the prospects of a military takeover could have been heightened, thereby undermining all the human rights reforms of the early 1990s.

Even before the 1997 crisis, Clinton's public diplomacy efforts in Thailand focused on strong trade relations with Bangkok as well as human rights promotion (Ungphakom 1993). Making US bilateral trade conditional on Thailand's human rights and democratic reforms dominated the trade negotiations of high-ranking officials from Bangkok and Washington. That emphasis on human rights-based trade diplomacy gained prominence in various high-profile events such as the APEC summits and many other official meetings of Thai and American leaders in the 1990s. During those events, President Clinton consistently characterized US-Thai links as part of a "bold new era in relations with the world's fastest-growing economies" and that the 1990s created "a new voice for the Asia-Pacific in world affairs" that "would help bring down global trade barriers" (Spetalnick 1993, 1, 8; see also Perlez 1999; Purdum 1996). Similarly, Prime Minister Chuan exhorted that "the Cold War is over . . . now is the era of the economic leading the political. I would like to pursue a policy of free trade . . . strengthen Thai businessmen to compete in the world market" (Cooney 1992, 16).

Illegal prostitution emerged as a key bilateral policy area for American and Thai government officials and civil society networks. The US State Department Report (1994) estimated that around 200,000 to 500,000 prostitutes worked in Thailand at that time, many of them underaged. Many of these prostitutes suffered from police abuse and sexually transmitted diseases including HIV/AIDS—issues that US-Thai cooperation heavily focused on (Greenhouse 1994). As Thailand experienced rapid economic growth and a tourism boom that followed thereafter, the continuous influx of predominantly Western tourists in the country stimulated the expansion of the local prostitution sector, involving mostly young women. Compared to the Cold War and the post-9/11 eras, when the Thai state alleged that it had solved drug trafficking and prostitution through extrajudicial killings (Asian Human Rights Commission 2014), the immediate post–Cold War years witnessed an approach that relied on promoting socioeconomic development initiatives. This shift in domestic policy was partly shaped by the Thai government's motivation to adapt to the US government's interests. US First Lady Hillary Clinton vigorously led public diplomacy efforts and civil society promotion initiatives that advocated for nonviolent and holistic approaches to Thai societal problems. In a landmark speech delivered in 1996 by First Lady Clinton at Chulalongkorn University, the "war on drugs and the sex industry," which were usually framed in militaristic terms during the Cold War, were approached differently in the post–Cold War era (Purdum 1996, 9):

> Expanding educational opportunities for children, curbing the spread of AIDS and ending the exploitation of young girls in [the] commercial sex industry will not only help individual Thai girls and their families, but Thai society as a whole.

Hillary Clinton vigorously lobbied for reforming Thai laws that dealt with the terms of imprisonment for all perpetrators of child prostitution, including the financially exploitative parents. Since then, USAID has funded several large-scale social welfare projects that were implemented by American and Thai NGOs. In cooperation with local Thai authorities, USAID provided substantial financial assistance to rural families in order to motivate them to abandon opium farming and to embrace crop substitution. From 1997 to 1999, the Clinton administration provided around 1.3 million USD to the crop substitution program. Some of these funds were spent on "an estimated 1,000 educational scholarships" that "were awarded to girls in risk groups in the four provinces of Chiang Rai, Chiang Mai, Lampang and Payao" (Vejpongsa 1996, 5). In 1999 US Secretary of State Madeleine Albright proudly reported that local farmers, who used to earn around 100 USD, had started to earn about 1,200 USD as a result of the USAID economic development incentives for farmers who abandoned opium farming (Perlez 1999, A14).

USAID provided substantial funding to many rural-based Thai and American NGOs that implemented vocational training and financial assistance programs that targeted many young women, who were rescued from the perils of prostitution and drug trafficking. The scheme was the well-known Women for Tomorrow Program funded by USAID and the US State Department and primarily implemented by Thai NGOs and local government units. Young women enrolled in this program took half-year vocational training classes that provided them the skills needed for employment in the booming formal Thai economy. Leading the Women for Tomorrow Program, Secretary of State Madeleine Albright, during her 1999 visit in Thailand, promoted the inspiring story of 21-year-old Chanpen Promsen, a prostitute who became a garment factory worker. In a widely televised interview, Albright sat with many young women in a rural village in northern Thailand and articulated how US aid was used to improve the lives of prostitutes and drug victims: "I'm doing things secretaries of state didn't do . . . partially because they interest me but more importantly because they are now elements of American foreign policy . . . combatting drugs is a job for the Secretary of State. . . . Here (in Thailand) we are saying no to narcotics and saying yes to vegetables" (Perlez 1999, 3). One must note, however, that "among the investors and managers of Thailand's large prostitution industry are Thai military officers" (Enloe 1993, 151), while American intelligence and military operatives used sexual labor during the US-Vietnam war to generate income (Truong 1990; Fineman 1997).

The US and Thai governments' nonmilitaristic approach in combatting drug trafficking and prostitution stood in clear contrast to the violent approaches implemented by the Thai government during the Cold War and the Thaksin era in the 2000s. The Women for Tomorrow Program showcased the US public diplomacy approach that highlighted economic livelihood as the key alternative path for women. The nonviolent approaches employed by the Thai and US governments in tackling the drug and prostitution problems reflected the emerging human rights norms at that time. The focus on the rehabilitation of young sex workers substantially undermined Thai security agencies' violent policy approaches toward prostitutes. This holistic approach underscored the importance of economic security and nonviolence as legitimate responses to a complex problem: particularly, the need to curb Thailand's enduring role in the "Golden Triangle" (with Myanmar and Laos) that was known for illegal drug production and trafficking, prostitution, and police abuse (Ford and Koetsawang 1991; Kulsudjarit 2006).

Domestic Politics and Policy Priorities: Toward a Pro-Human-Rights Agenda

The human rights agenda that emerged in the 1990s manifested in several concrete and transformative political initiatives: (1) the constitutional reforms that explicitly guaranteed human rights to Thai citizens; (2) the emergence of independent Thai media outlets; (3) the institutional reforms within the military; and (4) the unprecedented expansion of the Thai civil society sector. Influenced by political pressures and financial incentives from the US government and the demand from the Thai domestic public, those domestic initiatives represented a collective effort between Bangkok's political elites and the Thai government to push for stronger human rights protection in the country.

First, the promulgation in 1997 of the new constitution called the People's Constitution was widely seen as a huge step forward in integrating the human rights agenda in the core mandate of the Thai state. A UN Development Program report in 2000 affirmed the importance of Thailand's new constitution, which represents "a major change in Thailand, where the main safeguard of human rights and human development is the 1997 Constitution, the country's first democratic one" (Uniyal 2000, 7). Arguing that the reforms in the 1997 charter were not "simply cosmetic," Thai constitutional law expert Vitit Muntarbhorn hailed the 1997 Constitution as "the only one that can claim to be most democratic" because it provides unprecedent opportunities for civil society to flourish (Uniyal 2000, 9). Specifically, it provides "a high degree of contestation among different interest groups, whose agendas ranged from the deeply conservative to the highly progressive" (McCargo 1998, 10). Driven by broad-based political support from domestic and American civil society groups based in the country, the significant reforms in the 1997 Constitution "set out to re-engineer the political system in order to reduce the power of the bureaucracy, make politicians more responsive to the popular will, and to undercut old monopolies in business and government" (Pathmanand 2001, 25). The constitution laid "the ground rules for transforming Thailand from a bureaucratic polity prone to abuse of citizen rights and corruption, to a participatory democracy in which citizens will have greater opportunities to chart their destiny" (Klein 1998, 4). The constitution, in Article 56, guaranteed all citizens the opportunity to sue government agencies for harming the environment (McCargo 1998, 27). Although the enactment of the 1997 Constitution was the fifteenth time that a new charter had been drafted since 1932, the People's Constitution was unique because of the progressive political guarantees that it provided to all Thai citizens. The 1997 Constitution represents the "culmination of five years of political reforms designed to exorcise the ghosts of frequent military coups, patronage, money politics, and vote-buying that long plagued the country's politics of representation" (Pongsudhirak 2003a, 277).

Remarkably, the 1997 Constitution was the first Thai constitution that was comprehensively based upon the principles of democratic governance, civilian rule over the military, and human rights (Uwanno and Burns 1998). As such, the 1997 People's Constitution "catalogued human rights, established a range of new institutions to check the abuse of power, set out roadmaps for decentralization, media reform, and other items on the activist agenda, and even included some provisions for direct democracy" (Phongpaichit 2004, 2). Consequently, the Thai electorate, for the first time, had the power to elect all 200 members of the Senate. The Senate was established in 1947, and before 1997 all of its members were appointed by the prime minister and the Thai monarchy (Maisrikrod 2007, 343). Based on the 1997 Constitution, the fully elected Senate gained various forms of constitutional functions that had previously been entrusted to royally appointed members. Those functions included "selecting, appointing, advising, or endorsing the appointments to the following office[s]: the Election Commission, the Ombudsman, the Human Rights Commission, the Constitutional Court, members of the Justice Commission, the

Administrative Court, the National Counter-Corruption Commission, and the Auditor-General" (Maisrikrod 2007, 343). To prevent the emergence of political dynasties, the tenure of a Senate member is limited to two consecutive terms, with each term lasting six years. According to the principle of compulsory voting that was first introduced into Thai politics through the 1997 Constitution, the Election of Act of 1999 compels relevant state agencies to enable all eligible Thais to vote regardless of their location (Maisrikrod 2007).

Perhaps the most important institutional reform introduced by the 1997 Constitution was the creation of a permanent 11-member National Commission on Human Rights, which is tasked to "prepare an annual evaluation of the human rights situation for the National Assembly, propose policies and recommendations for amending laws to the National Assembly, promote measures to educate citizens on human rights, and investigate cases of human rights abuse" (US Department of State 1999, 76). The new commission appointed three ombudsman officers who were tasked with independently monitoring and investigating human rights violations (Human Rights Watch 1998).

In the 1990s, the Thai government had been consistent in introducing landmark reforms that severely undermined the military's interventionist stance in civilian politics. That agenda became dominant in the policy strategies of all prime ministers who served Thailand during the 1990s—particularly Prime Ministers Anand (1992), Banharn (1995–96), Chavalit (1996–97) and Chuan (1992–95; 1997–2001). Bangkok's liberal democratic politicians, mostly from the Democrat Party, justified these progressive reforms by contending that democratization is crucial for long-term economic stability. Thai political elites perceived that policy choice as beneficial because free and competitive markets, as the politicians claimed, can only flourish in a democratic society that respects human rights. The 1997 Asian financial crisis reinforced that perception, which positioned Thailand at the epicenter of the regional problem. The widespread belief in the direct link between economic growth and democracy facilitated the relative ease of implementing human rights reforms, especially in the 1990s. Kittipong Kittayarak (2003, 107), a high-ranking Ministry of Justice official, argued that the "pro-rights, pro-reform Constitution would not have passed the Parliament, had it not been that Thailand was hard hit by economic crisis during that same year." Subsequently, the perceptions of the Thai elites and the middle class upheld the causal belief that democracy and economic growth have a mutually reinforcing relationship (Englehart 2010, 254):

Economic growth in Thailand was based on foreign capital, and created a globalized economy sensitive to the confidence of international capital markets. A perception that these capital markets favored democratic regimes and political stability changed the political calculus in Thailand, shifting it firmly toward liberal democracy in the wake of the 1997 currency crisis.

Several significant reforms emerged within the military, which substantially undermined the Thai armed forces' control over civilian affairs. With the passage of the State Administration and Procedure Act in 1991, the Thai armed forces "was downsized and re-engineered with ideas of modern organizational management," which meant that the "great number of generals was reduced through early retirement, and the over-all size of the army trimmed by decreasing the annual recruitment" (Pathmanand 2001, 26). The sharp decrease in US military aid starting in the early 1990s led to the reduction in the Thai armed forces' organizational size and scale of operations, which in turn contributed to the decrease in collateral human rights abuses. The military's monopolistic control of Thai national media outlets, including 221 radio stations and 2 television channels, was also a key target for reform. The Thai population had demanded that the monopoly be ended, which in turn led to the formulation of Article 40 in the 1997 Constitution. It mandated that all electronic media organizations be in the public domain, that the media's independence be maintained, and that it advocates for the collective public interest (Pathmanand 2001, 28).

Thai citizens pushed for the depoliticization and reformation of the military and police agencies. Because of demands from the Thai monarchy and the US government for stability, General Suchinda stepped down from power, which was then followed by the landmark national election of a new prime minister and all members of the parliament. As early as 1992, the newly elected prime minister, Anand Panyarachun, compelled the military to apologize for its role in the Black May bloodbath and even started the "complicated process of extricating state companies from military control" (New York Times 1992b, 20). To constrain the power of the military, Anand established civilian government agencies in order to regulate contraband trade in the shared borders with Laos, Cambodia, and Burma. The emergence of civilian government control over the Thai military dramatically undermined the long-standing profiteering and rent-seeking behavior of military officers, particularly through "lucrative trading ties to Khmer Rouge warlords, drug lords, and operatives of Myanmar's thuggish State Law and Order Restoration Council" (1992b, 20). Many Thai citizens believed at that time that the profiteering and entrepreneurial activities of military border commanders were key sources of wealth of the Thai military (Branigin 1992; Manihandu and Sawatsawang 1996). By undermining the military's control over the borders, the Thai central government minimized the possibility of political adventurism by the military as well as limiting the propensity for human rights abuses at the borders. The civilian takeover of the government's anti-drug-trafficking agenda played a key role in the foreign policy strategy of the Clinton administration. While Prime Minister Thaksin Shinawatra (2001–06) attempted to solve the narcotics problem through the bloody 2003 war on drugs, in the 1990s President Clinton and Prime Minister Chuan focused on drug rehabilitation, education, and prevention. Because of that nonmilitaristic focus, the top US antidrug official, Barry McCaffrey, proudly reported that Thailand "had made great strides" not only in drug education but also in "the eradication of opium production" (Charles 1996, 2–3).

The Thai state abrogated some of the legal instruments that empowered the military and transferred some of those in the democratic branches of the government. For example, the state canceled the Internal Peacekeeping Directorate Act, which military and police officers regularly invoked in order to quell peaceful dissent. Afterwards, the Thai Senate and House approved the new law that required the approval of the civilian cabinet members before the military and the police could be tasked to control protests. The Chuan administration "declared the unconstitutionality of the military-backed seizure of assets," a political move that sought to professionalize the Thai armed forces by limiting its influence in civilian affairs, including business activities (Girling 1996, 86). Consequently, military officers seldom provided their unsolicited opinions "on the government's performance—a striking difference from earlier days" (Girling 1996, 86). The Thai military prohibited its officers from engaging with civilian politics, thereby depoliticizing the military in ways that reduced the likelihood of systematic abuses of peaceful political dissent. Those reforms "lulled Thais into thinking direct army takeovers were a thing of the past" (Amorn 1991, 1). The Thai Ministry of Defense's (1994, 1; see also McCargo 2002b) *Defence of Thailand* 1994 report stated that promoting liberal economic development and democratization reforms constituted the military's long-term strategy:

> The Armed Forces conducts its mission in accordance with the Constitution . . . a New World Order is emerging with greater emphasis on issues such as democracy, human rights, and environmental

conservation. At the same time, the world is entering an information age and there is greater economic competition. All these factors
have an effect on our long-term planning.

In the 1990s, a new cadre of younger and first-time national politicians and public servants emerged, and they eventually constituted the core
group advocating for democratization reforms in Thailand. These new
leaders vowed to make democracy, human rights, and equitable economic
development the key goals of the state. The Thai Democrat Party's chief of
policy planning, Savit Bhotiwihok, explained immediately after the Black
May incident that their "main task will be to strengthen political institutions so we don't go back to the coup-elections-coup syndrome which
plagued us in the past" (Ismartono 1992, 2). Likewise, Suchit Bunbongkarn, an influential academic from Chulalongkorn University, commented
that the "the May tragedy aroused a new democratic mood among Thais,
particularly those living in urban areas. They wanted a more stable democratic government and a withdrawal of the military from politics" (Ismart-
ano 1992, 6). In addition to advocating democratization reforms within
the country, Prasong Soonsiri, the chairperson of the National Security
Council and an influential political figure from the state security establishment, supported an activist Thai foreign policy committed to human rights
promotion in the region, considering that "the world is attaching greater
importance to issues such as human rights, democracy and the environment" (Mallet 1992, 13–14).

As early as 1992, Prime Minister Chuan Leekpai admitted that
reforms were necessary in order to make the Thai state more effective
in upholding the public interest (Phongpaichit and Piriyarangsan 1996,
109). Those reforms within the military gained more traction after
the 1997 Asian financial crisis. Many Thais believed that the crisis was
responsible for directing the country "on the road to political democracy," particularly when reforms were considered as crucial in "leading
to better economic development that will benefit people and not just the
elite" (Uniyal 2000, 24). Even President Clinton justified the 1.7 billion
USD worth of emergency aid to Thailand in 1997, based on the post–
Cold War US paradigm that linked the strength of US trade relations
with the human rights performance of partner states: "countries like
South Korea and Thailand have proven in this financial crisis that open
societies are more resilient; that elected governments have the authority
to make hard choices in hard times" (Agence France-Presse 1999, 16).
That statement exemplified how reforms toward political openness and

strong human rights protection were complementary. Thailand's position on the East Asian values debate was dramatically different from the stance held by other countries in the region where the governments of Singapore, Malaysia, and even Indonesia argued that human rights and democracy—as practiced in the West—were not compatible to Asian culture (Mauzy 1997; Emmerson 1995).

Thai civil society groups flourished in the 1990s and succeeded in undermining "the old socio-political order, while the military was simultaneously tamed" (Pathmanand 2001, 25). Thailand's booming civil society, a diverse group "ranging from affluent professionals to idealistic reformers and hard-pressed labor organizers, are nevertheless united as citizens in pursuit of a democratic society—all the more so when confronting the oppressive character of the bureaucratic polity and its surviving elements" (Girling 1996, 25). They contributed to the decrease in clientelism and undermined corruption in the state's coercive agencies (Laothamas 1992; Lucas 1997). They campaigned for reforms including "a fully sovereign parliamentary system, protection of human rights, decentralisation of power, media freedom, and more equitable economic policy" (Phongpaichit 2004, 1). Many civil society organizations persistently demanded political reforms, while the Thai armed forces became more tolerant toward civil society advocacies (Cook 2007, 162–63). A UN Development Program report in the 1990s applauded Thailand's reforms due to its "active press," which functioned as a "a constructive and critical avenue to monitor the work of state actors and others which have impacts on human rights" (Muntarbhorn 2000, 15). The military and the traditional Thai political establishment widely tolerated such peaceful activities, thereby making civil society activism a "recognizable feature of the Bangkok political scene" in the 1990s (Cook 2007, 163). In the 1990s, civil society leaders and prominent cultural personalities in Thailand strategically repackaged the political demand for human rights in a way so that it seemed a natural element of the Buddhist culture of Thailand (Barratt 2004, 148):

> Just as it is not difficult to find evidence of humanism and in principle support for human rights in modern Buddhism, there is also no shortage of evidence that many Buddhists are actively engaged in the quest for human rights, social justice and democracy. This phenomenon even has its own name: "Socially Engaged Buddhism," or just "Engaged Buddhism." It is based largely on the vaguely left wing, anti-capitalist, anti-authoritarian views of outspoken Buddhist monks.

Another focal point of domestic political reform pertains to the dramatic growth of civil society's influence over state policy (Phongpaichit 2004, 1). State economic planners embraced the "people-centered development" paradigm, whose goal is to ensure that economic growth is justly distributed across the society. The Ministry of Interior Affairs implemented decentralization reforms in order to empower local government units in effectively managing their fiscal affairs and development plans, while relevant government ministries promoted governance through decentralization in policy areas including health, education, and social provision as advocated by civil society groups. Highlighting the abuses of the military, the Black May incident in 1992 "exposed the military—and not civil society—as the divisive factor" in the country (Girling 1996, 20). The Black May incident also inspired the Thai public's sympathy for an emerging oppositionist civil society and served as a rallying point for a more active and peaceful criticism of government policies. Civil society groups eventually tamed the authoritarian tendencies of the Thai armed forces and other traditional elites from the "bureaucratic polity" (Bunbongkam 1991; Rhum 1996; Riggs 1966). Thai civil society groups' influence was even bolstered by the 1997 economic crisis that "has put authoritarianism on the defensive and empowered pro-democratic forces" (Acharya 1999, 420).

Many civil society groups received funding and technical support from USAID and American NGOs. The influence of human-rights-oriented NGOs is illustrated by the Thai state agencies' and business community's tolerant attitude toward labour unions. While many countries in the Global South had a business community that was generally disinterested, if not hostile, to labor interests and other social movements, Thailand during the 1990s was dramatically different. Indeed, the business community actively supported the emerging democracy movement that involved large numbers of student activists (Samarasinghe 1994, 16).

The US government strongly encouraged Thai prodemocracy business groups, which in turn contributed to human rights and democratization reforms. One of Thailand's most prominent civil society leaders, Parichart Chotiya, argued that "the most systematic and substantial program to promote provincial business came from foreign assistance, especially that from the US, which established a programme to strengthen the role of the private sector" (Chotiya 1997, 257). USAID provided financial resources to provincial chambers of commerce and business associations to promote management education, private enterprise, and the significance of responsible commercial activities in an open and democratizing society (Chotiya 1997, 257; Laothamas 1992, 82–83).

Notwithstanding increased US investments in Thailand, the influence of labor movements over the Thai state intensified. The Chuan government established the Ministry of Labour and Social Welfare on November 25, 1993. The new agency had 13,000 staff members and a substantial budget of 271 million Thai baht (6.89 million USD). The establishment of the Labour Ministry empowered labor movements in the formation of national economic policies (Hewison and Brown 1994, 509). The new ministry signified "the importance the administration attaches to labour and social welfare" (Leekpai 1993, 98–99) and was "suggestive of a transition from an authoritarian to a more representative regime" (Hewison and Brown 1994, 510). Consequently, a more conducive political climate emerged for labor movements without the fear of violent reprisals from the government. Such labor movements were clearly absent during the period of the Thai military junta (or the "National Peacekeeping Council"), which systematically and violently repressed any form of dissent during the Cold War.

The emergence of many civil society groups transformed state-society relations in Thailand, which experienced a "rapid shift from an administrative-centered to an interest-centered government, whereby individuals and groups from various quarters of society have penetrated the State and are increasingly shaping the goods and services it supplies" (Christensen and Siamwalla 1993, 3). The openness of the political system made it possible for a variety of interest groups to shape the democratic politics of the country in ways that were nearly impossible during the time of the military junta (Cook 2007, 168). This expansion of the public sphere empowered civil society groups, but it also forced military officers to confine themselves to the barracks rather than the halls of civilian politics (Kocak and Kode 2014; Samudavanija 1997).

Various sectors promoted the importance of human rights norms during this period. Grassroots activists and the general Thai public expressed their political demands for greater political openness and stronger human rights protection. Even the highly influential yet conservative Thai monarchy ended the 1992 Black May incident by pressuring the Thai military to give way to national elections that would install an elected civilian government. That move by the Thai monarchy was complemented by political pressures from the US government for the Thai military to embrace democratization reforms. Bangkok's leading foreign policy analyst, Kusuma Snitwongse (2001, 207), affirmed the importance of human rights reforms in post–Cold War US-Thailand relations: "Thai-U.S. relations have also improved because of the credentials of Thailand as a democratic country. The Chuan government used this to the country's benefit in dealing with the West. Prime Minister Chuan and President Clinton established a personal rapport that also helped bilateral relations."

American and Thai political elites realized their converging human rights interests through the US strategic support programs to Thailand, Bangkok's national policy priorities, and fundamental constitutional initiatives. Those political actors upheld that sustained economic development can only prosper within the framework of human rights and political openness. The election of Bill Clinton as president galvanized several changes in US foreign policy, which eventually motivated Thai officials to support a pro-human-rights agenda. Because "security-driven goals have become less critical and ideological goals more important with the passing of the Cold War," the US government during the 1990s was "increasingly rewarding democratic states with foreign aid while reducing assistance to strategically important nations" (Meernik, Krueger, and Poe 1998, 64; see also Baldwin 1995).

Patterns of Residual Human Rights Abuses

The emergence of shared expectations for a pro-human-rights agenda—particularly shared by the Clinton administration, the Chuan administration, the Thai monarchy, and the Thai population—was not enough to deter *all* human rights violations. There were two causal pathways in which institutional deficiencies in the armed forces and the judiciary contributed to human rights abuses. First, some rogue rank-and-file police officers and soldiers committed abuses without the fear of facing legal penalties. The central armed forces leadership either denied the institution's responsibility or even secretly condoned the perpetrators' actions. Considering that the Thai armed forces has a long history of abuses, some of its officers and soldiers remained dismissive of the emerging post–Cold War human rights norms and continued to view the military as the ultimate arbiter of the public interest (Chachavalpongpun 2011b; Dragsbaek 2007). Some state agents failed to realize the emerging post–Cold War demand in Thailand that "the point of civilian control is to make security subordinate to the larger purposes of a nation, rather than the other way around" (Kohn 1997, 141). Second, the enduringly ineffective Thai judicial system heightened the prospects for human rights abuses to pass without bringing perpetrators to justice. Many abusive Thai police and military agents did not face any legal penalties—and some of these officers even threatened the lives of judges and high-ranking civilian government officials to prevent them from publicly condemning abusive police officers.

During this period, extrajudicial killings, enforced disappearances, arbitrary detention, and other related violations of physical integrity rights were rare in Thailand. That was dramatically different from the severe and pervasive human rights violations during the Cold War, when Thailand, then governed by a military junta, became a hub for American military forces (Kislenko 2004; McCoy, Read, and Adams 1972). While strong human rights protections emerged in Thailand in the 1990s, several collateral human rights abuses persisted throughout the 1990s, albeit the number was much lower. The abuses did not enjoy the support of the US government and the Thai government. Thus, physical integrity rights abuses during this period can be classified into two distinct but not mutually exclusive types of actions carried out by agents of the Thai Royal Police and the Royal Thai Armed Forces: (1) abuses that emerged from regular criminal policing operations, and (2) abuses that emerged from police and military encounters with civil society activists.

Violations as Outcomes of Regular Policing Operations

The Thai state security agencies conducted their regular operations in the 1990s at a limited scale compared to the Cold War period and post-9/11 Thaksin era. In the absence of a perceived security threat, the Thai armed forces focused on problems such as prostitution, drug trafficking, illegal migration from neighboring countries, and other petty crimes such as theft and robbery. In response, the Thai government actively cooperated with civilian state agencies and the military and police forces, thereby framing those problems as issues of human welfare that require socioeconomic interventions, rather than the deployment of state violence. Moreover, human-rights-focused US foreign policy motivated the Thai armed forces to support civilian state agencies in promoting human rights and development. The US armed forces' engagements with the Thai military and police forces were limited to the annual COBRA Gold joint exercises, rather than expanding the Thai armed forces' magnitude of state operations comparable to the Cold War period.

Even so, several individual agents and small groups from the Thai Royal Police and the Royal Thai Armed Forces still committed human rights abuses. The Thai attorney-general revealed that 324 suspects and detainees without a final verdict perished in 1995 while they were in the custody of state agents (US Department of State 1997b). Several instances of abuses emerged from the unlawful killings of suspected criminals while they were under police responsibility or when police officers were arresting suspects (Human Rights Watch 2001). In 1995 the Thai Royal Police Force's information center documented 23 suspects who were killed during police arrests. In November 1996, Thai news media outlets reported the controversial arrest of six suspects for drug trafficking in the central province of Suphan Buri. Despite their peaceful surrender, the six suspects were killed a few moments later (US Department of State 1997b). Although the concerned local police command claimed that "they acted in self-defense since one of the suspects attempted to seize a weapon," other civilian government agency sources "questioned the credibility of the official police explanation" (US Department of State 1997b, 10).

Notwithstanding emerging human rights norms, the Thai armed forces continued to protect their own officers amid allegations of abuses. In the 1996 Suphan Buri incident, deputy Thai police director-general Salang Bunnag and 17 other officers failed to appear in the first hearing at court. Salang and his team were implicated as being fully responsible for the death of the six drug suspects in Suphan Buri. Yet, the Thai government prosecutor and senior investigating officer, Anothai Bamrungphong, confessed that "he had received threatening phone calls" and witnessed several "shooting incidents near his house," in which he claimed that "both had been carried out by officers involved in the Suphan Buri incident" (Human Rights Watch 1999, 10). Considering the institutional failures in launching a successful legal case against human rights abusers, the Thai attorney general referred to official government data and concluded that "90 cases of killings by all civil officials (including police and other civilian government officials, such as forestry and district officials) in 1995 resulted in 89 cases being dismissed by the courts" (US Department of State 1997b, 11). It is likely that intense pressures and death threats from police officers influenced the courts' decisions.

Several abuses involved police officers' inappropriate conduct during their pursuit of suspected criminals. For example, local civil society groups in Bangkok reported that, in 1993 alone, members of the Royal Thai Police killed 31 unarmed civilian suspects during an arrest (US Department of State 1995). One of the most widely known incidents of collateral abuse was the death in 1994 of the "wife and child of a key witness" in a highly controversial case about "jewelry and precious gemstones stolen by a Thai employee of a Saudi prince" (US Department of State 1995, 9). This case refers to the well-known Blue Diamond Affair (1989), an "international jewelry heist [that] captivated the world's attention because of its

unresolved murders, its implication of law enforcement and public officials from two divergent countries, and the resulting diplomatic tensions
between Thailand and Saudi Arabia" (McClincy 2012, 182). The incident
demonstrated the Royal Thai Police Forces' lack of discipline, professionalism, and "perpetuated corruption" (McClincy 2012, 182). The case
resulted in the unexplained murders of three Saudi diplomats in Bangkok,
Saudi businessmen, and several other Thai citizens up to the mid-1990s.
Locals believed that corrupt Thai police forces were involved in covering
up the crimes of Thai citizens and even gained some profits as a result. The
attempts of the Royal Thai Police Force to cover up the crime of the implicated Thai suspects resulted in the subsequent murders of key witnesses
and other crime suspects. As the *Economist* (2008, 1) claims, "In Thailand's
most sensational crimes, the prime suspects are often the police." Although
the senior police management is likely to be directly involved, several rank-
and-file police officers, one midlevel officer, and two senior police officers
were arrested due to the murders of key witnesses pertaining to the jewelry
heist (US Department of State 1995).

Another instance of documented abuse occurred when, on November
27, 1997, Bangkok-based police officers killed six Thai men who were suspected of being methamphetamine drug smugglers. Widely condemned
as one of the most notorious incidents of police abuse committed while
arresting suspects in the 1990s, that incident demonstrated that "corruption among police is common, and reportedly includes large-scale bribe
taking" (Cooper 1997, 4). According to Amnesty International and other
Bangkok-based NGOs, the police officers fired guns and killed the six suspects despite their surrender to the authorities. There were some procedural irregularities within the Royal Thai Police Forces because the dead
bodies of the six men "were cremated without autopsy and the police
destroyed evidence of the circumstances by burning down the house"
where they were killed (Cooper 1997, 14). Although the relevant civilian
state agencies, including the prime minister's office, criticized the police
force's misbehavior, the legal cases in the judicial courts did not prosper.
Similarly, on August 17, 1993, five agents of the Thai Royal Police Force
from Ban Pong district in the central Thai province of Rachaburi were
implicated in the killing of a vegetable trader, who was apparently beating
a traffic light (US Department of State 1994). Thailand's Interior Ministry
commissioned the autopsy and initiated an independent investigation into
the killing, yet the legal case against the police was eventually (and mysteri-
ously) discontinued in the court.

Due to the economic boom in the 1990s and the perceived stable political system, Thailand emerged as an attractive destination for economic migrants and political refugees. Despite the US government's continued emphasis on being more lenient with refugees for humanitarian reasons, some Thai state agents violated the physical integrity rights of those foreigners. In 1997 several Thai forestry bureau officials killed three ethnic refugees from the Karen indigenous minority in the rural hinterlands of northern Thailand. Thai state officials erroneously targeted the refugees as armed intruders in the Thai border and deemed it appropriate to fire guns (Cooper 1997). In August 1997, border police officers killed two Islamic religious leaders in the southern region of the country as the latter were mistaken for illegal refugees. In January 1998 Thai police officers killed three unarmed Cambodian children on the border regions in Sa Kaew Province, in a town thirty miles from the Thai-Cambodia border. In all of these incidents, the central command of the Thai Police Forces as well as the Office of the Prime Minister were quick to condemn the abuses of the implicated state actors.

During the 1997 Asian financial crisis and the international media hysteria that followed, some police officers and high-ranking government officials were suspected of undermining the freedom of speech of Thai citizens and media agencies. In July 1997 several agents of the Thai Royal Police Forces forcibly entered two American financial brokerage firms based in Bangkok, harassed their employees, and looked for documents containing incorrect financial information that were sent via fax (US Department of State 1997). Although Prime Minister Chavalit did not have a policy of undermining freedom of expression, the police obtained an arrest warrant that allowed them to search for faxed documents considered to be threatening to government stability (US Department of State 1997). Later on, Thai media agencies reported that the incident involved some high-ranking civilian officials and Bangkok-based police officers who attempted to hinder foreign media from reporting the Thai government's failures in the midst of the Asian financial crisis.

In such police abuses, government officials and business actors likely used "tea money" (Thai: *ngein chā*), or bribes, to contract police officers and other armed state agents for personal gain. Despite the professionalization reforms of the 1990s, some police officers continued to receive "tea money" in order to act as private security agents for high-ranking government officials and even influential Thai business elites. This is most likely the reason why, in the 1990s, some police officers killed some innocent civilians because they were deemed detrimental to many of these elites' rent-seeking activities that involved "tax evasion, gambling, immigrant trafficking, goods smuggling, and prostitution" (US Department of State 1997a, 4). Human Rights Watch (1994, 10) reported that some high-ranking officials from the Royal Thai Police Forces and the Royal Thai Armed Forces "made little effort to stop the trafficking of foreign girls and women, particularly Burmese and Chinese, into Thai brothels where the women faced debt-bondage, physical abuse and conditions akin to slavery."

In 1994, police officers rescued 148 Burmese women who were detained in prostitution houses encircled by electrified barbed wire. After the rescue mission, the women were transferred to an immigration detention center in the southern Thai province of Ranong. After two weeks, the local Thai police officers deported 58 of those women to Kawthaung in southern-most Burma, where it was believed that they were subsequently arrested on charges of prostitution and illegal drug trafficking. Those women suffered physical intimidation under the Thai government's custody. Because Thai police officers "are notorious for their cruelty" and some suspects were routinely tortured even in the 1990s (Thongpao 1997, 2), the deportation of the Burmese women trafficked into prostitution was widely considered an instance of human rights abuse. Similarly, in January 1997 Thai border control officers killed three minors from Cambodia as "as they were cross-ing the border from Sa Kaew Province in Thailand to Poipet town in Cam-bodia" (Human Rights Watch 1998, 5). In the Sa Kaew shooting incident, "Thai authorities have not clarified the circumstances of these shootings, and no investigation took place" (Human Rights Watch 1998). Despite the state's constitutional human rights guarantees, there was a lack of govern-ment interest in protecting the rights of refugees entering Thailand.

Isolated Abuses of State Agents

Despite the absence of a nationwide policy of domestic repression against peaceful dissent, several state agents harassed civil society activists. Such abuses were a response to environmental advocacy groups' public pro-tests and public expression of civilian government officials' highly critical views against the military; they involved the enforced disappearances of some civil society activists and the harassment of religious dissidents who challenged some traditional Thai cultural customs. Those abuses likely emerged because of the individual motivations of state agents rather than as the direct consequences of state policy. In general, however, a report from the early 1990s states that "human rights groups and other nongov-ernmental organizations are able to work openly in Thailand" (Human Rights Watch 1993, 15).

The 1992 death threat case of Chulalongkorn University rector Pradit Chareonthaitawee demonstrates how civilians could be targeted for violent repression because of their open criticism of the military. Following the Black May incident, the transitional civilian government appointed Pradit to chair an independent committee to investigate the nature of the protests and the whereabouts of the civilian activists (Associated Press 1992; Human Rights Watch 1993a). Pradit resigned after receiving death threats from military officers. Suspected agents from the Royal Thai Military issued death threats to Pradit and other committee members after the aforementioned targets publicly criticized the Thai armed forces for killing around 50 protesters during the 1992 Black May incident. Pradit claimed that his committee found evidence that the missing protesters' bodies were stored at an unknown Thai military base. Other civilian officials who openly castigated the military for its violent repression of the Black May protesters also received death threats (Associated Press 1992). Defying their constitutional obligations, some segments of the Thai armed forces' leadership refused to subject erring soldiers and officers to judicial processes, even after open criticism by the public and civilian government officials.

Policing operations during mass protests could escalate to violence, as demonstrated by the 1993 incident of police abuse in the northwestern province of Kamphaeng Phet (US Department of State 1994). Opposing high inflation rates, thousands of farmers and other grassroots activists peacefully protested in the main avenues and streets and marched to the provincial government building. The provincial police reported that some farmers violently provoked some police agents, who were then deployed in the area. In response, the police physically harassed the protesters, causing 25 reported cases of injuries and one death due to severe head contusion. Consequently, several provincial politicians investigated the incident, while the victims' relatives did not pursue a legal complaint against the provincial police. Local media reports discovered that each family of the victims received approximately 4,000 USD from the Kamphaeng Phet provincial government. Provincial government officials denied that compensation was given, and the local government vehemently denied the allegations of abuses.

Although environmental protection emerged as one of the core concerns of post–Cold War US-Thai bilateral relations, some state agents violently harassed and killed environmental activists. In October 1995, four local police officers killed Winai Chantamano in Satun Province, the southernmost province of Thailand. The police killed Winai due to his public protests against the wide-scale privatization of national forest lands

(US Department of State 1997b). Private investors of the development project were likely involved in commissioning local police officers to carry out the assassination.

There were other incidents of politically motivated killings involving local businessmen who paid groups of police officers to assassinate civil society activists. The targets included unarmed community activists who organized peaceful protests against the detrimental social and environmental costs of certain local business activities. The death of Joon Bhoonkkhuntod, a farmer and community activist in the northeastern Thai province of Chaiyaphum, is a prominent example of this kind of political killing in the 1990s (Coordinating Committee of Human Rights Organizations in Thailand/CCHROT 1996; US State Department 1997a). Joon was a member of the famous Forum of the Poor, a nationwide network of grassroots activists advocating for the rights of the most financially impoverished families in rural Thailand. He was known for organizing grassroots-based protests against the construction of the Pong Khun Phet Dam and for widely publicizing illegal logging operations that involved collusion between government officials from the Irrigation and Local Administration and local business tycoons. Condemned by police officers and local businessmen for his political advocacy, Joon was killed on July 22, 1996 by a gunshot from police Private Anuchet Chagruengklang. The official police report, later on published in the *Bangkok Post*, claimed that Anuchet killed Joon "because he resisted arrest . . . and in the confusion, the gun was fired accidentally" (CCHROT 1996, 2). The arrest was based on allegations that Joon was farming marijuana, although many sources believed that the police planted marijuana beside his body (CCHROT 1996). Yet testimony from the villagers and Joon's neighbors, including some young women who witnessed the shooting incident, strongly refuted the official and fabricated claims of the police. The witnesses confirmed that the police deliberately killed Joon. In an effort to threaten the women who tried to stop the killing, Anuchet and his accomplice yelled, "Stop or I'll shoot you." Despite the call from Prime Minister Anand for justice, the legal case against Anuchet and his accomplice did not prosper, and the Thai police's version of the case prevailed in the national media. A similar incident also happened to Thong-in Kaew-Wattha, who was shot and killed in 1996 by two policemen. The police killed Thong-in because of his vigorous public protests against a local chemical treatment plant that emitted toxic waste in a largely farming-based village. Local community leaders, human rights activists, and civilian government officials believed that "the suspects were hired by a local businessman whose interests were adversely affected by

Thong-in's environmental activism" (US Department of State 1997a, 8). Despite the main suspect's explicit admission of the crime, the Thai police considered the case closed and ended an internal investigation.

Moreover, some Thai government officials abused their official privileges as state officials, particularly when civil society activists protested against massive construction projects that involved public-private partnerships. For example, the protests in the 1990s against the building of the Yadana gas pipeline from Burma's Andaman Sea to Thailand's Kanchanaburi and Ratchaburi Provinces illustrates how some government agents undermined peaceful political opposition in the name of economic interests (Earth Rights International 2012; Human Rights Watch 1998). Some private companies paid Thai security forces in order to employ some Thai and Burmese citizens in coercive labor. In the 1990s, the Yadana gas pipeline project was "marred by serious and widespread human rights abuses committed by pipeline security forces on behalf of the companies, including forced labor, land confiscation, forced relocation, rape, torture, murder" of mostly Burmese and some Thai citizens residing in the affected areas (Earth Rights International 2012, 1). In 1996, many Thai NGOs organized regular and wide-scale protests in Bangkok throughout that year against the Thai government's involvement with the project. Many of these NGOs, however, "were closely monitored and, on occasion, restricted by the government" (Human Rights Watch 1998, 19). Another example of repression of peaceful political dissent occurred in May 1996. At that time, Thai intelligence agents imprisoned four Burmese students based in Bangkok for organizing peaceful protests outside the Malaysian Embassy as they advocated for Burma's denial of membership in ASEAN. Also, some Thai police officers imprisoned several Burmese students who staged protests during President Clinton's landmark visit to Bangkok in 1996. The students were imprisoned for almost a year in Bangkok's Special Detention Center, even after the UN High Commissioner for Refugees officially classified all of them as "persons of concern," a designation that grants them protected status under international law.

In addition, several high-ranking civilian government officials surreptitiously contracted police officers and other agents of the Thai Armed Forces in order to undermine opposition forces. This modus operandi is an exception in post–Cold War Thailand rather than a norm. Of particular interest is the case of Trairong Suwannakhiri, Thailand's deputy prime minister, who in July 1998 sent his private administrative assistant and "six gun-toting deputies," most likely from Bangkok's police forces, "to raid the *Thai Post* following its publication of a story describing how he had fled from protesting fishermen during a visit to southern Thailand" (Moeran 2001, 4). Although Trairong's representatives made some threatening remarks to the journalists and even demanded retraction of the article, the *Thai Post* did not yield to the demand. Similarly, *Newsweek* staff members faced intense pressure from some government agents to retract an article that cited a foreign diplomat who bluntly contended "that Thailand's economic advantages were 'sex and golf'—two hobbies much enjoyed by the Japanese, who now employ Thai and Filipina girls as 'hostesses' in their clubs and bars" (Moeran 2001, 4). Those incidents, however, did not constitute a systematic clampdown on media outlets. Rather, the incidents demonstrated that many state security agents at that time had yet to internalize fully the human rights reforms in the 1990s.

Conclusion: Stronger Human Rights Protection in the 1990s

What explains the improved human rights outcomes in Thailand throughout the 1990s? I demonstrated that the confluence of the pro-human-rights and less-militaristic interests of the Thai and US governments in the 1990s together with the strong domestic legitimacy of the elected government in Bangkok produced the lower number of state-initiated abuses.

The Black May incident in 1992 and the end of the Cold War represented two pivotal events that transformed the Thai public's perception of the need to moderate the powers given to the national security establishment in order to prevent human rights abuses. American and Thai political elites, meanwhile, framed the 1997 Asian financial crisis as a moment to recast economic crisis as a political problem by itself. Specifically, many Thai government officials in the 1990s promoted the causal idea that sustained and robust economic development depends on strong human rights protection and democratic reforms. The convergence of the pro-human-rights interests of the US and Thai governments produced domestic policies and foreign aid programs that contributed to entrenching human rights.

Remarkably, two key domestic policy patterns galvanized the human rights reforms in Thailand. The first pattern referred to the reclassification of counterterrorism, armed domestic rebellion, and other militaristic issues as low-priority concerns for the Thai state. Thai government officials shifted their attention and resources away from counterterrorism, while the US government reframed its public diplomacy and invested its material assistance toward economic development, civil society support, and other nonmilitary concerns. Those developments constrained the coercive capacities of the Thai armed forces, which severely limited the scale and frequency of their combat operations. The contraction of the armed forces' capacities and operations generated fewer human rights violations, which mostly came from routine policing and military operations. Second, as militaristic notions of state security lost traction, the Thai state widely tolerated the proliferation of civil society groups, which made the public discourse much more pluralistic and adversarial.

In closing, this chapter systematically analyzed the evidence from post–Cold War Thailand. During this time, strong human rights protection emerged from the Thai government's consistent and determined localization of emerging human rights norms, which sought to win the support of the US government as well as the Thai domestic public. The broader Thai society pressured the country's political elites to embrace human rights, democracy, and equitable economic development as key goals of the post–Cold War period. The confluence of the shared interests of US and Thai political elites on a diverse range of policy issues, together with the strong domestic legitimacy of the central government in Bangkok, led to the improvements in human rights. The next chapter probes the causes of the post-9/11 human rights crisis that emerged in Thailand.

SEVEN

From the War on Terror to Thaksin's War on Drugs and Dark Influences

> When the US makes war against terrorism, they do it with full commitment, pour in all their resources, and use every kind of influence they have, use every level of politics to deal with this matter. I think that task is more difficult than a domestic drug problem because they have to work all over the world. So today we have to make war on drugs, have to attack, and that is not beyond our ability. . . . I am really confident.
>
> —Thailand's Prime Minister Thaksin Shinawatra, speech at the Suan Dusit Ratchapat Institute, January 14, 2003[1]

> Inside your own country, you are pursuing dangerous terrorists and finding them—and America thanks you. . . . Thailand pledged to fight the war on terror, and that pledge is being honoured in full. . . . Thailand is also a force of good throughout Southeast Asia. Together, our two nations are fighting the drug trade by sharing intelligence that helps Thai law enforcement officials interdict shipments and catch drug traffickers.
>
> —US President George W. Bush, remarks to Thai troops, Royal Thai Army Headquarters, Bangkok, October 19, 2003[2]

Whereas the Philippines under the Arroyo administration branded armed Islamic and communist rebels as well as civilian activists as state enemies, the post-9/11 Thai government under Prime Minister Thaksin Shinawatra reframed the global war on terror as his own "war on drugs." That localization of the global war on terror discourses did not emerge only because of the Thaksin-led government's political interest—rather, US foreign strategic assistance fueled the human rights crisis in post-9/11 Thailand. How and to what extent did the Bush administration's strategic support to the Thai government shape the scope and extent of state repression implemented in Thailand from 2001 to 2006? In this chapter, I investigate how and under what combination of transnational and domestic conditions the deteriorated human rights deterioration emerged in post-9/11 Thailand. My core argument states that the convergence of the Thai and US governments on a counterterror agenda, combined with the weak domestic legitimacy of Prime Minister Thaksin Shinawatra, led to the increase in state-initiated human rights violations. The effect of interest convergence as well as the motivations of the Thai government for regime consolidation jointly facilitated the escalation of domestic repression, which, in turn, resulted in two transformative policy patterns. The first policy pattern refers to the expanded scale and increased frequency of military and police operations against armed Islamic rebel groups in the southern Thai provinces, which resulted in the prevalence in collateral human rights violations. The second pattern, meanwhile, pertains to the selective and widespread employment of state repression upon civilians, who were deemed state enemies. For example, the Thaksin administration strategically localized the global war on terror discourse into a local "war on drugs," thereby echoing the Bush administration's policy assertions that illicit drug trafficking fuels international terrorism. The Thai military and police, in cooperation with local government officials, implemented extrajudicial killings and physical harassment of civilians, many of whom were perceived as local political opposition members and critics of the Thaksin administration. Aiming to consolidate his weak domestic legitimacy, Thaksin deployed the military and police institutions to crack down on unarmed political dissidents and armed rebels. Taken together, those factors jointly generated the prevalence of intended and deliberate state-sanctioned abuses.

This chapter is organized into five parts. First, I discuss the overall human rights situation vis-à-vis America's foreign policy goals and bilateral aid to Thailand from 2001 to 2006. Next, I examine various policy discourses that embodied the shared policy expectations of American and Thai political elites as well as the broader Thai public in light of the post-9/11 security context. Third, the chapter demonstrates that a terror-oriented policy agenda was realized in the various domestic policies strategically crafted by the Thaksin administration as well as the programs funded by the US government. Consequently, I provide an analytical survey of the types of human rights violations that emerged during this historical period. The chapter concludes by explaining the theoretical implications of the evidence from post-9/11 US-Thai counterterror cooperation.

Overview: Human Rights Situation and US Foreign Policy in Post-9/11 Thailand (2001–2006)

The human rights situation in Thailand under Prime Minister Thaksin Shinawatra (2001–6) dramatically deteriorated compared to the previous decade. In the 1990s, Thai local civil society groups flourished, liberal democratic elites took power, and Thai military officials deliberately refrained from directly intervening in civilian politics. By the turn of the new millennium, "Thailand has made great strides since the army brutally suppressed pro-democracy protesters in 1992" (Streckfuss and Templeton 2002, 73). In contrast to the 1990s, when extrajudicial killings and disappearances rarely occurred, the post-9/11 Thai society witnessed a much more widespread and systematic commission of state-inflicted human rights violations. Human rights abuses reached a peak after 2003, when the Thaksin-led Thai government publicly supported the US-led war on terror (Gadavanij 2020, 54, 56). As I explain later, the Thai government actively localized global war on terror discourses based on Thailand's long-standing internal security threats vis-à-vis the long-term regime consolidation strategy of Thaksin and his Thai Rak Thai party.

Thaksin's government systematically killed suspected drug addicts and other civilians, while the Thai military implemented widespread counterterror operations against armed Islamic rebels. For instance, the post-9/11 Thaksin government reported 1,300 cases of extrajudicial killings during the "war on drugs" in 2003 alone, while Human Rights Watch claimed that the number could have been as high as 2,500. Local media outlets reported that the "three-month climate of fear resulted in 58,000 arrests, 2,274 deaths, and surrenders to authorities by more than 42,000 alleged drug traffickers" (Mutebi 2004, 80). Besides, Thai police officers and military agents killed around 4,700 civilians in the southern provinces from 2004 to 2006, when counterterror operations were officially launched against the armed Islamic insurgents. The Uppsala Conflict Data Program recorded 1,832 incidents of civilian deaths due to state-based violence during the period from 1989 to 2016. The majority of the state-based civilian deaths occurred after 2003 in the Muslim-dominated southern provinces, where the US-Thai counterterror operations were intensively implemented. Accordingly, Thai agents reportedly killed 1,772 civilians in the southernmost region, 4 in Bangkok, 8 in the northwestern provinces, and 48 in the northeastern region.

According to Human Rights Watch (2004c, 20), Thailand's National Human Rights Commission "was deluged with complaints of false arrests,

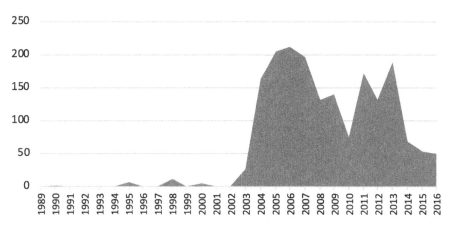

Fig. 7.1. Annual Statistics of Civilian Deaths by the Thai State, 1989–2016.
The data used to create this figure is available on our Fulcrum platform at
https://doi.org/10.3998/mpub.12036762.cmp.17

improper inclusion in drug blacklists, and related violations of due process" (see also Panaspornprasit 2004). Based on the Uppsala Conflict Data
Program, as shown in figure 7.1, the number of recorded state-sanctioned
civilian deaths dramatically increased in mid-2000s, when the Thaksin
government joined the US-led war on terror. While the exact number of
the victims of the war on drugs would be difficult to ascertain, the dramatic
increase of state-led human rights abuses during the time of Thaksin is
undeniable.

As the Thai government implemented its war on drugs, the country fell
from 59th place in 2004 to 107th out of 167 states in 2005 in the Press Freedom Index of Reporters without Borders. The proliferation of state-initiated
abuses during Thaksin's term is widely considered as the worst human rights
record in Thailand's recent political history. Figure 7.1 illustrates the substantial increase in the severity of state repression and human rights violations in the 2000s, when compared to the levels recorded in the 1990s.

Under Thaksin's leadership, Thai government agents violated the rights
of people from "hill-tribes, the Muslim population in the 'deep south,'
convicts and suspects, refugees, human rights defenders seeking justice,
and communities and groups in the midst of environmental or resource
conflict" (Connors 2011, 103). Notably, Thaksin's US-supported war on
terror was "not a discrete abuse of group, time and place—such as the
localised killings of over 20 human rights defenders in the last decade—but
a nationally mobilised policy by an elected government" (Connors 2011,

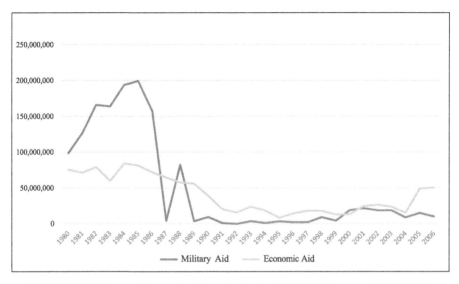

Fig. 7.2. US Military and Economic Aid to Thailand, 1980–2006 (constant 2016 USD). The data used to create this figure is available on our Fulcrum platform at https://doi.org/10.3998/mpub.12036762.cmp.17

104; see also National Human Rights Commission of Thailand 2004). State agents committed human rights abuses in the post-9/11 period in the context of the systematic and well-funded state policy of Thaksin's government, which enjoyed the political support of the Bush administration.

The combined amounts of US bilateral aid to Thailand increased in the 2000s, at levels that were higher than those recorded in the 1990s (see fig. 7.2). The amount of US military and economic aid to Thailand doubled from an annual average of 22.5 million USD for the period from 1993 to 2001 to 50.3 million USD for the period from 2002 to 2009. The total amount of US aid from 1993 to 2001 was only 202 million USD, which was much lower compared to 403 million USD for the years 2002 to 2009. Thus, figure 7.2 reveals the substantial increase of US bilateral aid to Thailand after 2001. As I discuss later, the notable changes in the amount of US bilateral aid to Thailand represented a transformation in the overall purpose of US foreign policy after 2001. Whereas US aid in the 1990s was allocated to a wide variety of militaristic and nonmilitaristic goals, including stronger human rights protection and democracy promotion, US bilateral assistance for the years 2001 to 2004 was primarily geared toward Thailand's own domestic counterinsurgency efforts and the arbitrary policy decisions of Thaksin and his political party. Thus, the deterioration in

Thailand's human rights situation in the post-9/11 period correlated with the increase in US bilateral aid. My investigation of Thailand's post-9/11 human rights crisis (2001–6) begins by examining how the Thaksin administration strategically localized US war on terror discourses in ways that bolstered his domestic security agenda.

US Foreign Policy Discourses and Bangkok's Strategic Localization of the Post-9/11 Threat

Although the US government focused only on targeting armed rebels, Thaksin's government included suspected drug addicts, criminals, civil society activists, and other civilians as targets of violent repression. Why did Thaksin and his allies deviate from the US government's intended purpose of counterterror support? This section analyzes the nonmaterial and sociolinguistic strategies used by Thaksin and his allies to strategically localize the global war on terror in the context of Thailand. I contend that domestic politics played a key role here. First, to bolster their legitimacy, Thaksin and his Thai Rak Thai (TRT) party co-opted with state security agencies in an effort to include civilians as targets of counterterror operations. The Thaksin administration reengaged the military and police agencies in civilian politics through financial incentives and the appointment of loyalists to key leadership posts. In return, military and police agencies effectively implemented its counterterror operations, targeting both armed and unarmed political opposition. Second, by carefully reframing the armed conflict in southern Thailand as a necessary component of the US counterterror strategy in Southeast Asia, the Thaksin administration aimed to unify national support for the administration amid weak political backing from Bangkok's elites and the monarchy. By focusing on a militaristic agenda, Thaksin hoped that a "tough line will even win votes in other, strongly nationalist, parts of the country that regard southerners as habitual troublemakers" (Cumming-Bruce 2004, 11). Thus, systematic killings and physical harassment occurred especially during the 2003 war on drugs, when state agents attempted to swiftly kill most of these "internal security threats" (Chachavalpongpun 2011a, 49–50). Other forms of repression included the harassment of media personnel and civil society activists.

The Thai government's participation in the US-led war on terror constituted a well-timed and careful use of rhetorical strategies that sought to justify Thaksin's terror-oriented policy agenda. Evading the potential antagonism from the Muslim minority in southern Thailand, Thaksin and his other political allies persistently referred to the 2003 arrest of Riduan Isamuddin or "Hambali" as justification for its counterterror partnership with the US government. In a joint operation in Ayutthaya, 75 kilometers from Bangkok, the Thai police and the CIA captured Hambali in August 2003 (Chambers 2004, 469; Busbarat 2016, 244). Hambali was known in the international intelligence community as the "Osama bin Laden of Southeast Asia" as he was widely believed to have been responsible for the 2002 Bali bombings in Indonesia that killed around 200 people, including American citizens. Thaksin rhetorically framed the capture of Hambali as the key basis for Bangkok's participation in the US-led war on terror. Consequently, the majority of the Thai population believed that increased counterterror operations were needed at the time. As Croissant (2007, 13) contended, "given the overwhelming support TRT and Thaksin gained from the majority of Thai voters, electoral incentives for a change in the government's heavy-handed counter-insurgency policy in the South towards non-military measures are weak." While increased counterterror cooperation began as early as 2001, which exemplified Thaksin's commitment to quelling armed Islamic insurgency in southern Thailand, the Thai government insisted on initially concealing its role in the US-led war on terror (Chambers 2004). Just a few months before the capture of Hambali, CNN reported that Thailand was the "silent partner" in the US-led war on terror, while Thaksin "refused to confirm or deny the story, telling Thai journalists that Thailand might not need to state an official position" (Chambers 2004, 467). It was only after the capture of Hambali and the 2003 official visit of Thaksin to the White House that the Thai government publicly expressed its political support for the global war on terror.

Although the White House agreed not to force Thaksin to inform the Thai public about the nature of the US-Thailand counterterror partnership, American news media outlets reported that the Bush administration was not pleased with Thaksin's "quiet approach" to public diplomacy (The Nation—Thailand 2001c, 2001a). Referring to Thaksin, a high-ranking White House official spoke anonymously about the sentiments in the Bush administration about Thaksin's strategy: "It is not enough to be with us in the war on terrorism, but you have to trumpet it" (Bonner 2003, 4). Compared to the Philippine government, which offered support to the Bush administration right after the 9/11 attacks, the Thaksin administration delayed its public support of the US government. The "low-key approach to terrorism" of Prime Minister Thaksin Shinawatra "was partly attributable to fear of frightening away the tourist trade, inciting Thai Muslims against him, and provoking an Al-Qaeda-like attack" (Chambers 2004,

468). Another strategic reason was to allegedly deceive terror plotters to go to Thailand in order for the Counterterrorism Intelligence Center and the CIA to fully monitor their actions without raising suspicion (Lopez and Crispin 2003).

Shortly after the capture of Hambali in 2003, the US and Thai governments publicly admitted their intensified post-9/11 bilateral military cooperation. During the 2003 state visit of Thaksin to the White House, President George W. Bush sidelined all other nonmilitaristic themes of bilateral cooperation and instead catapulted counterterrorism as the new strategic focus (Office of the Press Secretary, White House 2003, 6):

> We must fight terrorism on many fronts. We must stay on the offensive until the terrorist threat is fully and finally defeated. To win the war on terror, we must hunt a scattered and resourceful enemy in dark corners around the world. We must break up their cells, shut off their sources of money. We must oppose the propaganda of hatred that feeds their cause. . . . Nations that choose to fight terror are defending their own safety and securing the peace of all mankind.

The remarks of President Bush identified terrorism as the most compelling policy problem that democratic states ought to urgently address. Referring to the so-called "offensive" approach, Bush underscored increased armed counterterror operations as the appropriate policy response in the aftermath of the 9/11 attacks. By citing those countries "where resentment and terrorism" transpired, as mentioned above, Bush referred to southern Thailand's long-standing armed Islamic insurgency, which persistently called into question the legitimacy of the elected government based in Bangkok. Referring to states that adopted a predominantly militarized approach to the post-9/11 terror threat, Bush provided normative justifications in support of a bilateral counterterror agenda, particularly by framing US security as dependent upon the cooperation and security of American allies (Office of the Press Secretary, White House 2003, 7):

> The United States of America has made its choice. The Kingdom of Thailand has made its choice. We will meet this danger and overcome this evil. Whatever is asked of us, no matter how long it takes, we will push on until our work is done. Three months after my country was attacked on September the 11th, 2001, Prime Minister Thaksin came to America and offered Thailand's help in the war on

terror. Since then, Thailand has committed military forces outside Southeast Asia for the first time in more than 50 years.

President Bush characterized the post-9/11 US-Thailand bilateral relationship as mutually beneficial to both countries and hoped that such cooperation could effectively eliminate the danger of international terrorism. He implied that US-Thailand counterterror operations did not have limits, and that such operations would persist until the terror threat was gone. He also sought to legitimize this militaristic approach to the post-9/11 threat by invoking the long-standing and thriving relationship of the United States with Thailand. By designating Thailand as a key non-NATO ally of the United States, President Bush also conferred nonmaterial benefits on Thaksin's government and the Royal Thai Armed Forces. The designation as a major non-NATO ally was widely seen in Thailand and in policy circles in Washington, DC as a political reward given by the Bush administration to the Thai government for capturing Hambali (Associated Press 2003). Also, Thaksin contended that Thailand's designation as a major non-NATO ally of the United States signaled that the "military relations" between the two countries "will be more convenient" (Associated Press 2003, 7). That statement alluded to several important benefits to Thailand: access to US-made weapons and funding for counterterror exercises and training opportunities between the two countries' armed forces. In effect, the designation of Thailand as a "major non-NATO ally" boosted the Thaksin-led government's domestic legitimacy and amplified the importance of bilateral military cooperation with the US government. By providing military aid and other forms of counterterror assistance to Thailand, President Bush ignored the historically dismal human rights record of the Thai armed forces. Instead, Bush highlighted the US government's reengagement with the Thai armed forces in terms of its pragmatic value to international counterterror efforts. Bush expressed his gratitude to the Thai state and the Thai military during the 2003 press conference with Thaksin in the White House (Office of the Press Secretary, White House 2003, 9–16):

Thailand pledged to fight the war on terror and that pledge is being honored in full. . . . We're confident in the strength of our alliance and I have acted to designate Thailand a major non-NATO ally of the United States. . . . American and Thai forces serve together and train together and study at military academies in each other's countries. . . . Thailand and the United States lie thousands of miles apart. Yet in the ideals we serve, we will always be close. America is grateful for your friendship.

Because the TRT party's political support primarily came from the rural poor, Thaksin expected that the intensification of US-Thai security cooperation would result in considerable support from the Thai monarchy and other political elites (Chachavalpongpun 2011b). Before his tenure as Thailand's top official, Thaksin "did not have a genuine interest in rural issues or the plight of the poor" (Phongpaichit and Baker 2008b, 64). Thaksin is a fourth-generation member of a Chinese migrant family to Thailand and was in deep financial trouble in the early 1990s. He was able to recover and accumulate wealth when his company reached monopolistic control in the telecommunications industry. During the 2000 national elections, Thaksin's campaign promises on "slow liberalization and increased distribution" gained support from working-class Thais who were still recovering from the effects of the Asian financial crisis (Doner, Ritchie, and Slater 2005, 352). Except for Thaksin's TRT party, most members of the establishment elites, including the monarchy and high-ranking bureaucrats, "see the United States as a benign and stabilizing power," a belief that is "close to axiomatic in foreign policy circles" in Bangkok (Hamilton-Hart 2012, 2). That dominant belief among members of the Thai political establishment motivated Thaksin and the TRT party, notwithstanding its nationalist and pro-rural Thailand rhetoric, to reengage in a military security-focused cooperation with the US government in order to appease these influential and traditionally pro-US elites based in Bangkok.

Thaksin's justification for Thailand's role in the global counterterror effort was much more restrained at first. Specifically, Thaksin initially resorted to economic justifications in order to secure the support of the broader Thai public as well as Bangkok's elites. For example, Surat Horaichakul (2003) exposed the two main justifications that Thaksin gave to the Thai public, both of which show the quid pro quo bilateral relations between the two countries: (1) the long-standing US-Thailand alliance requires Bangkok's assistance in response to the terror attacks, and (2) the United States is the largest export market for Thai products.

There were several instances when the Bush administration provided economic incentives for Thaksin to embrace counterterrorism as a key policy priority. For example, in 2003 the US government awarded Thailand's Army Corps of Engineers with multimillion-dollar reconstruction contracts in Iraq, where the United States was waging war. When the parliament of Thailand rejected the Thaksin administration's request to allocate sufficient funds for travel and living allowances for nearly 1,000 Thai troops in Iraq, the Bush administration covered the expenses (Crispin and Wagstaff 2003, 26).

Thailand's participation in the US-led war on terror took shape in two ways: (1) quelling the armed Islamic insurgency in the southern provinces and (2) addressing the threat of drug trafficking and other forms of social ills that included political opposition members. The first objective referred to the publicly agreed policy expectations that the main and sole targets of state repression were the armed Islamic rebels in the southern provinces, many of whom were perceived as linked to Al Jemmayah al Islamiyah, the Al-Qaeda supported armed group that advocates the establishment of a pan–Southeast Asian Islamic caliphate. Second, what was notable during the post-9/11 period was the Thai government's expansion of the scope and magnitude of violent repression. Aiming to entrench the dominance of the TRT political party and his authority, Thaksin tagged various categories of civilians as "undesirable," making them targets of state violence. Those civilians included suspected drug traffickers, prostitutes, activists, and other political opposition members in the rural provinces. In addition, Thaksin branded them as "dark influences" who are suffering from endemic "social ills" (Dabhoiwala 2003; Kuhonta and Mutebi 2006; Mutebi 2004).

This localization of the global war on terror into the Thai war on drugs emerged from the partially converging interests and policy preferences of the Bush and Thaksin administrations. As early as December 2001, President Bush explicitly linked international terrorism to illegal drug trafficking (Associated Press 2001, 1): "If you quit drugs, you join the fight against terrorism. . . . And abroad, it's important for Americans to know that *trafficking of drugs finances the world of terror, sustaining terrorists*" (emphasis added). Similarly, the Thai government emphasized the illegal drug problem as the most important national security concern. As one of the most influential figures in the Thai national security establishment, retired general Teerawat Putamanonda told Thaksin during a national security meeting (held a month before Thaksin's visit to Washington, DC in late 2001): "Assistance from the US is necessary to combat narcotics. We have to think seriously about how to maintain such help" (The Nation—Thailand 2001a, 1). Because the US and Thai authorities recognized the "huge increase in use in methamphetamine stimulant tablets which Thais call *yaa baa* or crazy pills smuggled in from neighboring Burma" since the late 1990s, even the influential Thai king Bhumibol Adulyadej expressed his serious concerns and therefore "called on the government to take action" without compromising basic rights (Adams 2003, 1). Using the US war on terror as a pretext, Thaksin, at a meeting with other high-ranking government officials in mid-January 2003, "spoke of the necessity to eradicate drug traffickers as a matter of national security" (Connors 2011, 209).

Although the US State Department criticized Thaksin's 2003 war on drugs in its annual human rights report, the White House refrained from publicly criticizing Thaksin and the Thai armed forces. Immediately after launching the "war on drugs," Thaksin made an official state visit to the White House in June 2003. During this visit, "President Bush did not publicly mention extra-judicial killings, instead praising the campaign's success" and it momentarily appeared in the international media that the US government was "willing to ignore Thailand's human rights record in return for closer cooperation against terrorism and Iraq" (Chambers 2004, 472). Bush referred to the war on drugs as Thailand's version of an effective counterterror strategy, thereby contending that Thailand's connection to Southeast Asian Islamic terrorism was strongly linked to illegal drugs. That claim emerged amid a lack of convincing evidence that illegal drugs and terrorism were directly linked. Bush acknowledged Thailand as the foremost regional model in the global war on terror, in referring to the intensified collaboration among Southeast Asian countries that was key to averting terror attacks and the detention of the key terrorists from the Jemmayah Islamiyah network (White House—Office of the Press Secretary 2003).

The most explicit admission from Thaksin about his cooperation with the Bush administration came only in 2003, or almost two years after the collaboration started. Perhaps the careful timing was due to two factors. First, the Thai government avoided immediately castigating "six million Thai-Muslims, a concentrated and key voting bloc for Thaksin's Thai Rak Thai party" (Chambers 2004, 467). In the view of Thaksin and his allies, the arrest of Hambali in 2003 was an opportune time to justify to the Muslim population that US-Thai counterterror cooperation was politically necessary. Second, this late admission lent some credibility to the 2003 war on drugs, which was carried out shortly after Thaksin's state visit to the White House. That was likely because "Thaksin cannot afford to miss the boat in the war on terror because he has regional leadership ambitions . . . with no visible threat to derail plans for a second term in office," considering that he was "preoccupied with raising his international profile and regional stature" (Pongsudhirak 2003b, 29). In particular, the Thai government reaped the benefits of assisting in the reconstruction of postwar Afghanistan and Iraq and gained some leverage in negotiating a Thai-US free trade area (Pongsudhirak 2003b, 29).

Yet transnational and domestic civil society networks demanded that the White House pressure Thaksin to comply with human rights norms. In response, in 2003, shortly after Thaksin's state visit to the United States, the White House sent "an official letter of reproach" that demanded an explanation for the killings (Chambers 2004, 472). Although the letter cited the US Leahy Amendment that could potentially undercut funding to Thai security forces due to its human rights abuses, US military aid was temporarily canceled only after the 2006 military coup, when Thaksin was removed from power. The US government pressured the Thaksin government to halt its abuses, not by openly criticizing the regime, but through the US Embassy in Bangkok (Simon 2003).

With the terror-oriented US foreign strategic support, Thaksin launched two types of counterinsurgency operations. The first referred to the war on "several intractable social ills" (Mutebi 2004). On January 28, 2003, Thaksin ratified a law that provided detailed guidelines on leading a "concerted effort of the nation to overcome drugs" (Mutebi 2004, 80). Although it only specified guidelines that primarily dealt with nonviolent approaches including educational programs and public awareness campaigns against illegal drugs, the law that authorized the war on drugs in 2003 suggested a much more ambitious goal (Shinawatra 2003, 2): "to quickly, consistently and permanently eradicate the spread of narcotic drugs and to overcome narcotic problems, which threaten the nation." In practice, the law permitted Thaksin's government to compel all police officers and soldiers to efficiently kill suspected illegal drug users and traffickers through the use of attractive financial compensation: "At three baht [US $0.07] per methamphetamine tablet seized, a government official can become a millionaire by upholding the law, instead of begging for kickbacks from the scum of society" (Dabhoiwala 2003; Human Rights Watch 2004a, 50). Thaksin characterized all suspected civilians involved in drug trafficking and use as having "intractable social ills." In effect, the Thai government provided its state agents permission to kill and to physically harass unarmed civilian suspects who were deemed as "social ills," consequently bolstering the capacities of the Thai armed forces and the police. Thaksin attempted to justify his US-funded war on drugs by borrowing statements from Phao Sriyanon, who was the former head of the Thai Royal Police Force and was known for leading numerous political assassinations in the 1950s (Human Rights Watch 2004b, 8; Chaloemtiarana 2007, 73):

There is nothing under the sun, which the Thai police cannot do, he says. Because drug traders are ruthless to our children, so being ruthless back to them is not a bad thing. It may be necessary to have casualties. . . . If there are deaths among traders, it's normal.

The second phase of Thaksin's war on terror was locally called the "war on dark influences." On May 21, 2003 the Thai government officially declared that a joint police-military campaign would be launched against "some 15 types of criminal activity: the drug trade, influence peddling to fix [the] outcome of bidding contests, extortion at factories, illegal control of motorcycle taxis and other vehicles for hire, oil and goods smuggling, gambling dens and underground lottery rackets, trafficking in women and children, job scams, smuggling of laborers, tourism scams, hired gunmen, forced debt collection, illegal arms trade, and illegal encroachment on public land" (Mutebi 2004, 81). Thaksin made frequent trips within the country during this campaign against "dark influences," while promising rural Thai citizens a "country safe from corruption, flooding, drought, poverty, drugs, and other 'dark forces' within six years" (Mutebi 2004, 81).

Thaksin ignored all the human rights reforms introduced in the 1990s and vigorously "called for law enforcement to be conducted on the basis of an 'eye for an eye'" (Adams 2003, 1). A few months before the official launch of the 2003 war on drugs, Thailand's interior minister, Wan Muhamad Noor Matha, warned anybody who was involved in illegal drugs, regardless of the nature of their engagement, that "they will be put behind bars or even vanish without a trace. Who cares? They are destroying our country" (Adams 2003, 1). The Thai government characterized illegal drug use and trafficking as the root cause of all other problems associated with it, such as "armed insurgency near border areas, illegal arms trade, vehicle stealing, illegal labour trade, terrorism, and transnational organized crime" (Office of the Narcotics Control Board, Justice Ministry of Thailand 2003, 30). These statements showed how the Thai government strategically persuaded the Thai public by harping on two important messages: (1) anybody who was involved in illegal drugs deserved to be killed by the state and that (2) the drug problem in the country was directly linked to terrorism and other problems that destabilize national security.

Several Thai government officials used various sorts of discursive excuses amid criticisms pertaining to abuses of state power. For instance, Thai police commissioner General Sant Suranont contended that the "police would only fire in self-defense" (Mutebi 2004, 80). Similarly, Thai interior minister Wan Mohamad Noor Matha supported that stance when he claimed that the "the police would abide by the law in their campaign against drug trafficking" (Mutebi 2004, 80). Emphasizing the severity of the problem, Thai defense minister Thamarak Isarankula persistently defended the killings: "some three million people are methamphetamine-abusers, 5 per cent of the population. If we allow the situation to continue, we may end up a nation of crazy people" (The Nation—Thailand 2003a, 1). Responding to UN criticisms of Thaksin's human rights record, a Thai foreign ministry spokesperson declared to the media: "We want the international community to see our side of the story. It's necessary for the government to take decisive action to deal with the drug problem" (Dabhoiwala 2003, 16). In response, Thaksin derisively asserted that "the United Nations is not my father" (Dabhoiwala 2003). Rejecting allegations that he designed the counterinsurgency operations in order to gain the respect of Thai elites and the US government, Thaksin urged his critics to be more reasonable: "Just imagine terrorists bombing the houses of people who oppose the decrees and let's see what they make of that. . . . The government has issued the laws constitutionally" (Asian Tribune 2003).

Attempting to satisfy his critics, Thaksin established two independent committees that sought to ensure that the rule of law would be observed during counterinsurgency operations, but its members did not receive compliance reports from police and military officials (Cheesman 2003). Nonetheless, Thaksin warned that "critics of the campaign should now direct their empathy to our children who are victims of the drug menace, instead of sounding the alarm for falling traffickers" (Cheesman 2003, 26). In the most extreme form of defending the killings, Thaksin justified that "summary execution is not an unusual fate for wicked people" (Phongpaichit 2004, 81). In response to the US State Department's human rights report highlighting the human costs of the war on drugs, the Thai government "claimed that many of the killings resulted from dealers fighting each other" (US Department of State 2004b, 7).

Thaksin's government justified its systemic disregard for human rights by framing increased state repression as necessary for efficiently wiping out all forms of "social ills," which included armed rebels, ordinary drug traffickers, and political opposition members. Hence, the post-9/11 Thai government "de-emphasized human rights and democratization, instead stating that Thai foreign policy would in future be 'business-driven.' The pragmatism-over-ideology approach seemed characteristic of a corporate CEO" (Chambers 2004, 464). This sense of policy pragmatism was translated into state-initiated extrajudicial killings and disappearances of suspected criminals and drug addicts, many of whom were just ordinary opposition activists. Toward the end of the multiphase, ten-month war on drugs, Thaksin proudly remarked that the campaign was a clear success and justified its purpose once again: "to maintain the strong communities and the strength of the people for the sustainability in overcoming the drug problem in every area throughout the country" (Human Rights Watch 2004a, 12).

Notably, criticisms of Thailand's counterinsurgency campaign and its human rights abuses were not absent. For instance, the government's human rights body, an agency founded during the 1990s, strongly criticized the Thaksin administration for its human rights abuses during the "war on drugs" and the "war on dark influences." Right after the two "wars" launched by Thaksin, Pradit Chareonthaitawee, the chief of Thailand's National Human Rights Commission, claimed that the Thai government was spearheading widespread human rights abuses and that, as a consequence, "people are living in fear all over the kingdom" (Adams 2003). Pradit also wrote highly critical reports of Thaksin's counterinsurgency operations to the UN Commissioner for Human Rights in February 2003. In response, Thaksin called Pradit "ugly" and "sickening." Pradit received serious threats of impeachment from Thaksin's Thai Rak Thai party as well as anonymous phone calls from Thaksin's staff who warned Pradit to "stop speaking to the United Nations or die" (Human Rights Watch 2004a, 21). Pradit criticized the Thaksin administration and its US-supported war on drugs for Thailand's failed bid to win its candidacy for the UN Human Rights Council.

The Thaksin administration usually ignored criticisms from established political figures. One of the most prominent critics of Thaksin's repressive policies was Chuan Leekpai—the leader of the Democrat Party and the long-standing prime minister who spearheaded the human rights reforms in the 1990s. He reminded Thaksin that the legal and nonviolent measures were needed to counter the illegal drug problem (Connors 2011, 112):

> Our country is governed by a democracy not a dictatorship or tyranny.... It is true that in some cases ... people have disgust towards drug traffickers because they are a source of much evil in society, but there is no exception to allow arbitrary processes above the law. Legal powers are capable of handling such people. Even though it may be slow ... it is a guarantee for the innocent.

Similarly, the UN and international drug experts condemned Thaksin's war on drugs. These international actors suggested instead focusing on "supply reduction strategies." Particularly, these international actors, together with other US-based organizations such as Human Rights Watch, highlighted the need to "focus on its own military and police, many of whose members allegedly profit greatly from facilitating the smuggling chain from Burma" (Adams 2003, 1). Even prominent public intellectuals in Bangkok resisted Thaksin's localized version of the war on terror. Surapol Nitikraipoj, an influential legal scholar from Bangkok's Thammasat University, criticized how Thaksin's wars were demonstrative of an authoritarian-style leadership: "The country is just too big to be governed by a lone individual or 36 people" (Asian Tribune 2003). Various civil society groups representing rehabilitated drugs users, many of whom benefitted from USAID-funded programs in the 1990s, critically spoke against the war on drugs. For example, the leader of the Thai Drug Users' Network, Paisan Suwannawong, maintained that the drug problem should be considered an issue of public health rather than a problem of crime (Human Rights Watch 2004a):

> We are part of the solution, not the problem. . . . Yet as long as we are seen as criminals in the eyes of our political leaders and communities, we can never be healthy.

In sum, Thaksin's version of the war on terror was carried out amid widespread discourses of opposition both from international and domestic actors, including the US State Department. The overarching theme of anti-Thaksin discourses pertained to the detrimental consequences of the counterinsurgency operations to the Thai state's human rights commitments. Thus, Somchai Homlaor, a long-time human rights advocate in Thailand, rightly observed that "in many provinces, there are death squads roaming around killing drug dealers," and because of that "the rule of law and democracy could disappear overnight" (Human Rights Watch 2004a, 3). Even recovering drug addicts expressed their fears of Thaksin's repressive policies. For instance, 26-year-old Odd Thanunchai from Chiang Mai lamented: "Why do you have to kill people? It's better to help drug users find ways to change their behavior instead of killing them. There are not enough graves to bury us all" (Human Rights Watch 2004a, 1).

Thaksin's effective public diplomacy on the drug problem and the successful discursive linkage of illegal drugs with international terrorism provided some semblance of credibility to the counterinsurgency operations during this time. Thaksin and his allies characterized the conflict in southern Thailand as the "product of underworld collusion (illegal drug traffickers)" (Askew 2007, 9). As a victim himself of death threats from drug kingpins, who were more supportive of the political opposition, Thaksin maintained that illegal "drug trade and smuggling is linked to the financing of terrorist activities, creating a relationship between terrorists and drug groups operating out of southern Thailand" (Cheow 2003, 12).

Despite the human rights crisis, many Thais believed that illegal drugs had to be combatted using state violence. Preliminary surveys conducted by independent Bangkok-based opinion polling agencies revealed that "90 percent of the public supported the crackdown, even though 40 percent said they were afraid of being falsely accused, and 30 percent said they were afraid of being killed" (Mydans 2003, 16). Similarly, a 2003 survey conducted by the Bangkok-based Assumption University academics found that 84.2 percent of people living in Bangkok wholeheartedly supported the war on drugs, yet "of those same people, 65.3 percent expressed their fear that corrupt police could frame-up innocent people" (Ilchmann 2003, 9). It was likely that the overwhelming public belief that illegal drug use constituted a national security problem helped Thaksin in deflecting criticism from opposition politicians and human rights defenders. Remarkably, "Thaksin's political party . . . believes that Thaksin's tough line will even win votes in other, strongly nationalist, parts of the country that regard southerners as habitual troublemakers" (Cumming-Bruce 2004, 11). Thaksin's discursive association of the domestic terror problem with the post-9/11 international terror threats was amplified by the preexisting yet dominant stereotype among many Thais that Muslims in the south undermine political stability and social order.

Resource Mobilization: US Counterterror Assistance and the Expansion of the Thai Armed Forces' Activities

How did terror-oriented political discourses from the Bush and Thaksin administrations manifest in domestic policies and foreign aid programs? How did the changes in discourses transform the Thai state's security apparatus and the patterns of domestic repression? The terror-oriented strategic support from the US government provided the impetus for Thaksin's government to channel unprecedented amounts of material resources and political support to the Thai armed forces and police agencies. These resources were necessary to carry out the killings, torture, and enforced disappearances—all of which generated the human rights abuses in Thailand after late 2001.

After promoting political discourses that sought to justify Thailand's role in the war on terror, the Bush administration provided Thaksin's government enormous amounts of counterterror financial assistance and other forms of military assistance. The US government granted wide administrative discretion to the Thai government, particularly in the identification of targets of domestic repression as well as in the spending strategy concerning counterterror aid. Despite the abuses of the Thai armed forces since 2001, Bush "in a press conference before the Asia-Pacific Economic Cooperation meeting in Bangkok months after Hambali's arrest referred to Thai special branch counterterrorism chief General Tritos Ranaridhvichai as 'my hero' for his role in the sting operation" (Crispin 2008, 4). The US government was much more concerned with the goal of capturing terror suspects, even if a militaristic approach systematically undermined the US commitment to push its partner countries for strong human rights protection.

Administrative discretion in the use of terror-oriented US aid was given in exchange for Thailand's contribution to the advancement of the post-9/11 strategic interests of the US government. The Bush administration asked the Thai government to regularly cooperate with the US authorities in capturing the members of key Al-Qaeda linked terror groups based in mainland Southeast Asia, particularly by providing intelligence regarding the whereabouts of the key Al-Qaeda leaders and other terror groups (White House—Office of the Press Secretary 2003). Bush asked Thaksin, in late 2001, to allow the CIA to bring Al-Qaeda suspects from Thailand to the United States, to use Thai military bases for the wars in Iraq and Afghanistan, and for Thailand to participate in "Pentagon's new strategy of 'forward positioning,' establishing sites where American forces can store equipment and from which they can come and go as needed" (Bonner 2003, 8). The White House compelled the Thaksin administration to persuade other ASEAN leaders to engage in US-led multilateral counterterror intelligence sharing and other forms of military training. One of the landmark initiatives involving Bangkok and Washington was the Container Security Initiative, an agreement signed by Tom Ridge, the US secretary of homeland security, and Surakiart Sathirathai, the Thai foreign affairs minister. The aim of the initiative was to protect commercial shipping against terrorists (White House—Office of the Press Secretary 2003). The US government dramatically increased the number of training programs, whereby Thai police and military officers learned the latest and most advanced counterterror techniques. Many Thai military and police officers benefited from US counterterror training and assistance programs through the International Military Education and Training program, the Foreign Military Financing program, and Foreign Military Sales, all of which increased their program budgets after 2001 (Lohman 2011, 3). US foreign strategic assistance facilitated the participation of Thai officials and state agents in the Pentagon's Counter Terrorism Fellowship Program, which aimed to bolster the interagency approach of counterterror efforts (US Department of State 2004c, 81–87). In exchange for those benefits, the US government sought guarantees from Thaksin that the Thai government would not turn over any US citizens suspected of war crimes to The Hague–based International Criminal Court and that the US military would be able to store their equipment and launch operations in Thailand (Phongpaichit 2004, 83).

The post-9/11 US-Thailand bilateral cooperation was indeed a two-way street, whereby the Thai government gained a certain level of political legitimacy and substantial military resources in exchange for its counterterror assistance to the US government. US-Thailand foreign relations after 9/11 adopted a quid pro quo approach (Chambers 2004, 476):

A new era of strengthened Thai-U.S. relations has begun. Each country wants something from the other. For the United States, Thailand offers military facilities, token troops, and moral support in Washington's foreign policy endeavors. A close alliance with America offers Thailand a fast track to closer economic ties, the transfer of resources to the state, and assistance against Thai Muslim insurgents.

One of the most controversial post-9/11 bilateral initiatives was the establishment in late 2001 of the US-funded Counterterrorism Intelligence Center based in Bangkok (Crispin 2008). Remarkably, around "20 CIA officials are attached to the unit, which has received between $10 million and $15 million in U.S. funding" since late 2001 for personnel and equipment expenses (Lopez and Crispin 2003, 8). The Counterterrorism Intelligence Center enabled efficient and reliable intelligence sharing among the US, Thai, and other Southeast Asian government authorities in pursuit of armed terrorists linked to Al-Qaeda. This made Thailand the regional hub for all major US intelligence operations, and it also boosted the Thai armed forces' access to technologies and other counterterror equipment from the United States. The US embassy in Thailand is one of the five largest diplomatic missions of the United States, both in terms of the size of the building and the number of personnel. In late 2001, the CIA and the Drug Enforcement Administration began using "Thailand as a base from which to monitor neighboring countries such as Burma, Laos and Cambodia" (Lopez and Crispin 2003). The Counterterrorism Intelligence Center included three main Thai security agencies—the National Intelligence Agency, the Special Branch of the Thai police, and the elite Armed Forces Security Center—and those three agencies depended heavily on the CIA for strategy, funds, and logistics. The post-9/11 US-Thai cooperation demonstrated that "nowhere else in Southeast Asia are U.S. intelligence officials working as closely on the ground with a host government on matters of counterterrorism and intelligence" (Lopez and Crispin 2003, 3).

Critics of US counterterror assistance to Bangkok also harped on the intensity of the engagement of US armed forces with Thaksin's war on drugs. In late 2001, the US military already had been "training Task Force 399, a combined force of army personnel and border police, to fight drug trafficking along borders" (The Nation—Thailand 2001, 1; Chambers 2004, 464). Twenty instructors from the US Special Forces 1st Group assisted and led the 200 Task Force 399 officers, who came from the Thai Special Forces and the Thai Border Patrol Police based in Mae Rim (Chiang Mai). A leading historian of drug trafficking, Pierre Arnoud Chouvy (2010, 112), observed that "as it does elsewhere to support its global war on drugs and terror, the United States not only offered technical and financial aid to Thailand's counter-narcotics programme but also directly improved the drug interdiction capacity of the Thai military by providing it with military equipment." The US government provided the Thai armed forces with state-of-the-art surveillance technologies, combat equipment, Black Hawk helicopters, and night-vision goggles (Montlake 2002).

Thaksin redirected such US foreign strategic support to the state security establishment for counterterror operations. Bangkok "launched an aggressive counterinsurgency campaign expending 63 million USD, almost half of all US aid to Thailand, to expand the police from fifty-one thousand officers armed with M-16 rifles and an armada of thirty-seven helicopters" (McCoy 2009, 537). Those resources contributed to the perpetration of Thaksin's domestic insurgency campaign against Islamic armed rebels in the south and other unarmed targets during the 2003 war on drugs.

Besides foreign aid, the US armed forces had varying degrees of involvement in the Thai military and police forces' commission of human rights violations. The Bush administration influenced Thai politicians to legislate counterterror laws, an effort that resulted in the enactment of Thaksin-sponsored laws that made the war on drugs and "dark influences" possible. In July 2004, "US Secretary of State Colin Powell visited Bangkok to thank Thailand for its backing of Washington's global anti-terror campaign but also to gauge the level of Thaksin's continued commitment and press for full passage of the anti-terrorism bills" (Chambers 2004, 467). In 2003, the Thaksin government invoked national security and unilaterally pressed for new counterterrorism laws through executive decree, thereby bypassing legislative approval (Crispin and Wagstaff 2003, 8). That move was controversial to the extent that the executive branch dramatically changed the criminal codes without any involvement from the elected legislative members. Yet that initiative was resisted by various politicians, legal scholars, and human rights activists, all of whom feared that the Thai administration might use those laws for its own political gains rather than reasons directly related to public security. As the Law Society of Thailand official Danai Anantiyo argued, "the new laws violate the Thai constitution" as they "make it easier for the government to curb people's freedoms" (Crispin and Wagstaff 2003, 9).

All joint military exercises between armed forces units of the United States and Thailand "focused on counterterrorism techniques rather than conventional warfare" for the first time since the end of the Cold War (Lopez and Crispin 2003, 16). This was the case with the COBRA Gold Thai-US military exercises that started in the 1990s. Whereas the focus before 9/11 was on peacekeeping and other civilian development functions of the military, post-9/11 COBRA Gold training shifted to counterterrorism, whereby surveillance, torture, and interrogation techniques in a rural-based counterinsurgency context became its prominent qualities (Simon 2003). From 2002 until 2006, "several U.S. agencies, such as the Drug Enforcement Administration, the CIA and the military use[d] Thailand as a base from which to monitor neighboring countries such as Burma, Laos and Cambodia" (Simon 2003). Moreover, American officers and high-tech equipment from the United States facilitated, albeit covertly, the implementation of increased state repression in Thailand after 2001. As Crispin and Wagstaff (2003, 16) reported, "Thai counter-terrorism and U.S. Federal Bureau of Investigation agents were on occasion at loggerheads, as senior Thai officials complained that their U.S. counterparts were pushing them to arrest and interrogate terror suspects in ways that violated civil liberties protected under Thai law." Those instances most likely contributed to the perception that "the US is driving Thai policy, with greater emphasis on security and less on democracy" (Crispin and Wagstaff 2003, 18).

There were other ways in which the US government had left its mark on the armed insurgency in the southern provinces of the Pattani region. For instance, "rights advocates monitoring southern Thailand's conflict note a striking similarity between the torture techniques US agents are known to have used against terror suspects held in both Iraq and Guantanamo Bay,

Cuba with those now in practice by Thai security forces against suspected Thai Muslim militants" (Crispin 2008, 5). Thus, Thai forces deliberately adopted American war techniques and practices that they learned during bilateral counterterror exercises. The audacity of Thai state agents to deviate from their human rights obligations intensified especially after Thaksin explicitly "instructed police and local officials that persons charged with drug offenses should be considered 'security threats' and dealt with in a 'ruthless' and 'severe'" manner" (Human Rights Watch 2004a, 1–3). The systematic identification, harassment, detainment, and eventual killing of drug suspects or "dark influences" initially started with "blacklists" or "watch lists." Many pro-Thaksin provincial politicians registered the names of their local political enemies on such lists and implicated such enemies as somehow involved in illegal drugs even in the absence of credible evidence.

The aim was not only to consolidate a given local politician's legitimacy, but also to strengthen the TRT party's political power at the national scale (Human Rights Watch 2004a). Using US military aid, Thaksin's government provided hefty amounts of money to motivate state agents to kill as many suspected drug dealers and political enemies as possible. For each methamphetamine tablet seized, Thai police officers were awarded around 3 Thai baht (USD 0.7). Thaksin also resorted to several nonviolent strategies of political coalition building. The TRT party absorbed several smaller opposition parties through financial incentives and political compromises. Consequently, this measure solidified Thaksin's political control of the House of Representatives. In effect, the TRT party members in the legislative branch pushed for counterterror laws that were left unopposed, while securing a reliable political coalition and policy continuity during Thaksin's tenure (Mutebi 2003, 101).

In late 2003, Thaksin officially reported that the wars on drugs and on "dark influences" constituted a "victory" and "presented cash awards to agencies and officials who had taken part in the campaign" (Human Rights Watch 2004a, 12). The reward ranged from 50,000 Thai baht to 100,000 Thai baht (US$1,275 to $2,550) for each official "who had been injured in the course of combating the drug trade and children of those killed in the campaign" (Human Rights Watch 2004a, 29). Police officers and state security agents who turned in a "major drug dealer into government custody—'dead or alive'—received a bounty of one million baht (23,600 USD)" (Ilchmann 2003). The interior minister of Thailand threatened local elected authorities and police officers that their political careers would be jeopardized if they failed to produce the intended results for Thaksin's administration. The US State Department (2004d, 6; see also 2004b) reported that Thailand's Interior Ministry played a leading role in forcing local authorities to create their own lists of targets for the war on drugs:

> Instructed local authorities to update "blacklists" of individuals suspected of being involved in illegal drug trafficking, sale, or use and the Prime Minister told the governors and provincial police that those who failed to eliminate a prescribed percentage of the names from their "blacklists," would be fired. The Government threatened retaliation against local officials who did not produce results.

Thaksin expanded his executive powers by restructuring the bureaucratic apparatus. The goal was to efficiently facilitate interagency cooperation in the context of the war on drugs and counterterror operations, thereby making all agencies directly accountable to Thaksin's executive office. The other goal was to make all the key leaders of Thailand's national security agencies personally accountable to Thaksin. That bureaucratic restructuring within the Thai state apparatus facilitated the reorientation of the military leadership's loyalty toward Thaksin (Kocak and Kode 2014, 91). Thaksin politicized the military by only promoting his closest allies and by reclassifying strategic units under his own personal command. The restructuring began in October 2002, when the new fiscal budgeting year commenced in the Thai fiscal calendar. During this time, two important laws were ratified, the Bureaucratic Restructuring and the National Administration Acts, "collectively billed as Thailand's biggest bureaucratic shakeup in more than a century" (Mutebi 2003, 107). Thaksin considered this bureaucratic restructuring the "big bang" of Thai state politics (Painter 2006, 39). Six new ministerial offices and several other departments were created, with many civil servant positions filled by retired high-ranking military officers and active officers who had close relations with Thaksin. For instance, General Chaisit Shinawatra, Thaksin's cousin, was appointed as the army chief in 2003, while another close relative, General Uthai Shinawatra, became the permanent defense secretary. Many other former classmates and friends of Thaksin in the police academy were appointed to key ministerial agencies, which were normally headed by an experienced civilian bureaucrat. Perhaps an even more blatant example that showed this unprecedented scale of bureaucratic reshuffling was the appointment of Thaksin's brother-in-law to the much-coveted position of assistant police chief, thereby bypassing 14 other more senior police leaders (McCargo

2005, 229). In effect, Thaksin intervened in "the army's internal affairs by promoting his loyalists, two of whom were his own relatives, to key military posts" (McCargo and Pathmanand 2005, 147). Another vivid example of how Thaksin and his allies repoliticized the military is the appointment of Chaisit Shinawatra as an army commander in 2003, the same year the war on drugs and the human rights crisis were at their peak.

The proliferation of cronies in key government and military posts "undermined the professionalism and neutrality among Thai soldiers" (Chachavalpongpun 2011a, 46). Thus, Thaksin not only interfered with the seniority norm of the armed forces by appointing his relatives and allies to top positions, but "also aimed at bringing strategic units under his personal command" (Kocak and Kode 2014, 91). In effect, Thaksin gained a unique advantage in efficiently leading the military and police in the counterterror operations, thereby swiftly killing and harassing armed and unarmed political opponents of the TRT party. These examples of politicization of the military and police agencies showed that Thaksin "increased his scope for patronage politics and maneuvered his supporters into key government positions, perhaps to further his stated aim of ruling for four consecutive terms—16 years" (Mutebi 2004, 107). In effect, the Thai state effectively became more militaristic and beholden to the political whims of the TRT party and Thaksin.

One of the key reasons why it was viable for Thaksin's political coalition to expand the scope of state violence was because of the dual-level support he received at the domestic and international levels. Thaksin and his Thai Rak Thai party secured domestic support for expanded counterterror efforts against armed rebels and suspected criminals from important sectors in the Thai polity (Mydans 2003). Moreover, Thaksin won the conditional support of the Thai monarchy. This was the case especially for King Bhumibol, who was not supportive of Thaksin's populist politics, but was still very much in favor of increased US support for counterinsurgency in the southern provinces. By promising financial incentives to local politicians and police officers in exchange for support in the war on drugs, Thaksin also secured the political loyalties of these important local political actors. Because of the predominantly Buddhist majority of the Thai population, many were keen on supporting sustained military operations in the Muslim rebel-controlled Pattani region.

Despite the rapid economic development of Thailand in the past decades, the Thai armed forces still had to rely to the US government for military assistance (Kislenko 2004). This was for two key reasons. First, there were enduring personal and institutional links between the

Thai armed forces and the US government, starting in the years imme-diately after World War II. Many high-ranking military and police offi-cers received advanced training from US military training institutions, and even Thaksin, a former police officer, holds a PhD in criminal justice from a US university. These ties created the entrenched expectation among the Thai national security elites that the United States is a reliable ally. Of course, the 1954 Mutual Defense Treaty (through the 1954 Manila Pact of the former Southeast Asian Treaty Organization) between Thailand and the United States reinforced these institutional ties. This institutional dependency of the Thai armed forces on the US government reinforced the belief among Thai political elites that its armed forces agencies have heavily depended on US assistance. Second, because the US government repackaged its military assistance from a conventional warfare focus (pre-9/11) to an internal domestic counterinsurgency approach (post-9/11), the Thai government easily channeled counterterror resources to the armed operations that targeted drug traffickers and armed rebels, both of which were branded as terrorists. Without US counterterror assistance, the unprecedented scale of expansion of the Thai armed forces' counterter-ror operations after 2001 would have been relatively difficult. As the US State Department acknowledged in 2006, US government aid to Thailand "strengthens Thailand's efforts to combat terrorism, narcotics trafficking and other international crime, and reinforces military cooperation" and the various Foreign Military Financing programs of the Pentagon "boosted the counterterrorism capabilities of Thailand's Special Forces units" (Lum 2007, 24). Thus, the influx of terror-oriented resources from the United States to Thailand exhibited how "American advisers and Thai autocrats converged in their commitment to building a powerful police force that was mobile, lethal, and amplified with civilian auxiliaries" (McCoy 2009, 537). With US foreign strategic support, Thaksin and his allies deployed state violence against many forms of political opposition.

Intervening Factors: The US-Led War on Terror and Domestic Politics

Why did Thaksin and his political allies decide to target both armed Islamic rebels in the south and suspected drug users for extrajudicial kill-ings? What was Thaksin's motivation for including suspected drug users and political opposition members, composed mostly of civilians, as targets for violent repression? The influx of terror-oriented US strategic support to the Thai government reinforced Thaksin's preexisting motivations to consolidate his political rule and legitimacy in the face of pervasive public insecurity in Thailand. By joining the US-led war on terror, Thaksin and his political allies considered increased state repression as a powerful display of authority that would secure the support of Thailand's traditional elites, who were keen on violently addressing the armed insurgency problem in southern Thailand. These elites included the Thai monarchy and the "royalist elites, sections of the military and many middle-class Bangkokians" (Ünaldi 2014, 8). Many Bangkok-based elites were generally hostile to Thaksin's populist politics, which included "promised programmes such as 1 million baht (US$22,700) in revolving loans for each village, 30 baht (67 cents) medical visits, a People's Bank extending loans of up to 15,000 baht collateral-free, a 'one *tambon* (sub-district) one product' scheme for increasing rural production, and a three-year moratorium on farmers' debt repayment to the state Bank for Agriculture and Agricultural Co-operatives" (Funston 2002, 306).

Shortly before 9/11, Thaksin and his allies strategically consolidated their populist base by casting the Democrat Party as elitist, while Thaksin's TRT "came to power promising a war on drugs, and the establishment of a new 'moral order'" (The Nation—Thailand 2001b, 322; Mutebi 2004, 83). Thaksin's intention of entrenching the long-term dominance of his political party preexisted the influx of post-9/11 US strategic support. In early 2001, Thaksin confided that "Thailand was moving towards a two-party system," with his TRT party and the Democrat Party as the two major players (McCargo and Pathmanand 2005, 84). On other occasions, Thaksin confessed that his envisioned "one-party rule is necessary in order to achieve a great leap forward of economic growth into first world status" (Phongpaichit 2004, 4). During its first two years in power, the Thaksin administration prioritized the "neutralization of domestic challenges and the consolidation of Thaksin's political power base within the Thai polity" (Panaspornprasit 2004, 258). Thaksin and the TRT party implemented various policies that were seen as directly appealing to the interests of the rural population—a strategy that was in marked contrast with previous traditional Thai politicians who were generally focused on appeasing the Thai monarchy and the middle class in Bangkok. These policies included a "rural debt moratorium, the revolving village fund, and the 30-baht healthcare system (per hospital visit), Think Anew and Act Anew was again put into practice by his declaration of wars on drugs, poverty, shanty towns, and illiteracy" (Panaspornprasit 2004, 257). Thaksin also aimed to solidify his rule over the rural Thai population through the consolidation of political parties under his party coalition and projection of a "soft authoritarian image tempered by a populist touch" (Chambers 2004, 86).

Thaksin's long-term strategy was to build a one-party "developmental state" in Thailand, similar to that in Singapore (Pongsudhirak 2003a, 288). To lay the groundwork for an eventual one-party state, Thaksin and his political allies aimed at narrowing the space for political competition in Thailand by enticing other smaller parties to join the TRT, by restricting media coverage of the opposition, and by the blatant corruption of its senior government officials (Cotton 2003, 163). In 2004, Thaksin "openly declared that his TRT ruling party will remain in power for the next twenty years" (Bangkok Post 2003, 1). It is clear that Thaksin and his TRT party's strategy was to secure their long-term political dominance over all of Thailand. As Thithinan Pongsudhirak (2003a, 278) rightly described it, the "TRT has monopolized the party system, marginalized the opposition, co-opted and coerced the media, extended its controlling tentacles over the military and the police, and shunned the dissenting voices of civil society groups." It is unsurprising that Thaksin had openly articulated his high regard for well-known authoritarian leaders in the region: Malaysia's Mahathir Muhammad and Singapore's Lee Kuan Yew (Phongpaichit 2004, 2).

Domestic party politics played a crucial role in why Thaksin reframed Pattani, in southern Thailand, as the hotspot of US-funded counterterror operations in the country. Thaksin's TRT party aimed to win the political support of the upper southern provinces that were under the political control of the Democrat Party (McCargo 2008, 9). Particularly, Thaksin became prime minister in 2001 with his TRT party's main bulk of support concentrated in the northern provinces. The power vacuum in the south and the need to eliminate the Democrat Party's dominance in the upper south motivated Thaksin to institute policies that appeared to be in the best interest of the southern regions, including Pattani.

Consequently, Thaksin's government attempted to capture southern Thailand as a potential TRT stronghold mainly through implementing two key policies, which were crucial components of the US-led war on terror in Thailand (Jitpiromrsi and McCargo 2008; McCargo 2008; Wheeler 2010). First, in mid-2002 Thaksin abolished the Southern Border Provinces Administrative Centre (SBPAC), an agency established in 1981 that had a reputation for achieving "a degree of success in building confidence in the Thai state among local Malay Muslim leaders" (Wheeler 2010, 208). As the civilian agency that sought to coordinate civil society and government work on peace and development, the SBPAC was crucial in maintaining the relative peace in the south until its eventual dissolution in 2002. By dissolving the SBPAC, regular police forces, headed by Thaksin-appointed commanders, took over the provincial administration of the southern region (Gunaratna and Acharya 2013). Second, amid increasing violence between armed rebels and government forces, Thai armed forces' agents and police officers sought to obliterate Pattani-based supporters of the Democrat Party and the Royal Thai monarchy. As such, "senior police officers loyal to Thaksin moved to eliminate former separatists who had long served as key informants for military intelligence, sometimes under the cover of the controversial 2003 war on drugs, an officially sanctioned policy of extrajudicial murder" (McCargo 2008, 9). These two policies reflected a carefully designed political strategy that sought to consolidate Thaksin's political legitimacy and the long-term dominance of the TRT party, especially in the southern provinces.

There were two reasons why the Thai state security apparatus cooperated with Thaksin on his counterterror agenda. First, many rank-and-file police and military agents considered the financial incentives for each recorded killing of terrorists and drug addicts as attractive incentives. Second, for high-ranking state security officials, the influx of post-9/11 military aid and the redirection of domestic state resources to counterterrorism enabled Thaksin to lure military and police generals in cementing the dominance of the TRT party in exchange for financial and professional incentives. In an effort to expand his influence within the national security establishment, Thaksin employed "inactive senior officers as advisers" (Funston 2002, 312; Chachavalpongpun 2011a, 49). Around 500 officers applied, but only 53 got a position. Their functions were "never spelt-out," except for helping the elected governors of each province to become "CEOs." Thaksin's "CEO-oriented" paradigm to public governance, in reality, compels all elected governors to be directly accountable to the prime minister (as the CEO). During Thaksin's time, the "military involvement in commercial enterprises declined markedly" because financial rewards primarily came from Thaksin's control over military financing, with preferential support for those who are loyal to him (Chambers and Waitoolkiat 2017, 53).

Thaksin's counterterror strategy empowered some factions of the Thai armed forces that were willing to implement Thaksin's repressive policies. This means that Thaksin systematically undermined the royalist factions within the Thai armed forces, which were primarily led by General Prem Tinsulanonda (McCargo 2005, 499). This military faction was part of the larger network of elites and bureaucrats who were loyal to the Thai king, Bhumibol Adulyadev (Ivarsson and Isager 2010). The military's co-optation by Thaksin's counterterror plan liberated many of the state security agents from "the barracks," which consequently gave them more freedom in intervening in civilian politics. This was an opportunity for high-ranking military and police leaders to regain their political influence, which had been lost since the 1990s, when the democratic and human rights reforms were first introduced. This post-9/11 phenomenon of the civilian government's co-optation of the military was what analysts of Thai politics called the "Thaksinization of the military" (Chachavalpongpun 2011a, 46). By appointing antiroyalist and pro-Thaksin officers to top offices in the national security agencies, Thaksin was able to cement his political legitimacy within the Thai armed forces. The loyalty of these pro-Thaksin officers was crucial to the post-9/11 counterterror operations. For example, Thaksin relied on a group of trusted police officers who were delegated to combat his so-called dark influences (McCargo and Pathmanand 2005, 228–30). One of Thaksin's cohort mates from Thai Police Cadet Academy Class 26, Police major general Surasit Sangkapong—a crucial Thaksin ally—assumed his post as the commissioner of the Crime Suppression Division and implemented "silent killings" (*kha tat ton*), which led to several thousand civilian deaths in the context of the war on drugs.

In effect, Thaksin had "deflected the possibility of being forced out of office by coups, a recurrent feature of Thai politics in the 1970s" (Ganesan 2004, 26–27). In return, the Thai armed forces and police agencies regained their power and influence in civilian politics in exchange for killing and harassing the political enemies of Thaksin and the TRT party. That mutually beneficial deal between Thaksin and his TRT party vis-à-vis the Thai armed forces was not the mere outcome of the self-interested motivations of Thaksin and his allies in the TRT party vis-à-vis the military officers in order to consolidate their long-term political rule. Instead, the Thai armed forces' deep-seated institutional propensity to intervene in civilian politics, a behavioral tendency that was undermined in the 1990s, facilitated the easy co-optation of state security agencies by Thaksin's political coalition. Indeed, the institutional shortcomings of the Thai armed forces are well understood (McCargo 1997, 19):

> a bloated officer corps abounding in supernumerary colonels and generals; internal factional conflict; inter-service rivalry; lack of military competence; the fanciful world-view of military officers, based on crude Cold War paradigms; excessive politicization; a strong

propensity to stage coups; and, most importantly, a complete inability to recognize its own shortcomings.

The Thai armed forces' leadership has persistently intervened in civilian politics primarily because of its lack of "nationalist credentials drawn from a heroic independence struggle" (Chachavalpongpun 2011a, 47). The Thai military's absence of revolutionary credentials stood in contrast to other Southeast Asian countries, which typically had a long-standing colonial experience from which their current armed forces agencies emerged. The downfall of the Thai monarchy in 1932 established the Thai armed forces' self-perception as the protector of Thailand's public interests. Because Thailand generally did not have a compelling external threat (e.g., colonial power), the Thai armed forces zeroes in on internal security threats as a way of boosting its social legitimacy. The identification of domestic enemies was an arbitrary exercise, whereby the military picked and chose threats based on its invoked concept of nation-building and the temporal political interests of its high-ranking leaders (Chachavalpongpun 2005, 58–65). Staging a coup is a process through which the Thai military arbitrarily frames the ruling elected government as a security threat to Thailand's political stability (Chachavalpongpun 2011a, 47). Also, the Thai military gains its institutional legitimacy and pride from its historically rich relationship with the US government. During the Cold War, the US government "provided arms, money, and political support to a succession of military regimes in Thailand, and, in return, those governments backed American diplomacy and collaborated in a variety of military operations" (Fineman 1997, 1–3)

The influx of US terror-oriented aid provided the Thai armed forces a promising opportunity to reclaim its powerful influence in Thai politics by judiciously cooperating with the Thaksin's regime consolidation strategy. The relative ease with which the Thai armed forces acceded to Thaksin's counterterror agenda was reinforced by what Duncan McCargo (2002a, 123) called the "culture of over-promotion" and the proliferation of financial incentives after 2001. During the post-9/11 period, there were "somewhere around 1,400 serving generals in an armed forces whose total strength seems to number about 300,000—an absurd ratio of something like one general to every 215 troops" (McCargo 2002a, 123). Despite the reforms of the 1990s, the military to some extent "retained its old self-esteem, a strong grip on broadcast media, and a close association with the palace, while resenting the decline in its budget and public role" (Phongpaichit and Baker 2008a, 20). The Thai military's identification of its domestic enemies "was a rather arbitrary and superficial exercise, with the military picking its enemies according to the constantly changing concept of nation-building" (Chachavalpongpun 2005, 58–65). As Thaksin sought to justify widespread state repression in order to bolster national security, the Thai military cooperated in the hope of reinforcing its legitimacy in the eyes of the domestic public.

The enduring corruption within the Thai judicial system facilitated Thaksin's repressive policies and hindered the successful persecution of abusive police and military officers. The lack of judicial independence or autonomy within the Thai justice system made the courts very susceptible to external political pressures. This lack of autonomy provided viable opportunities for Thaksin's government and the armed forces to implement their repressive operations without the fear of judicial reprisal. This meant that state agents suspected of committing human rights abuses did not face prosecution in the courts. Thai judges often receive death threats right after they accepted cases that directly prosecuted erring police officers and soldiers.

Impunity is entrenched in the political culture of the judiciary and the state security establishment. Crucial to Thailand's state formation, impunity refers to "the persistent and repeated failure to secure accountability for state violence, has been produced by means of the intimidation of citizens, weak institutional structures, the unwillingness of state officials to find their colleagues responsible" (Haberkorn 2018, 4). The culture of accepting bribery or "tea money" persisted in many judicial proceedings. Some Thai military and police officers bribed courts to secure an acquittal or dismissal of a case filed against their officers and agents. Many human rights victims were hindered from filing a case against government agents because of their fear of retaliation and the lack of financial means to pay for lawyers. In a 2004 survey, around 30 percent of the respondents who went to court to file a case were asked to provide bribes, whereby the requested amounts "were about the same size than [as] the normal court costs" (Warsta 2004, 10). A middleman mediates between the courts and the prosecutors so that a direct interaction between opposing parties is avoided. Consequently, those who paid bribes were generally unsure if their "tea money" would have any effect on the final court decision. Despite the overwhelming protests against Thaksin's human rights practices, "courts and independent constitutional bodies were too intimidated by Thaksin's power and wealth to investigate him" (Head 2007, 25). This was because judges are often afraid of death threats from pro-Thaksin soldiers and police officers.

Patterns of Human Rights Violations in Post-9/11 Thailand

Selective Political Repression of
Thaksin's "Enemies of the State"

In contrast to human rights abuses generated by erroneous counterterror operations that generated collateral deaths and physical injuries, many Thai government agents deliberately harassed, and often systematically killed, unarmed political opposition members, anti-Thaksin activists, suspected criminals, drug addicts, and other civilians. Those cases constituted Thaksin's statewide policy that extensively implemented selective political repression, which targeted all forms of political dissidence.

The first but perhaps most important example of the Thai government's deliberate and systematic effort to kill and harass civilians was the "war on drugs" in 2003. US counterterror strategic assistance was crucial to curbing the long-standing illegal drug problem in Thailand. While the White House was only supportive of nonviolent policy measures (drug rehabilitation and awareness campaigns), the Thaksin administration included any suspected drug addict, dealer, or supporter of illegal drugs as targets of counterinsurgency operations. In the published guidelines of the Thai government, the emphasis was on educational programs and public awareness campaigns against the detrimental effects of illegal drugs. In practice, Thaksin's war on drugs concretely included the systematic identification and killing of anybody who was suspected of involvement in illegal drug trafficking and use in Thailand. With US strategic support, the Thai government used a "combination of incentives and warnings" in order "to have [the] police eliminate as many suspected drug dealers, by whatever means possible, within three months designated" (Dabhoiwala 2003, 2).

The Thai police, soldiers, and local government officials enjoyed wide administrative discretion in freely determining who the suspected drug addicts were, especially in the identification of suspected criminals and drug addicts. The identification process started with the provincial politicians, village chiefs, and provincial or town district officers who compiled a list of targets from their geographical areas of responsibility (Dabhoiwala 2003). This list was then submitted to the Interior Ministry, which in turn passed on the list for approval to the National Command Centre for Combatting Drugs, which was headed by Deputy Prime Minister Chavalit Yongchaiyuth, a Thaksin loyalist and a former commander-in-chief of the Royal Thai Army. This system of identifying the targets "left the door wide open for those compiling the blacklists to use them to settle personal grudges or deal with business or political opponents" (Ilchmann 2003, 9). The process of identifying the targets of violence was highly arbitrary to the extent that many pro-Thaksin local officials nominated the names of people unrelated to the drug trade, including their political enemies, as potential targets of violence (Human Rights Watch 2004a, 23).

To avoid incriminating state agents in human rights abuses, the Thai government did not allow forensic experts and pathologists to conduct autopsies, while bullets were reportedly removed from all the corpses (Amnesty International 2003b, 2003a). Based on an independent study by Pornthip Rohanasunan, Thailand's leading forensic scientist, in "more than half of the cases seen by her the drugs appeared to have been planted on the victims after their deaths—jammed in pockets at unnatural angles" (Dabhoiwala 2003, 13). Thai police and other government agents deliberately targeted the local enemies of Thaksin and his allies: "casually planting evidence, mistaken identity, incompetent coronary[*sic*] reports and bureaucratic bungling in the compilation of suspect lists (blacklists) used to target victims" (Connors 2011, 108). Even worse, some local witnesses confessed that some police officers made arrests even when urine tests indicated a negative result for drug use. For instance, Tai, one of these witnesses, admitted that the police officers unjustly exercised their powers (Human Rights Watch 2004a, 26):

> It looked like the police wanted to make arrests. Sometimes, the police just pick up kids on the road, and even if they test negative, they just take their money and cell phone and threaten them with arrest.

There were at least 2,000 recorded killings during the 2003 war on drugs, and one of the most well-known cases was the death of the nine-year-old boy, Chakraphan Srisa-ard (Mydans 2003). On March 2003, Thai police arrested the father of Chakraphan for allegedly trading 6,000 methamphetamine tablets, while Chakraphan and his mother fled their house in Bangkok for fear of harassment from the police. While escaping, Chakraphan, who sat in the back seat of the car, was killed by two bullets in his back. This incident was widely covered in local media outlets, where Chakraphan's uncle, Chlaermpol Kerdungruang, angrily protested to the police (Mydans 2003, 19):

> The war on drugs is getting more violent every day. The police kept shooting and shooting at the car. They wanted them to die. Even a child was not spared.

In reaction to the brutality of the police killing of a minor, Charan Pak-
dithanakul, secretary to the Thai Supreme Court, called for "stop[ping]
these bloodthirsty police officers" who were responsible for the killings
(Mydans 2003, 20). Charan also warned Thaksin and the US government that "an innocent boy killed downtown surely will affect the country's image, and if attempts are being made to twist the case, Thailand
will now become a twilight zone" (The Nation—Thailand 2003b, 14).
Likewise, a prominent legal scholar and Thammasat University law professor, Somkid Lerpaitoon, protested the determination of the killings as
a "kangaroo court situation." Somkid also warned Thaksin and his TRT
party that "ignoring the checks and balances in the justice system was
sending a bad message to the society and international community" (The
Nation—Thailand 2003b, 19). Even worse, the supposedly independent
government prosecutors, including Deputy Attorney General Praphan
Naiyakowit, who led the investigation, claimed that the police refused to
cooperate by not providing any reports or testimonies to him. Thaksin
defended the police by saying that the killings were made in self-defense
(The Nation—Thailand 2003b).

The manner in which the police killed Chakraphan was also very similar to other incidents such as the death of Raiwan Khwanthongyen and her
16-month-old baby, as well as Daranee Tasanawadee, who was shot while
her two sons witnessed the killing (Mutebi 2003). In February 2003, the
Thai police killed a couple from the rural hinterlands outside of Bangkok,
thereby leaving their three children orphans. One of the relatives of the
couple reacted to Thai media by saying that the couple "had to die to help
make the state suppression records look good" (Mutebi 2003, 21). In all of
these incidents, there was no direct evidence that implicated the victims as
being involved in any way with illegal drugs.

Many unarmed activists and street protesters became persistent targets
for harassment and killing by the Thai police force. One of the most heavily criticized incidents of police behavior toward unarmed protesters was
the Tak Bai massacre that occurred on October 25, 2004 (Albritton 2005,
166; Connors 2011, 105; Pathmanand 2006, 74–75). In the southernmost
province of Tak Bai, around 1,000 unarmed street activists gathered near
the provincial government hall to protest the US-funded counterinsurgency operations in the Islamic rebel-controlled southern region. Government troops, police forces, and other armed provincial government agents
stopped the protest and took around 1,000 protesters to a nearby military camp. During the mass arrests, government agents deliberately killed
around 85 unarmed Muslim protesters, while 78 died en route to the mili-

tary camp, primarily because of suffocation and dehydration. Thai security forces fired directly into the crowd, killing seven people. Consequently, Thai state agents forcibly transported the protesters from the police station to a military base where they were tortured and were subjected to other forms of cruel punishment. During the transit, Thai state agents coercively stacked all protesters in small trucks, which consequently resulted in 78 deaths (Amnesty International 2006a). Thaksin expressed his regrets for the Tak Bai killings, but vigorously defended the government, saying it "had done nothing wrong" (Cumming-Bruce 2004, 4). Thai political analysts generally consider the Tak Bai incident as a key example of the Thai government's systematic rejection of peaceful political opposition.

Because of Thaksin's adoption of a counterterror policy agenda, various forms of state-inflicted violence against other minority groups became more prevalent. This was especially so in the case of immigrants and the indigenous peoples of Thailand, who had suffered from discrimination of the majority population even before 2001. On June 2002, several Thai police agents stormed into a garment warehouse in Bangkok and imprisoned 11 Burmese civil society activists based on charges of violating immigration laws (US Department of State 2004b). Although the UN Commissioner for Human Rights classified the imprisoned activists as "persons of concern," thereby conditionally protecting them from further persecution, the Thai immigration authorities disregarded their status and physically harassed the activists.

Also, Thai police and army officers subjected indigenous peoples living in the hills and mountainous regions of Thailand to extrajudicial killings and enforced disappearances. Local human rights reports stated that several hill tribe regions of Thailand were subsumed under direct government control. For instance, from 2001 to 2006, many elder tribesmen in the Chiang Rai region suffered physical harassment and torture from the police and other government authorities. Amnesty International (2003b) underscored the post-2001 increase in the number of incidents of killings and disappearances of rural and environmental activists in provinces and communities outside Bangkok. Most of these incidents included the killings of individuals who organized peaceful protests against the increase of commercial activities in their communities. For example, in July 2002, a human rights activist, who was lobbying for Thai citizenship of hill tribes people living in the Thai border regions, was subjected to violent harassment by state security forces (US Department of State 2003). The activist was detained by the Chiang Mai provincial police unit, which had officers who illegally searched the activist's house for narcotics and other prohibited drugs. Local residents believed that the police aimed to stop the lobbying work of the activist on behalf of indigenous peoples who do not hold Thai citizenship. Judicial prosecution of the implicated police officers was not initiated, despite separate investigations conducted by the Chiang Mai provincial police and the Bangkok-based National Human Rights Commission.

The Thaksin-led government also subjected media outlets to intimidation techniques. For example, the Special Branch of the Royal Thai Police wrote several "letters of cooperation" to media outlets to be "cautious when reporting sensitive political or social issues" (US Department of State 2004b, 48). The letters compelled media agencies to practice self-censorship, thereby covering only materials that were favorable, or at least neutral, to the Thai government. In contrast to the tolerant attitude of the government in the 1990s, the Thaksin administration systematically harassed various media outlets (Eng 2002; Mutebi 2003; US Department of State 2003). In February 2002, the government issued deportation threats to the *Far Eastern Economic Review*'s foreign journalists, who had penned a piece that was extremely critical of Thaksin and the TRT party (Chambers 2004, 473). Although some influential individuals in Washington, including Senator Jesse Helms, and international media outlets (*New York Times* and *Washington Post*) decried the threat, the targeted journalist "was ultimately forced to merely apologize for its 'transgression' and Thaksin continued his campaign against the foreign media" (Chambers 2004, 472).

In contrast to the experiences of foreign journalists based in Thailand, local press agencies suffered even more brutal persecution from the government. For example, a political scandal, dubbed Thaksingate, erupted in March 2003. The scandal was about the Anti-Money Laundering Office (AMLO), which is the post-9/11 spin-off government agency directly under Thaksin's supervision. The AMLO mandated that 17 banks supply data concerning all the financial activities of famous journalists and leaders of the biggest Bangkok-based civil society groups. The common denominator among all these targeted individuals was their open and persistent criticisms of Thaksin's repressive policies and the US government's latent support of his regime. When the news about this asset probe became public, several groups filed a case against the AMLO at the Thai Administrative Court. Consequently, AMLO canceled the asset probe just right before the court mandated a judicial warning to stop the financial investigation. Strangely enough, the AMLO was eventually absolved from any wrongdoing by the courts (US Department of State 2004b), an outcome that suggests the lack of autonomy of the Thai judicial system. Another notable example was the cancellation of several radio and TV programs in which respondents and interviewees often expressed critical remarks about Thaksin and the TRT party. In response to all the repressive measures imposed upon the media, a prominent Thai journalist, Suthichai Yoon, contended that such incidents "had political influence written all over it" (Eng 2002, 59). The newly established AMLO office "probed the bank records of no fewer than 247 prominent Thai journalists and civil society activists for financial wrongdoing" from 2001 until 2003 (Pongsudhirak 2003a, 286).

In post 9/11 southern Thailand, many human rights activists and researchers emerged as key targets of assassination attempts by state agents (Amnesty International 2006). One of the most notable cases of enforced disappearance of a human rights advocate was the incident involving Somchai Neelapaijit, a well-known lawyer representing Malay Muslims from the south in terrorism-related cases. The family and friends of Somchai reported him as missing on March 12, 2004, at the height of Thaksin's counterterror operations in the Pattani region (Amnesty International 2006a; Kummetha 2014). Similar to the Philippine military's modus operandi of turning over civilians to military custody during the tenure of Arroyo, five Thai police officers forced Somchai into a police car in eastern Bangkok (Haberkorn 2018, 4). A day before Somchai's disappearance, he filed a torture legal case on behalf of five Thai men suspected of committing national security crimes. Unfortunately, enforced disappearance is not a recognized category of crime in the Thai legal system, which meant that the suspected state agents were only charged with robbery, coercion, and assault (Haberkorn 2018, 4). After several years of court trials, the Thai Supreme Court spent only "15 seconds reading the ruling on Somchai Neelapaijit's disappearance" (Kummetha 2014), which prohibited all future trials related to the case and acquitted the four defendants (police officers) implicated in the disappearance. The example of Somchai's disappearance and the judicial process that followed thereafter showcased the entrenched institutional deficiencies in the judiciary. Surprisingly, the Thai Court of Appeals, which was later supported by a final ruling from the Supreme Court, posited that the "law only recognizes a murder case when there is a dead body" and acquitted the police offers (Kummetha 2014, 11).

Many local informers reported that the Thai police forces stationed in the southern region were responsible for assassinations, death threats, and physical harassment of activists. For instance, in early 2005, one human rights activist received a phone call from an unidentified caller who threatened him to stop his research on the region or else he would be killed. Other Bangkok-based civil society researchers and media personnel abandoned their posts in southern Thailand because of the regular issuance of death threats by the police. In that regard, Amnesty International (2006a, 48) interviewed a young Malay Muslim university student who explained: "Even though I'm a university student I am subject to abuse—what about the villagers? They suffer more. . . . Villagers are constantly losing—they suffer grief, loss, and pain. If you want peace you need to focus on justice and humanity." One of these local residents, who was most likely killed by the police, was Ibrahim Kayo, a Muslim bus conductor from Pawing Village in Yala Province in the southern region of Thailand (Amnesty International 2006a; Bhumiprabhas 2006). A group of 10 police officers captured Kayo from his residence at 2 a.m. on January 8, 2004, and the officers did not reveal any details about his detention. Consequently, relatives reported the incident to the local police unit; they made repeated visits, but the police dismissed the case. After almost four months, the dead body of Kayo was found in another province in the southern region. Although the post-Thaksin government ruled that Kayo's disappearance was the collateral result of the violence, which qualified his family members for government compensation, the family claimed that they did not receive any compensation (Bhumiprabhas 2006). Ae Soh, Kayo's wife, did not file a legal case because of the lack of evidence (the police refused to investigate) and the belief that the judiciary would not render an impartial decision anyway.

Thai state agents in conflict-prone areas erroneously tagged some civilian residents as terrorists based on their minoritized status, particularly in the case of Thai Muslims in the Pattani region. With political support from the US government, Thai security officials subjected Muslim detainees from the southern region to various forms of torture, "ranging from sleep deprivation, forced nudity, exposure to extreme temperatures and even the threat to release German Shepherd guard dogs on detainees during interrogations" (Crispin 2008, 18) For example, a Thai detainee was nearly killed after being left naked in a freezer for more than 24 hours in a military base in Pattani (Crispin 2008).

One of the best-documented cases of state-initiated assassinations of unarmed Islamic community leaders was Satopa Yusoh, an imam in Narathiwat Province in southern Thailand who was killed on August 29, 2005 (International Crisis Group 2005). Local witnesses reported that four government soldiers used automatic rifles to shoot Satopa, who had just returned to his residence after leading a religious service at the local mosque. A few hours before the imam was killed, residents witnessed several military helicopters circling above the local community. After a series of gunshots stopped, immediate family members and relatives helped Satopa to get inside the house. Notwithstanding multiple gunshots, Satopa managed to live for a few hours after the incident, and he revealed that government forces had indeed fired the gunshots. Satopa insisted an ambulance not be called because of his fear that he would be taken from the hospital by the military. Local residents and Satopa's family members insisted that Satopa had nothing to do with armed rebel groups in Narathiwat Province. Although no one from the community called the hospital or the police to report the incident, an ambulance arrived in the community together with 10 trucks filled with soldiers. Consequently, the arrival of soldiers reinforced the local residents' belief that government forces were primarily responsible for the killing of Satopa. As one villager bluntly asked, "How could they have known someone had been shot if it wasn't them [the military] or their agents?" (International Crisis Group 2005, 9).

Government officials in several constitutional and independent agencies were not spared from state violence. For instance, Pradit Chareonthaitawee, a high-ranking National Human Rights Commission member, received death threats and various forms of political harassment (Mutebi 2003, 105). As one of the most prominent critics of Thaksin within the National Human Rights Commission, Pradit attributed the proliferation of human rights violations to Thaksin and his instrumentalization of US aid to ensure the long-term rule of the TRT party. Thaksin branded Pradit's behavior "as sickening and questioned his legitimacy" to report the human rights situation to the United Nations. The TRT party spokesman also castigated Pradit and threatened him with impeachment because he was acting "against national interests" (Mutebi 2003, 105). Pradit consistently received phone calls from an anonymous caller who commanded him to "stop speaking to the United Nations or die" (Mutebi 2003, 105). The harassment of Pradit demonstrated that Thaksin's leadership strategy of eliminating political opposition was not only limited to nonstate actors but extended to dissenting government officials who became the targets of harassment.

Collateral Consequences of
Bangkok's Counterterrorism Policies

Many reported incidents of collateral deaths were largely concentrated in the southern region of Thailand, where government forces launched offensive operations against armed Islamic rebels. The Islamic minority

population of Thailand mainly resides in such southern provinces as Pattani, Narathiwat, Yala, and some regions of Songkla; they are mostly ethnic
Malays and speak the Bahasa dialect. Because of their historically troubled
relationship with Bangkok, the southern provinces have been a hotspot for
armed secessionist groups that seek independence from Thailand (Chalk
2001). After the 9/11 attacks, the number of violent incidents by unidentified and armed nonstate armed groups had dramatically increased. At the
peak of its steady increase since late 2001, "political violence in the Muslim
majority far South of Thailand escalated sharply after a raid on an army
camp there by an unidentified armed group on 4 January 2004" (Amnesty
International 2006a, 1). From January 2004 until 2006, "more than 1,000
people have been killed, including both civilians and members of the security forces" (Amnesty International 2006a). Faced with the surge of violence, the Thai government deployed "significantly increased numbers of
security forces in these provinces" and enlarged "their powers by enact-
ing new security legislation" (Amnesty International 2006a, 1). Operating
within the broader legitimating frame of the US war on terror, Thaksin's
government "has put Pattani, Yala, and Narathiwat under special national
security legislation and mobilized massive numbers of security and counterinsurgency forces into the south" (Human Rights Watch 2007a, 2).
In February 2005, the Thaksin administration disclosed that the southern region would be divided into several zones (red, yellow, and green),
whereby red zones constituted communities that were considered to be
supportive of armed rebels—a classification that would disqualify them
from government funding (Storey 2007, 6). Those red zones in southern
Thailand witnessed the highest number of collateral deaths and killings as
a result of persistent clashes between government and rebel troops.

Because southern Thailand was largely inaccessible to many media
personnel and even high-ranking civilian officials from Bangkok (McCargo 2008, xi), there was a lack of reliable open-source information that
accurately pinpointed the whereabouts and other personal information
of armed secessionist rebels in the southern provinces. Many state agents
relied on inaccurate intelligence as they mistakenly deemed civilian residents as armed combatants. In November 2002, the Thai police detained
25 foreigners based on a mere allegation of their involvement in terrorist
activities, but many of them were later released (Cotton 2003, 151). Even
former prime minister Anand Panyarachun (Amnesty International 2006)
stated in July 2005 that "in 85% of murder cases, the government does
not know who the perpetrators were, which shows the government has
failed to find the real wrongdoers." On April 13, 2006, several Thai sol-

diers based in the Pattani region "shot and killed two teenagers, reportedly mistaking them for militants" (US Department of State 2007, 66). The Thai army later accepted its responsibility in the death of the two civilians, and paid some financial compensation (total amount of 25,500 USD) to the families of the two teenagers. Although reliable local reports on civilian casualties do not seem to exist, McCargo (2008, xi; see note 8) pointed to the undated statistical document produced by Srisompob Jitpiromsri, a notable scholar of Thailand's southern politics. The report highlighted the large number of collateral deaths and physical injuries in southern Thailand: by the end of April 2008, around 3,000 people had been killed, while nearly 5,000 Thais incurred physical injuries during the military's bombing operations (McCargo 2008, xi).

Thai armed forces and local police units as well as Islamic rebels were responsible for the killings of Thai civilians (US Department of State 2007). Even Lt. Gen. Chalermdej Chomphunuj, a high-ranking official of the Royal Thai Police Force, later confessed that "some people might have been mistakenly blacklisted, perhaps due to the carelessness of officials" (Dabhoiwala 2003). Thai police forces' informers sometimes provided incorrect information to the state authorities. The information was later passed on to police officers and security agents, who then acted on the basis of such. An example of false identification was the detention of Yarang district's (Pattani Province) Abdul Roh Ning Yaha, who was accused and detained by the local police on February 7, 2003. Abdul was falsely accused of illegally obtaining 300 methamphetamine tablets. He was widely known in the community as a religious Muslim and was in no way involved in any kind of drug trade, thereby showing the arbitrariness of the drug wars. As Chandra-nuj Mahakanjana contended, Thaksin's "brutal campaign against drug dealers in early 2003 caused many southerners to feel that they were particularly favored victims of the extra-judicial killings" (Mahakanjana 2006, 11).

Because many collateral abuses occurred in the southern provinces, the Thai armed forces units stationed in those regions detrimentally impacted the lives of schoolchildren. Many of these security forces, particularly from the Thai Rangers, a state-sponsored paramilitary unit, chose to establish their temporary camps in school buildings. The transformation of civilian facilities for military-oriented purposes disrupted the academic activities of the schoolchildren. At its worst, the military deployments also attracted armed Islamic rebels in the Pattani region to carry out their attacks on schools, where children were caught in a potential cross fire between government and rebel forces. As a nine-year-old schoolgirl confessed to

Human Rights Watch (Human Rights Watch 2010a, 9): "I am scared. . . . What scares me is the thought that the school could be attacked because the soldiers are at the school, but that students and teachers would be the ones that get hurt."

Capitalizing on global counterterror discourses, the Thaksin-led government imposed emergency legal measures to justify increased state repression. Imposed in 2002, martial law provided the legal justification for increased state repression in the Islamic southern regions. On July 19, 2005, Thaksin imposed the Executive Decree on Public Administration in Emergency Situations in Narathiwat, Pattani, and Yala, which explicitly (1) granted law enforcement agents total immunity from judicial prosecution and (2) suspended the powers and jurisdictions of Thai courts to prosecute government officials for human rights violations (International Crisis Group 2005). Those legal measures weakened any incentive for soldiers and police officers to take extra precautionary measures in identifying their targets. Although the process of "blacklisting" was used to target unarmed political opponents especially during the 2003 war in drugs, blacklisting was also used in counterterror operations against armed rebels in the southern provinces. In the case of the latter, soldiers and law enforcement agents intended to only capture armed rebels, but the "blacklist" that identified their targets was "often based on weak intelligence and weaker evidence" (International Crisis Group 2005, 1). The Thaksin-led government's financial incentives vis-à-vis the newly placed national security laws motivated state agents to aim for monetary benefits in exchange for killing as many suspected armed rebels and drug addicts as possible. Yet the pre-9/11 institutions in southern Thailand (Civilian-Police-Military Command 43/CPM43 and the Southern Border Provinces Administrative Centre/SBPAC) were more effective in "fostering closer relations and mutual trust between the local community, security forces and government officials" (Nurakkate 2012, 12), thereby contributing to fewer abuses (Mahakanjana 2006, 14). Thaksin, on the other hand, employed a heavy-handed approach to the Muslim south and dissolved the CPM43 and SBPAC; instead, he transferred all of the policing and civilian governance functions to the Thai police forces.

Conclusion: Post-9/11 Human Rights Crisis in Thailand

I used my theory of interest convergence to uncover the causal story of human rights in post-9/11 Thailand. My causal explanation proceeded in four parts. The first step deals with the Thai government's strategic localization of counterterror discourses. I referred to the Thai government's strategic reframing of political discourses in order to capture terror-oriented strategic support from the US government and the Thai public and key domestic constituencies' support for increased state repression. The second step pertains to the instrumentalization of US counterterror assistance and the Thai state's domestic resources in order to increase state repression, thereby producing two principal policy patterns: (1) selective political repression that targeted civilian targets and (2) erroneous policing practices that produced collateral human rights violations.

Why did the Thai government reframe international counterterror discourses after the 9/11 attacks? The Thai government reinterpreted counterterror discourses, mostly borrowed from the US-led global war on terror, because of two intended effects. The first goal referred to attracting foreign strategic support from the US government, and the second pertained to winning domestic public support for increased state repression in order to combat internal security threats. This process is what I call the strategic localization of transnational counterterror discourses, whereby Thaksin and his allies argued that the long-standing illegal drug trafficking problem and international terrorism were linked. The Thai government maintained that Islamic armed rebel groups in southern Thailand are directly linked to the Al-Qaeda network. That discursive framing of the domestic security situation enabled Thaksin and the TRT party to attract US strategic support to Thailand and also to lay the normative justification for increased repression against armed and unarmed targets. Through strategic localization, the Thaksin administration linked the armed Islamic rebellion in the southern provinces to the global armed Islamic movement. This interpretation of the conflict in southern Thailand reinforced the Bush administration's case for providing substantial counterterror support to Thaksin's government. Similarly, when communicating to the Thai domestic public, the TRT party and Thaksin's political allies depicted the southern Muslim-dominated provinces as the focal point for illegal drug trafficking, Islamic terrorism, and transnational criminal activity.

The mobilization of US counterterror material resources and political support for the Thai military and police agencies led to two transformative policy patterns. The Thaksin-led government in Bangkok fully sanctioned such repressive policies, while the Thai military and police agencies implemented them at various localities. The first pattern pertains to selective political repression in which suspected drug addicts and criminals were castigated as security threats. Many of the killed or "disappeared" civilians during the 2003 war on drugs were local political opposition members, who were deemed unfavorable to Thaksin's TRT party. The second pattern, meanwhile, refers to the expansion of military and police operations in southern Thailand, where the primary aim was to combat armed Islamic secessionist groups. The escalation of state violence contributed to the proliferation of collateral deaths in the southern provinces.

This chapter systematically probed how my theory of interest convergence explained the emergence of the deteriorating human rights situation in Thailand after 2001. The case study showed that the confluence of the US and Thai governments' interests on a counterterror agenda, together with the regime-consolidating motivations of Thaksin, produced transformative domestic policies and foreign assistance program that led to the proliferation of human rights violations. This chapter also demonstrated that the political acceptability of a militaristic policy agenda in post-9/11 Thailand depended on the Thai government's strategic reframing of internal security threats as closely linked to international terrorism, which was a key concern for the Bush administration. I showed that the strategic localization of the external counterterror discourses was an effective political tactic that generated the needed political support from the US government and the Thai domestic public, particularly for intensified counterterror operations in Thailand. The inclusion of civilians as targets of the Thai armed forces and the police was driven by Thaksin's logic of consolidating his rule and ensuring the long-term dominance of the TRT party. US strategic support enabled Thai state security agencies to implement an unprecedented scale of state repression aimed at eliminating armed rebels and unarmed civilian targets. The next chapter concludes this book by situating the findings in the various case studies within the broader context of American power and the transnational politics of foreign aid.

EIGHT

Conclusion

Patterns and Possibilities— Foreign Aid and Human Rights

This book has been motivated by two important trends about US foreign relations with smaller states in the Global South. First, foreign strategic support, which refers to both foreign aid programs and public diplomacy, varies over time. In periods of transnational security shocks, foreign strategic support emphasizes state security and militaristic priorities. That was the case during the Cold War and post-9/11 years, when US strategic support focused on counterterrorism and subordinated even economic and civilian development aid under overarching militaristic and geostrategic considerations. During the early post–Cold War years, US strategic support focused on a comprehensive range of militaristic and nonmilitaristic concerns and, in many cases, highlighted the importance of human rights and democracy promotion abroad. Second, the variation in the amount and purpose of foreign strategic support correlates with the magnitude and scope of domestic state repression in recipient countries.

My investigation began with that puzzle and proceeded by revisiting the social science literature that addressed the relationship between foreign aid and human rights. Yet our social scientific knowledge about foreign aid and human rights is still in its early phase. The recent studies on foreign aid's political consequences primarily employ large-N, cross-national, statistical investigations. Besides, the contemporary political and social science scholarship is roughly divided between two camps, with each one of them focusing on a given set of variables to explain variations in human rights outcomes and domestic state repression over time (Regilme 2014b; Kalyvas, Shapiro, and Masoud 2008; Davenport 2007, 2). International Relations scholars emphasize extranational factors, while comparative politics scholars underscore intranational factors. Amid the Trump administration's waning interest in human rights rhetoric and foreign aid (Regilme 2019), investigating the relationship between foreign strategic support and its consequences to thousands, if not millions, of lives in the Global South is all the more necessary. The scholarly literature has yet to provide a full theoretical account of the causal processes that link foreign strategic support and human rights outcomes.

To redress that neglect, I developed a theoretically guided account of the political consequences of foreign aid on a recipient country's physical integrity rights situation. My interest convergence theory is integrative precisely because it combines useful constructivist, rationalist, and historical-institutionalist insights into a unified explanatory framework that links foreign strategic assistance programs and physical integrity rights. I analyzed how ideational factors—including state identities, shared expectations, and changing political beliefs—interacted with the strategic-motivational considerations of donor and recipient governments. Taken together, these ideational and material factors jointly shaped the ways in which foreign strategic support was used in recipient countries. Neither transnational nor domestic factors exclusively influence the ways in which foreign strategic support impacts human rights; rather, the interactions of transnational and domestic factors jointly produce variations in human rights outcomes at the local level. The previous chapters demonstrated that the convergence of the political expectations, interests, and beliefs of influential political elites in donor and recipient countries shapes the impact of foreign strategic support on human rights. Using interest convergence theory, this book traverses through various scales of analysis, ranging from extranational and national structures to the level of individual political agency of the abuser and the human rights victim.

The global politics of aid and human rights constitutes the global ecosystem of hierarchical power relations. Notwithstanding the rise of emerging powers and the purported decline of American hegemony (Regilme and Parisot 2017; 2020), the United States still remains the most powerful state actor in world politics today. This book zoomed in on the complex social and power relations through which the American imperium operates, particularly in the foreign aid provision sector. The previous chapters illustrated the subtleties, the scope, and the magnitude of the US government's supposedly philanthropic interactions with Thai and Filipino state and nonstate actors—particularly the ways in which such dynamics shaped physical integrity rights outcomes in Southeast Asia. Conceived as collaborators to the American aid imperium, various key institutions and principal political actors in the Philippines and Thailand were not mere passive agents of American power; rather, those actors strategically localized American political discourses to suit the domestic context and instrumentalized US foreign aid to consolidate their own domestic power. While the notion of aid imperium implies a hierarchical distinction between the giver and the receiver, or between the ruler and the ruled, I provided evidence that the American imperium emerges from the converging interests that mutually reinforce the claims for legitimacy and dominance of the United States with regard to its less powerful allies.

That convergence, however, is not always full and unconditional. During the global war on terror under the Bush administration, US officials turned a blind eye to the Thai and Philippine states' violent repression of *unarmed* political dissidents, as it was shown in chapters 4 and 7. If the American foreign aid imperium is truly committed to human rights norms, then why did it allow the Thai and Philippine governments at that time to diverge from the publicly stated aims of US strategic assistance? I offer two likely explanations. First, any form of imperium has an inherent propensity to maintain its dominant status regardless of moral considerations. The Bush administration's counterterror policy priorities and other geostrategic interests in the Asia-Pacific region trumped human rights considerations in its strategic partner countries. The second probable explanation refers to the fungible nature of foreign aid especially in the context of a security crisis, when recipient governments are likely to misuse aid for purposes that were unintended by the donor.

Key Patterns: US Strategic Assistance and Human Rights in Southeast Asia

To summarize, the convergence of interests of donor and recipient governments, together with the recipient government's level of domestic legitimacy, affects the scope and magnitude of state-initiated human rights abuses. In its quest to attract foreign strategic assistance, a prospective aid recipient government strategically adapts its discourses and policy preferences to the interests of the potential donor government and its own domestic public. Faced by the increasing domestic demand for the expansion of the public sphere and democratic spaces in the 1990s, the Thai and

Philippine governments welcomed US strategic support that was designed for nonmilitaristic purposes. This bilateral cooperation meant that domestic resources and US strategic support were used for a diverse range of militaristic and nonmilitaristic goals. That scheme of resource mobilization generated fewer physical integrity rights violations, many of which were collateral abuses. Without US strategic assistance in the 1990s, democratic reforms and improved human rights outcomes in the Philippines and Thailand would have been quite limited because American support for liberal democratization was crucial in forcing the military leadership to give up state control.

During the post-9/11 years, the Thai and Philippine governments strategically localized their public discourses and policy preferences in ways that linked the US-led war on terror to their own countries' struggles with armed separatist movements. Located within the Asia-Pacific security complex, Thailand and the Philippines played a pivotal role in the post-9/11 US strategy that framed Southeast Asia as the "second front on the war on terror," with the Middle East as the first front (Gershman 2002; Tan 2003). Foreign policy elites within the United States and the Asia-Pacific region viewed post-9/11 transnational terrorism as a grave threat to the long-established American dominance in the region. Beyond Asia, the US government dramatically increased its militaristic assistance to Pakistan, Colombia, and Uganda, among many others; many, if not all, of them experienced deterioration in their domestic human rights situation. As Jason Ralph argues (2013, 1), "there is nothing strange about the US being at war" in the context of the post-9/11 strategy, yet "the Bush administration's decision to wage war against a nonstate transnational network was unusual" (2013, 1). That unique feature of the Bush strategy pertains to the willingness to view the Al-Qaeda threat through the lens of an armed conflict instead of a domestic law and security enforcement issue. Such a strategy discursively paved the way for other US allies, including Thailand and the Philippines, to wage their own "wars" against nonstate actors that those states arbitrarily deemed as domestic security threats.

By localizing their political discourses, those Southeast Asian governments bolstered their legitimacy in two ways: (1) by appeasing the United States as the donor government, (2) and by justifying to the Filipino and Thai public audiences that the local security problems could be resolved by participating in the US-led war on terror. That convergence of interests in counterterrorism and militarism shaped the ways through which the Philippine and Thai governments deployed domestic state resources and US strategic support. This increase in domestic state repression of armed political dissidents facilitated the proliferation of collateral human rights abuses. Because of serious challenges to their domestic authority, the Thaksin and Arroyo administrations diverged from the publicly stated US interest of only targeting armed rebel groups and included instead all forms of political dissidence. State repression constituted the identification of and crackdown on all forms of political opposition, including elected opposition members and civilian political activists—an outcome that led to the post-9/11 human rights crisis in Thailand and the Philippines.

The comparative evidence from Southeast Asia illustrates the role of foreign patrons in the domestic politics of smaller and less powerful states. As Jason Brownlee (2007, 211) maintains, "external powers may constrain or buttress the domestic control" of national leaders. Yet, the evidence herein suggests that the role of US strategic assistance should not be overstated. Whether it was in the 1990s or during the war on terror period, US strategic assistance amplified the interests and policy preferences of the ruling governments in the Philippines and Thailand. That reinforcement effect means that even without US counterterror assistance, Thaksin's quest for regime consolidation and Arroyo's quest for political survival would likely have still entailed the repression of all forms of political opposition. Without US counterterror aid in the 2000s, the Thai and Philippine governments could have solicited the external support of the Chinese government, which has been active in the last 15 years or so in pulling Southeast Asian governments away from the American sphere of influence. After the fall of Thaksin in 2006 and the series of political crises that followed thereafter, Thailand "has been strengthening its ties with China" (Chachavalpongpun 2016, 9). The US government's criticisms of the military junta and advocacy for a return to open democratic elections were followed by the Thai military's increasingly closer ties with Beijing. Consequently, the US government reduced the scale of joint military exercises and cooperation with the Royal Thai Armed Forces, and Bangkok's military-led government "responded by forging closer ties with Asian giant China" (Reuters 2017, 7). Although Arroyo strengthened bilateral ties with the United States, Chinese influence was not fully sidelined. In fact, Arroyo, "compared to past presidents, clinched the greatest number of bilateral agreements with China in the two countries' 30-year relationship," although those deals were primarily commercial and economic in nature (Esmaquel 2017, 9). This foreign policy hedging strategy illustrates how the Philippine government under Arroyo depended on Washington, DC for matters of high politics (particularly military support), while Beijing contented itself with stronger commercial ties with Manila. In the absence of counterterror US strategic assistance, it is likely that Beijing would probably have supported Arroyo in ways that could have led to increased domestic repression of all forms of political dissidence.

Thailand and the Philippines in the 1990s

In the 1990s, the US government provided strategic support to its partner countries for a wide range of goals including economic development, trade expansion, human rights protection, and democratization. Various policy goals such as human rights promotion in aid recipient countries gained traction especially during the immediate post–Cold War years (Meernik, Krueger, and Poe 1998; Cingranelli and Richards 1999). In chapter 3, I showed that nonmilitaristic US strategic support to the Philippines in the 1990s reinforced the Philippine government's efforts to institutionalize democratic reforms and human rights protection. To justify its democratization reforms and nonmilitaristic US strategic support, the Ramos administration strategically reframed emerging international human rights norms as crucial in ensuring long-term economic development. The Ramos administration's preference for democratic reforms and human rights commitments converged with the US government's post–Cold War emphasis on a nonmilitaristic foreign policy in the Asia-Pacific region. By framing human rights as crucial to economic development, the Ramos administration effectively responded to the growing domestic public demand for stronger human rights protection. The democratization reforms, the constitutionalization of human rights guarantees, and the substantially less militaristic US strategic support contributed to the improved human rights outcome in the 1990s. The Philippine government tolerated legal and peaceful political opposition, introduced key reforms to professionalize the military and police agencies, and integrated former armed rebels into mainstream politics. Publicly condemned by both the Philippine and US governments, several collateral human rights abuses emerged primarily because of the erroneous intelligence and policing practices of individual state agents.

Similarly, in chapter 6, I demonstrated that Thai and US government officials and politicians in the 1990s upheld a policy agenda that was supportive of human rights and democratization. Many Thai politicians of the Democrat Party strategically localized emerging human rights norms as essential in sustaining Thailand's rapid economic development. Several transformative local events strengthened the political appeal of the pro-human-rights agenda of Thai and American government officials. Thai liberal democrats strategically framed the Black May incident in 1992, when Thai soldiers physically harassed thousands of civilian protesters in Bangkok, killing more than 50 people, as a vivid reminder that the military's authoritarian rule had to be ended in light of the emerging post–Cold War demand for human rights and democratic governance. At that time, the liberal democratic politicians and Bangkok's civilian elites blamed the Thai military regime's authoritarian practices for hindering the economic progress of the country. For example, the Thai government strategically reinterpreted the Asian financial crisis in 1997 as a reminder that human rights and democratization reforms in the country should be further expanded in order to prevent financial crises in the future. Moreover, the Thai government undermined the once-powerful role of the Thai armed forces and police agencies in civilian politics and promoted widespread government toleration for peaceful political opposition. Funded and implemented by the US and Thai governments, socioeconomic development programs addressed several domestic policy concerns—including prostitution, illegal drug trafficking, and the Islamic Malay minority in the southern provinces. That policy approach stood in marked contrast with the militaristic policy stance upheld by American and Thai elites during the Cold War and the post-9/11 periods. Because of those developments, the physical integrity rights situation in Thailand in the 1990s dramatically improved. Nevertheless, some collateral human rights abuses emerged because of the prevailing corrupt tendencies in several pockets of the Thai military and police forces that colluded with individual politicians and business actors. Similar to the Philippines in the 1990s, most of the Thai state agents who committed human rights violations remained free from any form of judicial prosecution.

Thailand and the Philippines after 2001

After the 9/11 attacks, the US and Southeast Asian governments' prioritized counterterrorism as the overarching policy paradigm. To justify US counterterror aid and increased counterterror operations, Southeast Asian governments strategically localized counterterror and militaristic public discourses from the Bush administration by framing both unarmed and armed political opposition as existential threats to state security. That policy pattern is generated by selective political repression, a process in which state-initiated human rights abuses emerge because of an explicit state policy that upholds widespread and violent repression of unarmed civilian targets. In addition, the convergence of the US and Southeast Asian governments' interests toward militarism resulted in the expansion of counterterror operations, which consequently generated collateral human rights abuses emerging from erroneous intelligence and policing practices. The decision to harass and to kill systematically unarmed political opposition emanated from the need of the Thaksin and Arroyo administrations to consolidate their rule amid weak domestic legitimacy. Taken together, the widespread selective political repression in the post-9/11 period and the entrenched culture of impunity from human rights abuses jointly contributed to the overall human rights deterioration in Thailand and the Philippines.

Chapter 4 demonstrated that the Philippine government under President Arroyo framed the long-standing armed Islamic rebellion in southern Philippines as directly linked to the Al-Qaeda network. Her government also incriminated armed communist rebellion as a fundamental threat to state security. That kind of strategic reinterpretation led to two transformative outcomes intended by the Arroyo administration: (1) the influx of militaristic strategic support from the Bush administration, which upheld a strong counterterror agenda; and (2) the emergence of Filipino public support (at least initially) for increased military and police repression against the domestic armed rebellion of communist and Islamic fundamentalist groups.

Faced by growing public resistance against her leadership, Arroyo sought to repress political opposition in the hope of consolidating her authority. Arroyo used discretionary counterterror funds from the US government as well as from domestic sources to buy the military's political support in exchange for violently eliminating armed and unarmed political opposition. Her administration rebranded legal political opposition, most especially left-wing political parties, as complicit to armed communist rebellion, thereby violently killing and harassing members of peaceful political opposition parties that were highly critical of Arroyo's leadership. The magnitude of state violence against armed communist and Islamic rebel groups thereby expanded, which generated an increase in collateral killings and injuries of civilians precisely because of the numerous erroneous policing and counterterror practices that emerged after 2001. In sum, the intensified selective political repression and the proliferation of counterterror operations precipitated the human rights crisis in the Philippines during Arroyo's tenure.

Chapter 5 confirmed that, notwithstanding interest convergence on nonmilitaristic policy agendas vis-à-vis the strong political legitimacy of the recipient governments, collateral human rights abuses could still emerge due to the enduring institutional shortcomings in the judiciary and the state security establishment. Although the US government was still actively engaged in counterterror operations in many places elsewhere in the world during that period, the Obama and Aquino administrations' policy agendas covered a wide array of bilateral policy priorities. Their policy concerns shifted from their predecessors' focus on domestic security (counterterrorism) to external security, with the emphasis on China's reemergence as a global power and the broad range of nonmilitaristic issues including human rights protection, economic development, and good governance. This transformation in security perceptions facilitated the momentary downsizing of domestic counterterror operations in the Philippines, which led to a decrease in the number of collateral violations. Above all, the strong domestic political legitimacy of Philippine president Aquino, particularly within the state security establishment as well as in the broader Filipino society, eliminated the necessity for increased state violence against political dissidence. In effect, the modest scale of counterterror operations and the absence of selective political repression during this period generated comparatively fewer state-initiated human rights abuses.

In chapter 7, I examined the human rights situation in Thailand from 2001 to 2006, particularly during the tenure of Prime Minister Thaksin Shinawatra and his government's participation in the US-led war on terror. Thaksin and Bush advocated for a counterterror-oriented bilateral agenda. Thaksin aimed to consolidate his power, which was strongly challenged by the Thai political establishment including the royal family, factions within the military leadership, and royalist supporters (see Chachavalpongpun 2011b). Faced by weak support from the Thai political establishment, Thaksin and his local allies used domestic state resources and US foreign strategic support in ways that diverged from the US interest in only curbing armed terrorists. Thus, the Thai government violently harassed and killed civilians, including political opposition members, especially in the context of the "war on drugs." Regime consolidation, in the view of Thaksin and his TRT party, was necessary precisely because they did not enjoy the political support of influential and traditional Bangkok-based elites, the Thai middle class, and the Thai monarchy. To legitimize his militaristic policy agenda and the influx of American counterterror assistance, Thaksin strategically framed the long-standing Islamic armed rebellion in the southern Thai provinces as directly linked to the Al-Qaeda movement and other regional terror networks. Intensifying state violence against armed rebel groups, Thaksin sought to bolster his political legitimacy in the southern Thai provinces, which were once a traditional political bailiwick of the rival Democrat Party. By winning the political support of the Bush administration, Thaksin secured some conditional and temporary acceptance from some of the Bangkok-based elites, including the Thai monarchy. Nonetheless, the escalated level of state repression in the southern provinces generated an unprecedented increase in the number of collateral human rights abuses. Using counterterror support from the United States, in 2003 the Thaksin-led government launched the war on drugs, which branded suspected drug addicts, criminals, and many local political opposition members as security threats. These "socially undesirable" civilians became victims of Thaksin's policy of extrajudicial killings and enforced disappearances.

Theoretical and Policy Implications

This book develops a theoretical framework that brings ideational factors and their interactions with strategic-motivational interests into the analysis of foreign aid and its political consequences. By spelling out relevant yet previously understudied mechanisms of influence, I show why and how shared interests and political expectations matter in interstate cooperation (see Regilme 2018b, 2018c). The investigation here is the most comprehensive account of the political consequences of post–cold war US foreign strategic assistance to human rights in the Global South; it brought together the interactions between ideational and materialist variables as well as domestic and transnational factors into a unified explanatory framework.

The case studies herein confirm the expectations of my interest convergence theory. First, the causal link between foreign strategic support and human rights outcomes in recipient countries is contingent on the widely shared ideas and beliefs of donor and recipient governments. Particularly, the shared ideas and political beliefs shape the intended purposes and implementation patterns of (1) foreign strategic support and (2) the domestic policies of the aid recipient government. The analysis here distinguishes itself from the current literature on foreign aid, which often focuses on the strategic-motivational considerations of donor and recipient governments. It confirms that the relationship between *ideas* (shared policy expectations, beliefs, and intentions) and *material factors* (policies, military aid, economic assistance, internal state resources) is both causal and constitutive. The relationship is *causal* because my case studies show that the mutually shared political expectations and ideas of donor and recipient governments shape the substantive content and implementation patterns of foreign strategic support programs and the domestic policies of aid recipient governments. Also, the relationship is *constitutive* because foreign aid, as a material resource, represents the much broader and overarching political strategy and purposes of donor and recipient governments. Hence, widely shared ideas about the purpose of foreign aid affect the ways in which aid will be used.

Second, domestic political conditions influence the recipient government's decision whether foreign strategic support and internal state resources would be used to escalate domestic repression against armed and unarmed political opposition. Ruling governments with strong political support from within and beyond the formal state apparatus are likely to tolerate nonviolent political opposition and critics. The strong political legitimacy of the Ramos-led government in the Philippines and the Chuan-led government in Thailand in the 1990s eliminated the need for curbing peaceful political opposition. In contrast, the Arroyo administration in the Philippines and the Thaksin administration in Thailand persistently faced severe challenges to their domestic legitimacy right from the very start of their leadership tenure, and even before the 9/11 attacks that precipitated the US-led global war on terror. This problem with political legitimacy motivated the Arroyo and Thaksin administrations to expand the range of targets for state repression and to tag legal political opposition members and activists as enemies of the state.

In the midst of a security crisis, donor governments should only provide militaristic aid to recipient governments that enjoy strong domestic legitimacy. In that way, foreign strategic assistance is likely to be used only for the repression of *armed* rebels and not civilians and unarmed political dissidents. To minimize the risk that state agents erroneously target civilians as armed rebels, foreign aid should support the long-term professionalization and institutional development of the judicial system, the armed forces, and police agencies.

Another lesson is that the principal strategic interests of the core states of the international system can still influence the scope and extent of domestic state repression in the Global South—notwithstanding several decades of formal decolonization and the norm of state sovereignty. Since the end of World War II, the highly politicized practice of aid giving is now a widely accepted and highly entrenched norm in contemporary world politics (Riddell 2008; Lancaster 2007). Unfortunately, the literature on political violence, including in political science, has neglected the transnational underpinnings of state violence (Kalyvas, Shapiro, and Masoud 2008; Davenport 2007, 2).

Yet imperium-building, including its constitutive politics of aid giving, is a two-way street. Recipient governments accept aid because their political interests and expectations appear to converge with some of the core policy preferences of the donor governments, in addition to other symbolic and material benefits of foreign aid. The historical evidence here shows the dynamic interactions in the structures of power between the US aid imperium and its subordinate states. I demonstrate how such interactions profoundly impact vulnerable political actors in the subordinate state, including civilians.

Despite interest convergence on human rights, residual abuses may still persist. Such residual abuses emerge because of the enduring institutional deficiencies within the state security agencies and ineffective judicial institutions. Many, if not all, of the suspected state abusers during the postwar on terror period in the Philippines have yet to be formally prosecuted in courts, despite the pro-human-rights rhetoric and policies of the US government and the Aquino administration. The state of impunity sends a wrong message to prospective state violators, who assume that they can easily evade legal penalties, thereby engendering more collateral violations. In policy terms, foreign strategic support should undermine the entrenched culture of impunity from human rights abuses by implementing long-term institutional reforms in the judiciary and the armed forces.

My case studies illustrated that states are not monolithic entities, and that their leaders' interests, normative beliefs, and policy predispositions can radically change even in such a short period of time. Critical junctures, such as the 9/11 attacks in the United States, have motivated influential political actors in Southeast Asia to reconsider their policy ideas and normative beliefs that could impact the magnitude of state violence. That was the case in Thailand and the Philippines during the post-9/11 period. It was in the 2000s when seemingly entrenched values concerning human rights and democracy, which gained traction in the 1990s, suddenly became subservient to state security and counterterrorism. My case studies demonstrated that the dominant counterterror agenda that emerged after 2001 gravely undermined the gains resulting from human rights reforms in the 1990s. Although the United States did not publicly advocate for these two Southeast Asian countries to systematically undermine human rights after 2001, the evidence indicated that the Bush administration was dismissive of the deteriorating human rights records of the Arroyo and Thaksin governments.

US Strategic Support in Other World Regions

Ultimately, this book calls for further exploration of how foreign aid is related to state repression and human rights outcomes in recipient countries. The current International Relations scholarship suggests that foreign strategic support and physical integrity rights outcomes are directly related, especially when one considers the experiences of several Global South countries (Branch 2011; Regilme 2018b, 2018c). Among these potential cases for further investigation is Colombia, a Mutual Defence Treaty ally of the United States (Rio Treaty of 1947) and arguably Washington's most important ally in South America. An independent preliminary report confirms the correlation between increased US military funding to Colombia and the number of civilian killings and harassment perpetrated by the Colombian army "based on 5,763 reported executions in Colombia and extensive documentation of U.S. assistance to the Colombian military" from 2000 until 2010 (Fellowship of Reconciliation 2014, 2; see also Regilme 2018b).

Similarly, Pakistan has been one of the biggest recipients of foreign aid since the US-led war on terror began. Important for its strategic location and geostrategic role in dismantling terror networks in the Afghan border regions, Pakistan has provided crucial support for US counterterror strategy against jihadi groups and the Al-Qaeda network. Thus, the Pakistani government received more than 10 billion USD worth of civilian and military aid from 2002 to 2016 (Walsh and Pidd 2010). Under the government of President Pervez Musharaff (2001 to 2009), the Pakistani military and police forces implemented the violent suppression of peaceful protests, with many lawyers and other critics subjected to torture and severe physical harassment. The proliferation of enforced disappearances and the widespread use of torture emerged after the Pakistani government openly welcomed counterterror US strategic support (Human Rights Watch 2007b; DeYoung 2010).

Kenya has been one of the largest recipients of US strategic assistance on the African continent, where American foreign policy constitutes the strategic deployment of diplomatic pressures and customized aid programs

(Prestholdt 2011, 3, 20). After the democratic transition in 2002, Kenya has maintained close bilateral relations with the United States. Faced with serious security threats posed by armed Islamic rebel groups, most notably the Al-Shabaab, Kenya's police and military agencies have required external counterterror assistance to bolster their coercive capacities (US Department of State, Bureau of African Affairs 2020). For that reason, US counterterror assistance to Kenya dramatically increased from 24 million USD in 2010 to 100 million USD in 2015 (Security Assistance Monitor 2015). In an open letter to President Barack Obama, Human Rights Watch (2015) and its partner NGOs in Kenya warned that "Kenyan security forces, including, but not limited to, the Anti-Terrorism Police Unit" were involved "in extrajudicial killings and enforced disappearances of terrorism suspects in Nairobi, on the coast and in the northeastern region" (Human Rights Watch 2015, 10). Supported by US counterterror aid, Kenyan security forces have systematically subjected civilians to harassment based on their ethnicity and religious background. Particularly, Kenyan government agents have mistakenly targeted civilians of ethnic Somali Kenyan background as well as Somali refugees as allegedly being affiliated to the terror group Al-Shabaab.

Those three vignettes of US foreign strategic support to Colombia, Pakistan, and Kenya demonstrate the transnational and global scope of the American foreign aid imperium as well as its ability to shape the domestic politics of subordinate states. There is a considerable case to apply, to falsify, or even to modify interest convergence theory in light of these additional cases outside Southeast Asia. While contemporary human rights literature in the social sciences (Merry 2006; Farmer 2005) tends to be macro-oriented as in the case of large-N statistical research, this book analyzes the relationship between foreign strategic support and human rights at various levels of analysis. I investigated the interactions between extranational and domestic political leaders' beliefs and expectations vis-à-vis the impact of their policy decisions upon local state repression and individual human rights. I presented concrete stories of individual human rights victims and explored how structural *discursive* and *material* conditions at the international and domestic levels jointly generated a particular human rights outcome at a given historical period. One direction for future research is to focus on the micro-level, by examining the individual motivations for abuses among high-ranking domestic and international actors, rank-and-file state agents, and nonstate actors. By focusing at the micro-level, future research can falsify the various theories of human rights outcomes produced by macro- and meso-oriented studies.

Limits and Possibilities of the US Foreign Aid Imperium

In this book, I aimed to dispel two inaccurate claims that are common to public and scholarly understanding concerning foreign aid. The first narrative pertains to the *Western-centric* myth, which portrays aid from the Global North as primarily beneficial to recipient countries. It characterizes the detrimental consequences of foreign aid as the fault of poor, irresponsible, and corrupt states in the Global South. The second narrative, meanwhile, refers to the *critical view*, which posits that any Western intervention—including foreign and human rights diplomacy initiatives—is nothing but evil, imperialistic, and detrimental to the emancipatory politics of peoples beyond the West. Both narratives are fundamentally wrong. One might argue that the solution to a crisis caused by failed intervention programs could be found *within* the US foreign aid imperium's toolkit—more precisely, by adopting the paradigms and strategies espoused by the imperium. Yet, I maintain that a sustainable and legitimate path for the protection of human dignity cannot be fostered through incremental reforms found within the US aid imperium and the international system that it dominates. That system, unfortunately, engenders profound material inequalities within and across nation-states, in racialized hierarchical relations among states, and in unjust gendered social relations within and beyond its core leadership. For that reason, we ought to rethink whether the protection of human dignity and effective aid giving practices are sustainable within deeply hierarchical and imperium-like structures consisting of powerful states as donors and subordinate governments as recipients.

Yet the reliance upon powerful donor states for human rights protection is not a faultless proposition. Emilie M. Hafner-Burton suggested that reforming the global human rights regime should include the establishment of "an exclusive club of steward states engaged in human rights promotion—to share information, set common standards, and coordinate the use of state power where possible" (2013, 188). She proposes that these "steward states"—Western states including the United States—must implement a "triage strategy," whereby resources are optimized in specific human rights promotion programs that are proven by evidence to be the most effective. Hafner-Burton assumes that there are inherently "good" and "bad" states when it comes to human rights protection. On the contrary, states are *not* monolithic and independent entities preprogrammed only for human rights protection. Many of these states are led by elected governments whose leaders are constrained by a vast array of pressures from various interest groups within and beyond its territory. A strong human rights commitment from yesterday could be trumped by other geostrategic aims the following day. Fueling the war on terror that led to a human rights crisis in many places worldwide, the fear that emerged in the post-9/11 years sabotaged the human rights commitments and democratic reforms introduced in the 1990s. Human rights principles in modern US foreign policy have always been provisional, as they arguably only gained traction in the 1970s during the Carter administration, which aimed to delegitimize the Soviet Union during the Cold War (Keys 2014).

Advocates of the aid imperium often frame foreign strategic assistance and human rights promotion as being in the *best* interest of the people in recipient countries. As Barnett (2012, 520) maintains, "paternalism is an enduring feature of global life," and "it permeates the discourses, practices, and institutions that govern the past, present, and future world orders." This book shows the paternalistic nature of the American aid imperium with its intrusive and, at times, coercive social engineering of societies through material support and the unjust imposition of a dominant narrative in global human rights discourses. Those policies, although enabled and strategically localized by the elites in the subordinate state, are sometimes devoid of deliberative and meaningful participation by the marginalized peoples they supposedly intend to help. While the US aid imperium is in retreat, the Chinese government has bolstered its aid interventions in the Global South—including in the civil wars and in a diverse range of investments in Africa (Hodzi 2018; Benabdallah 2020; Regilme and Hodzi 2021; Regilme and Hartmann 2018) and the war on drugs in the Philippines (Regilme 2020b, 7; Flores 2017). Those potential power shifts suggest that geostrategic interests shape the politics of aid in the era of great power rivalry, thereby sidelining the welfare of the most vulnerable communities in aid recipient states.

As Samuel Moyn (2017, 274) observes, "Imperialism still haunts contemporary liberalism in many ways, at a minimum in the functional replacement of formal empire with the promotion of human rights." Supported by the Global South's local elites, which are keen on consolidating their domestic authority, the United States and its supportive elites in the Global South—in their persistent imperium-building mode—instrumentalize foreign aid programs through the language of human rights. Human rights discourses are part of contentious politics, and even before the age of decolonization, Western imperial powers and local actors in the colonies invoked human rights to advance specific political objectives (Ibhawoh 2006; see also Mutua 2002; Regilme 2018d). In that sense, imperium-like models of global order need to vanish in order to give way to a world order where individuals and political communities realize human dignity through the prism of global justice. The politics of foreign aid emerges from deep-seated logics of domination and moral superiority, thereby laying the preconditions for violence. Such perverse political logics ought to give way to a post-imperium world order that is constitutionalized by nonviolence, justice, care-based economies, and universal humanity.

Appendix

1. In measuring the magnitude of state-initiated human rights violations, I use these two sources: (1) the Uppsala Conflict Data Program/UCDP (Pettersson, Högbladh, and Öberg 2019) and (2) the Political Terror Scale/PTS Scale (Gibney et al. 2017).
2. For the Political Terror Scale (PTS), a rating of 5 represents the worst classification in terms of the severity of human rights violations. It means that "terror has expanded to the whole population" and a clear example of this is North Korea, while a rating of 3 means "extensive political imprisonment" and that "execution or other political murders may be common." Contemporary Zimbabwe and Bangladesh typify this level of violence. The lowest levels of violence are represented either by a rating of 2 ("limited amount of imprisonment for nonviolent political activity" and "political murder is rare") or 1 ("torture is rare" and "political murders are rare"). Since the start of the PTS rating, Switzerland, Germany, and Sweden have been consistently rated with either a 1 or a 2 in any given year.
3. Data on human rights violations in the Philippines came from KARAPATAN (www.karapatan.org), the country's largest network of human rights organizations. Since the late 1990s, KARAPATAN has been producing an annual report on the human rights situation in the Philippines based on carefully aggregated data culled from local sources. Domestic statistical sources on Thailand's human rights violations are unavailable primarily because of the overall

absence of long-standing and widespread "cultural discourses" on enforced disappearances, torture, and the like. Alternatively, I refer to the UCDP and the PTS in assessing Thailand's human rights situation.

4. For the data on the Philippines (see the figures in chapter 3), local human rights reports recorded a slight increase in the number of enforced disappearances in the year 2000 (Asian Federation Against Involuntary Disappearances 2007; Clarke 1998, 190; Silliman 1994, 107), which was primarily due to the short-term local counterinsurgency campaign of the Estrada administration that enjoyed modest political support from the US government. Nonetheless, the number of enforced disappearances consistently increased after 2002 and reached its peak in 2005 and 2006, coinciding with the turbulent electoral and postelectoral scandals faced by the Arroyo administration in the mid-2000s. The number of disappearances substantially decreased from 2008 until 2010, corresponding with the growing human rights advocacy in the country and political pressures from the US government.

5. The data on US bilateral aid came from the US Agency for International Development (USAID) Greenbook (https://eads.usaid.gov/gbk). Annual measures of US military and economic aid from 1946 to 2016 were based on 2016 "constant dollars," unless stated otherwise.

6. Data on public opinion surveys in the Philippines came from the Manila-based Social Weather Station, the country's largest opinion poll organization. The SWS maintains archived statistical summaries of the SWS website unless stated otherwise (www.sws.org.ph).

Notes

1. https://www.nytimes.com/1978/12/07/archives/excerpts-from-carters-speech-on-anniversary-of-human-rights.html

2. My theory is analytically eclectic, which allows me to "complement, engage, and selectively utilize theoretical constructs embedded in contending research traditions to build complex arguments that bear on substantive problems of interest to both scholars and practitioners" (Sil and Katzenstein 2010, 411). For examples of this approach, see Regilme (2018a) and Katzenstein and Okawara (2002).

3. For examples of studies on US foreign policies' ideational foundations, see Mayroz (2019) on genocide; Doty (1996) on imperial representations; Parmar (2012) on philanthropic foundations; and Solomon (2015) and Holland (2012) on contemporary war on terror discourses.

4. For example, see Trisko (2012).

5. Figure 1.1 tests and updates the data analysis from Callaway and Matthews (2008, 81–82), which only covered the period from 1978 to 2003.

6. See appendix, footnote 4, for data sources.

7. See Engerman's (2018) historical research on US aid to India during the Cold War. That work does not explicitly analyze the broader theoretical insights concerning the causes and consequences of foreign aid.

8. The role of discourse in foreign aid gained more traction in the last two decades. See the following: on foreign aid and its impact on human rights (Regilme 2018b, 2018c); the motivating factors of foreign aid (van der Veen 2011); and the relationship between discourse and foreign aid (Phillips 2020).

9. See the work of Haberkorn (2018, especially 136–46 on the role of the United States) on Thailand during the Cold War era as well as Simpson (2008) on Indonesia-US relations in the 1960s.

10. On Asia, see Christie (1995) and Jetschke (2010). On Africa, see Branch (2011).

CHAPTER 2

1. http://www.latimes.com/world/africa/la-fg-us-africa-aid-2017-story.html

2. Milan Svolik's (2012) theory on authoritarian coalitions does not apply in the intended empirical scope of this book. Specifically, I focus on two countries that do not have full-blown authoritarian systems.

3. For a detailed discussion of state capacities in Thailand and the Philippines, see Crone (2011), Slater (2010), and McCoy (2009).

4. See Kinsella (2011) for a rich historical account of the distinctions between combatants and civilians. I consider civilians as those individuals who are not directly involved in armed rebellion against the state. My definitional choice is analytic, rather than explicitly normative.

CHAPTER 3

1. http://www.officialgazette.gov.ph/1993/12/10/speech-of-president-ramos-at-the-human-rights-day-with-the-indigenous-people/

CHAPTER 4

1. This is the same strategy in the case of Thaksin Shinawatra, as demonstrated in chapter 6, as well as Philippines president Rodrigo Duterte (2016–present), who was Arroyo's most loyal local politician when Duterte was still the mayor of Davao City. As of December 2018, more than a third of Duterte's presidential cabinet were former military and police generals (Ranada 2018).

2. Cacho Olivarez was one of the country's veteran journalists. She was a staunch critic of Marcos, Arroyo, and Aquino III, and she persistently defended press freedom throughout her career (Rappler 2020).

3. This recruitment tactic by the Philippine military can also be seen in the US-funded counterterror operations in Colombia during the same period. Poor people from the slums as well as indigenous peoples were recruited by the Colombian military, which later on killed those civilians and presented the dead bodies as rebel casualties. See Regilme (2020b, 12; 2018b, 358) concerning the false positives scandal in Colombia.

CHAPTER 6

1. Human rights group in Thailand only began documenting cases of military and police officers' physical harassment and killings of civilians in the 1990s. Incidents of physical integrity rights violations were recorded if they occurred during police riots or single mass events in which state security forces inflicted violence upon civilians.

2. The Communist Party of Thailand was active from 1942 until the early 1990s.

3. For a more detailed comparison of the statistical data on state-initiated civilian deaths between the post–Cold War and the war on terror periods, see also figures 1.4 (chapter 1) and 7.2 (chapter 7).

CHAPTER 7

1. Translated by Chris Baker and Pasuk Phongpaichit, http://pioneer.netserv. chula.ac.th/~ppasuk/t2/thaksinspeechondrugwar14january2003.pdf (accessed July 4, 2017).

2. White House, Office of the Press Secretary, https://2001-2009.state.gov/p/ eap/rls/rm/2003/25352.htm (accessed July 4, 2017).

Bibliography

Abaya, Antonio. 2007. "Extra-Judicial Blah." *Manila Standard Today* 3 (July 26), A4.
Abella, Jerrie. 2010. "Family Cries Foul Play in Pinoy's Death among US Troops." GMA News Online. March 15. http://www.gmanetwork.com/news/story/1861 26/news/nation/family-cries-foul-play-in-pinoy-s-death-among-us-troops
Abinales, Patricio. 2005. "Life after the Coup: The Military and Politics in Post-Authoritarian Philippines." *Philippine Political Science Journal* 26 (49): 27–62.
Abinales, Patricio, and Donna Amoroso. 2017. *State and Society in the Philippines.* Lanham, MD: Rowman and Littlefield.
Acharya, Amitav. 1999. "Southeast Asia's Democratic Moment." *Asian Survey* 39 (3): 418–32.
Acharya, Amitav. 2003. "Democratisation and the Prospects for Participatory Regionalism in Southeast Asia." *Third World Quarterly* 24 (2): 375–90.
Acharya, Amitav. 2009. *Whose Ideas Matter? Agency and Power in Asian Regionalism.* Ithaca: Cornell University Press.
Acharya, Amitav. 2014. "Global International Relations (IR) and Regional Worlds." *International Studies Quarterly* 58 (4): 647–59.
Acharya, Amitav, and Richard Stubbs. 2006. "Theorizing Southeast Asian Relations: An Introduction." *Pacific Review* 19 (2): 125–34.
Acharya, Amitav, and See Seng Tan. 2006. "Betwixt Balance and Community: America, ASEAN, and the Security of Southeast Asia." *International Relations of the Asia-Pacific* 6 (1): 37–59.
Acop, Dencio. 2006. "Assessing the Expanded Role of the Armed Forces of the Philippines in Nation-Building." *Asia-Pacific Social Science Review* 6 (2): 131–52.
Acop, Dencio. 2012. "The Expanded Nontraditional Role of the AFP: A Reassessment." *Prism: A Journal of the United States' National Defense University* 3 (2): 99–114.
Adams, Brad. 2003. "Thailand's Crackdown: Drug 'War' Kills Democracy, Too." *International Herald Tribune*, April 24. http://www.hrw.org/news/2003/04/23 /thailands-crackdown-drug-war-kills-democracy-too-0

Adriano, Joel. 2008. "Arroyo's Risky Politics of Patronage." *Asia Times Online*, December 9. Accessed January 5, 2015. http://www.atimes.com/atimes/South east_Asia/JL09Ae01.html

Agabin, Pacifico. 2012. *The Political Supreme Court*. Quezon City: University of the Philippines Press.

Agence France-Presse. 1992. "U.S. Cancels Military Maneuvers with Thailand." May 19.

Agence France-Presse. 1995. "US Trade Campaign Zeroes in on Southeast Asian Nations." September 21.

Agence France-Presse. 1997. "Thailand Objects to US Human Rights Report." November 12.

Agence France-Presse. 1999. "Albright to Arrive in Thailand for Wide-Ranging Talks." March 2.

Agence France-Presse. 2003. "Bush Visit to Boost RP's Image as Trusted US Ally in War vs Terror." *Philippine Star*, October 16. http://www.philstar.com/headl ines/224369/bush-visit-boost-rp%C2%92s-image-%C2%91trusted%C2%92 -us-ally-war-vs-terror

Ahmed, Faisal. 2012. "The Perils of Unearned Foreign Income: Aid, Remittances, and Government Survival." *American Political Science Review* 106 (1): 146–65.

Ahmed, Faisal. 2019. "Foreign Aid and Repression." In *Lessons on Foreign Aid and Economic Development*, edited by N. Dutta and C. Williamson. Cham, Switzerland: Palgrave.

Albert-Corpuz, Gerry. 2002. "GMA's 'Strong Republic' a Rehash of Marcos' 'Bagong Lipunan.'" *Bulatlat*, July 21. http://www.bulatlat.com/news/2-24/2-24 -sona-gerry.html

Albritton, Robert. 2005. "Thailand in 2004: The 'Crisis in the South'." *Asian Survey* 45 (1): 166–73.

Alipala, J. S., and R. D. Rosauro. 2014. "Groups Cheer PH-MILF Peace Pact: MNLF Unhappy. *Inquirer*, January 26. http://newsinfo.inquirer.net/569673/pe ace-groups-cheer-ph-milf-peace-pact-mnlf-unhappy

Alston, Philip. 2007. *Preliminary Note on the Visit of the Special Rapporteur on Extrajudicial, Summary or Arbitrary Executions, Philip Alston, to the Philippines*. February 12–21. New York: UN Human Rights Council. https://www2.ohchr.org/en glish/bodies/hrcouncil/docs/8session/A.HRC.8.3.Add.2_sp.doc

Alston, Philip. 2008. *Report of the Special Rapporteur on Extrajudicial, Summary or Arbitrary Executions, Mission to the Philippines*. New York: UN Human Rights Council. https://www.hr-dp.org/files/2014/06/27/Mission_to_Philippines_20 08.pdf

Alston, Philip. 2010. "The Challenges of Responding to Extrajudicial Executions: Interview with Philip Alston." *Journal of Human Rights Practice* 2 (3): 355–73.

Amnesty International. 2002. *Unmatched Power, Unmet Principles: The Human Rights Dimensions of US Training of Foreign Military and Police Forces*. Amnesty International USA. July 29. http://www.amnestyusa.org/pdfs/msp.pdf

Amnesty International. 2003a. *Document—Thailand: Extrajudicial Killing Is Not the Way to Suppress Drug Trafficking*. Amnesty International, June 14. https://www .amnesty.org/en/documents/asa39/001/2003/en/

Amnesty International. 2003b. *Document—Thailand: Grave Developments-Killings and Other Abuses.* Amnesty International, June 20. https://www.amnesty.org/en/documents/ASA39/008/2003/en/

Amnesty International. 2006a. *If You Want Peace, Work for Justice.* Amnesty International, June 14. https://www.amnesty.org/download/Documents/76000/asa 390012006en.pdf

Amnesty International. 2006b. *Political Killings, Human Rights and the Peace Process.* August 15. London: Amnesty International. https://www.amnesty.org/en/documents/asa35/006/2006/en/

Amnesty International USA. 2014. *Pakistan Human Rights.* Amnesty International USA. http://www.amnestyusa.org/our-work/countries/asia-and-the-pacific/pakistan (accessed September 2, 2020).

Amorn, Vithoon. 1991. "Military Has Long Involvement in Thai Politics." *Reuters,* February 23.

Andrei, Mercedes. 1999. "Estrada, Clinton Meet Today to Promote 'New Era' in RP-US Relations." *Business World,* September 13, 1.

Aquino, Benigno, III. 2010. "Speech of President Aquino at the 62nd Anniversary of the Universal Declaration on Human Rights." *Official Gazette of the Republic of the Philippines,* December 10. https://www.officialgazette.gov.ph/2010/12/10/speech-of-president-aquino-at-the-62nd-anniversary-of-the-universal-declaration-on-human-rights/

Aquino, Benigno, III, and David Bradley. 2010. "A Conversation with Benigno S. Aquino III." September 23. https://www.cfr.org/event/conversation-benigno-s-aquino-iii

Arendt, Hannah. 1970. *On Violence.* Orlando, FL: Harvest Book.

Armed Forces of the Philippines. 1997. "AFP Campaign Plan 'KAISAGANAAN'—Letter of Instructions 14/97." Quezon City: Armed Forces of the Philippines. http://www.pdgs.org/Archivo/d000003e.htm

Arroyo, Gloria Macapagal. 2002. *Gloria Macapagal-Arroyo, Second State of the Nation Address, July 22, 2002.* Official Gazette of the Republic of the Philippines. https://www.officialgazette.gov.ph/2002/07/22/gloria-macapagal-arroyo-second-state-of-the-nation-address-july-22-2002/

Arroyo, Gloria Macapagal. 2006. "Text of Proclamation No. 1017." Official Gazette of the Republic of the Philippines. https://www.officialgazette.gov.ph/2006/02/24/proclamation-no-1017-s-2006/

Arugay, Aries. 2011. "The Military in Philippine Politics: Still Politicized and Increasingly Autonomous." In *Political Resurgence of the Military in Southeast Asia,* edited by Marcus Mietzner, 85–106. Abingdon, Oxford: Routledge.

Asia Foundation. 2002. *The Asia Foundation: Bilateral Conference on United States–Thailand Relations in the 21st Century.* Washington, DC: Asia Foundation.

Asian Federation Against Involuntary Disappearances. 2007. *Statistics on Enforced Disappearance in Asia.* Quezon City: Asian Federation Against Involuntary Disappearances. Accessed November 24, 2013. http://www.afad-online.org/rsl/stats_pg_263_283.pdf

Asian Federation Against Involuntary Disappearances. 2010. *Overall Results: FIND's Search and Documentation Work (November 1985 to July 31, 2010).* Quezon City: Asian Federation Against Involuntary Disappearances. Accessed October 8, 2013. http://www.afad-online.org/statistics/find_stat.htm

Asian Human Rights Commission. 2006. "Extrajudicial Killings and Human Rights Abuses in the Philippines." *Asian Human Rights Commission.* Accessed November 3, 2019. http://www.humanrights.asia/resources/journals-magazin es/article2/0505/extrajudicial-killings-human-rights-abuses-in-the-philippines

Asian Human Rights Commission. 2014. "Thailand: Crime of the State: Enforced Disappearance, Killings and Impunity." March 27. http://www.humanrights.as ia/news/forwarded-news/AHRC-FAT-006-2014

Asian Tribune. 2003. "Thai PM Defends Anti-Terrorism Decrees." *Asian Tribune,* August 15. http://www.asiantribune.com/news/2003/08/15/thai-pm-defends-anti-terrorism-decrees

Askew, Marc. 2007. *Conspiracy, Politics, and a Disorderly Border: The Struggle to Comprehend Insurgency in Thailand's Deep South.* Washington, DC: East-West Center.

Associated Press. 1992. "Member of Fact-Finding Committee Resigns after Threats." Associated Press News Archive. Accessed April 1, 2014. http://www .apnewsarchive.com/1992/Member-of-Fact-Finding-Committee-Resigns-Aft er-Threats/id-46552d7586c646c94ca3d92956aac333

Associated Press. 1994. "U.S., Philippines to Sign Ship Servicing Agreement." November 10. http://www.lexisnexis.com/de/business/delivery/DownloadD oc.do?delFmt=QDS_EF_PDF&fileSize=5000&dnldFilePath=%2Fl-n%2Fsh ared%2Fprod%2Fdiscus%2Fqds%2Frepository%2Fdocs%2F0%2F21%2F2 825%3A420170210%2Fformatted_doc&zipDelivery=false&dnldFileName= _U.S.%2C_Philippines_to_Sign_Ship_Servicing_Ag&jobHandle=2825%3A4 20170210

Associated Press. 1999. "Thai Human Rights Said to Improve." January 19. Retrieved from Factiva database.

Associated Press. 2001. "Bush: War on Drugs Aids War on Terror." December 14. https://www.cbsnews.com/news/bush-war-on-drugs-aids-war-on-terror/

Associated Press. 2003. "Bush Declares Thailand a Major Non-NATO Ally." *New Straits Times,* October, 20.

Bacani, Luis. 2013. "Courts Congested with over 1 Million Cases Yearly—NSCB. *Philippine Star,* June 14. http://www.philstar.com/headlines/2013/06/14/9539 27/courts-congested-over-1-million-cases-yearly-nscb

Balana, Cynthia. 2009. "US Ups Foreign Aid to Philippines." *Philippine Daily Inquirer.* Accessed December 22, 2012. http://newsinfo.inquirer.net/breakingn ews/nation/view/20090513-204846/US-ups-foreign-aid-to-Philippines

Baldwin, David. 1995. "Review Article: Security Studies and the End of the Cold War." *World Politics* 48 (1): 117–41.

Bamrungsuk, Surāchat. 1988. *United States Foreign Policy and Thai Military Rule, 1947–1977.* Bangkok: Editions Duankamol.

Bangkok Post. 1993. "Thais Slam Use of Rights as Protectionist Motives." *Bangkok Post,* March 31, 1–2.

Bangkok Post. 1996. "Human Rights Violation." *Bangkok Post,* April 21.

Bangkok Post. 2003. "TRT Set for 20 Years in Power, PM Tells Faithful." *Bangkok Post,* April 28, 1.

Banlaoi, Rommel. 2010. *Philippine Security in the Age of Terror: National, Regional, and Global Challenges in the Post-9/11 World.* Boca Raton, FL: CRC Press.

Barboza, David. 2010. "China Passes Japan as Second-Largest Economy." *New*

York Times, August 15, 1–5. http://www.nytimes.com/2010/08/16/business/gl obal/16yuan.html?pagewanted=all

Barcenas, Democrito. 2014. "Tell It to Sunstar: Jovito Palparan." *Sun Star*, August 25. http://www.sunstar.com.ph/cebu/local-news/2014/08/25/tell-it-sunstar-jo vito-palparan-361834

Barnett, Michael. 2011. *Empire of Humanity: A History of Humanitarianism*. Ithaca: Cornell University Press.

Barnett, Michael. 2012. "International Paternalism and Humanitarian Governance." *Global Constitutionalism* 1 (3): 485–521.

Barr, Michael D. 2007. "Lee Kuan Yew and the 'Asian Values' Debate." *Asian Studies Review* 24 (3): 309–34.

Barratt, Bethany. 2004. "Aiding or Abetting: British Foreign Aid Decisions and Recipient Country Human Rights." In *Understanding Human Rights Violations: New Systematic Studies*, edited by Sabine C. Carey and Steven C. Poe, 43–62. Surrey: Ashgate.

Barratt, Bethany. 2008. *Human Rights and Foreign Aid: For Love or Money?* New York: Routledge.

Bauzon, Kenneth. 1999. "The Philippines: The 1996 Peace Agreement for the Southern Philippines: An Assessment." *Ethnic Studies Report* 17 (2): 253–81.

Baviera, Aileen. 2012. "Aquino: Pushing the Envelope, Single-Mindedly." *Southeast Asian Affairs* 1: 241–56.

BBC. 1993. "Thailand's National Security Chief Interviewed on Burma, Cambodia." BBC Monitoring Service: Asia-Pacific, August 21.

BBC. 2010. "Aquino to Invite More Investors to Philippines during US Visit Sep." *BBC World Service*, February 20.

Beach, Derek. 2012. *Analyzing Foreign Policy*. London: Palgrave Macmillan.

Beach, Derek, and Pedersen, Rasmus. 2013. *Process-Tracing Methods: Foundations and Guidelines*. Ann Arbor: University of Michigan Press.

Beehner, Lionel. 2010. "Bloodshed in Mindanao." *Foreign Policy*, May 11, 1–3. Accessed October 10, 2013. http://www.foreignpolicy.com/articles/2010/05 /11/chaos_in_mindinao?page=full

Bell, Stephen. 2011. "Do We Really Need a New 'Constructivist Institutionalism' to Explain Institutional Change?" *British Journal of Political Science* 41 (4): 883–906.

Bello, Walden, Herbert Docena, Marissa de Guzman, and Marylou Malig. 2004. *The Anti-Development State: The Political Economy of Permanent Crisis in the Philippines*. Quezon City: University of the Philippines, Department of Sociology and Focus on the Global South.

Benabdallah, Lina. 2020. *Shaping the Future of Power: Knowledge Production and Network-Building in China-Africa Relations*. Ann Arbor: University of Michigan Press.

Bennet, James. 1998. "Clinton Urges Asia Investors to Aid Lands Like Thailand." *New York Times*, March 14, A5.

Bennett, Colin. 1991. "What Is Policy Convergence and What Causes It?" *British Journal of Political Science* 21 (2): 215–33.

Bernas, Joaquin. 2007. *A Living Constitution: The Troubled Arroyo Presidency*. Quezon City, Manila: Ateneo University Press.

Bhattacharji, Preeti. 2009. *Terrorism Havens: Philippines*. Washington, DC: Council on Foreign Relations.

Bhumiprabhas, Subhatra. 2006. "Women Ask NHRC for News of Kin." *The Nation—Thailand*, March 11. Accessed June 25, 2014. http://www.nationmulti media.com/2006/03/11/national/national_20002515.php

Bienert, Anja. 2018. "Command Responsibility and the Use of Force by the Police." In *The Police and International Human Rights Law*, edited by R. Alleweldt and G. Fickenscher. Cham, Switzerland: Springer.

Blair, Harry, and Gary Hansen. 1994. *Weighing in on the Scales of Justice: Strategic Approaches for Donor-Supported Rule of Law Programs*. Washington, DC: USAID Development Information Services Clearinghouse.

Blanton, Shannon. 2000. "Promoting Human Rights and Democracy in the Developing World: U.S. Rhetoric versus U.S. Arms Exports." *American Journal of Political Science* 44 (1): 123–31.

Blanton, Shannon. 2005. "Foreign Policy in Transition? U.S. Arms Transfers, Democracy and Human Rights." *International Studies Quarterly* 49 (4): 647–67.

Blum, William. 2004. *Killing Hope: US Military and CIA Interventions since World War 2*. London: Zed Books.

Bodansky, Daniel. 1999. "The Legitimacy of International Governance: A Coming Challenge for International Environmental Law?" *American Journal of International Law* 93 (3): 596–624.

Bodansky, Daniel. 2008. "The Concept of Legitimacy in International Law." In *Beiträge zum ausländischen öffentlichen Recht und Völkerrecht*, edited by Rüdiger Wolfrum and Volker Röben, 309–17. Berlin: Springer.

Böhnke, Jan, and Christoph Zürcher. 2013. "Aid, Minds and Hearts: The Impact of Aid in Conflict Zones." *Conflict Management and Peace Science* 30: 411–32.

Bonner, Raymond. 2003. "Thailand Tiptoes in Step with the American Antiterror Effort." *New York Times*, June 8, N29.

Boutton, Andrew. 2019. "Military Aid, Regime Vulnerability and the Escalation of Political Violence." *British Journal of Political Science*, September 26. https://dx .doi.org/10.1017/s000712341900022x

Bower, Ernest. 2012. "President Aquino's U.S. Visit Will Cap Revitalization of Alliance." Center for Strategic and International Studies, June 4. https://csis .org/publication/president-aquinos-us-visit-will-cap-revitalization-alliance

Branch, Adam. 2011. *Displacing Human Rights: War and Intervention in Northern Uganda*. New York City: Oxford University Press.

Branigin, William. 1992. "Prospect of Clinton Win Worries Southeast Asians." *Washington Post*, October 25, A35.

Bräutigam, Deborah A., and Stephen Knack. 2004. "Foreign Aid, Institutions, and Governance in Sub-Saharan Africa." *Economic Development and Cultural Change* 52 (2): 255–85.

Breuil, Brenda, and Ralph Rozema. 2009. "Fatal Imaginations: Death Squads in Davao City and Medellín Compared." *Crime, Law, and Social Change* 52 (4): 405–24.

Bridges, Brian. 1999. "Europe and the Asian Financial Crisis: Coping with Contagion." *Asian Survey* 39 (3): 456–67.

Brinkley, Douglas. 1997. "Democratic Enlargement: The Clinton Doctrine." *Foreign Policy* 106: 110–27.

Briscoe, C. H. 2004. "Balikatan Exercises Spearheaded ARSOF Operations." *Special Warfare* 17 (1): 6–25.

Briscoe, David. 1993a. "Ramos Urges Clinton to Take 'New Look' at Philippines." Associated Press. Accessed January 7, 2013. http://www.apnewsarchive.com/19 93/Ramos-Urges-Clinton-to-Take-New-Look-at-Philippines/id-b0aace6eb3 ca30f1645ba3599622db17?SearchText=philippines%20united%20states%20h uman%20rights;Display_

Briscoe, David. 1993b. "Security, Aid Issues No Longer Dominate US-Philippine Relations." Associated Press. Accessed January 7, 2013. http://www.apnewsarc hive.com/1993/Security-Aid-Issues-No-Longer-Dominate-US-Philippine-Re lations/id-15a7bd5dbdd97c6c599aede9ba86e6de?SearchText=philippines%20 united%20states%20human%20rights;Display_

Brodeur, Jean-Paul. 1983. "High Policing and Low Policing: Remarks about the Policing of Political Activities." *Social Problems* 30 (5): 507–20.

Brodeur, Jean-Paul. 2007. "High and Low Policing in Post-9/11 Times." *Policing* 1 (1): 25–37.

Brown, Stephen, and Jörn Grävingholt. 2016. "Security, Development, and the Securitization of Foreign Aid." In *The Securitization of Foreign Aid*, edited by Stephen Brown and Jörn Grävingholt, 1–18. Basingstoke, UK: Palgrave.

Brownlee, Jason. 2007. *Authoritarianism in an Age of Democratization.* Cambridge: Cambridge University Press.

Bueno de Mesquita, Bruce, and Alastair Smith. 2007. "Foreign Aid and Policy Concessions." *Journal of Conflict Resolution* 51 (2): 251–84.

Bueno de Mesquita, Bruce, and Alastair Smith. 2009. "Political Survival and Endogenous Institutional Change." *Comparative Political Studies* 42 (2): 167–97.

Bueno de Mesquita, Bruce, Alastair Smith, Randolph Siverson, and James D. Morrow. 2005. *The Logic of Political Survival.* Cambridge, MA: MIT Press.

Bulatlat. 2009. "Military Refuses to Leave 15 Lumad Communities in Surigao Del Sur." *Bulatlat*, August 5. Accessed June 27, 2013. http://bulatlat.com/main /2009/08/05/military-refuses-to-leave-15-lumad-communities-in-surigao-del -sur/

Bulatlat. 2010. "Download Fact-Finding Report on the Death of Gregan Cardeño." *Bulatlat*, March 11. Accessed June 26, 2020. https://www.bulatlat.com/2010/03 /11/download-fact-finding-report-on-the-death-of-gregan-cardeno/

Bunbongkam, Suchit. 1991. "Toward an End to 'Thai-Style' Democracy." *Wall Street Journal*, December 11, 6.

Bunbongkarn, Suchit. 1993. "Thailand in 1992: In Search of a Democratic Order." *Asian Survey* 33 (2): 218–23.

Bureau of Economic and Business Affairs, State Department. 2000. *Country Commercial Guide: Philippines for Fiscal Year 2000, US Department of State.* Washington, DC: US Department of State. http://1997-2001.state.gov/www/about_sta te/business/com_guides/2000/eap/philippines_CCG2000.pdf

Busbarat, Pongphisoot. 2016. "'Bamboo Swirling in the Wind': Thailand's Foreign Policy Imbalance between China and the United States." *Contemporary Southeast Asia* 38 (2): 233–37.

Busbarat, Pongphisoot. 2017. "Thai-US Relations in the Post–Cold War Era: Untying the Special Relationship." *Asian Security* 13 (3): 256–74.

Bush, George W. 2003. "President Discusses War on Terror in Thailand." October 19. US State Department. http://2001-2009.state.gov/p/eap/rls/rm/2003/253 52.htm

Bush, George W., and Gloria Macapagal Arroyo. 2001a. "Joint Statement between President George W. Bush and President Gloria Macapagal-Arroyo of the Philippines on the 50th Anniversary of the U.S.-Philippine Alliance." November 20. US Government Printing Office: 1697–1700. http://www.gpo.gov/fds ys/pkg/WCPD-2001-11-26/pdf/WCPD-2001-11-26-Pg1697-2.pdf

Bush, George W., and Gloria Macapagal Arroyo. 2001b. "Remarks Following Discussions with President Gloria Macapagal-Arroyo of the Philippines and an Exchange with Reporters." November 20. US Government Printing Office: 1694–97. http://www.gpo.gov/fdsys/pkg/WCPD-2001-11-26/pdf/WCPD-20 01-11-26-Pg1694.pdf

Buzan, Barry, and Ole Waever. 2003. *Regions and Powers: The Structure of International Security*. Cambridge: Cambridge University Press.

Buzan, Barry, Ole Waever, and Jaap de Wilde. 1998. *Security: A New Framework for Analysis*. Boulder: Lynne Rienner.

Caballero-Anthony, Mely. 2003. "The Winds of Change in the Philippines: Whither the Strong Republic?" *Southeast Asian Affairs* 2003 (1): 213–27.

Calica, Aurea, and Marichu Villanueva. 2002. "US to Netherlands: Freeze CPP Funds." *Philippine Star*, August 13. http://www.philstar.com/headlines/171848 /us-netherlands-freeze-cpp-funds

Callaghy, Thomas. 1987. "The State as Lame Leviathan: The Patrimonial Administrative State in Africa." In *The African State in Transition*, edited by Zaki Ergas. London: Macmillan.

Callaway, Rhonda L., and Elizabeth G. Matthews. 2008. *Strategic US Foreign Assistance: The Battle between Human Rights and National Security*. Burlington, VT: Ashgate.

Calonzo, Andreo. 2014. "DFA Chief: US Bound to Defend PHL in Case of Attack in West Philippine Sea." *GMA News Online*, April 30. http://www.gmanetwo rk.com/news/story/358978/news/nation/dfa-chief-us-bound-to-defend-phl-in -case-of-attack-in-west-philippine-sea

Capulong, Eduardo. 2002. "Philippines: Arroyo Turns the 'War on Terrorism' Into War on the Left." *International Socialist Review*, September/October. http:// www.thirdworldtraveler.com/Asia/Arroyo_WarOnLeft.html

Carcamo, Dennis, and Camille Diola. 2013. "SC to AFP Chief: Locate Men in Burgos Disappearance." *Philippine Star*, April 12. http://www.philstar.com/hea dlines/2013/04/12/929858/sc-afp-chief-locate-men-burgos-disappearance

Cardenas, Sonia. 2004. "Norm Collision: Explaining the Effects of International Human Rights Pressure on State Behavior." *International Studies Review* 6 (2): 213–32.

Carleton, David, and M. Stohl. 1985. "The Foreign Policy of Human Rights: Rhetoric and Reality from Jimmy Carter to Ronald Reagan." *Human Rights Quarterly* 7 (2): 205–29.

Carleton, David, and M. Stohl. 1987. "The Role of Human Rights in U.S. Foreign Assistance Policy: A Critique and Reappraisal." *American Journal of Political Science* 31 (4): 1002–18.

Carnegie, Allison, and Nikolay Marinov. 2017. "Foreign Aid, Human Rights, and Democracy Promotion: Evidence from a Natural Experiment." *American Journal of Political Science* (January 18): 1–13.

Casauay, Angela. 2012. "It's a First in Asia: 'Desaparecidos' Law." *Rappler*, December 21. http://www.rappler.com/nation/18363-first-in-asia-desaparecidos-law

Casino, Teddy. 2007. "The Philippines after 9–11: Focus on Mindanao as the 'Second Front' of the US' War on Terror." *Arkibong Bayan*, 1–4. Accessed June 10, 2013. http://www.arkibongbayan.org/2007-09Sept11-911forum/doc/lecture%20on%209-11%20final.doc

Chachavalpongpun, Pavin. 2005. *A Plastic Nation: The Curse of Thainess in Thai-Burmese Relations.* New York: University Press of America.

Chachavalpongpun, Pavin. 2011a. "Thaksin, the Military, and Thailand's Protracted Political Crisis." In *The Political Resurgence of the Military in Southeast Asia*, edited by Marcus Mietzner, 45–62. Abingdon, Oxford: Routledge.

Chachavalpongpun, Pavin. 2011b. "The Necessity of Enemies in Thailand's Troubled Politics." *Asian Survey* 51: 1019–41.

Chachavalpongpun, Pavin. 2016. "Thailand in Sino-U.S. Rivalry. At the Crossroads of the Thai Internal Conflict." Southeast Asian Studies at the University of Freiburg. Accessed 20 January 2021. https://www.southeastasianstudies.uni-freiburg.de/documents/occasional-paper/op29.pdf

Chacko, Priya, and Kanishka Jayasuriya. 2017. "Trump, the Authoritarian Populist Revolt and the Future of the Rules-Based Order in Asia." *Australian Journal of International Affairs* 71 (2): 121–27.

Chalk, Peter. 2001. "Separatism and Southeast Asia: The Islamic Factor in Southern Thailand, Mindanao, and Aceh." *Studies in Conflict and Terrorism* 24 (4): 241–69.

Chaloemtiarana, Thak. 2007. "Distinctions with a Difference: The Despotic Paternalism of Sarit Thanarat and the Demagogic Authoritarianism of Thaksin Shinawatra." *Crossroads: An Interdisciplinary Journal of Southeast Asian Studies* 19 (1): 50–94.

Chambers, Paul. 2004. "U.S.-Thai Relations after 9/11: A New Era in Cooperation?" *Contemporary Southeast Asia: A Journal of International and Strategic Affairs* 26 (3): 460–79.

Chambers, Paul. 2012. "A Precarious Path: The Evolution of Civil–Military Relations in the Philippines." *Asian Security* 8 (2): 138–63.

Chambers, Paul, and Napisa Waitoolkiat. 2017. "Arch-Royalist Rent: The Political Economy of the Military in Thailand." In *Khaki Capitalism: The Political Economy of the Military in Southeast Asia*, edited by Paul Chambers and Napisa Waitoolkiat, 40–92. Copenhagen: NIAS Press.

Charles, Deborah. 1996. "U.S. Drug Chief Lauds Thais, Slams Burmese." *Reuters*, November 22.

Cheesman, Nick. 2003. "Murder as Public Policy in Thailand." Asian Legal Resource Centre. Accessed May 25, 2014. http://www.article2.org/mainfile.php/0203/86/

Cheng, Willard. 2011. "Clinton Heaps Praise on Pacquiao, Reaffirms US Support for PH." ABS-CBN News.com, November 16. http://www.abs-cbnnews.com/nation/11/16/11/clinton-heaps-praise-pacquiao-reaffirms-us-support-ph

Chenoweth, Erica, and Maria Stephan. 2011. *Why Civil Resistance Works: The Strategic Logic of Nonviolent Conflict.* New York: Columbia University Press.

Cheow, Eric. 2003. "Terrorists Regroup in Southern Thailand." *Asia Times Online.* Accessed June 15, 2014. http://www.atimes.com/atimes/Southeast_Asia/EH1 9Ae05.html

Children's Rehabilitation Center. 2008. *GMA's War on Terrorism: Children Made as Sacrificial Lambs.* Accessed June 27, 2013. http://www.childrehabcenter.org/res ources/documents/gmas-war-terrorism-children-made-sacrificial-lambs

Choi, Seung-Whan, and Patrick James. 2017. "Are US Foreign Policy Tools Effective in Improving Human Rights Conditions?" *Chinese Journal of International Politics* 10 (3): 331–56.

Chorev, Nitsan. 2020. *Give and Take: Developmental Foreign Aid and the Pharmaceutical Industry in East Africa.* Princeton: Princeton University Press.

Chotiya, Parichart. 1997. "The Changing Role of Provincial Business in the Thai Political Economy." In *Political Change in Thailand: Democracy and Participation,* edited by Kevin Hewison, 251–61. London: Routledge.

Chouvy, Pierre Arnoud. 2010. *Opium: Uncovering the Politics of the Poppy.* Cambridge, MA: Harvard University Press.

Christensen, Scott, and Amar Siamwalla. 1993. *Beyond Patronage: Tasks for the Thai State.* Bangkok: Thailand Development Research Institute Foundation.

Christie, Kenneth. 1995. "Regime Security and Human Rights in Southeast Asia." *Political Studies* 43: 204–18.

Cibulka, Frank. 1999. "The Philippine Foreign Policy of the Ramos Administration: The Quest for Security of a Weak State." *Asian Journal of Political Science* 7 (1): 108–34.

Cingranelli, David, and Thomas E. Pasquarello. 1985. "Human Rights Practices and the Distribution of U.S. Foreign Aid to Latin American Countries." *American Journal of Political Science* 29 (3): 539–63.

Cingranelli, David, and David Richards. 1999. "Respect for Human Rights after the End of the Cold War." *Journal of Peace Research* 36 (5): 511–34.

Ciorciari, John. 2012. "Institutionalizing Human Rights in Southeast Asia." *Human Rights Quarterly* 34: 695–725.

Clapano, Jose. 2003. "Pimentel Wants US Payments for Overflights." *Philippine Star,* March 23. http://www.philstar.com/headlines/199968/pimentel-wants-us -payments-overflights

Clarke, Gerard. 1998. *The Politics of NGOs in South-East Asia: Participation and Protest in the Philippines.* London: Routledge.

Clinton, Hillary. 2011. "America's Pacific Century." *Foreign Policy,* October 11. http://www.foreignpolicy.com/articles/2011/10/11/americas_pacific_century

Clinton, William. 1993. "The President's News Conference with President Fidel Ramos of the Philippines." November 22. https://www.govinfo.gov/content /pkg/PPP-1993-book2/html/PPP-1993-book2-doc-pg2047.htm

Clinton, William. 1994. "William J. Clinton: Remarks to the International Business Community in Jakarta." https://www.govinfo.gov/content/pkg/WCPD -1994-11-21/pdf/WCPD-1994-11-21-Pg2404.pdf

Cole, Benjamin. 2006. "The Philippines Media: Agent of Stability or Restraint?"

In *Conflict, Terrorism and the Media in Asia*, edited by Benjamin Cole, 61–81. Abingdon, Oxford: Routledge.

Conde, Carlos. 2005. "Philippine Death Squads Extend Their Reach." *New York Tiimes*, March 23. http://www.nytimes.com/2005/03/22/world/asia/22iht-phils .html

Conde, Carlos. 2009. "Abuse Charges Persist in Philippines' Fight against Communists." *New York Times*, August 13. http://www.nytimes.com/2009/08/13/wo rld/asia/13iht-phils.html

Conde, Carlos H. 2014. "What Senators' Silence on Duterte Threat Means." *Rappler*. Accessed February 7, 2014. http://www.rappler.com/nation/49946-hum an-rights-duterte-senate-hearing?utm_source=feedburner&utm_medium=fee d&utm_campaign=Feed%3A+rappler+(Rappler)

Connors, Michael. 2011. "Ambivalent about Human Rights: Thai Democracy." In *Human Rights in Asia*, edited by Thomas Davis and Brian Galligan, 103–22. Cheltenham: Edward Elgar.

Cook, Nerida. 2007. "Democratisation in Thailand Revisited." *Asian Studies Review* 9: 157–73.

Cooley, Alexander. 2008. *Base Politics: Democratic Change and the U.S. Military Overseas*. Ithaca: Cornell University Press.

Cooney, Kevin. 1992. "Thai Pro-Democracy Parties Stick to Alliance." Reuters, September 15.

Cooper, Michael. 1997. "Amnesty Worried at Extrajudicial Killings in Thailand." Agence France-Presse, May 19.

Coordinating Committee of Human Rights Organizations in Thailand/CCHROT. 1996. "Thailand: Another Community Activist Murdered." Accessed February 5, 2021. https://web.archive.org/web/20090228111924/http://www.hrsolidari ty.net/mainfile.php/1996vol06no03/

Corpus, John. 2010. "Oplan Bantay Laya: Blue Print for State Terror." In *Oplan Bantay Laya*, 6–15. Manila: Ibon Foundation.

Corpuz, Gerry. 2002. "GMA's 'Strong Republic' a Rehash of Marcos' 'Bagong Lipunan'." Karapatan: Alliance for the Advancement of People's Rights 2 (24). Accessed September 2, 2020. http://www.bulatlat.com/news/2-24/2-24-sona -gerry.html

Corpuz, Gerry. 2003. "Taking Cues from SC Decision Voiding PEA-Amari Deal: Militants Want Halt to All Reclamation Projects in Manila Bay." Karapatan: Alliance for the Advancement of People's Rights. Accessed October 8, 2013. http://www.bulatlat.com/news/3-15/3-15-peaamari.html

Corvera, Ann. 2003a. "AFP Chief Admits Corruption in Military." *Philippine Star*, August 1. http://www.philstar.com/headlines/215651/afp-chief-admits-corrup tion-military

Corvera, Ann. 2003b. "New York Times Editorial: US Aid Helping Militants Because of AFP Corruption." *Philippine Star*, October 19. http://www.philstar .com/headlines/224696/new-york-times-editorial-us-aid-helping-militants-be cause-afp-corruption

Cotton, James. 2003. "Southeast Asia after 11 September." *Terrorism and Political Violence* 15 (1): 148–70.

Crisostomo, Isabelo. 1997. *President Fidel v. Ramos: Builder, Reformer, Peacemaker.* Quezon City: J. Kriz Publishing.

Crispin, Shawn. 2008. "US and Thailand: Allies in Torture." *Asia Times Online.* Accessed May 25, 2014. http://www.atimes.com/atimes/Southeast_Asia/JA25 Ae01.html

Crispin, Shawn, and Jeremy Wagstaff. 2003. "The Terror War's Next Offensive." *Far Eastern Economic Review* 166 (34): 12–16.

Croissant, Aurel. 2007. "Muslim Insurgency, Political Violence, and Democracy in Thailand." *Terrorism and Political Violence* 19 (1): 1–18.

Croissant, Aurel, and David Kuehn. 2009. "Patterns of Civilian Control of the Military in East Asia's New Democracies." *Journal of East Asian Studies* 9 (2): 187–217.

Croissant, Aurel, David Kuehn, and Philip Lorenz. 2012. *Breaking with the Past? Civil-Military Relations in the Emerging Democracies of East Asia.* Honolulu: East-West Center.

Crone, Donald. 2011. "State, Social Elites, and Government Capacity in Southeast Asia." *World Politics* 40 (2): 252–68.

Cruz, Booma. 1993. "Ramos-Clinton Exchange of Letters Show Better Ties." *Manila Chronicle* 33 (687) (December 21): 2.

Cumming-Bruce, Nick. 2004. "Some Neighbors Fault Hard-Line Approach in Thailand's South: Thaksin and Unrest Stir Doubt in Region." *New York Times,* November 11. https://www.nytimes.com/2004/11/11/news/in-southern-thaila nd-a-crossroads-of-terror.html

Cupin, Bea, and Richard Falcatan. 2014. "RTC Judge Shot Dead in Zamboanga." *Rappler.* Accessed May 24, 2014. http://www.rappler.com/nation/51780-zamb oanga-shooting-rtc-judge

Curato, Nicole. 2013. "Deliberative Capacity as an Indicator of Democratic Quality: The Case of the Philippines." *International Political Science Review* 36 (1): 99–116.

Curato, Nicole, and Aries Arugay. 2010. "Militarised Politics and Politicised Military: Society-Military Relations under the Arroyo Regime." In *Project 2010: Gloria Macapagal-Arroyo's Legacy.* Quezon City: Focus on the Global South.

Curtis, Polly, and Martin Hodgson. 2008. "Student Researching Al-Qaida Tactics Held for Six Days." *The Guardian,* May 24. http://www.guardian.co.uk/educati on/2008/may/24/highereducation.uk

Dabhoiwala, Meryam. 2003. "A Chronology of Thailand's 'War on Drugs'." Asian Human Rights Commission. Accessed February 26, 2014. http://www.human rights.asia/resources/journals-magazines/article2/0203/a-chronology-of-thaila nds-war-on-drugs

Davao Today. 2007. "Philippines: Satur Back on Campaign Trail; Palace, AFP Finally Admit Roles in Anti-Bayan Muna Drive." *Davao Today,* April 9, 1–2. Accessed May 25, 2013. http://davaotoday.com/2007/04/09/philippines-satur -back-on-campaign-trail-palace-afp-finally-admit-roles-in-anti-bayan-muna -drive/

Davao Today. 2013. "'Outrageous' Fiscal's Dismissal vs. Army Suspects Marks Tampakan Massacre 1st Anniversary." *Davao Today,* October 20. Accessed March 8, 2014. http://davaotoday.com/main/2013/10/20/outrageous-fiscals-di smissal-vs-army-suspects-marks-tampakan-massacre-1st-anniversary/

Davenport, Christian. 2007. "State Repression and Political Order." *Annual Review of Political Science* 10 (1): 1–23.

Debusman, Bernd. 2011. "Pakistan and Questions over Foreign Aid." Reuters, May 13. http://blogs.reuters.com/bernddebusmann/2011/05/13/pakistan-and -questions-over-foreign-aid/

De Castro, Renato. 1999. "Adjusting to the Post-US Bases Era: The Ordeal of the Philippine Military's Modernization Program." *Armed Forces & Society* 26 (1): 119–38.

De Castro, Renato Cruz. 2000. "Managing 'Strategic Unipolarity': The ASEAN States' Responses to the Post–Cold War Regional Environment." In *Southeast Asian Perspectives on Security*, edited by Derek Da Cunha. Institute of Southeast Asian Studies. https://doi.org/10.1355/9789812307064-007

De Castro, Renato. 2004. "Addressing International Terrorism in Southeast Asia: A Matter of Strategic or Functional Approach?" *Contemporary Southeast Asia* 26 (2): 193–217.

De Castro, Renato Cruz. 2012. *Future Challenges in the US-Philippines Alliance*. Asia Pacific Bulletin—East-West Center: 1–2.

De Jesus, Julliane. 2014. "First Woman 2-Star General Heads Newly Formed Human-Rights Panel." *Philippine Daily Inquirer*, February 13. http://newsinfo .inquirer.net/577785/first-woman-2-star-general-heads-newly-formed-human -rights-panel

Del Rosario-Malonzo, Jennifer. 2010. "Blood Trail: The US' Active Role in OBL." In *Oplan Bantay Laya*, 49–61. Manila: Ibon Foundation.

de Mesquita, Ethan, and Eric S. Dickson. 2007. "The Propaganda of the Deed: Terrorism, Counterterrorism, and Mobilization." *American Journal of Political Science* 51 (2): 364–81.

Demirel-Pegg, Tijen, and J. Moskowitz. 2009. "US Aid Allocation: The Nexus of Human Rights, Democracy, and Development." *Journal of Peace Research* 46 (2): 163–80.

de Quiros, Conrado. 2014. "Impunity." *Philippine Daily Inquirer*, March 4. http:// opinion.inquirer.net/72208/impunity-2

DeYoung, Karen. 2010. "Human Rights Report Threatens Aid to Pakistan." *Washington Post*, April 6. http://www.washingtonpost.com/wp-dyn/content/article /2010/04/05/AR2010040504373_pf.html

Diamond, Jared, and James Robinson. 2011. "Afterword: Using Comparative Methods in Studies of Human History." In *Natural Experiments of History*, edited by Jared Diamond and James Robinson, 257–75. Cambridge: Belknap Press of Harvard University Press.

Dietrich, Simone, and Amanda Murdie. 2016. "Human Rights Shaming through INGOs and Foreign Aid Delivery." *Review of International Organizations* 12 (1): 95–120.

Dimond, Paul. 2006. "The Philippines: Fragile Democracy or Strong Republic?" *Asian Affairs* 37 (2): 210–19.

Dixon, Robyn. 2017. "With 20 Million People Facing Starvation, Trump's Foreign Aid Cuts Strike Fear." *Los Angeles Times*, March 19. http://www.latimes.com /world/africa/la-fg-us-africa-aid-2017-story.html

Djankov, Simeon, Jose Montalvo, and Marta Reynal-Querol. 2008. "The Curse of Aid." *Journal of Economic Growth* 13 (3): 169–94.

Docena, Herbert. 2007a. "The U.S. Troops' 'Unconventional' Presence." Philippine Center for Investigative Journalism, 1–4. Accessed January 30, 2021. https://www.alainet.org/es/node/119631?language=es

Docena, Herbert. 2007b. *Unconventional Warfare: Are US Special Forces Engaged in an "Offensive War" in the Philippines?* Quezon City: Focus on the Global South.

Docena, Herbert. 2008. "In the Dragon's Lair." Transnational Institute, February 26. https://www.tni.org/en/article/in-the-dragons-lair

Doner, Richard, Bryan Ritchie, and Dan Slater. 2005. "Systemic Vulnerability and the Origins of Developmental States: Northeast and Southeast Asia in Comparative Perspective." *International Organization* 59 (2): 327–61.

Donilon, Tom. 2011. "America Is Back in the Pacific and Will Uphold the Rules." *Financial Times*, November 27. Accessed March 5, 2020. http://www.ft.com/in tl/cms/s/0/4f3febac-1761-11e1-b00e-00144feabdc0.html

Doty, Roxanne. 1996. *Imperial Encounters: The Politics of Representation in North-South Relations.* Minneapolis: University of Minnesota Press.

Dragsbaek, Johannes. 2007. "The Great Power Game and Thai Military Rule." *Asia Insights* 3: 15–18.

Dube, Oeindrila, and Suresh Naidu. 2015. "Bases, Bullets, and Ballots: The Effect of US Military Aid on Political Conflict in Colombia." *Journal of Politics* 77: 249–67.

Duffield, Mark. 2007. *Development, Security and Unending War: Governing the World of Peoples.* Cambridge: Polity Press.

Dutta, Nabamita, Peter T. Leeson, and Claudia Williamson. 2013. "The Amplification Effect: Foreign Aid's Impact on Political Institutions." *Kyklos* 66 (2): 208–28.

Eadie, Pauline. 2011. "Legislating for Terrorism: The Philippines' Human Security Act 2007." *Journal of Terrorism Research* 2 (3): 24–33.

Earth Rights International. 2012. *The Yadana Pipeline.* Accessed May 5, 2014. http://www.earthrights.org/campaigns/yadana-pipeline

Easterly, William. 2008. "Foreign Aid Goes Military!" Brookings Institution, November 6, 1–14. https://www.brookings.edu/opinions/foreign-aid-goes-mi litary/

Economist. 2008. "The Thai Police: A Law unto Themselves." April 17. http://www.economist.com/node/11058580

Egco, Joel. 2001. "RP-US 'War-Pact' to Fight Terrorism." *Manila Standard* 15 (174), November 14, 2.

Emmerson, Donald. 1995. "Singapore and the 'Asian Values' Debate." *Journal of Democracy* 6 (4): 95–105.

Eng, Peter. 1997. "Thai Democracy: The People Speak." *Washington Quarterly* 20 (4): 169–89.

Eng, Peter. 2002. *Thailand's Incomplete Information Revolution.* Development Dialogue 1. Accessed April 1, 2014. http://www.dhf.uu.se/pdffiler/02_01/02_1_p art6.pdf

Engel, Susan. 2014. "The Not-So-Great Aid Debate." *Third World Quarterly* 35 (8): 1374–89.

Engerman, David. 2018. *The Price of Aid: The Economic Cold War in India.* Cambridge, MA: Harvard University Press.

Engle, Karen. 2016. "A Genealogy of Human Rights Agenda." In *Anti-Impunity and the Human Rights Agenda*, edited by Karen Engle, Zinaida Miller, and D. M. Davis. Cambridge: Cambridge University Press.

Engle, Karen, Zinaida Miller, and D. M. Davis, eds. 2016. "Introduction." In *Anti-Impunity and the Human Rights Agenda*. Cambridge: Cambridge University Press.

Englehart, Neil. 2010. "Democracy and the Thai Middle Class: Globalization, Modernization, and Constitutional Change." *Asian Survey* 43 (2): 253–79.

Enloe, Cynthia. 1993. *The Morning After: Sexual Politics at the End of the Cold War*. Berkeley: University of California Press.

Ermita, Eduardo. 2004. "National Defense." In *The Macapagal-Arroyo Presidency and Administration, Record and Legacy (2001–2004)*, edited by J. Abueva, V. Bautista, M. Domingo, and E. Nicolas, 195–202. Diliman: University of the Philippines Press.

Esmaquel, Paterno. 2017. "Why China Prefers Arroyo over Aquino." *Rappler*. Accessed September 16, 2017. https://www.rappler.com/nation/9128-how-china-views-aquino,-arroyo

Fajardo-Heyward, Paola. 2015. "Understanding the Effect of Security Assistance on Human Rights: The Case of Plan Colombia." *Latin Americanist* 59 (2): 3–27.

Fariss, Christopher. 2010. "The Strategic Substitution of United States Foreign Aid." *Foreign Policy Analysis* 6: 107–31.

Farmer, Paul. 2005. *Pathologies of Power: Health, Human Rights, and the New War on the Poor*. Berkeley: University of California Press.

Fearon, James. 1991. "Counterfactuals and Hypothesis Testing in Political Science." *World Politics* 43 (2): 169–95.

Fellowship of Reconciliation and Colombia-Europe-U.S. Human Rights Observatory. 2014. "The Rise and Fall of 'False Positive' Killings in Colombia: The Role of U.S. Military Assistance, 2000–2010." May 13. https://omeka.as.kent.edu/items/show/733

Ferrara, Federico. 2010. *Thailand Unhinged: Unraveling the Myth of a Thai-Style Democracy*. Singapore: Equinox Publishing.

Feyzioglu, Tarhan, Vinaya Swaroop, and Min Zhu. 1998. "A Panel Data Analysis of the Fungibility of Foreign Aid." *World Bank Economic Review* 12: 29–58.

Filipino Express. 1997. "No More Bases: Envoy Says U.S. Is Not Interested in Building in Mindanao." *Filipino Express* (Jersey City, NJ), January 27, 4.

Filipino Reporter. 2010. "Aquino Bags $2.8-B, Mends Investors' Trust." *Filipino Reporter* 38 (43): 1 and 12. Accessed February 20, 2014. http://search.proquest.com/news/docview/758616980/6B95BE9C70D74098PQ/183?accountid=15172

Filipino Reporter. 2012. "Obama Toasts Aquino." *Filipino Reporter*. Accessed February 20, 2014. http://search.proquest.com/news/docview/1024820236/6B95BE9C70D74098PQ/7?accountid=15172

Fineman, Daniel. 1997. *A Special Relationship: The United States and Military Government in Thailand, 1947–1958*. Manoa: University of Hawai'i Press.

Finnemore, Martha, and Kathryn Sikkink. 1998. "International Norm Dynamics and Political Change." *International Organization* 52 (4): 887–917.

Fisher, Richard. 1999. *Rebuilding the US-Philippine Alliance*. Washington, DC: Heritage Foundation.

Fiss, Owen. 1993. "The Limits of Judicial Independence." *University of Miami Inter-American Law Review* 25 (1): 57–76.

Flick, Uwe. 2014. *An Introduction to Qualitative Research*. London: SAGE.

Flores, Helen. 2017. "China Urges UN to Support Philippines' War on Drugs." *Philippine Star*, May 12. https://www.philstar.com/headlines/2017/05/12/1699 401/china-urges-un-support-philippines-war-drugs

Floyd, Rita. 2006. "Securitization Theory and Securitization Studies." *Journal of International Relations and Development* 9 (1): 53–61.

Fonbuena, Carmela. 2013. "Allegations of Human Rights Violations Declining—AFP." *Rappler*. Accessed November 20, 2013. http://www.rappler.com/nation /33506-military-human-rights-violations-declining

Foot, Rosemary. 2005. "Collateral Damage: Human Rights Consequences of Counterterrorist Action in the Asia-Pacific." *International Affairs* 81 (2): 411–25.

Ford, Nicholas, and Suporn Koetsawang. 1991. "The Socio-Cultural Context of the Transmission of HIV in Thailand." *Social Science & Medicine* 33 (4): 405–14.

Francia, Luis. 2007. "GWOT: the Philippines." *The Nation*, December 13. http:// www.thenation.com/article/gwot-philippines

Franco, Jennifer, and Patricio Abinales. 2007. "Again, They're Killing Peasants in the Philippines." *Critical Asian Studies* 39 (2): 315–28.

Frank, Robert. 2000. "The Corruption in the Philippines Keeps Getting Worse with Estrada's Tactics and Cronyism." *Wall Street Journal*, September 20. http://www.sexwork.com/philippines/wsjcorruption.html

Funston, John. 2002. "Thailand: Thaksin Fever." *Southeast Asian Affairs*: 305–25.

Gadavanij, Savitri. 2020. "Contentious Polities and Political Polarization in Thailand: Post-Thaksin Reflections." *Discourse & Society* 31 (1): 44–63.

Ganesan, N. 2004. "Thaksin and the Politics of Domestic and Regional Consolidation in Thailand." *Contemporary Southeast Asia* 26 (1): 26–44.

GEM Program Office, Philippines, USAID. 2002. *Growth with Equity in Mindanao Program Report, Phase 1 Completion Report*. October 1995 to September 2001.

Gershkoff, Amy, and Shana Kushner. 2005. "Shaping Public Opinion: The 9/11-Iraq Connection in the Bush Administration's Rhetoric." *Perspectives on Politics* 3 (3) 525–37.

Gershman, John. 2002. "Is Southeast Asia the Second Front?" *Foreign Affairs* 81 (73): 60–74.

Gibney, Mark, Linda Cornett, Reed Wood, Peter Haschke, Daniel Arnon, and Attilio Pisanò. 2017. "The Political Terror Scale 1976–2016." Political Terror Scale website, http://www.politicalterrorscale.org

Gill, Lesley. 2004. *The School of the Americas: Military Training and Political Violence in the Americas*. Durham: Duke University Press.

Girling, John. 1996. *Interpreting Development: Capitalism, Democracy, and the Middle Class in Thailand*. Ithaca, NY: Cornell University, Southeast Asian Studies Program.

Glennie, Jonathan. 2011. "Giving Aid to Poor Countries Is Hardly a Great Act of Generosity." *Guardian*, June 14. https://www.theguardian.com/global-develo pment/poverty-matters/2011/jun/14/aid-is-hardly-an-act-of-great-generosity -effectiveness

Gloria, Glenda. 2013. "Jonas Burgos: Trapped in a Web of Lives." *Rappler*. Accessed June 25, 2020. http://www.rappler.com/newsbreak/25355-jonas-burgos-trapped-in-a-web-of-lives

Gloria, Glenda, Aries Rufo, and Gemma Bagayaua-Mendoza. 2011. *The Enemy Within: An Inside Story on Military Corruption*. Quezon City, Philippines: Public Trust Media Group.

Go, Julian. 2011. *Patterns of Empire: The British and American Empires, 1688 to the Present*. New York: Cambridge University Press.

Goh, Evelyn, et al. 2012. "Review of Natasha Hamilton-Hart, *Hard Interests, Soft Illusions: Southeast Asia and American Power*. Ithaca: Cornell University Press, 2012." *H-Diplo and the International Studies Association's Security Studies Section (ISSS)* 4 (8). https://issforum.org/ISSF/PDF/ISSF-Roundtable-4-8.pdf

Goldmann, Kjell. 2005. "Appropriateness and Consequences: The Logic of Neo-Institutionalism." *Governance* 18 (1): 35–52.

Goldstein, Judith, and Robert O. Keohane. 1993. "Ideas and Foreign Policy: An Analytical Framework." In *Ideas and Foreign Policy: Beliefs, Institutions, and Politics*, edited by Judith Goldstein and Robert O. Keohane. Ithaca: Cornell University Press.

Gonzalez, Daisy. 2005. "The Rise and Rise of Rodrigo Duterte." *Davao Today*, 5, no. 40 (November 13–19). http://www.bulatlat.com/news/5-40/5-40-duterte.htm

Gonzalez, Mia. 2001a. "GMA Gets Call from Bush, Global Backing." *Today* 2551 (June 25): 1.

Gonzalez, Mia. 2001b. "GMA Ok'd America's Use of RP Airspace 'as Needed'." *Today* 2798 (October 2): 1.

Government of the Philippine Republic. 2012. "Republic Act 10353: An Act Defining and Penalizing Enforced or Involuntary Disappearance and for Other Purposes." Official Gazette. https://web.archive.org/web/20130118211322/http://www.gov.ph/2012/12/21/republic-act-no-10353/

Greenhouse, Steven. 1994. "State Department Finds Widespread Abuse of World's Women." *New York Times*, February 3. http://www.nytimes.com/1994/02/03/world/state-dept-finds-widespread-abuse-of-world-s-women.html

Grewal, Inderpal. 2017. *Saving the Security State: Exceptional Citizens in Twenty-First-Century America*. Durham: Duke University Press.

Grynaviski, Eric. 2014. *Constructive Illusions: Misperceiving the Origins of International Cooperation*. Ithaca: Cornell University Press.

Guevarra, Marina. 2007. "Sustaining an Unpopular Regime." May 31. http://www.publicintegrity.org/2007/05/31/5763/sustaining-unpopular-regime

Gunaratna, Rohan, and Arabinda Acharya. 2013. *The Terrorist Threat from Thailand: Jihad or Quest for Justice?* Washington, DC: Potomac Books.

Gunness, Christopher, and Gloria Macapagal-Arroyo. 2001. "Philippines President Gloria Arroyo on the War against Terrorism—Interview." *BBC World Service*, December 5. http://www.bbc.co.uk/worldservice/asiapacific/eastasiatoday/indepth/011120_arroyo.shtml

Gupta, Sanjeev, Luiz Mello, and Raju Sharan. 2001. "Corruption and Military Spending." *European Journal of Political Economy* 17: 749–77.

Haberkorn, Tyrell. 2013. "Getting Away with Murder in Thailand: State Violence and Impunity in Phatthalung." In *State Violence in East Asia*, edited by N. Ganesan and Sung Chull Kim, 185–208. Lexington: University Press of Kentucky.

Haberkorn, Tyrell. 2018. *In Plain Sight: Impunity and Human Rights in Thailand.* Madison: University of Wisconsin Press.

Hafner-Burton, Emilie. 2005. "Right or Robust? The Sensitive Nature of Repression to Globalization." *Journal of Peace Research* 42 (6): 679–98.

Hafner-Burton, Emilie. 2009. *Forced to Be Good: Why Trade Agreements Boost Human Rights.* Ithaca: Cornell University Press.

Hafner-Burton, Emilie. 2013. *Making Human Rights a Reality.* Princeton: Princeton University Press.

Hafner-Burton, Emilie. 2014. "A Social Science of Human Rights." *Journal of Peace Research* 51 (2): 273–86.

Hafner-Burton, Emilie, Susan D. Hyde, and Ryan S Jablonski. 2014. "When Do Governments Resort to Election Violence?" *British Journal of Political Science* 44 (1): 149–79.

Hafner-Burton, Emilie, and James Ron. 2007. "Human Rights Institutions: Rhetoric and Efficacy." *Journal of Peace Research* 44 (4): 379–84.

Hafner-Burton, Emilie, and James Ron. 2009. "Seeing Double: Human Rights Impact through Qualitative and Quantitative Eyes." *World Politics* 61 (2): 360–401.

Hagelin, Bjorn. 1988. "Military Dependency: Thailand and the Philippines." *Journal of Peace Research* 25 (4): 431–48.

Hall, Rosalie Arcala. 2006. "Politics in the Frontline: Local Civil-Military Interactions in Communist Counterinsurgency Operations in the Philippines." *Philippine Political Science Journal* 27 (50): 1–30.

Hall, Rosalie Arcala. 2010. "Boots on Unstable Ground: Democratic Governance of the Armed Forces under Post 9/11 US-Philippine Military Relations." *Asia-Pacific Social Sciences Review* 10 (2): 25–42.

Hamilton-Hart, Natasha. 2010. "External Influences on Political Violence in Southeast Asia." In *Political Violence in South and Southeast Asia: Critical Perspectives,* edited by Itty Abraham, Edward Newman, and Meredith Weiss, 112–40. Tokyo: United Nations University Press.

Hamilton-Hart, Natasha. 2012. *Hard Interests, Soft Illusions: Southeast Asia and American Power.* Ithaca: Cornell University Press.

Hamilton-Hart, Natasha. 2017. "Deal-Makers and Spoilers: Trump and Regime Security in Southeast Asia." *Contemporary Southeast Asia: A Journal of International and Strategic Affairs* 39: 42–49.

Hansen, Lene. 2006. *Security as Practice: Discourse Analysis and the Bosnian War.* London: Routledge.

Harrigan, Jane, and Chengang Wang. 2011. "A New Approach to the Allocation of Aid among Developing Countries: Is the USA Different from the Rest?" *World Development* 39: 1281–93.

Harris, Bryant, Robbie Gramer, and Emily Tamkin. 2017. "The End of Foreign Aid as We Know It." *Foreign Policy,* April 24, 1–7. http://foreignpolicy.com/20 17/04/24/u-s-agency-for-international-development-foreign-aid-state-depart ment-trump-slash-foreign-funding/

Hattori, Tomohisa. 2001. "Reconceptualizing Foreign Aid." *Review of International Political Economy* 8 (4): 633–60.

Hay, Colin. 2006. "Constructivist Institutionalism." In *The Oxford Handbook of*

Political Institutions, edited by R. A. W. Rhodes, Sarah A. Binder, and Bert Rockman, 56–74. Oxford: Oxford University Press.

Hayes, Jarrod. 2012. "Securitization, Social Identity, and Democratic Security: Nixon, India, and the Ties That Bind." *International Organization* 66 (1): 63–93.

Hayes, Jarrod. 2013. *Constructing National Security: US Relations with India and China*. New York: Cambridge University Press.

Head, Jonathan. 2007. "A Fit and Proper Premiership?" *BBC Sport*, July 31. http://news.bbc.co.uk/sport2/hi/football/teams/m/man_city/6922650.stm

Hedman, Eva-Lotta, and John Sidel. 2000. *Philippine Politics and Society in the Twentieth Century: Colonial Legacies, Post-Colonial Trajectories*. London: Routledge.

Hernandez, Carolina. 1995. *ASEAN Perspectives on Human Rights and Democracy in International Relations*. Quezon City: University of the Philippines CIDS and the University of the Philippines Press.

Hernandez, Carolina. 2006. *The AFP's Institutional Responses to Armed Conflict: A Continuing Quest for the Right Approach*. Makati City, Metro Manila: Philippine Institute for Development Studies.

Hernandez, Carolina, and Maria Ubarra. 1999. *Restoring and Strengthening Civilian Control: Best Practices in Civil-Military Relations in the Philippines*. Institute for Strategic and Development Studies, December 31. https://www.ndi.org/node/22335

Hewison, Kevin. 1997. "Introduction." In *Political Change in Thailand: Democracy and Participation*, edited by Kevin Hewison, 1–20. London: Routledge.

Hewison, Kevin, and Andrew Brown. 1994. "Labour and Unions in an Industrializing Thailand." *Journal of Contemporary Asia* 24 (4): 483–514.

Hodzi, Obert. 2018. *The End of China's Non-Intervention Policy in Africa*. Cham, Switzerland: Palgrave.

Holden, William. 2009. "Ashes from the Phoenix: State Terrorism and the Party-List Groups in the Philippines." *Contemporary Politics* 15 (4): 377–93.

Holden, William, and Daniel Jacobson. 2013. *Mining and Natural Hazard Vulnerability in the Philippines: Digging to Development or Digging to Disaster?* New York: Anthem Press.

Holland, Jack. 2012. *Selling the War on Terror: Foreign Policy Discourses after 9/11*. London: Routledge.

Horaichakul, Surat. 2003. "The Far South of Thailand in the Era of the American Empire, 9/11 Version, and Thaksin's 'Cash and Gungho' Premiership." *Asian Review*. http://horachaikul.blogspot.com/2007/09/far-south-of-thailand-in-era-of.html

Human Rights Committee. 2004. *General Comment 31. Nature of the General Legal Obligation on States Parties to the Covenant*. UN Doc. CCPR/C/21/Rev.1/Add.13 https://www.refworld.org/docid/478b26ae2.html

Human Rights Now. 2008. *Report on Extrajudicial Killings and Enforced Disappearances in the Philippines*. Tokyo: Human Rights Now.

Human Rights Watch. 1993a. "Human Rights Report: 1993." http://www.hrw.org/reports/1993/WR93/Asw-11.htm#P397_166328

Human Rights Watch. 1993b. "Philippines, 1993: Human Rights Watch." http://www.hrw.org/reports/1993/WR93/Asw-09.htm#TopOfPage

Human Rights Watch. 1994. "Human Rights Report: Thailand." http://www.hrw
.org/reports/1994/WR94/Asia-11.htm#P446_157551

Human Rights Watch. 1998. "Human Rights Report: Thailand." http://www.hrw
.org/legacy/worldreport/Asia-11.htm#P981_250969

Human Rights Watch. 1999. "HRW World Report 1999: Thailand: Human Rights
Developments." http://www.hrw.org/legacy/worldreport99/asia/thailand.html

Human Rights Watch. 2001. "Human Rights Watch World Report 2001: Thailand: Human Rights Developments." http://www.hrw.org/legacy/wr2k1/asia
/thailand.html

Human Rights Watch. 2004a. *Thailand: Not Enough Graves: The War on Drugs,
HIV/AIDS, and Violation of Human Rights. Human Rights Watch* 16 (8): 1–58.
http://www.hrw.org/reports/2004/thailand0704/thailand0704.pdf

Human Rights Watch. 2004b. "Timeline of Thailand's War on Drugs." https://
web.archive.org/web/20090218111618/http://www.hrw.org/legacy/english/do
cs/2004/07/07/thaila9014.htm

Human Rights Watch. 2004c. "Human Rights Abuses and the War on Drugs."
https://www.hrw.org/reports/2004/thailand0704/4.htm

Human Rights Watch. 2007a. *"It Was Like Suddenly My Son No Longer Existed":
Enforced Disappearances in Thailand's Southern Border Provinces.* https://www.hrw
.org/reports/2007/thailand0307/

Human Rights Watch. 2007b. "US: Suspend Non-Humanitarian Aid to Pakistan."
Human Rights Watch. https://www.hrw.org/news/2007/11/08/us-suspend-non
-humanitarian-aid-pakistan

Human Rights Watch. 2009. *"You Can Die Any Time": Death Squad Killings in Mindanao.* New York City: Human Rights Watch.

Human Rights Watch. 2010a. *"Targets of Both Sides": Violence against Students,
Teachers, and Schools in Thailand's Southern Border Provinces.* New York: Human
Rights Watch.

Human Rights Watch. 2010b. *"They Own the People": The Ampatuans, State-Backed
Militias, and Killings in the Southern Philippines.* New York: Human Rights
Watch. https://www.hrw.org/report/2010/11/16/they-own-people/ampatuans
-state-backed-militias-and-killings-southern-philippines#_ftnref201

Human Rights Watch. 2012a. "Philippines: Milestone Law Criminalizes Forced
Disappearances." http://www.hrw.org/news/2012/12/21/philippines-milesto
ne-law-criminalizes-forced-disappearances

Human Rights Watch. 2012b. "Philippines: Obama Should Press Aquino to Tackle
Abuses." http://www.hrw.org/news/2012/06/07/philippines-obama-should-pr
ess-aquino-tackle-abuses

Human Rights Watch. 2013a. *Letter to President Aquino re: State of the Nation Address
and Human Rights.* New York City: Human Rights Watch.

Human Rights Watch. 2013b. "World Report 2013: Philippines." http://www.hrw
.org/world-report/2013/country-chapters/philippines?page=3 (February 18,
2014).

Human Rights Watch. 2013c. *You Are All Terrorists": Kenyan Police Abuse of Refugees
in Nairobi.* http://www.hrw.org/sites/default/files/reports/kenya0513_ForUplo
ad_0_0.pdf

Human Rights Watch. 2015. "Joint Policy Letter to President Obama ahead of

Visit to Kenya." *Human Rights Watch*, July 15, 1–8. https://www.hrw.org/news/2015/07/15/joint-policy-letter-president-obama-ahead-visit-kenya

Human Rights Watch. 2017. "The Dangerous Rise of Populism." January 12. https://www.hrw.org/world-report/2017/country-chapters/dangerous-rise-of-populism

Huntington, Samuel P. 1957. *The Soldier and the State: The Theory and Politics of Civil-Military Relations*. Cambridge: Harvard University Press.

Hyde, Susan. 2011. *The Pseudo-Democrat's Dilemma: Why Election Observation Became an International Norm*. Ithaca: Cornell University Press.

Ibhawoh, Bonny. 2006. *Imperialism and Human Rights*. Albany: State University of New York Press.

IBON Foundation. 2005. "Aid Militarization and Arroyo's Policy of Repression." In *A New Wave of State Terror in the Philippines*, edited by IBON Foundation, 32–36. Manila: IBON Foundation.

IBON Foundation. 2006. *Stop the Killings in the Philippines*. Manila: IBON Foundation.

IBON Foundation. 2007. *Stop the killings, Abductions, and Involuntary or Enforced Disappearances in the Philippines*. Manila: IBON Foundation.

Ibrahim, Azeem. 2009. "How America Is Funding Corruption in Pakistan." *Foreign Policy* website, August 11. https://foreignpolicy.com/2009/08/11/how-america-is-funding-corruption-in-pakistan/

Ignatieff, Michael. 2004. *The Lesser Evil: Political Ethics in an Age of Terror*. Princeton: Princeton University Press.

Ikenberry, John, David Lake, and Michael Mastanduno. 1988. "Conclusion: An Institutional Approach to American Foreign Economic Policy." *International Organization* 42 (1): 219–43.

Ilchmann, Susanne. 2003. "Thousands of Dead as a Result of Thailand's 'War on Drugs.'" World Socialist website, May 19. http://www.wsws.org/en/articles/2003/05/thai-m09.html

Indigenous Peoples' Rights-Monitor Philippines, Tebtebba Foundation Indigenous Peoples' International Centre for Policy, Philippines, Philippine Indigenous Peoples' Link/PIPLINKS in London, United Kingdom. 2008. *The Human Rights Situation of Indigenous Peoples in the Philippines*. New York: Office of the United Nations High Commissioner for Human Rights. http://lib.ohchr.org/HRBodies/UPR/Documents/Session1/PH/IPRM_PHL_UPR_S1_2008_IndigenousPeopleRightsMonitor_uprsubmission.pdf

Inquirer News. 2014. "You Vowed to Help, Edita Burgos Reminds Aquino." *Inquirer News*, April 28. http://newsinfo.inquirer.net/597779/you-vowed-to-help-edita-burgos-reminds-aquino

InterAksyon. 2012. "Anti-Mining, Human Rights Groups Blame Sagittarius for 3 Killings in Davao Del Sur." *Interaksyon*, October 25. https://web.archive.org/web/20121129031058/http://www.interaksyon.com/article/46488/anti-mining-human-rights-groups-blame-sagittarius-for-3-killings-in-davao-del-sur

International Coordinating Secretariat in Utrecht and IBON Foundation. 2007. *Repression and Resistance: the Filipino People vs Gloria Macapagal-Arroyo, George W. Bush, et al.* Utrecht: International Coordinating Secretariat in Utrecht; Quezon City: IBON Foundation.

International Crisis Group. 2005. *Thailand's Emergency Decree: No Solution*. Accessed September 2, 2020. https://web.archive.org/web/20160707040551/http://www.crisisgroup.org/~/media/Files/asia/south-east-asia/thailand/105_thailand_s_emergency_decree_no_solution_web.pdf

Inter-Press Service. 1992. "Asia: Pushing to Redefine 'Human Rights'." November 11. Inter Press Service Global Information Network. Retrieved from Factiva database.

Ismartono, Yuli. 1992. September 22. "Thailand: Democratization a Priority for First-Time Politicians." InterPress Service: 1–2. Retrieved from Factiva database.

Ivarsson, Søren, and Lotte Isager. 2010. "Introduction: Challenging the Standard Total View of the Thai Monarchy." In *Saying the Unsayable: Monarchy and Democracy in Thailand*, edited by Søren Ivarsson and Lotte Isager, 1–26. Copenhagen: NIAS Press.

Jablonski, Ryan S. 2014. "How Aid Targets Votes: The Impact of Electoral Incentives on Foreign Aid Distribution." *World Politics* 66 (2): 293–330.

Jacobson, Richard. 2013. "Modernizing the Philippine Military." *Diplomat*, August 22. http://thediplomat.com/2013/08/modernizing-the-philippine-military/?all=true

Jadoon, Amira. 2017. "Persuasion and Predation: The Effects of U.S. Military Aid and International Development Aid on Civilian Killings." *Studies in Conflict & Terrorism* 41 (10): 776–800.

Jaleco, Rodney. 2010. "Aquino Wrote Obama before Getting MCC Agreement." *ABS-CBN News*, October 10. http://www.abs-cbnnews.com/nation/08/10/10/aquino-wrote-obama-getting-mcc-agreement

Jervis, Robert. 2005. *American Foreign Policy in a New Era*. New York: Routledge.

Jervis, Robert. 2010. *Why Intelligence Fails: Lessons from the Iranian Revolution and the Iraq War*. Ithaca: Cornell University Press.

Jervis, Robert, Francis J. Gavin, Joshua Rovner, and Diane Labrosse. 2018. "Introduction." In *Chaos in the Liberal Order*, edited by Robert Jervis, Francis J. Gavin, Joshua Rovner, and Diane Labrosse. New York: Columbia University Press.

Jetschke, Anja. 1999. "Linking the Unlinkable? International Norms and Nationalism in Indonesia and the Philippines." In *The Power of Human Rights: International Norms and Domestic Change*, edited by Thomas Risse, Stephen C. Ropp, and Kathryn Sikkink, 134–71. Cambridge: Cambridge University Press.

Jetschke, Anja. 2010. *Human Rights and State Security Indonesia and the Philippines*. Philadelphia: University of Pennsylvania Press.

Jha, Pankaj. 2007. "The Philippines Human Security Act: Will It Be Successful?" Institute of Peace and Conflict Studies, July 23. https://web.archive.org/web/20150503191910/http://www.ipcs.org/article/terrorism/the-philippines-human-security-act-will-it-be-successful-2338.html

Jitpiromrsi, Srisompob, and Duncan McCargo. 2008. "A Ministry for the South: New Governance Proposals for Thailand's Southern Region." *Contemporary Southeast Asia: A Journal of International and Strategic Affairs* 30 (3): 403–28.

Johnson, Darryl, and Surakiart Sathirathai. 2003. "Exchange of Letters between US Ambassador to Thailand and the Thai Foreign Affairs Minister Regarding Article 98 of the Rome Statute." Thai Ministry of Foreign Affairs and the US Embassy in Bangkok.

Jones, Lee. 2010. "ASEAN's Unchanged Melody? The Theory and Practice of 'Non-Interference' in Southeast Asia." *Pacific Review* 23 (4): 479–502.

Jones, Lee. 2011. "Beyond Securitization: Explaining the Scope of Security Policy in Southeast Asia." *International Relations of the Asia-Pacific* 11 (3): 403–32.

Jones, Lee. 2012. *ASEAN, Sovereignty and Intervention in Southeast Asia.* London: Palgrave Macmillan.

Jorgensen, Nick. 2009. "Impunity and Oversight: When Do Governments Police Themselves?" *Journal of Human Rights* 8 (4): 385–404.

Kalyvas, Stathis. 1999. "Wanton and Senseless? The Logic of Massacres in Algeria." *Rationality and Society* 11 (3): 243–85.

Kalyvas, Stathis. 2006. *The Logic of Violence in Civil War.* New York: Cambridge University Press.

Kalyvas, Stathis, Ian Shapiro, and Tarek Masoud, eds. 2008. *Order, Conflict, and Violence.* Cambridge: Cambridge University Press.

Karapatan. 1997. "The Ramos Presidency and Human Rights." http://webcache .googleusercontent.com/search?q=cache:XltWQZaEkwYJ:www.hartford-hwp .com/archives/54a/039.html+&cd=11&hl=en&ct=clnk&gl=nl

Karapatan. 2009. *Oplan Bantay Laya: Blueprint for Terror and Impunity.* 2009 Report on the Human Rights Situation in the Philippines. http://www.bulatlat.com /main/wp-content/uploads/2010/03/Karapatan-2009-Human-Rights-Report.pdf

Karapatan. 2010. *2010 Year-End Report on the Human Rights Situation in the Philippines.* Quezon City: Karapatan Alliance for the Advancement of People's Rights.

Karapatan. 2011. *KARAPATAN Monitor, July-September 2011.* Quezon City, Metro Manila: Karapatan Alliance for the Advancement of People's Rights.

Karapatan. 2013. *KARAPATAN Monitor—January to April 2013.* Quezon City, Metro Manila: Karapatan: Alliance for the Advancement of People's Rights. http://www.karapatan.org/files/Karapatan_Monitor_Issue1_2013_web.pdf

Karapatan. 2014. 2013 *Karapatan Year-End Report on the Human Rights Situation in the Philippines.* Quezon City: Karapatan Alliance for the Advancement of People's Rights.

Karnitschnig, Matthew. 2017. "Donald Trump Leaves Europe in the Cold." *Politico,* January 20. http://www.politico.eu/article/donald-trump-leaves-europe-in -the-cold-in-inauguration/

Katigbak, Jose, and Roel Pareño. 2002. "Reyes: US Military Aid to Focus Less on Direct Missions in RP." *Philippine Star,* August 15. http://www.philstar.com/he adlines/172142/reyes-us-military-aid-focus-less-direct-missions-rp

Katzenstein, Peter J. 2005. *A World of Regions: Asia and Europe in the American Imperium.* Ithaca: Cornell University Press.

Katzenstein, Peter J., and Nobuo Okawara. 2002. "Japan, Asian-Pacific Security, and the Case for Analytical Eclecticism." *International Security* 26 (3): 153–85.

Keith, Linda. 2002. "Judicial Independence and Human Rights Protection around the World." *Judicature* 85 (4): 195–200.

Kelly, Philip. 1997. "Globalization, Power and the Politics of Scale in the Philippines." *Geoforum* 28 (2): 151–71.

Kendall, Sue. 1994. "Clinton Says He Will Pursue Human Rights at APEC Summit." Agence France-Presse, November 10.

Kerry, John. 2014. *Finalization of the Philippines-Moro Islamic Liberation Front*

Framework Agreement on the Bangsamoro. US State Department. https://2009-2017.state.gov/secretary/remarks/2014/01/220622.htm

Keys, Barbara. 2014. *Reclaiming American Virtue.* Cambridge, MA: Harvard University Press, 2014.

King, Daniel, and Jim LoGerfo. 1996. "Thailand: Toward Democratic Stability." *Journal of Democracy* 7 (1): 102–17.

Kinsella, Helen. 2011. *The Image before the Weapon: A Critical History of the Distinction between Combatant and Civilian.* Ithaca: Cornell University Press.

Kirk, Donald. 2005. *Philippines in Crisis: U.S. Power versus Local Revolt.* Manila: Anvil Publishing.

Kislenko, Arne. 2004. "A Not So Silent Partner: Thailand's Role in Covert Operations, Counter-Insurgency, and the Wars in Indochina." *Journal of Conflict Studies* 24 (1): 65–96.

Kittayarak, Kittipong. 2003. *The Thai Constitution of 1997 and Its Implication on Criminal Justice Reform.* United Nations Asia and Far East Institute for the Prevention of Crime and Treatment of Offenders—Annual Report for 2001 and Resource Material Series: 107–17. https://web.archive.org/web/20140714171116/http://www.unafei.or.jp/english/pdf/PDF_rms/no60/ch06.pdf

Klein, James. 1998. *The Constitution of the Kingdom of Thailand, 1997: A Blueprint for Participatory Democracy.* Working Paper Series. San Francisco: Asia Foundation.

Kocak, Deniz, and Johannes Kode. 2014. "Impediments to Security Sector Reform in Thailand." In *Security Sector Reform in Southeast Asia*, edited by Felix Heiduk. Basingstoke, UK: Palgrave.

Kohn, Richard. 1997. "How Democracies Control the Military." *Journal of Democracy* 8 (4): 140–53.

Kono, Daniel, and Gabriella R. Montinola. 2009. "Does Foreign Aid Support Autocrats, Democrats, or Both?" *Journal of Politics* 71 (2): 704–18.

Krasner, Stephen. 2010. "Revisiting 'the Second Image Reversed.'" Paper prepared for a conference in honor of Peter Gourevitch, University of California, San Diego, April 23–24.

Kratochwil, Friedrich, and John Ruggie. 1986. "International Organization: A State of the Art on an Art of the State." *International Organization* 40 (4): 753–75.

Kuhonta, Erik, and Alex Mutebi. 2006. "Thaksin Triumphant: The Implications of One-Party Dominance in Thailand." *Asian Affairs: An American Review* 33 (1): 39–51.

Kuhonta, Erik, Dan Slater, and Tuong Vu. 2008. "Introduction: The Contributions of Southeast Asian Political Studies." In *Southeast Asia in Political Science: Theory, Region, and Qualitative Analysis*, 1–54. Stanford, CA: Stanford University Press.

Kulsudjarit, Kongpetch. 2006. "Drug Problem in Southeast and Southwest Asia." *Annals of the New York Academy of Sciences* 1025 (1): 446–57.

Kummetha, Thaweeporn. 2014. "After 3 Years of Waiting, Supreme Court Spends 15 Seconds Reading Ruling on Somchai Neelapaijit Disappearance." *Prachatai*, May 21. http://www.prachatai.com/english/node/3978

Lagniton, Francis. 2002. "Filipinos Satisfied with US Help—SWS." *Philippine Star*, August 7. http://www.philstar.com/headlines/171103/filipinos-satisfied-us-help-sws

Lai, Brian. 2003. "Examining the Goals of US Foreign Assistance in the Post–Cold War Period, 1991–96." *Journal of Peace Research* 40 (1): 103–28.

Lancaster, Carol. 2007. *Foreign Aid: Diplomacy, Development, Domestic Politics.* Chicago: University of Chicago Press.

Landau, Mark. 2004. "Deliver Us from Evil: The Effects of Mortality Salience and Reminders of 9/11 on Support for President George W. Bush." *Personality and Social Psychology Bulletin* 30 (9): 1136–50.

Landler, Mark. 2001. "Philippines Offers U.S. Its Troops and Bases." *New York Times*, October 3, A5.

Landler, Mark. 2012. "Obama Shows Support for Philippines in China Standoff." *New York Times*, June 8. http://www.nytimes.com/2012/06/09/world/asia/obama-shows-support-for-philippines-in-china-standoff.html

Landman, Todd. 2005. "The Political Science of Human Rights." *British Journal of Political Science* 35 (3): 549–72.

Laothamas, Anek. 1992. *Business Associations and the New Political Economy of Thailand.* Boulder: Westview Press.

Larkins, Christopher. 1996. "Judicial Independence and Democratization: A Theoretical and Conceptual Analysis." *American Journal of Comparative Law* 44 (4): 605–26.

Laude, Jaime. 2002. "GMA Issues 10-Point Guideline for Conduct of RP-US Games." *Philippine Star*, January 27. http://www.philstar.com/headlines/1484 97/gma-issues-10-point-guideline-conduct-rp-us-%C2%91games%C2%92

Laude, Jaime. 2004. "US, RP Will Remain Allies—Ricciardone." *Philippine Star*, July 16. http://www.philstar.com/headlines/257689/us-rp-will-remain-allies -%C2%97-ricciardone

Lebovic, James, and Erik Voeten. 2009. "The Cost of Shame: International Organizations and Foreign Aid in the Punishing of Human Rights Violators." *Journal of Peace Research* 46 (1): 79–97.

Lebow, Richard. 2010. *Forbidden Fruit: Counterfactuals and International Relations.* Princeton: Princeton University Press.

Lee, Hyun. 2011. "The Impact of U.S. Foreign Aid on Human Rights Conditions in Post–Cold War Era." MPA diss., Iowa State University.

Leekpai, Chuan. 1993. "Sunthonphot Khong Naiyokratchamontri Mang Krasuang Raengngan Lae Sawafikansangkhom." In *raengngan thai 2536: soknatakam lae wikritakan (Thai Labour 1993: Tragedy and Crisis)*, edited by Banthit Thonchaisetawut, 98–99. Bangkok: Arom Phongphagnan Foundation and Friedrich Ebert Stiftung.

Legro, Jeffrey. 2005. *Rethinking the World: Great Power Strategies and International Order.* Ithaca: Cornell University Press.

Lehner, Urban, and Cynthia Owens. 1992. "Thai Premier Says Democracy Is Chief Concern." *Wall Street Journal*, 28 September. Retrieved from Factiva database.

Lehrer, Jim, and Gloria Macapagal Arroyo. 2001. "Newsmaker: Philippine President Gloria Arroyo." *PBS Newshour*, November 19. http://www.pbs.org/newshour/bb/asia-july-dec01-arroyo_11-19/

Linantud, John. 2008. "Pressure and Protection: Cold War Geopolitics and Nation-Building in South Korea, South Vietnam, Philippines, and Thailand." *Geopolitics* 13 (4): 635–56.

Lobo, Fred. 1999. *Fidel Valdez Ramos, the Centennial President: Vision, Action and Statesmanship.* Manila: Manila Bulletin.

Locsin, Joel. 2001. "Arroyo, Bush Swaps Congrats." *Manila Standard*, January 25.

Lohman, Walter. 2011. "Reinvigorating the U.S.–Thailand Alliance." Heritage Foundation, September 28. http://www.heritage.org/research/reports/2011/09 /reinvigorating-the-u-s-thailand-alliance

Lopez, Leslie, and Shawn Crispin. 2003. "U.S. and Thai Agents Collaborate in Secret Cold-War-Style Alliance." *Wall Street Journal*, October 1. http://online .wsj.com/article/SB106496138273373900.html

Lucas, John. 1997. "The Politics of Business Associations in the Developing World." *Journal of Developing Areas* 32 (1): 71–96.

Lucas, Vanessa, and Azadeh Shahshahani. 2014. "How US Aid Fosters Human Rights Violations in the Philippines." *The Nation*, February 19. http://www.th enation.com/blog/178453/how-us-aid-fosters-human-rights-violations-philip pines

Lum, Thomas. 2007. *U.S. Foreign Aid to East and South Asia: Selected Recipients.* Washington, DC: Congressional Research Service.

Lutz, Ellen, and Kathryn Sikkink. 2000. "International Human Rights Law and Practice in Latin America." *International Organization* 54: 633–59.

Lutz, Ellen, and Kathryn Sikkink. 2001. "The Justice Cascade: Evolution and Impact of Foreign Human Rights Trials in Latin America." *Chicago Journal of International Law* 2: 1–33.

Maaten, Jules, and Pauline Sanchez. 2011. "Aquino Administration's Human Rights Direction: Traversing a Straight Path?" *Observer: A Journal on Threatened Human Rights Defenders in the Philippines* 3 (1): 1–4.

Mahakanjana, Chandra-nuj. 2006. *Decentralization, Local Government, and Sociopolitical Conflict in Southern Thailand.* Washington, DC: East West Center Washington.

Mahoney, James, and Dietrich Rueschemeyer. 2003. "Comparative Historical Analysis: Achievements and Agendas." In *Comparative Historical Analysis in the Social Sciences*, edited by James Mahoney and Dietrich Rueschemeyer. New York: Cambridge University Press.

Maisrikrod, Surin. 2007. "Learning from the 19 September Coup: Advancing Thai-Style Democracy?" *Southeast Asian Affairs* (1): 340–60.

Mallet, Victor. 1992. "Survey of Thailand (9): Low Profile Preferred—Foreign Relations." *Financial Times*, December 4, 34. Retrieved from Factiva database.

Managbanag, Nicole J. 2014. "Marcos-Era Human Rights Victims to Get P50,000 Payment Anew." *Sun Star*, January 13. http://www.sunstar.com.ph/cagayan-de -oro/local-news/2014/01/14/marcos-era-human-rights-victims-get-p50000 -323131

Manihandu, Anuraj, and Nussara Sawatsawang. 1996. "Analysis / Thai-US Relations—First among Equals." *Bangkok Post*, November 25, 13.

Maniruzzaman, Talukder. 1992. "Arms Transfers, Military Coups, and Military Rule in Developing States." *Journal of Conflict Resolution* 36: 733–55.

March, James, and Johan Olsen. 2006. "The Logic of Appropriateness." In *The Oxford Handbook of Public Policy*, edited by Michael Moran, Martin Rein, and Robert E. Goodin, 689–708. Oxford: Oxford University Press.

Maren, Michael. 1997. *The Road to Hell: The Ravaging Effects of Foreign Aid and International Charity*. New York: Free Press.

Marsh, Ian. 2006. "Democratization and State Capacity in East and Southeast Asia." *Taiwan Journal of Democracy* 2 (2): 69–92.

Mascarinas, Erwin. 2012. "Lumad Evacuees from Agusan Military Ops Seek Refuge in Butuan City." *Interaksyon*. Accessed March 12, 2014. http://www.inter aksyon.com/article/28000/lumad-evacuees-from-agusan-military-ops-seek-ref uge-in-butuan-city

Mauzy, Diane. 1997. "The Human Rights and 'Asian Values' Debate in Southeast Asia: Trying to Clarify the Key Issues." *Critical Asian Studies* 10 (2): 210–36.

Mayroz, Eyal. 2019. *Reluctant Interveners: America's Failed Responses to Genocide from Bosnia to Darfur*. New Brunswick, NJ: Rutgers University Press.

McBride, James. 2018. "How Does the U.S. Spend Its Foreign Aid?" Council on Foreign Relations, October 1. https://www.cfr.org/backgrounder/how-does-us -spend-its-foreign-aid

McCargo, Duncan. 1997. *Chamlong Srimuang and the New Thai Politics*. New York: St. Martin's Press.

McCargo, Duncan. 1998. "Alternative Meanings of Political Reform in Contemporary Thailand." *Copenhagen Journal of Asian Studies* 13 (1): 5–30.

McCargo, Duncan. 2002a. "Democracy under Stress in Thaksin's Thailand." *Journal of Democracy* 13 (4): 112–26.

McCargo, Duncan. 2002b. "Security, Development and Political Participation in Thailand: Alternative Currencies of Legitimacy." *Contemporary Southeast Asia* 24 (1): 50–67.

McCargo, Duncan. 2005. "Network Monarchy and Legitimacy Crises in Thailand." *Pacific Review* 18 (4): 499–519.

McCargo, Duncan. 2008. *Tearing Apart the Land: Islam and Legitimacy in Southern Thailand*. Ithaca: Cornell University Press.

McCargo, Duncan, and Ukrist Pathmanand. 2005. *The Thaksinization of Thailand*. Copenhagen: Nordic Institute of Asian Studies.

McCarthy, Terry. 2000. "Trouble in Paradise." *Time Magazine*, May 8. http://cont ent.time.com/time/world/article/0,8599,2053657,00.html

McClincy, Meghan. 2012. "A Blue Thai Affair: The Blue Diamond Affair's Illustration of the Royal Thai Police Force's Standards of Corruption." *Penn State Journal of Law and International Affairs* 1 (1): 182–201.

McCormick, James, and Neil Mitchell. 1988. "Is U.S. Aid Really Linked to Human Rights in Latin America?" *American Journal of Political Science* 32 (1): 231–39.

McCoy, Alfred. 1999. *Closer Than Brothers: Manhood at the Philippine Military Academy*. New Haven: Yale University Press.

McCoy, Alfred. 2006. *A Question of Torture: CIA Interrogation, from the Cold War to the War on Terror*. New York City: Henry Holt and Company.

McCoy, Alfred. 2009. *Policing America's Empire: The United States, the Philippines, and the Rise of the Surveillance State*. Madison: University of Wisconsin Press.

McCoy, Alfred, Cathleen B. Read, and Leonard P. Adams. 1972. *The Politics of Heroin in Southeast Asia*. New York: Harper and Row.

Mearsheimer, John, and Stephen Walt. 2013. "Leaving Theory Behind: Why Simplistic Hypothesis Testing Is Bad for International Relations." *European Journal of International Relations* 19 (3): 427–57.

Meernik, James, Eric Krueger, and Steven Poe. 1998. "Testing Models of U.S. Foreign Policy: Foreign Aid during and after the Cold War." *Journal of Politics* 60 (1): 63–85.

Melo, Jose. 2007. *The Melo Commission Report: Independent Commission to Address Media and Activist Killings (Created under Administrative Order No. 157, Series of 2006)*. Manila: Melo Commission, Government of the Republic of the Philippines.

Merry, Sally. 2006. *Human Rights and Gender Violence: Translating International Law into Local Justice*. Chicago: University of Chicago Press.

Merry, Sally. 2016. *The Seductions of Quantification: Measuring Human Rights, Gender Violence, and Sex Trafficking*. Chicago: University of Chicago Press.

Mertus, Julie. 2008. *Bait and Switch: Human Rights and U.S. Foreign Policy*. 2nd ed. New York: Routledge.

Merueñas, Mark. 2011. *Pork Barrel—a Continuing Poison in the System*. Transparency Reporting Philippines, 1–5. Accessed May 25, 2103. http://www.transpa rencyreporting.net/index.php?option=com_content&l.arrel-a-continuing-pois on-in-the-system&catid=44:stories&Itemid=94

Messick, Richard. 1999. "Judicial Reform and Economic Development: A Survey of the Issues." *World Bank Research Observer* 14 (1): 117–36.

Mietzner, Marcus. 2011. "Conflict and Leadership: The Resurgent Political Role of the Military in Southeast Asia." In *The Political Resurgence of the Military in Southeast Asia: Conflict and Leadership*, edited by Marcus Mietzner, 1–23. Abingdon, Oxford: Routledge.

Millennium Challenge Corporation. 2010. "Millennium Challenge Compact between the United States of America Acting through the Millennium Challenge Corporation and the Republic of the Philippines." https://www.mcc.gov /resources/doc/closed-compact-report-philippines

Miller, Brad. 2008. "Philippines: Mindanao Tribals Caught between Army, Insurgents." *Inter Press Service*, January 9. http://www.ipsnews.net/2008/01/philippi nes-mindanao-tribals-caught-between-army-insurgents/

Miller, Terry, Kim R. Holmes, Edwin J. Feulner. 2012. *2012 Index of Economic Freedom*. Washington, DC: Heritage Foundation and Wall Street Journal.

Moeran, Brian. 2001. "The Field of Asian Media Productions." In *Asian Media Productions*, edited by B. Moeran, 1–38. London: Routledge.

Mogato, Manny. 2002. "Beyond War Games." *Newsbreak* 2 (5) (February 13). Accessed June 10, 2013. http://archives.newsbreak-knowledge.ph/2002/02/12 /beyond-war-games/

Mogato, Manuel. 2015. "Philippines Seeks Help from U.S. in South China Sea Dispute." Reuters, April 15. https://www.reuters.com/article/us-southchinasea -philippines-usa/philippines-seeks-help-from-u-s-in-south-china-sea-dispute -idUSKBN0N616A20150415

Montemayor, Jocelyn. 2001. "US Use of Former Bases Okayed." *Malaya* 20 (242) (September 19): 1.

Montiel, Cristina. 2006. "Political Psychology of Nonviolent Democratic Transitions in Southeast Asia." *Journal of Socio-Economics* 62 (1): 173–90.

Montlake, Simon. 2002. "Diplomatic Pitfalls Frustrate Thailand's Antidrug Fight."

Christian Science Monitor, December 3. http://www.csmonitor.com/2002/1203/p07s02-wosc.html/(page)/3

Morada, Noel. 2003. "Philippine-American Security Relations after 11 September: Exploring the Mutuality of Interests in the Fight against International Terrorism." *Southeast Asian Affairs* 2003 (1): 228–38.

Morea, Gary. 2008. "From Enduring Strife to Enduring Peace in the Philippines." *Military Review* (June): 38–48.

Morgenthau, Hans. 1962. "A Political Theory of Foreign Aid." *American Political Science Review* 56 (2): 301–9.

Morrison, Wayne. 2013. *China's Economic Rise: History, Trends, Challenges, and Implications for the United States*. Washington, DC: Congressional Research Service.

Moyn, Samuel. 2017. "Human Rights and the Crisis of Liberalism." In *Human Rights Futures*, edited by Stephen Hopgood, Jack Snyder, and Leslie Vinjamuri, 261–82. Cambridge: Cambridge University Press, 2017.

Moyo, Dambisa. 2009. *Dead Aid: Why Aid Is Not Working and How There Is a Better Way for Africa*. New York: Farrar, Straus and Giroux.

Muntarbhorn, Vitit. 2000. *Human Rights and Human Development: Thailand Country Study*. United Nations Development Program. http://hdr.undp.org/sites/default/files/vitit_muntarbhorn-thainland.pdf

Mutebi, Alex. 2003. "Thailand in 2002: Political Consolidation amid Economic Uncertainties." *Asian Survey* 43 (1): 101–12.

Mutebi, Alex. 2004. "Thailand in 2003: Riding High Again." *Asian Survey* 44 (1): 78–86.

Mutua, Makau. 2002. *Human Rights: A Political and Cultural Critique*. Philadelphia: University of Pennsylvania Press.

Mydans, Seth. 2003. "A Wave of Drug Killings Is Linked to Thai Police." *New York Times*, April 8, 1–3.

Nathan, Andrew. 2012. "Capsule Review: Hard Interests, Soft Illusions: Southeast Asia and American Power." *Foreign Affairs*, September/October. http://www.foreignaffairs.com/articles/137962/natasha-hamilton-hart/hard-interests-soft-illusions-southeast-asia-and-american-power

The Nation—Thailand. 2001a. "No Red Carpet for Thaksin in the US." *The Nation—Thailand*. Accessed September 4, 2020. http://www.nationmultimedia.com/opinion/No-red-carpet-for-Thaksin-in-the-US-52715.html

The Nation—Thailand. 2001b. "Thailand and Terror: US Shift May Take Heat Off Narcotics." *The Nation—Thailand*. Accessed July 14, 2013. http://www.nationmultimedia.com/The%20Region/THAILAND-AND-TERROR-US-shift-may-take-heat-off-nar-51288.html

The Nation—Thailand. 2001c. "War on Terror Divides South East Asian Grouping." *The Nation—Thailand*. Accessed September 4, 2020. http://www.nationmultimedia.com/opinion/War-on-terror-divides-S-East-Asian-grouping-49774.html

The Nation—Thailand. 2003a. "Thaksin Sets Up 2 Panels to Monitor Drug War." *The Nation—Thailand*. Accessed May 25, 2014. http://www.nationmultimedia.com/home/Thaksin-sets-up-2-panels-to-monitor-drug-war-74831.html

The Nation—Thailand. 2003b. "War on Drugs: Police Chief: Govt Blacklist Flawed." *Asian Tribune*. Accessed June 15, 2014. http://www.asiantribune.com/news/2003/02/26/war-drugs-police-chief-govt-blacklist-flawed

National Human Rights Commission of Thailand. 2004. *21 Nakdosu-Pheau-Sithi-Manutsuchon ('21 Human Rights Defenders')*. Bangkok: National Human Rights Commission, Thailand.

Natsios, Andrew. 2006. "Focus on the Future of USAID: USAID in the Post-9/11 World." *Foreign Service Journal* (June): 19–24.

New York Times. 1992a. "Hints of Hope in Manila." *New York Times*, June 1, 16.

New York Times. 1992b. "Help Thailand's Quiet Revolution." *New York Times*, July 25. http://www.nytimes.com/1992/07/25/opinion/help-thailand-s-quiet-revolution.html

Nielsen, Richard, Michael G. Findley, Zachary S. Davis, Tara Candland, and Daniel L. Nielson Brigham. 2011. "Foreign Aid Shocks as a Cause of Violent Armed Conflict." *American Journal of Political Science* 55 (2): 219–32.

Norwegian Refugee Council. 2002. "More Filipinos Displaced in War on Terror—Philippines." http://reliefweb.int/report/philippines/more-filipinos-displaced-war-terror

Nurakkate, Chumphot. 2012. "The Conflict in Southern Thailand." Centre for Defence and Strategic Studies—Shedden Papers. March. https://data.opendevelopmentmekong.net/library_record/the-conflict-in-southern-thailand

Obama, Barack. 2011. "Remarks by President Obama to the Australian Parliament." http://www.whitehouse.gov/the-press-office/2011/11/17/remarks-president-obama-australian-parliament

Obama, Barack. 2013. "Barack Obama: Press Briefing by Press Secretary Jay Carney." American Presidency Project—Online by Gerhard Peters and John T. Woolley. http://www.presidency.ucsb.edu/ws/index.php?pid=103990&st=philippines&st1=

Office of the Narcotics Control Board, Justice Ministry of Thailand. 2003. *War on Drugs' Concept and Strategy*. Accessed May 25, 2014. http://www.ahrn.net/Evidence/ONCB%20-%20War%20on%20Drugs.pdf

Office of the Presidential Adviser on the Peace Process. 2013. *Guidebook on Conflict-Sensitive and Peace-Promoting Local Development Planning*. OPAPP Manila and UNDP. http://www.undp.org/content/philippines/en/home/library/crisis_prevention_and_recovery/guidebook-on-conflict-sensitive-and-peace-promoting-local-devel/

Office of the President of the United States/Office of Management and Budget. 2017. *America First: Budget Blueprint to Make America Great Again*. White House. https://www.whitehouse.gov/sites/whitehouse.gov/files/omb/budget/fy2018/2018_blueprint.pdf

Office of the Press Secretary, White House. 2003. "President Discusses War on Terror in Thailand." October 19. http://2001-2009.state.gov/p/eap/rls/rm/2003/25352.htm

Official Gazette of the Government of the Republic of the Philippines. 2004. "Speech of President Arroyo during the Commissioning and Blessing of the Newly Acquired Cyclone Class Navy Vessel." March 8. https://www.officialgazette.gov.ph/2004/03/08/speech-of-president-arroyo-during-the-commissioning-and-blessing-of-the-newly-acquired-cyclone-class-navy-vessel-brp-general-mariano-alvarez-ps38/

Official Gazette of the Government of the Republic of the Philippines. 2012a. "Philippine Government Action Plan for the Open Government Partnership." Official Gazette of the Republic of the Philippines, 1–13. http://www.gov.ph /documents/20147/247768/Draft-Philippine-OGP-Action-Plan.pdf

Official Gazette of the Government of the Republic of the Philippines. 2012b. "The Aquino Administration's Human Rights Initiative." December 10. https://www .officialgazette.gov.ph/2012/12/10/the-aquino-administrations-human-rights -initiatives/

Olea, Ronalyn. 2003. "Proposed 2004 National Budget: A Sign of Insecurity." *Bulatlat* 3, no. 29 (August 24–30). http://www.bulatlat.com/news/3-29/3-29-bu dget.html

Olea, Ronalyn. 2009. "US Congress Withholds Military Aid to the Philippines Due to Human Rights Abuses." *Bulatlat*, November 5. http://bulatlat.com/ma in/2009/11/05/us-congress-withholds-military-aid-to-the-philippines-due-to -human-rights-abuses/

Olsen, Tricia, Leigh Payne, and Andrew Reiter. 2010. "The Justice Balance: When Transitional Justice Improves Human Rights and Democracy." *Human Rights Quarterly* 32 (4): 980–1007.

Ong, Perry, and Nina Ingle. 2011. "A National Treasure: Leonard L. Co (1953–2010)." *Social Science Diliman* 7 (1): 117–19.

Ople, Blas. 1994. *Global but Parochial: Selected Writings and Speeches on Foreign Policy.* Quezon City: Institute for Public Policy.

Opotow, Susan. 2001. "Reconciliation in Times of Impunity: Challenges for Social Justice." *Social Justice Research* 14 (2): 149–70.

Orentlicher, Diane. 1991. "Settling Accounts: The Duty to Prosecute Human Rights Violations of a Prior Regime." *Yale Law Journal* 100 (8): 2537–2615.

Orentlicher Diane. 2005. *Report of the Independent Expert to Update the Set of Principles to Combat Impunity, Diane Orentlicher: Addendum.* Geneva: Commission on Human Rights.

Oreta, Jennife, Alma Salvador, and Kathline Tolosa. 2012. *Defense Budget and Spending: Alignment and Priorities (Philippine Defense Spending 2001 to 2012).* Metro Manila: Friedrich Ebert Stiftung/AusAID/Ateneo De Manila University, Department of Political Science.

Owen, John M., IV. 2010. *The Clash of Ideas in World Politics: Transnational Networks, States, and Regime Change, 1510–2010.* Princeton: Princeton University Press.

Painter, Martin. 2006. "Thaksinisation or Managerialism? Reforming the Thai Bureaucracy." *Journal of Contemporary Asia* 36 (1): 26–47.

Pamintuan, Ana. 2003. "A Two-Way Street." *Philippine Star*, October 17. http:// www.philstar.com/opinion/224477/two-way-street

Panaspornprasit, Chookiat. 2004. "Thailand: Politicized Thaksinization." *Southeast Asian Affairs*: 257–66. http://www.jstor.org/stable/10.2307/27913264

Pangalangan, Raul. 2011. "Human Rights Discourse in Post-Marcos Philippines." In *Human Rights in Asia*, edited by Thomas Davis and Brian Galligan, 56–69. Cheltenham: Edward Elgar.

Pangilinan, Christian. 2012. "American Aid and Human Rights in the Philippines." *Georgetown Journal of International Affairs* 13: 119–26.

Parmar, Inderjeet. 2012. *Foundations of the American Century: The Ford, Carnegie, and Rockefeller Foundations in the Rise of American Power*. New York: Columbia University Press.

Parmar, Inderjeet. 2016. "Racial and Imperial Thinking in International Theory and Politics: Truman, Attlee and the Korean War." *British Journal of Politics and International Relations* 18 (2): 351–69.

Pathmanand, Ukrist. 2001. "Globalization and Democratic Development in Thailand: New Path of the Military, Private Sector, and Civil Society." *Contemporary Southeast Asia* 23 (1): 24–42.

Pathmanand, Ukrist. 2006. "Thaksin's Achilles' Heel: The Failure of Hawkish Approaches in the Thai South." *Critical Asian Studies* 38 (1): 73–93.

Patino, Patrick, and Djorina Velasco. 2004. *Electoral Violence in the Philippines*. Friedrich-Ebert-Stiftung. http://library.fes.de/pdf-files/bueros/philippinen/50 071.pdf

Pattugalan, Gina. 1999. "A Review of Philippine Foreign Policy under the Ramos Administration." *Kasarinlan: Philippine Journal of Third World Studies* 14 (3).

Penney, Joe. 2011. "The 'War on Terror' Rages in the Philippines." *Al Jazeera*, October 5. http://www.aljazeera.com/indepth/inpictures/2011/10/201110414 5947651645.html

Perez, Analyn, and T. J. Dimacali. 2009. "The Ampatuan Massacre: A Map and Timeline." *GMA News*, November 25. http://www.gmanetwork.com/news/st ory/177821/news/specialreports/the-ampatuan-massacre-a-map-and-timeline

Perlez, Jane. 1999. "Thais Show Albright the Fruits of American Aid: Meaningful Jobs and Legal Crops." *New York Times*, March 4, A14.

Petras, James. 1997. "Imperialism and NGOs in Latin America." *Monthly Review* 49 (7): 10–27.

Petras, James, and Henry Veltmeyer. 2002. "Age of Reverse Aid: Neo-Liberalism as Catalyst of Regression." *Development and Change* 33 (2): 281–93.

Pettersson, Therese, Stina Högbladh, and Magnus Öberg. 2019. "Organized Violence, 1989–2018, and Peace Agreements. *Journal of Peace Research* 56 (4): 589–603.

Pew Research Center. 2013. "Philippines: Opinion of the United States—Global Indicators Database." Accessed September 2, 2020. https://www.pewresearch .org/global/database/indicator/1/country/ph/

Philippine Commission on Human Rights. 2000. "On the Revival of the Civilian Armed Forces Geographical Units (CAFGUs)." Commission on Human Rights, May 9. https://web.archive.org/web/20130611221657/http://www.chr .gov.ph/MAIN%20PAGES/about%20hr/advisories/abthr006-010.htm#cafgu

Philippine Commission on Human Rights. 2009. "In the Matter of the Disappearance and/or Arrest and Detention of Muhamidya K. Hamja'." Accessed September 3, 2020. https://web.archive.org/web/20130611220011/http://www .chr.gov.ph/MAIN%20PAGES/about%20hr/position%20papers/Reso_CHR _A2009-172.htm

Philippine Daily Inquirer. 2011. "What Went Before: Abduction of UP Students Karen Empeño and Sherlyn Cadapan." December 17. http://newsinfo.inquirer .net/112599/what-went-before-abduction-of-up-students-karen-empeno-and -sherlyn-cadapan

Philippine Daily Inquirer. 2012. "What Went Before: Death of a Botanist." December 20. https://newsinfo.inquirer.net/327149/what-went-before-death -of-a-botanist

Philippine Presidential Management Staff. 2003. *Beating the Odds: Major Accomplishments of the Arroyo Administration*. Manila: Philippine Presidential Management Staff, Office of the President of the Republic of the Philippines.

Philippine Star. 2002. "SWS Poll: 84% of Pinoys Back Aid from US Troops." *Philippine Star*, January 30. http://www.philstar.com/headlines/148815/sws-poll -84-pinoys-back-aid-us-troops

Philippine Star. 2003a. "AFP Calls for More US Aid to Buy Weapons vs Terror." *Philippine Star*, May 20. http://www.philstar.com/headlines/206899/afp-calls -more-us-aid-buy-weapons-vs-terror

Philippine Star. 2003b. "US Military Aid at Highest Level." *Philippine Star*, December 7. http://www.philstar.com/headlines/230680/us-military-aid-highest-level

Philippine Star. 2006. "US Intelligence Chief Praises RP Commitment to Democracy." *Philippine Star*, February 4. http://www.philstar.com/headlines/319963 /us-intelligence-chief-praises-rp-commitment-democracy

Philippine Star. 2007. "Militants Slam Negroponte Visit, US Intervention in SE Asia." *Philippine Star*, August 2. http://www.philstar.com/nation/10020/militan ts-slam-negroponte-visit-us-intervention-se-asia

Phillips, Sarah. 2020. *When There Was No Aid*. Ithaca: Cornell University Press.

Philpott, Daniel. 2001. *Revolutions in Sovereignty: How Ideas Shaped Modern International Relations*. Princeton: Princeton University Press.

Phongpaichit, Pasuk. 2004. *Thailand under Thaksin: Another Malaysia?* Perth: Asia Research Centre, Murdoch University.

Phongpaichit, Pasuk, and Chris Baker. 1995. *Thailand, Economy and Politics*. Kuala Lumpur: Oxford University Press.

Phongpaichit, Pasuk, and Chris Baker. 1997. "Power in Transition: Thailand in the 1990s." In *Political Change in Thailand: Democracy and Participation*, edited by Kevin Hewison. London: Routledge.

Phongpaichit, Pasuk, and Chris Baker. 2008a. "Thailand: Fighting over Democracy." *Economic and Political Weekly* 43 (50): 18–21.

Phongpaichit, Pasuk, and Chris Baker. 2008b. "Thaksin's Populism." *Philippine Political Science Journal* 38 (1): 62–83.

Phongpaichit, Pasuk, and Sungsidh Piriyarangsan. 1996. *Corruption and Democracy in Thailand*. Chiang Mai, Thailand: Silkworm Books.

Pierson, Paul. 2004. *Politics in Time: History, Institutions, and Social Analysis*. Princeton: Princeton University Press.

Poe, Steven. 1990. "Human Rights and US Foreign Aid: A Review of Quantitative Studies and Suggestions for Future Research." *Human Rights Quarterly* 12 (4): 499–512.

Pongsudhirak, Thitinan. 2003a. "Thailand: Democratic Authoritarianism." *Southeast Asian Affairs*: 277–90.

Pongsudhirak, Thitinan. 2003b. "Behind Thaksin's War on Terror." *Far Eastern Economic Review* 166 (38): 29.

Pongsudhirak, Thitinan. 2016. "An Unaligned Alliance: Thailand-U.S. Relations in the Early 21st Century." *Asian Politics & Policy* 8 (1): 63–74.

Prestholdt, Jeremy. 2011. "Kenya, the United States, and Counterterrorism." *Africa Today* 57: 3–27.

Przeworski, Adam, Michael E. Alvarez, Jose A. Cheibub, and Fernando Limongi. 1996. "What Makes Democracies Endure?" *Journal of Democracy* 7 (1): 39–55.

Purdum, Todd S. 1996. "Clinton Hails Thais in Visit at Conclusion of Asia Trip." *New York Times*, November 27, 1.

Putnam, Robert D. 1988. "Diplomacy and Domestic Politics: The Logic of Two-Level Games." *International Organization* 42 (3): 427–60.

Qian, Nancy. 2014. "Making Progress on Foreign Aid." *Annual Review of Economics* 7 (1): 277–308.

Quimpo, Nathan Gilbert. 2007. *The US and the Southern Philippines' Quagmire.* Perth: Asia Research Centre, Murdoch University.

Racelis, Mary. 2000. "New Visions and Strong Actions: Civil Society in the Philippines." In *Funding Virtue: Civil Society Aid and Democracy Promotion*, edited by M. Ottaway and T. Carothers, 159–87. Washington, DC: Carnegie Endowment for International Peace.

Radyo ng Bayan Quezon City. 1992. "Ramos Interviewed on His Leadership Strategy," July 5, 1–10.

Ralph, Jason. 2013. *America's War on Terror: The State of the 9/11 Exception from Bush to Obama.* Oxford: Oxford University Press.

Ramalingam, Ben. 2013. *Aid on the Edge of Chaos.* Oxford: Oxford University Press.

Ramos, Fidel. 1995. "Fidel v. Ramos, Fourth State of the Nation Address, July 24, 1995—'the Best Is Soon to Come'." Official Gazette of the Republic of the Philippines, July 24. https://www.officialgazette.gov.ph/1995/07/24/fidel-v-ra mos-fourth-state-of-the-nation-address-july-24-1995/

Ramos, Fidel. 1998. *Developing as a Democracy: Reform and Recovery in the Philippines, 1992–1998.* New York: St. Martin's Press.

Ramos, Fidel. 2010. "Democratic Control of the Armed Forces: Lessons from East Asia." *Asia-Pacific Review* 8 (1): 37–41.

Ramos, Fidel. 2013. *Nation-Building Is Never-Ending.* Manila: Ramos Peace and Development Foundation.

Ranada, Pia. 2018. "List: Duterte's Top Military, Police Appointees." *Rappler.* December 15. https://www.rappler.com/newsbreak/iq/218702-list-duterte-top -military-police-appointees-yearend-2018

Rappler. 2012. "Weak Judiciary, Corruption Limit PH Economy." Rappler, September 30. https://rappler.com/business/ph-still-among-mostly-unfree-econo mies-worldwide

Rappler. 2020. "Daily Tribune Founding Chair Ninez Cacho-Olivares Dies." *Rappler*, January 3. https://www.rappler.com/nation/248455-daily-tribune-foundi ng-chairperson-ninez-cacho-olivares-dies

Rauhala, Emily. 2010. "The Maguindanao Massacre: Still No Justice One Year Later." *Time Magazine.* Accessed June 23, 2013. http://www.time.com/time/wo rld/article/0,8599,2032802,00.html

Regalado, Edith. 2007. "CIA, FBI, Aussie Agents Operating in South." *Philippine Star*, January 20. http://www.philstar.com/headlines/380828/cia-fbi-aussie-age nts-operating-south-%C2%97-afp

Regalado, Edith. 2012. "Dabawenyos Dismiss CHR Findings vs Duterte." *Philip-*

pine Star, August 17. http://www.philstar.com/nation/2012/08/17/838902/dab awenyos-dismiss-chr-findings-vs-duterte

Regilme, Salvador. 2014a. "Bringing the Global Political Economy Back In: Neoliberalism, Globalization, and Democratic Consolidation." *International Studies Perspectives* 15 (3): 277–96.

Regilme, Salvador. 2014b. "The Social Science of Human Rights: The Need for a 'Second Image' Reversed?" *Third World Quarterly* 35 (8): 1390–1405.

Regilme, Salvador. 2018a. "Beyond Paradigms: Understanding the South China Sea Dispute Using Analytic Eclecticism." *International Studies* 55 (3): 1–25.

Regilme, Salvador. 2018b. "A Human Rights Tragedy: Strategic Localization of US Foreign Policy in Colombia." *International Relations* 32 (3): 343–65.

Regilme, Salvador. 2018c. "Does US Foreign Aid Undermine Human Rights? The 'Thaksinification' of the War on Terror Discourses and the Human Rights Crisis in Thailand, 2001 to 2006." *Human Rights Review* 19 (1): 73–95.

Regilme, Salvador. 2018d. "The Global Politics of Human Rights: From Human Rights to Human Dignity?" *International Political Science Review* 40 (2): 279–90.

Regilme, Salvador. 2019. "The Decline of American Power and Donald Trump: Reflections on Human Rights, Neoliberalism, and the World Order." *Geoforum* 102: 157–66.

Regilme, Salvador. 2020a. "Human Rights and Humanitarian Interventions in the International Arena." In *The SAGE Handbook of Political Science*, 1456–73. London: SAGE.

Regilme, Salvador. 2020b. "Visions of Peace amidst a Human Rights Crisis: War on Drugs in Colombia and the Philippines." *Journal of Global Security Studies*. https://doi.org/10.1093/jogss/ogaa022

Regilme, Salvador, and Henrik Hartmann. 2018. "Mutual Delegitimization: American and Chinese Development Assistance in Africa." *The SAIS Review of International Affairs*, March 30. https://saisreview.org/china-america-development -assistance/

Regilme, Salvador, and Obert Hodzi. 2021. "Comparing US and Chinese Foreign Aid in the Era of Rising Powers." *The International Spectator*. https://doi.org/10 .1080/03932729.2020.1855904

Regilme, Salvador, and James Parisot. 2017. "Introduction: Debating American Hegemony—Global Cooperation and Conflict." In *American Hegemony and the Rise of Emerging Powers: Cooperation or Conflict*, edited by James Parisot and Salvador Santino Regilme, 3–18. New York: Routledge.

Regilme, Salvador, and James Parisot. 2020. "Contested American Dominance: Global Order in an Era of Rising Powers." In *The Routledge Handbook of Transformative Global Studies*, edited by S. A. Hamed Hosseini, James Goodman, Sara C. Motta, Barry K. Gills, 181–93. New York: Routledge.

Regilme, Salvador, and Carmina Untalan. 2016. "The Philippines 2014–2015: Domestic Politics and Foreign Relations, a Critical Review." *Asia Maior* 26: 133–56.

Reid, Robert. 1992. "Philippines Looking for Better Relations under Clinton Presidency." Associated Press, November 5.

Remmer, Karen. 2004. "Does Foreign Aid Promote the Expansion of Government?" *American Journal of Political Science* 48 (1): 77–92.

Reuters. 1991. "US Urges Thailand to Restore Democracy." Reuters, March 6. Accessed April 1, 2013. http://global.factiva.com/aa/?ref=lba0000020011124d n3601c77&pp=1&fcpil=en&napc=p&sa_from=

Reuters. 2014. "Philippines, Muslim Rebels Sign Final Peace Deal to End Conflict." March 27. Accessed September 2, 2020. http://www.reuters.com/article /2014/03/27/us-philippines-rebels-idUSBREA2Q1W220140327

Reuters. 2017. "U.S. Army Pacific Chief in Bangkok amid Regional Security Concerns." June 5. https://www.reuters.com/article/us-usa-asia-thailand/u-s-ar my-pacific-chief-in-bangkok-amid-regional-security-concerns-idUSKBN18 W104

Rhum, Michael. 1996. "'Modernity' and 'Tradition' in 'Thailand'." *Modern Asian Studies* 30 (2): 325–55.

Richardson, Michael. 1993. "Washington's Emphasis on Human Rights Issues Could Hurt Relations: Value Clash Looms for U.S. and Asia." *New York Times*, May 3. Accessed September 4, 2020. http://www.nytimes.com/1993/05/03/ne ws/03iht-clas.html

Riddell, Roger. 2008. *Does Foreign Aid Really Work?* Oxford: Oxford University Press.

Riggs, Fred. 1966. *Thailand: The Modernization of a Bureaucratic Polity.* Manoa: University of Hawai'i Press.

Risse, Thomas. 1995. "Bringing Transnational Relations Back In: Introduction." In *Bringing Transnational Relations Back In: Non-State Actors, Domestic Structures and International Institutions*, edited by Thomas Risse, 3–36. Cambridge: Cambridge University Press.

Risse, Thomas. 2000. "'Let's Argue!': Communicative Action in World Politics." *International Organization* 54 (1): 1–39.

Risse, Thomas, and Kathryn Sikkink. 1999. "The Socialization of International Human Rights Norms into Domestic Practices: Introduction." In *The Power of Human Rights International Norms and Domestic Change*, edited by Thomas Risse, Stephen C. Ropp, and Kathryn Sikkink, 1–38. Cambridge: Cambridge University Press.

Rivera, Temario. 2005. "The Philippines in 2004: New Mandate, Daunting Problems." *Asian Survey* 45 (1): 127–33.

Robinson, William. 1996. *Promoting Polyarchy: Globalization, US Intervention, and Hegemony.* Cambridge: Cambridge University Press.

Rodriguez, Robyn, and Nerissa Balce. 2004. "American Insecurity and Radical Filipino Community Politics." *Peace Review: A Journal of Social Justice* 16 (2): 131–40.

Rodrik, Dani. 1999. "The Asian Financial Crisis and the Virtues of Democracy." *Challenge* 42 (4): 44–59.

Romero, Alexis. 2013. "Army Reaffirms Commitment to Human Rights." *Philippine Star*, December 2. http://www.philstar.com/headlines/2013/12/02/12634 21/army-reaffirms-commitment-human-rights

Romero, Paolo. 2007. "1st Targets: Rogue AFP, Red Terrorists." *Philippine Star*, July 11. http://www.philstar.com/headlines/5028/1st-targets-rogue-afp-red-te rrorists

Romualdez, Babe. 2003. "Bright Future for RP-US Relations." *Philippine Star*, May 25. http://www.philstar.com/opinion/207453/bright-future-rp-us-relations

Ronas, Malaya. 2013. "The Philippines in 2012: Pursuit of Good Governance, Improved Business Confidence, Strained Relations with China." *Philippine Political Science Journal* 34 (2): 188–98.

Russett, Bruce. 1993. *Grasping the Democratic Peace: Principles for a Post–Cold War World*. Princeton: Princeton University Press.

Sabillo, Kristine. 2014. "Aquino Satisfaction Rating Slightly Recovers–SWS." *Inquirer*, December 10. http://newsinfo.inquirer.net/656383/aquino-satisfacti on-rating-slightly-recovers-sws

Sales, Peter. 2009. "State Terror in the Philippines: The Alston Report, Human Rights and Counter-Insurgency under the Arroyo Administration." *Contemporary Politics* 15 (3): 321–36.

Samarasinghe, SWR. 1994. *Democracy and Democratization in Developing Countries*. Boston: Data for Decision Making Project, Harvard School of Public Health.

Samudavanija, Chai-Anan. 1997. "Old Soldiers Never Die, They Are Just Bypassed: The Military, Bureaucracy, and Globalisation." In *Political Change in Thailand: Democracy and Participation*, edited by K. Hewison, 42–57. London: Routledge.

Sandholtz, Wayne. 2016. "United States Military Assistance and Human Rights." *Human Rights Quarterly* 38: 1070–1101.

Sandoval, Gerardo, Mahar Mangahas, and Linda Guerrero. 1998. "The Situation of the Filipino Youth: A National Survey." Paper presented at the 14th World Congress of Sociology, Working Group 3/Sociology of Childhood, Montreal, Canada, July 26–August 1. https://web.archive.org/web/20140714194238/htt p://www.sws.org.ph/youth.htm

San Juan, E., Jr. 2007. *U.S. Imperialism and Revolution in the Philippines*. Basingstoke: Palgrave Macmillan.

Santolan, Joseph. 2012. "Impeachment Trial of Chief Justice Opens in the Philippines." WSWS/International Committee of the Fourth International. Accessed September 4, 2020. http://www.wsws.org/en/articles/2012/01/phil-j16.html

Santos, Matikas. 2014. "US, Canada Laud PH-MILF Peace Deal." *Inquirer*, January 28. http://globalnation.inquirer.net/97867/us-canada-laud-ph-milf-peace-deal

Santos, Tina. 2011. "US Hails Aquino Admin's Commitment to Human Rights." *Inquirer Global Nation*, December 10. http://globalnation.inquirer.net/20623 /us-hails-aquino-admin%E2%80%99s-commitment-to-human-rights

Savun, Burcu, and Daniel Tirone. 2011. "Foreign Aid, Democratization, and Civil Conflict: How Does Democracy Aid Affect Civil Conflict?" *American Journal of Political Science* 55 (2): 233–46.

Schirmer, Daniel. 1997. *Fidel Ramos—the Pentagon's Philippine Friend, 1992–1997*. Durham, NC: Friends of the Filipino People.

Schmidli, William. 2013. *The Fate of Freedom Elsewhere: Human Rights in US Cold War Policy toward Argentina*. Ithaca: Cornell University Press.

Schmidt, Vivien. 2008. "Discursive Institutionalism: The Explanatory Power of Ideas and Discourse." *Annual Review of Political Science* 11 (1): 303–26.

Schmitz, Hans. 2004. "Domestic and Transnational Perspectives on Democratization." *International Studies Review* 6 (3): 403–26.

Schoultz, Lars. 1981a. *Human Rights and United States Policy toward Latin America*. Princeton: Princeton University Press.

Schoultz, Lars. 1981b. "US Foreign Policy and Human Rights Violations in Latin

America: A Comparative Analysis of Foreign Aid Distributions." *Comparative Politics* 13 (2): 149–70.

Security Assistance Monitor. 2015. "US Counterterrorism Aid to Kenya: Focusing on a Military with Motivation and Corruption Problems." Security Assistance Monitor. http://securityassistance.org/fact_sheet/us-counterterrorism -aid-kenya

Selby, Don. 2018. *Human Rights in Thailand*. Philadelphia: University of Pennsylvania Press.

Senate of the Philippines. 2007. "Loren Warns Manobo Evacuees Face Humanitarian Disaster." Senate, Government of the Republic of the Philippines, December 3. http://www.senate.gov.ph/press_release/2007/1203_legarda1.asp

Shatkin, Gavin. 2000. "Obstacles to Empowerment: Local Politics and Civil Society in Metropolitan Manila, the Philippines." *Urban Studies* 37 (12): 2357–75.

Shinawatra, Thaksin. 2003. *Prime Minister's Order No. 29/2546Re: The Fight to Overcome Narcotic Drugs*. Bangkok: Office of the Prime Minister of Thailand.

Sidel, John. 1999. *Capital, Coercion, and Crime: Bossism in the Philippines*. Stanford, CA: Stanford University Press.

Sidel, John. 2007. *The Islamist Threat in Southeast Asia: A Reassessment*. Washington, DC: East-West Center.

Sikkink, Kathryn. 1993. "Human Rights, Principled Issue-Networks, and Sovereignty in Latin America." *International Organization* 47: 411–41.

Sikkink, Kathryn. 2004. *Mixed Signals: U.S. Human Rights Policy and Latin America*. Ithaca: Cornell University Press.

Sikkink, Kathryn. 2011. *The Justice Cascade: How Human Rights Prosecutions Are Changing World Politics*. New York: W.W. Norton.

Sil, Rudra, and Peter Katzenstein. 2010. *Beyond Paradigms: Analytic Eclecticism in the Study of World Politics*. London: Palgrave Macmillan.

Silliman, Sidney. 1994. "Human Rights and the Transition to Democracy." In *Patterns of Power and Politics in the Philippines: Implications for Development*, edited by James F. Eder and Robert L. Youngblood, 103–46. Tempe: Program for Southeast Asian Studies, Arizona State University.

Silliman, Sidney, and Lela Garner. 1998. "Introduction." In *Organizing for Democracy: NGOs, Civil Society, and the Philippine State*, edited by G. Sidney Silliman and Lela Garner, 3–25. Honolulu: University of Hawai'i Press.

Simangan, Dahlia. 2018. "Is the Philippine 'War on Drugs' an Act of Genocide?" *Journal of Genocide Research* 20 (1): 68–89.

Simon, Sheldon. 2002. *Southeast Asia and the U.S. War on Terrorism*. Seattle: National Bureau of Asian Research.

Simon, Sheldon. 2003. "U.S.–Southeast Asia Relations: Southeast Asia Solidifies Antiterrorism Support, Lobbies for Postwar Iraq Reconstruction." *Comparative Connections: A Quarterly E-Journal on East Asian Bilateral Relations*: 11.

Simpson, Bradley. 2008. *Economists with Guns: Authoritarian Development and US-Indonesian Relations, 1960–1968*. Stanford: Stanford University Press.

Singh, Bilveer. 2007. *The Talibanization of Southeast Asia: Losing the War on Terror to Islamist Extremists*. Westport, CT: Praeger Security International.

Sison, Bebot, and Cecile Felipe. 2003. "Tribune Publisher-Editor Arrested on

Libel Charges." *Philippine Star*, August 5. https://www.philstar.com/metro/20 03/08/05/216136/tribune-publisher-editor-arrested-libel-charges

Skocpol, Theda. 1979. *States and Social Revolutions: A Comparative Analysis of France, Russia, and China*. Cambridge: Cambridge University Press.

Slater, Dan. 2010. *Ordering Power: Contentious Politics and Authoritarian Leviathans in Southeast Asia*. New York: Cambridge University Press.

Snitwongse, Kusuma. 2001. "Thai Foreign Policy in the Global Age: Principle or Profit?" *Contemporary Southeast Asia* 23 (2): 189–212.

Social Weather Station. 2001. "SWS: Media Release: Filipinos, Much Worried about Terrorism, Offer Mainly Moral Support to the US." *Social Weather Station*: 1–4. Accessed May 13, 2013. http://www.sws.org.ph/pr122801.htm

Social Weather Station. 2010. "Third Quarter 2010 Social Weather Survey: Net Satisfaction with General Performance of National Administration Is a Record-High 'Very Good' +64." *Social Weather Station*. Accessed September 4, 2020. https://web.archive.org/web/20160802004142/http://www.sws.org.ph /pr20101202.htm

Social Weather Station. 2012. "The 2012 SWS Annual Survey Review." *Social Weather Station*. Accessed September 4, 2020. https://web.archive.org/web/201 20826141342/http://www.sws.org.ph/pr20120118.htm

Soliven, Max. 2003. "$1-Billion Military Aid Package May Await GMA's State Visit to Washington, DC." *Philippine Star*, April 24. http://www.philstar.com/opin ion/203538/1-billion-military-aid-package-may-await-gma%C2%92s-state-vi sit-washington-dc

Solomon, Ty. 2015. *The Politics of Subjectivity in American Foreign Policy Discourses*. Ann Arbor: University of Michigan Press.

South China Morning Post. 1998. "Chuan's Trip to US Pays Dividends in Shape of Aid." *South China Morning Post*, March 15.

Spetalnick, Matt. 1993. "Clinton Declares New Era in Pacific Rim Relations." Reuters, November 21.

Spillius, A. 2000. "Hostages Tell of Escaping Philippine Jungle Trek." *Telegraph*, September 21. http://www.telegraph.co.uk/news/worldnews/asia/philippines /1356275/Hostages-tell-of-escaping-Philippine-jungle-trek.html

Stohl, M., D. Carleton, and S. Johnson. 1984. "Human Rights and U. S. Foreign Assistance from Nixon to Carter." *Journal of Peace Research* 21 (3): 215–26.

Storey, Ian. 2007. *Ethnic Separatism in Southern Thailand: Kingdom Fraying at the Edge?* Honolulu: Asia-Pacific Center for Security Studies.

Streckfuss, David, and Mark Templeton. 2002. "Human Rights and Political Reform in Thailand." In *Reforming Thai Politics*, edited by Duncan McCargo, 73–90. Copenhagen: NIAS Press.

Stritzel, Holger. 2012. "Securitization, Power, Intertextuality: Discourse Theory and the Translations of Organized Crime." *Security Dialogue* 43 (6): 549–67.

Sutter, Robert. 2009. "The Obama Administration and US Policy in Asia." *Contemporary Southeast Asia* 31 (2): 189–216.

Svolik, Milan. 2012. *The Politics of Authoritarian Rule*. New York: Cambridge University Press.

Swedlund, Haley. 2017. *The Development Dance: How Donors and Recipients Negotiate the Delivery of Foreign Aid*. Ithaca: Cornell University Press.

Sy, Marvin, and Benjie Villa. 2004. "CPP, NPA Want Arroyo to Ask US, Europe to Take Them off Terror Lists." *Philippine Star*, August 11. http://www.phils tar.com/headlines/260825/cpp-npa-want-arroyo-ask-us-europe-take-them-ter ror-lists

Talosig, Malou. 2001a. "RP, US 'Reviving' ACSA Basing Pact." November 16. *Today* 2843 (November 16): 1.

Talosig, Malou. 2001b. "Arroyo, US Defense Officials Meet on ACSA." *Today* 2844 (November 18): 1–1.

Talosig, Malou. 2001c. "State Dept Seeks Biggest US Military Aid since 1991." July 28. *Today* 2732 (July 28): 1–1.

Tan, Andrew. 2003. "Southeast Asia as the 'Second Front' in the War against Terrorism: Evaluating the Threat and Responses." *Terrorism and Political Violence* 15: 112–38.

Tarrow, Sidney. 2010. "The Strategy of Paired Comparison: Toward a Theory of Practice." *Comparative Political Studies* 43 (2): 230–59.

Task Force Detainees of the Philippines. 1998. "Philippines: Political Prisoners, the Forgotten Heroes." Accessed September 4, 2020. https://web.archive.org /web/20080514204525/http://www.hrsolidarity.net/mainfile.php/1998vol08n o08/1626/?print=yes

Tat, Ho. 1993. "U.S. Links Human Rights to Asian Security." Reuters, May 15, 1–2.

Teves, Oliver. 2010. "Aquino Promises Justice as Philippines President." Associated Press, June 9. http://www.apnewsarchive.com/2010/Aquino-promises-jus tice-as-Philippines-president/id-f077c3b9ee7a4033b9ef3e6d7266e19e?Search Text=philippines%20united%20states%20human%20rights;Display_

Thai Ministry of Defence. 1994. *The Defence of Thailand*. Bangkok: Thai Defence Ministry—Supreme Command Headquarters.

Thompson, Mark. 1996. "Off the Endangered List: Philippine Democratization in Comparative Perspective." *Comparative Politics* 28 (2): 179.

Thompson, Mark. 2001. "Whatever Happened to 'Asian Values'?" *Journal of Democracy* 12 (4): 154–65.

Thongpao, Thongbai. 1997. "Commentary—Time to Tackle Rights Abuses." *Bangkok Post*, July 27, 7.

Tible-Caoyonan, Elisa. 1994. *Development Diplomacy: Foreign Policy and Technological Transfer*. Diliman, Metro Manila: Asian Center, UP Diliman.

Tiglao, Rigoberto. 2012. "Unmasked: Akbayan Is Aquino's 'Dilawan'." *Philippine Daily Inquirer*, October 31. http://opinion.inquirer.net/39850/unmasked-akba yan-is-aquinos-dilawan

Tilly, Charles. 1975. "Revolutions and Collective Violence." In *Handbook of Political Science*, edited by F. Greenstein and N. Polsby, 483–555. Reading, MA: Addison-Wesley.

Tira-Andrei, Mercedes. 1994. "Clinton Seeks $72.6-M Aid for RP." *Filipino Reporter*, March 31, 11.

Today. 2001. "Bush Offers Help against Abu Sayyaf." *Today* 2848 (November 22): 1.

Toronto Star. 1992. "Legalize Communists, Filipino Leader Urges." *Toronto Star*, July 28, A14.

Trisko, Jessica. 2012. "Aiding and Abetting: Foreign Aid and State Coercion." PhD diss., Political Science, McGill University.

Truong, Thanh. 1990. *Sex, Money and Morality: Prostitution and Tourism in South-East Asia*. London: Zed Books.

Tyner, James. 2007. *America's Strategy in Southeast Asia: From Cold War to Terror War*. Lanham, MD: Rowman and Littlefield.

Ufen, Andreas. 2008. "Political Party and Party System Institutionalization in Southeast Asia: Lessons for Democratic Consolidation in Indonesia, the Philippines and Thailand." *The Pacific Review* 21 (3): 327–50.

Ünaldi, Serhat. 2014. "Thailand: A Coup, the Crown, and Two Middle Classes." *The Diplomat*, May 23. http://thediplomat.com/2014/05/thailand-a-coup-the-crown-and-two-middle-classes/

Ungphakom, Peter Mytri. 1993. "Thais Aim to Keep Talks to Agenda." *Bangkok Post*, November 18, 1–2.

Uniyal, Mahesh. 2000. "Rights-Thailand: Human Rights Assumes a New Prominence." *InterPress Service*, July 5. Retrieved from Factiva.

US Department of State. 1994a. "US State Department 1993 Human Rights Report: Thailand." January 31. https://web.archive.org/web/20100711201745/http://dosfan.lib.uic.edu/ERC/democracy/1993_hrp_report/93hrp_report_eap/Thailand.html

US Department of State. 1994b. "U.S. Department of State Country Report on Human Rights Practices 1993—Philippines." January 30. http://www.refworld.org/topic,50ffbce40,50ffbce421,3ae6aa3c8,0,USDOS,,PHL.html

US Department of State. 1995. "US State Department 1994 Human Rights Report: Thailand." February. https://web.archive.org/web/20160303184028/http://dosfan.lib.uic.edu/ERC/democracy/1994_hrp_report/94hrp_report_eap/Thailand.html

US Department of State. 1997a. "US State Department 1996 Human Rights Report: Thailand." US Department of State, Bureau of Democracy, Human Rights, and Labor. January 30. https://web.archive.org/web/20090807062737/http://www.state.gov/www/global/human_rights/1996_hrp_report/thailand.html

US Department of State. 1997b. "US State Department 1997 Human Rights Report: Thailand." https://web.archive.org/web/20090807061807/http://www.state.gov/www/global/human_rights/1997_hrp_report/thailand.html

US Department of State. 1998. "1997 Human Rights Report: The Philippines." January 30. https://web.archive.org/web/20090807061822/http://www.state.gov/www/global/human_rights/1997_hrp_report/philippi.html

US Department of State. 1999. "1998 Human Rights Practices Report—Thailand." February 26. https://web.archive.org/web/20090807072552/http://www.state.gov/www/global/human_rights/1998_hrp_report/thailand.html

US Department of State. 2000. "Philippines." February 23. https://web.archive.org/web/20150715082449/http://www.state.gov/j/drl/rls/hrrpt/1999/303.htm

US Department of State. 2003. "Thailand." March 31. https://web.archive.org/web/20171126190548/https://www.state.gov/j/drl/rls/hrrpt/2002/18265.htm

US Department of State. 2004a. "Philippines." February 25. https://web.archive.org/web/20171126190018/http://www.state.gov/j/drl/rls/hrrpt/2003/27786.htm

US Department of State. 2004b. "U.S. Department of State Country Report on Human Rights Practices 2003—Thailand." February 25. https://www.refworld .org/docid/403f57bc10.html

US Department of State 2004c. *Foreign Military Training: Joint Report to Congress, Fiscal Years 2003 and 2004*. June. https://web.archive.org/web/20171128180800 /https://www.state.gov/t/pm/rls/rpt/fmtrpt/2004/34216.htm

US Department of State. 2007. "Thailand." March 6. https://2009-2017.state.gov /j/drl/rls/hrrpt/2006/78792.htm

US Department of State. 2008. "Philippines." March 11. https://web.archive.org /web/20171122211654/http://www.state.gov/j/drl/rls/hrrpt/2007/100535.htm

US Department of State. 2012. "Obama, Clinton Welcome Philippine President Aquino." June 8. https://web.archive.org/web/20151015060430/http://iipdigit al.usembassy.gov/st/english/article/2012/06/201206087140.html

US Department of State. 2013. April 19. "2012 Country Reports on Human Rights Practices—Philippines." April 19. https://www.refworld.org/docid/517e6dee 18.html

US Department of State—Bureau of African Affairs. 2020. "US Relations with Kenya." https://www.state.gov/u-s-relations-with-kenya/#:~:text=The%20Un ited%20States%20established%20diplomatic,enduring%20partnership%20si nce%20Kenya's%20independence

US Department of State—Office of the Coordinator for Counterterrorism. 2005. "Country Reports on Terrorism 2004." April 27. https://web.archive.org/web /20171127202043/http://www.state.gov/j/ct/rls/crt/45388.htm

Uwanno, Borwornsak, and Wayne D. Burns. 1998. "The Thai Constitution of 1997: Sources and Process." *University of British Columbia Law Review* 32 (2): 227–47.

van der Kroef, Justus. 1986. "Private Armies and Extrajudicial Violence in the Philippines." *Asian Affairs: An American Review* 13 (4): 1–21.

van der veen, Maurits. 2011. *Ideas, Interests, and Foreign Aid*. New York: Cambridge University Press.

van de Wetering, Carina. 2016. *Changing US Foreign Policy toward India: US-India Relations since the Cold War*. New York: Palgrave.

van de Wetering, Carina. 2017. "Policy Discourses and Security Issues: US Foreign Policy toward India during the Clinton Administration." *Foreign Policy Analysis* 13 (2): 460–79.

Vejpongsa, Yassanee. 1996. "Hillary Hails Anti-Sex Trade Efforts." *Bangkok Post*, November 25, 2.

Villanueva, Marichu, and Pia Lee Brago. 2003. "Bush: RP Now Full Military Ally." *Philippine Star*, May 21. http://www.philstar.com/headlines/206968/bush-rp -now-full-military-ally

Villegas, Bernardo. 1987. "The Philippines in 1986: Democratic Reconstruction in the Post-Marcos Era." *Asian Survey* 27 (2): 194–205.

Viola, Lora. 2013. "Stratificatory Differentiation as a Constitutive Principle of the International System." In *Bringing Sociology to International Relations: World Politics as Differentiation Theory*, edited by M. Albert, B. Buzan, and M. Zürn, 112–31. Cambridge: Cambridge University Press.

Wah, Chin Kin. 2000. "Reflections on the Shaping of Strategic Cultures in Southeast Asia." In *Southeast Asian Perspectives on Security*, edited by Derek Da Cunha, 1–19. Singapore: Institute of Southeast Asian Studies.

Walldorf, Charles. 2008. *Just Politics: Human Rights and the Foreign Policy of Great Powers*. Ithaca: Cornell University Press.

Walley, Cherilyn. 2004. "Civil Affairs: A Weapon of Peace on Basilan Island." *Special Warfare* 17 (1): 30–35.

Wallis, William. 2009. "Foreign Aid Critic Spreads Theory Far and Fast." *Financial Times*. Accessed July 7, 2017. https://www.ft.com/content/d70b7cba-4732-11 de-923e-00144feabdc0

Walsh, Declan, and Helen Pidd. 2010. "US to Cut Aid to Pakistan Military Units over Human Rights Abuses." *Guardian*, October 22. http://www.theguardian .com/world/2010/oct/22/us-cut-pakistan-military-aid

Waltz, Kenneth. 2000. "Structural Realism after the Cold War." *International Security* 25 (1): 5–41.

Warsta, Matias. 2004. *Corruption in Thailand*. International Management Asia Conference at the Swiss Federal Institute of Technology, Zurich, April 22. http://ac eproject.org/ero-en/regions/asia/TH/Corruption_in_Thailand.pdf

Wattanayagorn, Panitan. 1998. "Thailand." In *Arms Procurement Decision Making, Volume I: China, India, Israel, Japan, South Korea and Thailand*, edited by R. Singh, 211–41. London: Oxford University Press; Stockholm: SIPRI.

Weissman, Robert. 1994. "'Development' and the Denial of Human Rights in Ramos's Philippines." *Harvard Human Rights Journal* 7: 251–68.

Wendt, Alexander. 1995. "Constructing International Politics." *International Security* 20 (1): 71–81.

Wendt, Alexander. 1999. *Social Theory of International Politics*. Cambridge: Cambridge University Press.

Whaley, Floyd. 2012. "Clinton Reaffirms Military Ties with the Philippines." *New York Times*, November 16, A8. http://www.nytimes.com/2011/11/17/world/as ia/clinton-reaffirms-military-ties-with-the-philippines.html

Wheeler, Matt. 2010. "People's Patron or Patronizing the People? The Southern Border Provinces Administrative Centre in Perspective." *Contemporary Southeast Asia: A Journal of International and Strategic Affairs* 32 (2): 208–33.

Wheeler, Nicholas. 2000. *Saving Strangers: Humanitarian Intervention in International Society*. Oxford: Oxford University Press.

White House—Office of the Press Secretary. 2003. "Joint Statement between the United States of America and the Kingdom of Thailand." June 11. http://ge orgewbush-whitehouse.archives.gov/news/releases/2003/06/20030611-1.html

White House—Office of the Press Secretary. 2012. "Statement on the President's Meeting with President Aquino of the Philippines." June 8. https://obamawhit ehouse.archives.gov/the-press-office/2012/06/08/statement-president-s-meeti ng-president-aquino-philippines

Wickham, Daniel. 2014. "Top Ten US Aid Recipients All Practice Torture." *Left Foot Forward*. Accessed September 4, 2020. http://leftfootforward.org/2014/01 /top-ten-us-aid-recipients-all-practice-torture/

Wilson, Karl. 2010. "Gloria Arroyo, the 'Most Hated' Philippines Leader since Marcos." *The National*, May 9. https://www.thenationalnews.com/world/asia/ gloria-arroyo-the-most-hated-phillipines-leader-since-marcos-1.538409

Winn, Jane. 2009. "Globalization and Standards: The Logic of Two-Level Games." *I/S: A Journal of Law and Policy for the Information Society* 5 (2): 185–218.

Wood, Elisabeth. 2003. *Insurgent Collective Action and Civil War in El Salvador*. New York: Cambridge University Press.

World Bank. 2001. *Combatting Corruption in the Philippines: An Update*. Washington, DC: World Bank—Philippine Country Management Unit, East Asia and Pacific Regional Office.

World Bank. 2017. "GDP Growth of the Philippines." World Bank Data. Accessed September 4, 2020. http://data.worldbank.org/indicator/NY.GDP.MKTP.KD.ZG

Yeo, Andrew. 2011. *Activists, Alliances, and Anti-U.S. Base Protests*. New York: Cambridge University Press.

Yujuico, Emmanuel. 2011. "The Philippines." London School of Economics—IDEAS. http://eprints.lse.ac.uk/47503/1/The%20Philippines%28lsero%29.pdf

Zabriskie, Phil. 2002. "The Punisher." *Time Magazine*, July 19. http://content.time.com/time/subscriber/article/0,33009,265480-1,00.html

Zenko, Micah, and Michael Cohen. 2012. "Clear and Present Safety: The United States Is More Secure Than Washington Thinks." *Foreign Affairs* 91 (2): 79–93.

About the Author

Salvador Santino Fulo Regilme Jr. (born 1986) is a tenured International Relations scholar at the Institute for History, Leiden University in the Netherlands. His research agenda covers international human rights norms, United States foreign policy, and the transnational politics of the Global South. He is the coeditor, with James Parisot, of *American Hegemony and the Rise of Emerging Powers* (Routledge, 2018) and the author of peer-reviewed articles in *International Studies Perspectives*, *Journal of Global Security Studies*, and *Human Rights Review*, among many others. He is the 2019 Inaugural Winner of the Asia-Pacific Best Conference Paper Award of the International Studies Association and the 2022 Honorable Mention recipient of the American Sociological Association's Best Scholarly Article Award for Human Rights. Follow him on Twitter: @santinoregilme

Index